General Henry Baxter,
7th Michigan
Volunteer Infantry

General Henry Baxter, 7th Michigan Volunteer Infantry

A Biography

Jay C. Martin

McFarland & Company, Inc., Publishers
Jefferson, North Carolina

All images are from the author's collection unless noted otherwise

LIBRARY OF CONGRESS CATALOGUING-IN-PUBLICATION DATA [new form]

Names: Martin, Jay C., author.
Title: General Henry Baxter, 7th Michigan Volunteer Infantry : a biography / Jay C. Martin.
Description: Jefferson, North Carolina : McFarland & Company, Inc., Publishers, 2016. | Includes bibliographical references and index.
Identifiers: LCCN 2015049032 | ISBN 9781476663395 (softcover : acid free paper)
Subjects: LCSH: Baxter, Henry, 1821–1873. | Generals—United States—Biography. | United States—History—Civil War, 1861–1865—Biography. | United States—History—Civil War, 1861–1865—Campaigns. | United States. Army. Michigan Infantry Regiment, 7th (1861–1865) | Jonesville (Mich.)—Biography.
Classification: LCC E467.1.B298 M37 2016 | DDC 355.0092—dc23
LC record available at http://lccn.loc.gov/2015049032

ISBN (print) 978-1-4766-6339-5
ISBN (ebook) 978-1-4766-2386-3

BRITISH LIBRARY CATALOGUING DATA ARE AVAILABLE

© 2016 Jay C. Martin. All rights reserved

No part of this book may be reproduced or transmitted in any form or by any means, electronic or mechanical, including photocopying or recording, or by any information storage and retrieval system, without permission in writing from the publisher.

Front cover: Brigadier general Henry Baxter (Library of Congress)

Printed in the United States of America

McFarland & Company, Inc., Publishers
Box 611, Jefferson, North Carolina 28640
www.mcfarlandpub.com

For my family

Table of Contents

Acknowledgments **ix**

Introduction **1**

1. Along the Old Chicago Road **5**
2. Rush for Gold, 1849–1852 **16**
3. Building Family and Community, 1853–1860 **33**
4. Off to War, 1861 **42**
5. Action at Last, Early 1862 **57**
6. An Authentic Piece of Human Heroism, Late 1862 **76**
7. Stalemate, 1863 **96**
8. Pushing South, 1864 **115**
9. Traitors Defeated, Home Regained, 1865–1868 **124**
10. Mission to Honduras, 1869–1873 **145**
11. Ended All Too Soon **171**

Chapter Notes **177**

Bibliography **191**

Index **197**

Acknowledgments

The rivers of history run wide and frequently shallow. Rarely does one find the perfect collection of primary documents that chronicle an individual or an event completely and in depth. In the case of Henry Baxter, there are relatively few documents left by the man himself. Only one fragment of an 1849 Gold Rush letter survives in published form, a court deposition exists from the same year, part of his Civil War letters and reports exist, and most of his diplomatic correspondence is available. In all, it is not enough to fully express the subject's thoughts and feelings, hopes and desires. But with sources produced by those around him, I have been able to recreate Baxter's life, albeit sometimes in skeletal form. Even at that, this biography took more than three decades to piece together.

The journey that led to this biography of Henry Baxter was inspired by a brief summary of his career in a short history of Jonesville, Michigan, written by Leonard Scott, one of the fine teachers at Jonesville High School. Interest in the topic was fanned by Dr. Albert Castel, for whose Western Michigan University Civil War history class I chose Baxter as the subject of a term paper. Through this research I located and interviewed Henry Baxter descendent Dr. Charles Henderson. That paper later was refined into several articles that Bill Dunn, by way of encouraging a teenager interested in local history, published in the weekly *Jonesville Independent* in 1983.

I later relied upon Baxter descendent Charles Henderson and his wife Sherry who graciously answered many questions about family history. Special recognition is due Dick Morgan at the Grosvenor House Museum in Jonesville, Michigan, who dedicated days of his time to allow access to the records of E.O. Grosvenor and other prominent Jonesvilleites. Similarly, Jonesville historians Ralph "Monty" Powers and Chris Spencer lent their time and expertise to vet this work in the context of community history.

The journey led me to many archival repositories in Michigan, including the Clarke Historical Library at Central Michigan University, the Archives and Regional History Collection at Western Michigan University, the Bentley Historical Library at the University of Michigan, the Hillsdale County Clerk of Courts and Register of Deeds, Hillsdale's Mitchell Public Library, the Jonesville District Library, the Lenawee County Register of Deeds, the St. Joseph County Register of Deeds, the State of Michigan Archives, the State of Michigan Library, the Tecumseh District Library, and the White Pigeon Township Library. Outside Michigan I found the bulk of Baxter's extant papers at the L. Tom Perry Special Collections at Brigham Young University in Provo, Utah.

Acknowledgments

On the national level, both the National Archives and the Library of Congress provided critical documents regarding Baxter's military and diplomatic careers. The search for other vital documents led me to Tegucigalpa, Honduras, where the staff of the National Museum of History was quite helpful. Paul Schiftan not only assisted me with the language but helped me to understand the culture and traditions of Central America, for which I am grateful.

The extensive travel required for this project was largely self-funded, but in the final stages of the research the Office of Research and Sponsored Programs (ORSP) and the College of Humanities and Social and Behavioral Sciences (CHSBS) at Central Michigan University were critical supporters. I would like to thank CHSBS Dean Dr. Pamela Gates and ORSP Director Dr. John McGrath and Interim Director Dr. Ian Davison for their support. Thanks are due to Christine Joyner and Caity Sweet for facilitating my research and travel. Sheree Hall assisted with proofing parts of the final draft.

Several of my colleagues read and made important comments upon early versions of the manuscript. I would like to thank my friend Marc Lapham for sharing his expertise in Jonesville history and Dr. Leroy Barnett for his encyclopedic knowledge of Michigan history. Several Central Michigan University students assisted with manuscript preparation, particularly Travis Farrington, Farrah McDaniel, Samantha Sullivan, Brad Collins, and Andrew Paquette. Andrea Puskas assisted with final research and created the manuscript index.

No journey this long can be maintained without a passion for the subject matter. I owe much to my parents, Joseph and Sarah Martin, for encouraging my interest in history. I wish to thank my wife Rebecca and son James for sharing trips to Baxter-related sites and for giving me the many hours necessary to complete this project.

Introduction

It was a cold December day in Fredericksburg, Virginia, when hell, or at least the Rappahannock River, froze over. For on that frigid day in 1862 Lieutenant Colonel Henry Baxter ordered the 7th Michigan Volunteer Infantry to use the butts of their Springfield rifles to propel their boats across the icy river. They did so under an intense enemy fire in what became the first frontal daylight amphibious assault on an entrenched enemy position in American military history.[1] The mission was called the "Forlorn Hope" because it was considered suicidal.

Though the successful crossing and initial assault would occur with remarkably few casualties, in the end the Battle of Fredericksburg was a bloody Union defeat. Victory was not the lasting legacy Baxter and his men attained. What they did was inspire thousands of witnesses with their bravery and ingenuity in the face of withering enemy fire. Winifred Lyster of Detroit was so stirred that she penned what became the unofficial state anthem, "Michigan, My Michigan," a poem—and later song—in which the 7th Michigan is specifically memorialized. That her haunting words were inspired by the heroic acts of brave Michiganders fighting for American unity and the elimination of slavery gave them even deeper meaning for those who lost loved ones in America's most iconic conflict. Even today, those verses set to the tune of "Maryland, My Maryland" impart an appreciation for what ordinary Americans, motivated by visionary leadership, can accomplish in the midst of great adversity:

> Dark rolled the Rappahannock's flood,
> Michigan, my Michigan,
> The tide was crimsoned with thy blood,
> Michigan, my Michigan.
> Although for us the day was lost,
> Still it shall be our proudest boast:
> At Fredericksburg our Seventh crossed!
> Michigan, my Michigan.[2]

Stanza eight captures the public response to the heroic actions of Baxter and his men. These pages attempt to capture the essence of Henry Baxter, because his extraordinary ability to learn from what he experienced, inspire his countrymen, and accomplish great deeds in the midst of tremendous obstacles set him apart.

America was energized in the nineteenth century, literally crawling with humans intent upon shaping their destinies using imagination, business acumen, and personal initiative. This collective vigor refused to be contained, bursting forth in great expressions of creativity. One by-product of this movement was the establishment of the foundations—political entities, transportation networks, economies, family lineages—we know today. A second outcome was the nurturing of a spirit that valued creativity and innovation in a world where opportunities literally lay in every direction.

Many aggressive, self-motivated Americans audaciously converted the wilderness into productivity. They were intent upon maintaining American virtue, the essential vitality of the institutions that managed the natural and the built environment.[3] For many, this attitude came from religious convictions as well as secular beliefs that highly valued "equal rights, equality of opportunity in the capitalist market place, security of property, and a laissez-faire philosophy of government."[4] Progress involved boldly building, harnessing, and controlling resources. Henry Baxter was typical of these Americans who played transformative roles in frontier communities.

Like many of his contemporaries, Baxter had seen a lot of America. Born in upstate New York, he emigrated with his family to the Michigan Territory during his youth, built multiple business enterprises, and became part of the political elite as statehood was achieved. But unlike his siblings, he was adventurous and confident of his place within the natural world. As a young man he participated in the California Gold Rush, then returned to his Michigan business, politics, and family. When the Civil War began he was determined to make a difference. And what a difference he made. He repeatedly distinguished himself in battle, briefly achieving national notoriety at Fredericksburg, and rising to general officer. In the post-war era, he played important roles in local, state, and national politics, ultimately earning a diplomatic appointment to Honduras. This firmly placed him on the leading edge of America's emergence as a transformative force on the international stage. At the time of his death he was slated to take up a more important European diplomatic post through which his family fortunes would have continued to grow. But without their most adventurous, charismatic, and dynamic member, the Baxters no longer had a presence on the national level and their prospects waned.

Born into a middle class family, he reinforced the rags to riches mythology that anyone could attain their dreams in America. Becoming something bigger in America meant taking advantage of "providence," the combination of religion, opportunity, and good luck that so many in the antebellum world felt moved with them across the continent.[5] Opportunities and challenges abounded, luring those with the courage, ambition, stamina, vision, and ability to stretch themselves to achieve either their personal potential or utter ruin.

Many have traced the concept of "manifest destiny" and this book will not bury itself in that well-plowed field. Instead, it argues that the concept of "manifest destiny" alone was not so compelling, not so cherished that it could have thrived without *walking, talking proof* that dramatic advancement was possible. Here is where Baxter and those like him were important. They arose at a time when great opportunity surrounded those with the imagination to see it. Their culture encouraged them to seize the chance, and with the ability to learn and adapt quickly, their tenacity and confidence permitted them to accomplish great things, implementing a loosely shared vision for America. At the same time, their efforts built up a reservoir of "local knowledge" of places, concepts, practical engineering, and leadership techniques that enabled them to overcome obstacles as the frontier was rapidly transformed.

The national impulse toward westward movement encouraged the building of "extended local knowledge" through frequent relocation on a grand geographic scale and a significant emphasis upon acquisition and retention of information gained through observation and personal experience. Movement brought familiarity with many localities and fostered the skills necessary to analyze and interpret environments quickly and effectively despite widely differing circumstances. Not just surveyors, soldiers, farmers, railroad men, and adventurers like the 49ers, but Americans of every background gained extended local knowledge. This collective nurturing of talent spawned "venturists," quick learners who were a super-productive, highly capable group that populated the United States, fought the Civil War, and prepared America to be a leader on the world stage.

As they settled the western states, the venturists brought with them the ability to overcome obstacles through creative problem-solving in the service of capitalism, military necessity, or social responsibility. Challenges were met with resources close at hand, using labor, natural resources, and tools scrounged, invented, or acquired, often without significant outside assistance. This manifested itself most visibly in the built environment where agriculture, transportation, industry, commerce, and civic institutions grew at a pace unequaled in human history.[6]

But the frontier itself was not the defining catalyst of the American spirit, it was the freedom to gain and apply knowledge creatively in support of self-interest. With the combined power of imagination, accumulated extended local knowledge, and hands-on visionary management unencumbered by regulatory restraints, nineteenth century Americans had the freedom to cross the continent, found remote enterprises, build transportation networks, and fight battles by reading the topography, assessing the value of the resources at hand, and applying the executive abilities to achieve success. Since Americans had a strong affinity for "progress" (the itch to move forward toward bigger and better things) and "success" (achieving goals that bettered one's life or circumstances), these abilities were valued highly, leading to both financial and status rewards. Hence, a person who encapsulated the key characteristics of the venturist was the ideal American, the "rugged individualist" who personified the evolving Jeffersonian ideal of virtue as the bedrock of American culture.[7]

In the mid-nineteenth century "progress" was tied closely to "building," therefore like the scientists of later generations who made "progress" by harnessing the mantra of scientific method to create drugs, medical procedures, and technology to better American life, the venturists built things that illustrated both progress and gentrification.[8] They were the architects of a new power structure that alternated its focus between the physical and political structure, almost overpowering in its proportions. They advanced the states they founded, using interpersonal connections, family, and their own individual knowledge and charisma to build a power base that reached previously unparalleled heights during and after the Civil War. Their efforts are overshadowed by the national rift as the defining event in nineteenth century American history.[9]

Many of the leaders who achieved success during the Civil War were venturists. But the interpretation that the Mexican War was the cradle of leadership for the Civil War has prevailed because it fit the designs of the army elite who so often wrote military history. While the Mexican War shaped the experience of many West Pointers and some volunteers, resourceful and dynamic Civil War leaders also came from among the venturists who gained practical knowledge of engineering, logistics, provisioning, preventative medicine, creative problem solving, and leadership in private life, often on the frontier. Certainly this was true of Henry Baxter and it is the reason that one Civil War historian credits him with having won the respect of his contemporaries based upon his "gritty up-front style of leadership."[10] The post–Mexican War careers imply that many West Pointers were also venturists.

Too often the early lives of Civil War soldiers and sailors are viewed superficially as a prelude to the war itself. This book argues that the events of youth were the catalyst for success for those who played roles—both major and minor—in historical events, while post-war success confirms that those achievements were based on a talent that transcended each challenge, no matter what arena it was experienced in. In other words, true ability was apparent as a *lifelong* attribute, not as singular to the war effort.

1

Along the Old Chicago Road

The venutrist developed in reaction to his environment and the challenges faced. In this context Henry Baxter was favorably influenced by an older generation who were themselves venturists. Revolutionary War veterans graced both his maternal and paternal family trees. Before, during, and after the Revolution, the Johnston and the Baxter families were prominent pioneers of Delaware County, an area of fertile valleys nestled among the Catskill Mountains of eastern New York. Maternal great grandfather William Johnston (1710–1792) was an Irish immigrant and a Presbyterian minister who explored the Susquehanna River Valley in 1770 and settled there in 1771. The Johnston settlement was named for him.

His son Witter (1753–1839) was one of the first settlers in the Susquehanna River Valley. A Colonel in the Revolution, Witter survived the 1778 attack on the fort at Cherry Hill led by Loyalist Walter Butler and Mohawk Chief Joseph Brant. He was with Colonel Marinus Willet in the engagement at West Canada Creek on October 30, 1781, when Butler was killed, revenging his role in the Cherry Creek Massacre of November 11, 1778. After the war, Witter Johnston was "prosperous and public spirited, though reported to be 'set in his way,'" a trait apparent in his descendants.[1]

Paternal great grandfather Francis Baxter (1742–1827) was a veteran of the 1759 campaign to capture Quebec and a soldier in the Revolution. He was taken prisoner by the "Tories and Indians, and after suffering much ill usage and abuse was confined in the memorable 'sugar house' in New York."[2] His grandfather Levi Baxter, Sr. (1764–1851) was "a man of great energy and character" who rose from private to captain during the Revolution.[3]

After the war, Levi Baxter, Sr., married Mary Washburn (1767–1859) and in 1786 settled in Delhi, New York. Together they had three sons: John, William, and Levi, Jr. Levi, Sr., became a prominent citizen and illustrated his role as a venturist. He owned a tavern, dabbled in brick making, was an overseer of highways, and assessor, before moving on to Sidney Plains in 1805. He built a mill near the mouth of Carr's Creek, entered politics, and became a justice of the peace.

Henry Baxter's father, Levi Baxter, Jr., was born at East Windsor, Connecticut, on October 5, 1788. The family moved to Delhi while Levi was still a child and stayed there until the 1803 move to Sidney. The village was located on the eastern bank of the Susquehanna River and there Levi, Jr., first became a venturist of his own through assorted businesses, including farming, lumbering, and "mercantile pursuits."[4]

On January 12, 1814, Levi, Jr., married Lois Johnston (born January 19, 1792), daughter of Witter and Jane Campbell Johnston, at Sidney Plains. Levi's brother John married Lois' sister Mary, further deepening the family connection. Levi and Lois ultimately had ten children: Benjamin Levi (born April 7, 1815); Witter Johnston (born June 18, 1816); Mary Jane (born April 2, 1818); Nancy Ann (born 1819); James Henry (born September 8, 1821); Francis (born November 2, 1823); Narcissa (born July 17, 1825); Henry (born 1827); Helen N. (born December 18, 1829); and Lois Francis (born August 1, 1834). They also adopted Anna Bella McInnis (1804–1828), a native of Scotland.

The growing family suffered tragedy in the summer of 1828 when five were lost in two weeks: Francis (August 6); Nancy Ann (August 10); Narcissa (August 11); nine-month-old baby Henry (August 12); and Anna Bella (August 23). The sudden death of four of the children and Anna Bella—the children's caretaker—suggests an epidemic, but there is no record of what malady swept the family. In 1830 the household held only five children: Benjamin, Witter, Mary Jane, James Henry, and Helen.

The death of so many children in 1828 may have influenced the decision to leave New York. More likely western prospects appeared promising to a man of ambition, so 42-year-old Levi decided to emigrate. In 1831 he and his Sidney business partner Selleck C. Boughton moved to Michigan with the intention of opening a mercantile store in the central Lower Peninsula town of Jackson. But when they arrived in Detroit they were told that Jackson had an unhealthy climate. Fresh from the loss of so many children, Baxter reconsidered. Boughton and Baxter met General Joseph W. Brown, who convinced them to move to Tecumseh on July 4, 1831, where the partners started business under the name Baxter & Boughton. Later that year they bought the "first mills of any size west of Monroe" from General Brown. Known as "Tecumseh" or "Red Mills," the firm was located on the Raisin River in Brownsville, just north of Tecumseh. The mill had substantial capacity and a virtual monopoly in the early years, drawing business from a 50-mile radius.[5]

Levi became a miller, just as his father had in New York. This was a very important position since newly settled areas with agriculture-based economies required capital-intensive milling operations to grind grain into a consumable and saleable product like flour or meal. The *Laws of the Territory of Michigan* (1833) show that the miller's toll (fee) was set at one-eighth (corn) to one-twelfth (wheat, rye, or other) of the quantity of grain ground.[6] The product thus tolled by the miller was retailed to the public

An 1831 emigrant to Michigan, Judge Levi Baxter built a power base in lower tier counties and sired a family that became influential in mid- to late-nineteenth century Michigan business and politics. Levi was the first chairman of the new Republican Party in Michigan and made the decision to move the first meeting in Jackson out "under the oaks."

or shipped elsewhere for the wholesale market. The increasing agricultural output of Michigan, the scarcity of competing milling operations, and the growth of maritime transportation, good roads, and later railroads made the miller one of the most influential and affluent members of the community. By involving ten-year-old Henry at the mill in small ways, Levi was developing a protégé who would learn at his elbow.

Tecumseh and Brownsville were a good locality for aspiring merchants. Set among rolling hills at the western edge of the flatlands that cover most of extreme Southeastern Michigan and Northwest Ohio, the Raisin River had a good descending grade. Excellent mill sites were in close proximity to an abundance of fertile farm land. Since between Tecumseh and Monroe there were few rivers suitable for milling, there was little competition. The mill, fed by Red Mill Pond, did very well.

Tecumseh/Brownsville were in Lenawee County, which was laid out in 1822, but was administratively part of Monroe County until 1826. Tecumseh was founded in 1824. Only 30 miles up the La Plaisance Bay Pike (built between 1832 and 1835 and later known as the Monroe Trail) from the disembarkation of emigrants arriving by lake boat at Monroe, the village was close to the intersection with the Chicago Road 16 miles west at Cambridge Junction. The Chicago Road was the primary east-west road across southern Michigan in the 1830s. Tecumseh was therefore a town with a bright future for milling, commerce, and land speculation, all of which Levi Baxter excelled in.

In 1831 Baxter was appointed the third chief-justice of the court of Lenawee County by Territorial Governor Lewis Cass, thus becoming known for the rest of his life as "Judge Baxter." At the time there were no circuit courts, and since most of the population was concentrated in the extreme southeastern counties, his position made him a member of the power elite. There were few organized counties and since Lenawee County controlled lands to the west, his position gave him far reaching influence.

Levi's substantial business income and his $1,200 annual salary as judge funded judicious land speculation. Tecumseh was a major thoroughfare for west bound emigrants and Levi acquired and resold good land for a substantial profit. He made liberal use of the courts to collect his debts. Yet, there was only so much undeveloped land and after a time emigrants passed by Tecumseh in favor of communities further down the Chicago Road.

Levi held responsibility for lands to the west in the lower tier of counties that were administered by Lenawee County. One of these was Hillsdale County, Lenawee County's western neighbor, described at the time as

> in the northern portion of the county are oak openings, but the rest of the county is heavily timbered. It is traversed south by heads of St. Joseph's river flowing into the Maumee, and north by heads of St. Joseph's river emptying into Lake Michigan. The surface is undulating, with occasional marshes, and some of the highest land in the peninsula, and the county, in its appearance, may well be called hills and dale. The general soil of the county is black sandy loam, rich and very productive of grain, but less adapted to grazing.[7]

The county was created as a separate political entity by the Michigan legislature on October 29, 1829, but remained under Levi's authority until a county seat was established. In the winter of 1830 Jonesville applied to become county seat and was ultimately selected in July 1830.

The headwaters of many important rivers lay within the borders of Hillsdale County.

Spring fed and located among the highest elevations of southern lower Michigan, the rivers flowed north, south, east, and west. The St. Joseph, the Grand, and the Kalamazoo all flowed into Lake Michigan. One tributary flowed into the Maumee. Both the Maumee and the Raisin flowed into Lake Erie. As a miller, Levi Baxter's interest was piqued by this significant confluence of waterways. Hillsdale County was also unique because of its central position in the southern tier, the only county sharing borders with both Ohio and Indiana, making it an important north-south crossroads. Since the county was transected by the Chicago Road, it was on the most important east-west route crossing Michigan's Lower Peninsula.

In his position as Chief Justice of the Court of Lenawee County, Levi frequently dealt with the affairs of Hillsdale County. He made regular trips westward and saw the opportunities that the county offered. He arranged for oldest son Benjamin to teach school in Jonesville during the winter of 1833–34, illustrating his intent to move further west.[8]

With his term as Chief Justice at an end in 1833 and business in Tecumseh going well, in 1834 Levi Baxter formed a partnership with Cook Sisson, a fellow New York emigrant, to build a large water-powered mill at Jonesville on the south side of the important Chicago Road, using both the natural grade of the St. Joseph River and artificial means to generate a fall of 12 feet. They called it "Fayette Mill" for the township in which it lay.[9]

This road was the key to the success of Jonesville and other young communities in southern Michigan. In 1824 Congress set aside money for roads of military importance via the General Survey Act. The Chicago Road was laid out in 1825 following the Native American Sauk Trail across the lower tier counties. Although originally intended to support military communication and transport of supplies between Detroit and Fort Dearborn (Chicago), its utility soon made it a well-traveled east-west thoroughfare. The road crossed the St. Joseph River at a convenient ford where Jonesville would later be located.[10]

In 1836 Harriet Martineau described the Chicago Road as a transportation route along which the traveler had to frequently leave a coach in order to walk around obstacles:

> Juggernaut's car would have been "broke to bits" on such a road [and beyond Jonesville it was] more deplorable than ever ... such hopping and jumping, such slipping and sliding; such looks of despair from the middle of the pond; such shifting of logs, and carrying of planks, and handing along the fallen trunks of trees.[11]

Such slow and challenging roads left the coach traveler battered and exhausted, making frequent stops to rest, make repairs, and change horses critically important.

In the fall of 1828 Benaiah Jones and his wife Lois founded the community that bore their name as a stage coach stop west of the St. Joseph River ford. With its prime location almost exactly in the middle of the southern Lower Peninsula, Jonesville quickly became an important crossroads for both east-west and north-south travel.

The town was situated in a picturesque valley, surrounded by hills that from the east, west, north, and south provided spectacular views, especially when the tree leaves turned to hues of orange, red, and yellow each fall. The rolling hills, small lakes, and occasional swamps made the valley good for farming and hunting, as well as a fine place to harvest lumber and run stock. Jonesville was, in fact, the kind of place that emigrants dreamed of. With abundant natural resources and good communication with the outside world, it was a spot where a person could prosper as the community grew.

Eventually roads radiated from Jonesville into the hinterland, connecting to Hillsdale,

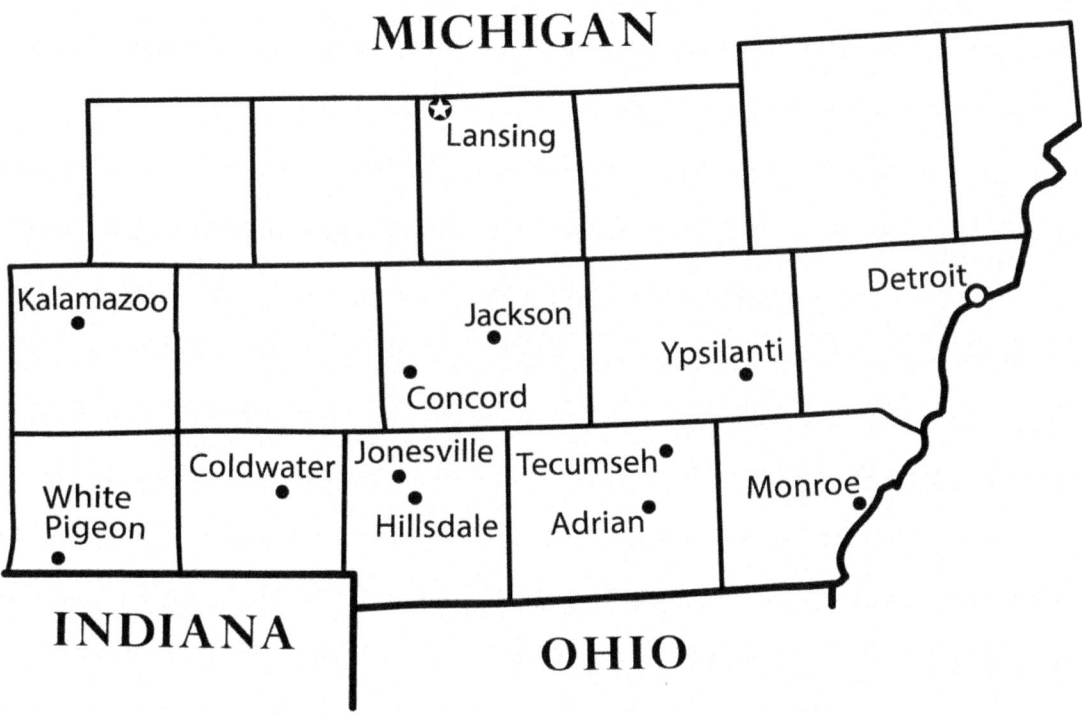

When statehood was achieved in 1837, the southeastern tiers of Michigan counties and the Detroit metropolitan area were most populous and therefore most influential in state politics. Levi Baxter and his sons chose locations of advantage to build their influence: Levi in Tecumseh, White Pigeon, and Jonesville; Benjamin in Tecumseh; Witter in Detroit, White Pigeon, and finally Jonesville; and Henry in Jonesville. The rivalry between Hillsdale and Jonesville warped Hillsdale County politics for decades. Map by Dakota Camarena.

Osseo, Pittsford, and Hudson to the south and southeast, Reading to the southwest, Mosherville, Concord, and Jackson to the northeast, North Adams to the east, and Litchfield and Homer to the northwest. But in 1828, the Chicago Road was the only reliable means of inland travel in the extreme southern Michigan Territory.

Jonesville was well situated in other ways. The Chicago Road brought with it good communication with other important towns throughout Michigan, Indiana, and Illinois via stage coach. Starting in 1830, General Joseph Brown's Great Western Stage Company developed regular service from Detroit through Ypsilanti, Saline, Tecumseh, Jonesville, White Pigeon, Niles, Michigan City, and into Chicago—a trip of approximately 280 miles. The journey was expected to take four and a half days one way, but frequently took six because of the roughness and dilapidated state of the corduroyed road.

Remarkable changes marked Jonesville in its first half century:

> This whole county was one vast unbroken wilderness ... only inhabited by the native Indian. To-day we see in every nook and corner, thrift, intelligence, and progress. Look at these fine farms, brick and frame houses, convenient and costly barns and store houses, the rich mill property, these splendid roads, these great railroad thoroughfares, the flourishing and prosperous villages and large towns, the comfortable school houses, the numerous colleges and all the various institutions of learning; and its millions of dollars in church property with its numerous costly

places of worship and fine churches, with their spires pointing heavenward. Behold the vast and almost inconceivable changes that have taken place within the recollection of your humble speaker, covering only a space of time of fifty three years.[12]

Whether Levi's wife Lois ever saw Jonesville is unknown. Her death at Tecumseh on October 26, 1834—only two months after giving birth to Lois Frances—left Levi with a large family, but no consort. For an active man of business building a geographically diverse empire, continuing on alone was impracticable. He turned to an old acquaintance. Thirty-year-old Elizabeth M. Orton (1805–1872) was the daughter of Miles Orton (1774–1813) and Lydia Gibbs (1770–1852). She grew up in Litchfield, Connecticut, but often visited her oldest brother, the Reverend Samuel G. Orton who officiated at Presbyterian churches in Sidney Plains and Delhi, New York, between 1826 and 1833. Levi was a former member of her brother's flock. They married in Albany, New York, on June 22, 1835, and ultimately had seven children: Antoinette (born January 19, 1838); Elizabeth (born April 12, 1840); Susan E. (born c. 1841); unnamed infant (unknown birth date); Clara (born April 1, 1842); Charles E.K. (born November 21, 1844); and Florence (born September 26, 1846).[13]

Levi was deeply involved in education. In April 1833 he was appointed by the Territorial Legislature as one of the first trustees of the newly incorporated Michigan Manual Labor School. The first meeting was in Ann Arbor on April 27, 1833. This school was part of a national movement dedicated to teaching students practical skills and was intended to be supported by the products created by its students.

Levi took some pains with the education of his children, particularly the boys. Oldest son Benjamin spent three years at Dartmouth College and then returned to run the state Normal School branch at Tecumseh. Second son Witter's education came from "common school and academical [sic] education at the State University branches at Tecumseh, White Pigeon, and Detroit."[14] He began teaching in 1836, but he switched to the study of law in Detroit in 1841. Third son Henry had the most basic education, attending the state university branch at White Pigeon for only a short time. Though his later correspondence and reports show good composition and penmanship, Henry was an outdoorsman, not particularly suited for indoor pursuits. He worked closely with his father at the mills, learning from Levi as he developed an extended commercial empire in southern Michigan.

⸺

On January 8, 1834, Jonesville hosted a Territorial Convention aimed at placing the southern counties on the first western railroad. At the time, traveling via Lake Huron and Lake Michigan was the most rapid, inexpensive, comfortable, and reliable method of transportation from Detroit to Chicago. But the all water route was 850 miles long, sometimes dangerous, and not open in the winter because the freshwater lakes froze. The Chicago Road was difficult and near impassible during the winter. The aim of the delegates to the 1834 convention was to petition the federal government for the construction of a 300 mile railroad to traverse the base of Michigan's Lower Peninsula. The railroad would cut the travel time from days to hours and make the trip possible year round. The petition addressed to President Martin Van Buren on January 19, asked Congress to appropriate funding to examine, survey, and construct a railroad from western Lake Erie to southern Lake Michigan, hopefully passing through Jonesville. The delegates assured the President that their interest was "unshackled by local or sectional interests & such as shall be thought, most conducive to the general good."[15] The petition was introduced in Congress by Territorial Representative Lucius Lyon, but was unsuccessful.

Levi Baxter was not a delegate to this convention, but Thomas Sisson—a relative of his business partner Cook Sisson—represented Lenawee County. Baxter was associating himself with men who had strong ambitions for Michigan.

In the spring of 1835 Levi's partner Selleck Boughton was a Lenawee County delegate to the state constitutional convention in Detroit. That same year Levi dissolved his partnership with Boughton, but continued to operate in Tecumseh for another year while the partners settled accounts. To keep abreast of the opportunities presented by westward expansion, in 1836 Levi moved his family to White Pigeon, 95 miles west of Tecumseh and 55 miles beyond Jonesville. Here in 1839 he built an extensive mill with Henry's help.

Located in western St. Joseph County, White Pigeon was only three miles from the Indiana border. The township was settled in 1827 within the productive prairie that characterizes northern Indiana to the south, making it ideal for farming. The town of White Pigeon was laid out in 1830 when there were 600 citizens. Like Jonesville, White Pigeon had good east-west connections along the Chicago Road, and good north-south access via the Kalamazoo Road. A federal land office was established on the south side of the Chicago Road near the intersection of Kalamazoo Street and between 1831 and 1834 more than a quarter million acres were conveyed through its books.

The six acre commercial property that Levi purchased for $1,600 on October 1, 1839, did not include rights to use water for power. An additional investment of $3,500 acquired rights to draw water from the mill race created by Neal McGaffey. The financial burden of the venture was eased later that month by a $2,000 sale of water rights for a lumber mill adjacent to the property. Levi built the first grist mill in White Pigeon with four run of stones at the foot of St. Joseph Street, just south of River Street, where the White Pigeon Paper Company is today.[16]

Levi Baxter now owned businesses in two growing communities—White Pigeon and Jonesville—while maintaining his connections in Tecumseh. There were many changes in Hillsdale County in 1836, and Henry Baxter—working closely to represent his father's interest in the Fayette Mill—was in an ideal position to observe

> emigration as it poured into and through our county[,] the Chicago turnpike being the only thoroughfare at that time. Along this road came the emigration that settled some of the counties of Northern Indiana turning southward at Allen's Prairie and other points a line of wagons almost continuous passing through the village daily.... [Jonesville] was then the county seat, the county jail occupying the public square [on the] north side of Chicago road. A grist mill had been erected [by Baxter] the year before 1835. An Indian trail up the valley of the St Joseph branching towards Baw Beese and Sand Lakes was the only road south of Jonesville. The first saw mills were built one a mile and a half up stream from Jonesville and run by the late Jonathan Lockwood the other still a mile above by James Olds and others.[17]

By 1837 "Jonesville was still the only important village center in Hillsdale County" and "was one of the most important points on the Chicago Road."[18]

However, competition was growing to the south. Just five miles closer to the center of Hillsdale County, a new community was founded. Platted in 1835, Hillsdale consisted of little until the first mill, inn, and store were erected in 1838. But the organizers had chosen their site to take advantage of available water power and named the place strategically. They pursued railroad access with zeal, achieving success in 1843. Local politics were consumed by the rivalry over the location of the county seat, which led to the election of pro–Jonesville and pro–Hillsdale candidates to the Michigan legislature. For three years the county seat was even removed to tiny Osseo in an attempt to settle the controversy over the permanent location. Finally on January 30, 1843, the legislature voted to move the county seat to Hillsdale. The *Hillsdale County Gazette*, which was founded in Jonesville in 1839, moved to Hillsdale. Sharp competition between the two towns contorted county politics for decades.

Michigan entered the Union as the 26th state on January 26, 1837, with a population of 200,000. The euphoria over statehood did little to sooth the economic challenges of the Panic of 1837. Created by rampant land speculation, lack of available specie (hard money) on the frontier, huge debts incurred for internal improvements, and an unfavorable balance of trade, the economy of Michigan was hit hard. The resulting depression slowed the progress of railroads and stopped canal construction. The mania for canal construction would never revive. Still, by 1838 Jonesville was described as "newly settled, but it is very flourishing, and handsomely located on the east bank of the [St. Joseph] river, and has the prospect of being a place of much business."[19]

The young state needed good roads to bring the products of interior lands to market. In the spring of 1839 the legislature authorized an impressive array of internal improvements, including two roads through Jonesville. The first road started at Jonesville and went 14 miles north through Concord to the Grand River. A second road connected Jonesville with Union City about 26 miles west. Together, these roads cemented Jonesville's role as the central connection to the critical east-west Chicago Road.

The tide of emigration continued and business in Michigan kept pace. In 1840 Levi Baxter decided to expand his Jonesville mill in partnership with H.L. Hewitt of Tecumseh. During construction a large timber fell and crushed Levi's left leg, an injury that never healed properly. He walked with a limp for the rest of his life, his slowed gait marking a shift from the pursuit of a commercial empire to a greater influence in state politics.

This change came when Levi's White Pigeon household included nine people: Levi, wife Elizabeth, and children Witter, Henry, Helen, Lois, Antoinette, Elizabeth, and Susan. Henry and his sister Helen were students at the University of Michigan branch at White Pigeon. His older brother Witter was an assistant tutor at the state university. Twenty-year-old daughter Mary Jane was now on her own, having married 31-year-old George Kellogg (March 11, 1807–April 30, 1888) on February 6, 1839. Kellogg had arrived in White Pigeon in 1832 as a partner in a store with his brothers Edwin and Charles, distant cousins of the founders of the Battle Creek cereal empire. In June 1841 Levi sold his grist mill to George and his brothers for $17,000.[20]

By 1843 Benjamin Baxter had finished Dartmouth College and begun management of the Tecumseh branch of the University of Michigan through the influence of his father, a member of the Board of Trustees. The branch operated in the old court house—the county seat having relocated to Adrian—from 1838 until it was discontinued in 1842. Benjamin then taught at a private entity called the Tecumseh Literary Institute which carried on the work of the branch. He studied law with Perley Bills, with whom he had a law practice in Tecumseh for 25 years. Second son Witter steered a similar course, first teaching and then studying law in Detroit under Zephaniah Platt, who was then Attorney General of Michigan, before being admitted to the bar in 1844.

The long apprenticeship of third son Henry appeared to be drawing to a close. In 1843 Levi placed the mill in Jonesville in the care of his 21-year-old son. Just weeks after his 22nd birthday, Levi sold Henry one-quarter ownership of the mill property for $1,000. On March 28, 1845, Levi sold Henry an additional one quarter for $3,500, establishing his son as an equal partner at age 23. Henry and Levi added additional acreage for an enlarged mill pond in 1845–46, continuing to increase the capacity of their joint business enterprise. Henry—the budding venturist—had achieved basic parity with his mentor, though it was some time before he would be truly independent.

The mill was growing to meet the demands of maturing agricultural interests. Maintaining a sufficient supply of water to run the mill was paramount, leading Levi and Henry to cache the waters of the St. Joseph River. This limited the volume available to the competing "Genesee Mills"—about a mile downriver—owned by John Gardner. In running Fayette Mills, Henry managed to alternately hold and discharge water in a manner that damaged the mill dam of his downstream rival. The resulting 1847 law suit brought jury trials in July and August in the Hillsdale County Circuit Court. W.W. Murphy represented the Baxters and

The primary source of Baxter family prosperity was Levi Baxter's milling operations, first in Tecumseh, then Jonesville and White Pigeon. Eventually family holdings were concentrated in Fayette Mill at Jonesville, in which Levi and third son Henry became equal partners. The railroad siding that ran between the mill and Chicago Street linked Baxter products (grain, flour, and furniture) directly to a nationwide market.

subpoenaed virtually every prominent member of the Jonesville business community to testify. Gardner was awarded damages in the amount of $500. This settlement spawned a second suit that tied up Levi and Henry's joint real estate and business holdings into 1849.

Meanwhile, Levi Baxter continued to build political influence. In 1847 he with Edwin and Charles Kellogg, Elias S. Swan, John Redfern, and George W. Beisel of St. Joseph County received a charter from the state for the "White Pigeon Academy," the purpose of which was to be "an institution of learning for the instruction of persons in the various branches of literature and the arts and sciences."[21] The academy replaced the branch of the Michigan university system when it closed.

The start of the Mexican War in May 1846 interested Henry. The conflict mobilized many who saw that opportunities would follow the anticipated American victory. However, the Baxters were Whigs and their support for the war was limited because they opposed the acquisition of more territory for new slave states. The end of the war in 1848 and the resulting additions to American territory would have a profound impact on Henry's life.

Like his father, Henry was active in the community. He was a charter member of the Independent Order of Odd Fellows Fayette Lodge Number 16 organized on October 3, 1846. Earlier that same year his brother Witter—who had previously joined the lodge in Detroit—was elected Secretary of the Grand Lodge of Michigan.

Pursuing philanthropy in a small community was another method of establishing ascendency. In 1847 Henry was the leading contributor to the Presbyterian Church annual pew rental fundraiser, giving $23.50 of the $82 total, or 29 percent of what was raised from among a dozen of the community elite. The following year Levi and Witter joined the church and hence forth were among the leading contributors. Henry was replaced by Levi as a key church leader.[22]

Henry built ventures on his own. Horse-trading was a sideline that led to travel through southern lower Michigan, northern Indiana and Ohio. He "was the sole light of the younger people" with an affability and manliness that was recognized by other men his entire life.[23]

Levi moved his family to Jonesville in 1848 and continued to develop business interests there. He hoped to continue Henry's management of the mill since it added to his available capital, yet left him free so that he could pursue other economic and political ventures.

Levi's role as judge in Lenawee County wetted his appetite for political power. He was "prominently connected with the Whig party until the organization of the Free-Soil party, in 1848, when he enlisted in that movement, and was made their party candidate for the office of State senator."[24] He defeated Democrat Salmon Sharp—the first settler in Adams Township—and served in the Michigan Senate from January 1, 1849, through December 31, 1850, representing the Third District including Monroe, Lenawee, Hillsdale, and Branch Counties. Among his accomplishments was "securing the passage of the Michigan Southern Railroad through Jonesville, and thus secured to the village benefits that told largely on its subsequent growth, prosperity, and business importance."[25] This accomplishment was significant. After the state sold the Michigan Southern in 1846, the extension from Hillsdale to Jonesville was the only additional track completed. Levi Baxter also forced the extension of the Lake Shore and Michigan Railway from Hillsdale to Jonesville by inserting a clause in enabling legislation that made completion of the extension to Jonesville by September 15, 1851, mandatory.

The Michigan Southern Railroad was a very important artery of commerce. Construction began in 1838 on the east-west route across the southern-most counties in the Lower

Peninsula. The line connected Jonesville directly with business interests in Monroe and Detroit. Like the Michigan Central Railroad that passed through the second tier of Michigan counties, the Michigan Southern Railroad was originally a venture of a Michigan government that desperately wanted to support business in the most populous part of the state. Though both railroads turned a profit, by 1846 they needed expensive repairs. To avoid the expense, Michigan sold them to private interests. At this time, the Michigan Southern had only been completed as far westward as Hillsdale.

To speed the extension, Jonesville residents led by Ransom Gardner took up a subscription to pay for the construction of the roadbed to Jonesville, the grade for which was ready for track and ties in 1849. The *Hillsdale Whig Standard* reported that the first locomotive of the Michigan Southern Railroad reached Jonesville the first week of September 1850, making it the temporary terminus for the line and opening the local harvest to distant markets. The collective Baxter family business interests increased in value now that the mill could ship product directly to market. Jonesville was on the primary route between Chicago and Detroit via the Chicago Road, and now connected to the Michigan Southern Railroad. The town lacked only a navigable waterway to make it a player in Michigan's economy.

Whether they worked in flour or lumber, land speculation or legal affairs, all the Baxters were doing extremely well. They continued to prosper as the Michigan Southern crept slowly westward, through Coldwater and White Pigeon by 1851. In 1852 both the Michigan Southern and the Michigan Central reached Chicago, securing the ability to cut across the Lower Peninsula and reach major ports on Lake Erie (Monroe and Toledo) and Lake Michigan (Chicago). By 1855 both railroads had access to New York City as well. Levi and Henry purchased a right of way and added a spur from the Lake Shore and Michigan that crossed the St. Joseph River on a bridge directly south of and parallel to the vehicular/pedestrian Chicago Street Bridge, allowing them to ship grain, flour, and other products directly from their mill to major national markets.

The ability to ship flour and other products competitively to distant markets significantly increased productivity. Production of corn increased 115 percent between 1850 and 1860 and production of wheat 69 percent during the same period as Michigan agriculture shifted sharply from subsistence to a market economy. Lumbering expanded rapidly in the 1840s and 1850s, becoming a leading industry. The flow of settlers migrating into Michigan increased 83 percent between 1850 and 1860. Industrial expansion mirrored the growth in settlement.[26]

The growth of agriculture by 1854 led Secretary of the Interior Robert McClelland—a Monroe attorney, Congressman (1838–1849), and Michigan Governor (1852–1853)—to predict that "the state will be one of the richest and most respectable in the union."[27] The Baxters and other agricultural, commercial, and industrial interests certainly expected this prediction would come true.

2

Rush for Gold, 1849–1852

Henry Baxter had accomplished much by his mid-twenties. He moved west with his father, helped build a successful family business, and achieved a leadership position in a new and growing agricultural-commercial town. He could have lived out his days in a position of respectability and comfort having established a thriving business and a substantial income. For many this would have been enough. But young Baxter chafed at a domesticated lifestyle, yearning to be acknowledged as a venturist, a solitary achievement that could not occur while in the shadow of his father.

Henry did not participate in the Mexican War because Whigs were against the spread of slavery. Still, he and others of his generation were being drawn westward. With the conclusion of the war and the addition of territory, it was up to a good Whig to make sure that the slave power did not gain control of the southeast. The discovery of gold at Sutter's Mill, California, on January 24, 1848, spawned lurid reports of gold caches uncovered and men made rich overnight, fueling a near delirium. Though not surprising that the dreamers would succumb to such tales, what is impressive is how many solid, conservative members of eastern communities caught "gold fever." Henry Baxter was one of them. He and those like him made the rash speculation of the Gold Rush respectable by the social decorum of the time.[1]

Interest in California already existed before fire swept Jonesville on January 31, 1849, leaving "the principal [sic] commercial block in the village of Jonesville, including nearly every dry goods store in the village ... burned to the ground."[2] The fire did not damage the Baxter mill, but the mercantile interests suffered, leaving many ambitious young clerks unemployed.

At the time, 27-year-old Henry Baxter was fighting a round of nasty law suits in the Hillsdale County Circuit Court concerning how he managed flow from their mill pond. The relocation of his overbearing father to Jonesville had created an atmosphere that was oppressive to a young man's independence. Having operated the mill for five years, he viewed closer fatherly supervision with distaste. This inspired him as much as the adventurous appeal of the trip to California, the potential wealth to be gained, or the challenge of the trip across country. He became the leader who shaped the opportunity for a small company of Jonesville men.

The group first met on the evening of Saturday, February 3, 1849, just days after the fire freed up the future of many young men. They discussed going to the gold fields near Sacramento by way of Independence, Missouri. For Henry Baxter this was a way to move beyond his father, allowing him to fully achieve the goals of the venturist on his own. Companies of young men from Adrian, Detroit, Kalamazoo, Marshall, and other Michigan towns were preparing to do the same. Once the idea was on the table, Baxter pushed forward quickly.

They called themselves the "Fayette Rovers" after their home township. Like other groups, the Fayette Rovers were founded along paramilitary lines, yet maintained a democratic government, meaning the group elected officers who exercised authority in the best interest of all. They had bound "ourselves together as to secure harmony, good feeling, and the profit and advantage of all concerned, and to provide as far as possible against the evils and dangers attendant upon such an expedition."[3]

The terms of the agreement showed both exclusivity (any applicant could be barred by one negative vote from existing members) and democratic governance (an equal vote for each company member). But only the affluent could join. There was a $25 application fee, which—upon acceptance of membership—could be applied toward the $300 each member was expected to pay into the treasury. All goods and equipment procured were considered community property and each member's share lived beyond his disablement or death, as long as this was not "occasioned by imprudence." The Sabbath would be observed on the trip, except "under circumstances rendering it absolutely necessary to do otherwise." Intoxication and gambling would not be tolerated. Once they arrived "at the Gold Regions, the members of the Company shall work together, and for the joint interests of all the members of the Company, and the monies, properties and effects which shall be accumulated by the Company, and ... shall not be divided until their arrival home; unless some member or members of the Company are desirous of remaining, in which case their share shall be apportioned to them before starting." Further, "each member of this Company shall consider himself legally, and morally bound, and pledges his honor, to fulfill as far as he can, his duties as a member of this Company, ... and to stand by and relieve, so far as in his power, any member in peril or distress."[4] They elected Henry Baxter, Captain; G.W. Halstead, First Lieutenant; H.W. Platt, Secretary; J.S. Lewis, Treasurer; C. Ralph, Steward.

Additionally, "A.S. Welch, Principal of the Jonesville Academy, is a member of the 'Rovers,' and will take with him a set of mineralogical and assaying instruments, and also those necessary to determine latitude and longitude."[5] Adonijah Welch was a particularly valuable member of the company. The organizing principal of the Jonesville Union School in 1847, he later became the first Principal of the Michigan State Normal School (1851–1865) at Ypsilanti, today known as Eastern Michigan University. He was the most faithful scribe of the company, sending parts of his expansive journal to the *Hillsdale Whig Standard*, the *Milwaukee Sentinel*, the *Detroit Advertiser*, and the *Monroe Commercial*.[6]

Baxter purchased supplies, using his "local knowledge" of travel in the Midwest to anticipate their needs on the trail. As Captain, Baxter was responsible for finalizing all preparations. In many respects, the group operated like a joint stock enterprise, with the concentration of capital, the establishment of articles and bylaws, and leadership structure all testimony to the symbiotic relationship between democracy and capitalism. Baxter's experience in managing funds, men, and the selection of horses made him an ideal leader.

The county was excited by the prospects of success, temporarily uniting citizens of Jonesville and Hillsdale. But the *Standard* spoke for the conservative element when it editorialized,

> We believe this gold seeking to be a wild and hazardous scheme, but those who are going in this company are of the right stamp, and will get a share of the root of all evil if it is to be had.[7]

The 15 Fayette Rovers left Jonesville on Monday, March 12, 1849, bound for Sacramento, California. Hundreds turned out to see them off. L.M. Jones—son of the town founder and owner of the Fayette House—threw a dinner in their honor. The *Standard* stated that they had "provided themselves with the best outfit that could be procured."[8] The company included Henry Baxter, George W. Halstead, H.W. Platt, J.S. Lewis, Calvin R. Ralph, A.S. Welch, A.J. Baker, Andrew Hartman, Ira Latham, G.C. Cooley, A.M. Dibble, J.T. Onderdonk (M.D.), Henry Gregory, Henry Gale, and Peter P. Aker. The latter four were from Kalamazoo.[9]

Henry did not get far. The unresolved mill pond law suit forced his return to Jonesville, where he was deposed on April 10 and 12 by W.W. Murphy. He rode hard to catch up with the balance of the company.[10]

News from the 49ers took time to reach Hillsdale County, leading to anxiety over their safety. The lack of news was bemoaned by the *Standard*:

> All sorts of reports have been circulated about this company of Californians, some to the effect that they had lost part of their members by the Cholera, and others that they were expected to return. We are happy to inform all interested in their welfare that on the 18th of last month they were at St. Francis, Missouri, all well and in fine spirits, and just on the point of starting for Salt Lake, in the company of a Morman [sic] train, many of the members comprising which are well acquainted with the road, having travelled it a number of times.[11]

The Rovers stopped in Council Bluffs, Iowa. The town supplied the Mormon emigrants—the "Saints" of the Church of Jesus Christ of Latter-Day Saints—traveling to their settlement at the Great Salt Lake. As word spread of the gold strikes in California, 49ers flooded the community, bringing with them behaviors the Saints discouraged, including drunkenness, gambling, and fighting. On the other hand, the gold seekers brought plenty of money and offered the Mormons a chance to unload their surplus at a premium. Since Council Bluffs was the

In the decades before the Civil War Henry Baxter achieved prominence as a prosperous Jonesville businessman and favorite among the younger citizens. This popularity led to his election as leader of the Fayette Rovers, a group of adventurers that trekked overland to the California gold country in 1849. This image—probably taken about the time of his journey to California—depicts a confident young man of conservative style and taste (courtesy Chris T. Spencer, Holland, Michigan).

last opportunity to re-provision before crossing the prairie, the 49ers had little choice but to pay an average 26 percent premium in prices.[12] The Rovers re-provisioned while they waited for cattle-sustaining grass to sprout on the plains. They needed to be underway by mid–June in order to arrive before snows made the mountains impassable.

Just as individuals banded together in Jonesville, so too did it become apparent that sharing resources with a larger group would be most advantageous on the longest stretch of the journey. Baxter led the Rovers in a May 12 meeting with groups from Illinois, Iowa, and Michigan that resulted in a consolidation of all under the name of the "Knox County, Illinois Company." Before their departure from Council Bluffs on May 23, new bylaws and a code of conduct were adopted. The leaders of each group were elected lieutenants, creating a second tier of command, including Baxter. Cephas Arms of the large Knox County group was elected overall Captain.[13]

There were five large companies that departed Kanesville in late May. The 574 people of the enlarged Knox Company ferried across the Missouri River on May 23–24. Only one company included women and was therefore a true emigrant train rather than a collection of adventurers bound for the gold fields. They stretched their imaginations to a new definition of "roughing it" during the coming weeks. Solving logistical problems became a daily requirement.

The outbound trip was quite eventful. They were strung out for miles, separated as they forded rivers, dealt with break downs, or hunted lost cattle. On May 28, the advanced unit camped on the banks of the Platte River after using "double teams to get through" terrible roads.[14] Several Pawnee Indians came into the camp that evening and were fed. Although they "seemed very friendly," Arms wrote, "they were the first Indians that had visited us, and nearly all we have seen. We begin to realize that we are in the Indian Country, and the importance of keeping a strict watch both day and night. I have increased the guard to-night."[15] The next day 11 of "our Indian friends returned to camp ... for their breakfast ... they seemed almost starved."[16] Still, Arms had heard that the Indians stole and killed cattle, and so he remained vigilant.

On June 1 they crossed the Cedar River and passed through the ruins of the Pawnee Mission and village. They were fascinated with the remnants of the block house and the village recently destroyed by the Sioux, but they did not tarry. Everyday sights and experiences captivated them. Arms wrote at length about the prairie dogs. He wrote less enthusiastically, but more often about the clouds of mosquitoes that dogged their every movement.[17] All of the travelers wrote of scenery. Their idea of the bigness of the country was being noticeably expanded, and so too progressively was their ability to read the landscape, to pay attention to provisioning, to solve a myriad of logistical problems, and to understand that in a democracy strong leadership skills were essential.

Welch's account of their journey between Council Bluffs and Fort Laramie provides a sense of how the "venturist" acquired and applied their extended local knowledge. While hunting on June 2 Baxter found a note with a description of the "death of Harrison Rowe, merchant at Plattsville, Iowa, who was murdered by the Sioux Indians, May 23, 1849."[18] The Rovers were warned about "leaving their train. When necessary, go in large numbers."[19]

Undeterred, Welch reported that the Rovers

> found the teams gathered on the banks of the Loup, the men being engaged ... preparatory to crossing. The stream is perhaps half a mile in width, but the direction of the ford is oblique and

up the river, which makes the distance in the water about a mile. The average depth where we crossed was two feet.... The current is rapid, and the bottom is a quicksand deposit, so that if a team stops it is liable to sink and be entirely buried. We forded with double teams.... It was a strange scene to see twenty teams, each drawn by eight yoke of oxen, with two or three drivers spouting at the top of their voices, while the cattle were struggling powerfully against the strong current and sinking at every step into the treacherous quicksand. The loaded wagons fill as the bottom was washed from under wheels and produced a sound not unlike the rumble of heavy stones. The ford is much more dangerous for horses than oxen. I came near losing mine while riding across, but he struggled out after a powerful effort. Captain Baxter, in riding in to follow a team, sunk up to his saddle. By three in the afternoon we were all across without accident.[20]

On Sunday, June 3, the company washed clothes, cleaned arms, and completed chores. Baxter and Welch joined Sabbath services at the neighboring Oscaloosa encampment. They found a large tent full of women and an adjacent awning with about 50 men "screaming" out the hymn "When I Can Read My Title Clear."[21] Whatever the comfort communal singing provided the emigrants gathered under the big blue skies on a broad prairie, the poorly delivered text "Treasures of wickedness profit nothing" left the Michiganders "puzzled" as to the speaker's meaning. Welch pronounced,

> The whole sermon was the greatest literary curiosity I ever heard—to say nothing of the silent comment the old man's journey to the gold mines furnished upon his text. I fear that the amusement excited by the sermon on the plains, contributed little to inspire those feelings of devotion with which we should ever listen to the word of God.[22]

They returned to camp glad for "a huge kettle of pork and beans, of which we partook with a relish known only to the 'voyageur.'"[23] Then came more serious business:

> This evening a meeting was held to amend two or three articles in our constitution.—One was ... added, providing for the appointment of four sub-captains to take charge of ten wagons each; this arrangement was strenuously urged by Mr. Miles, ... Baxter, 'of ours,' was selected one of the captains.[24]

Baxter was again recognized for his competence, leadership, and popularity.

On June 4 they started early and made good time thanks to favorable weather. They experienced a minor stampede, their first of the journey:

> A horse broke loose, and followed by a barking dog, ran at full speed, by one of the teams. The cattle sheered off and began to run—the alarm was spread, and in an instant, 20 wagons were wheeling with astonishing velocity across the plains. For a moment, the shouts of the drivers, and the rattle of the wheels, as they dashed together, were deafening; but by timely assistance from those in advance, order was soon restored.[25]

That night they camped on Prairie Creek, a small stream 24 miles up the trail. They made 26 miles on Tuesday, a day without incident except for another notice found stuck on a pole near a small stream. "The Iowa Rangers" warned that "three hunters were driven in by a large band of armed Indians, who pursued them at full speed until they came within three hundred yards of the camp, when, turning they were soon out of sight. Be cautious about hunting in small parties."[26] A healthy fear of Native Americans came from the conclusion "that the intentions of the Indians towards the emigrants, are decidedly hostile."[27] That night they camped near Grand Island, Nebraska.

They suffered calamity about 10 p.m. on June 10 when a stampede emptied the corral of cattle, Baxter led the Rovers out to look for them in the dark, as Welch recounted:

Away through the darkness we rode, at quick gallop, directing our course backward, according to the instructions of the guide, who had told us that in a stampede the cattle would make for "the settlements." The night was dark, but the Moon would rise in an hour. Holding a tight rein, we vaulted at a teaming rate over ditch and slough, bog and bank, expecting every moment to be precipitated headlong from our horses. But our animals proved true; and after an hour's hard ride, we heard the oxen looing [sic], off on the right, and soon came up with them. They had stopped, but were very uneasy. Several horsemen of the Knoxville "ten" joined us, and we surrounded them, endeavoring to keep them together, but a motion, commencing in the centre, communicating itself to the whole mass, and away they rolled with clashing horn and clattering hoof toward the north. On again went the horsemen, and, as the Moon had now risen, we soon succeeded in overtaking them. They now remained quiet and a guard being detained to stay, we returned to camp.... All were cheerful in camp, for we had survived a stampede without the loss of one ox. Three men had been run over but not seriously hurt.[28]

The following night another stampede with more serious consequences occurred. This account gives, as no other text can, a sense of the transient life in an emigrant train. Men and women—confident enough of their abilities back home—were suddenly thrust into an unfamiliar world where they used their skills and common sense to achieve success far away from the shelter or rescue of civilization.

As the guard[s] were driving the cattle into the corral last evening, after dark, a veteran ox was observed to raise his head and exhibit symptoms of disquiet without any apparent cause. The others seemed to watch attentively the movements of the sagacious patriarch for a moment, and then with a loud snuff the whole herd broke simultaneously with their resounding hoofs. Then again rose the cry from every quarter of the camp: "to horse! to horse!!"—and over the plain we flew at a break-neck pace, not knowing but that the next moment we should be dashed over the heads of our horses, or sent with them into the depths of some bottomless slough. Of all rides, it seems to me a night ride on the plains is the most perilous and exciting, especially as the ground is filled with holes of the praire [sic] dog and other animals, in which a horse is constantly liable to fall. Coursing on at full speed, we heard the looing [sic] of an ox about six miles from camp, near the Platte, and soon discovered through the darkness, a long single-file of oxen, running down the river and splashing the water furiously about as they crossed a deep slough. Baxter and Baker immediately rode across with them, while Cooley and I waited until the last were over....

The cattle, after crossing, took a coral [sic] close to the river, while Cooley and I, mistaking the direction, took the road which lies parallel. We galloped two hours before we again heard of them: then following the sound, found them near the river, still running in a long single file—sometimes on a brisk trot, and sometimes dashing off, with head and tail erect, on a swift gallop.

Flying on to the head of the line we tried to sooth them with our voice, crying out with the peculiar intonation of the western driver, s-o-o-k, while they answered looing [sic] more loudly than ever, and the neighboring bluffs echoeing [sic] back each s-o-o-k. At last we succeeded in turning them up the river, in which direction we followed them until we thought ourselves within six miles of the camp, and regarded the prospect of saving our cattle, fair. But our expectations were destined to disappointment. The dark cloud which had hung silently on the verge of the northern horizon suddenly rose, and soon obscured the whole canopy of heaven. The rain beat down upon us in such torrents that we soon had not a dry thread of clothing. No object could be seen half a yard distant except when the inpenetrable [sic] darkness was dispelled by a sudden flash of vivid lightning, which clothed the whole plain and river with a glare or unearthly light, rendering every object distinctively visible for miles distant—an instant then left us in darkness as blind as before.

We lost the points of the compass and abandoned all hope of driving the cattle to camp that night. Looking around us, we discerned in the distance the twinkling of a light, and rightly judging it a beacon raised to guide us back to camp....

Hard riding soon found us to camp, where we hoped to enjoy the luxury of a dry shirt and dry blanket. No such luxury awaited us; the ground under the tents was inundated. Halsted & Arcker [sic] were busily employed in ditching under one to keep the sick men dry, and in the other a few men lay shivering rolled in India rubber clothes. I looked at my watch by the light of a candle in the sick tent, and found it three in the morning. We then tied our weary horses, and soon found our way into a wagon, where, wrapped in our wet clothes, we shivered until we fell asleep.

When we awoke this morning the horses were gone, others having taken them and left camp early to renew the search—Baxter and Baker had brought in forty head of oxen about midnight, after a hard ride. A large number had been collected soon after the stampede by others.[29]

Of the 280 cattle, 127 were missing. Searches on June 13 were equally frustrating, but Baxter persisted in leading the Rovers out with rations for three days. In small groups through a night filled with thunder, lightning, and rain they used their knowledge of bovine behavior to locate and retrieve their charges. Welch remembered that the worst part was attempting to sleep in the rain:

> The rain increased to a torrent which left not a dry fibre upon us. The lightning's red glare made vivid in its quick flashes every object around us, while during the intervals, we were wrapt [sic] in darkness inpenetrable [sic]; and peal after peal of crashing thunder shook the very earth. It rained all night. Wrapping our weapons in a buffalo skin, we placed them under the saddles, and each of us taking a wet blanket and setting upon the ground threw it over his head, so as to form a kind of tent, of which he was the center pole, and in this position, tried to get a little rest.
>
> Vain attempt! No sleep visited our weary eye-lids…. On that lonely plain amid the crashing elements, an observer might have seen, by the lightning's vivid glare, four small white cone like objects in close proximity, silent and motionless, except when a solitary voice arose from one or another of them exclaiming, "well! This is going to Callyforny."[30]

The missing cattle were a serious problem, threatening to strand the group with their gear on the open plains short of locomotive power. Baxter agreed that they must jettisoned items in order to lighten the load, adapting to their changing circumstances and the rapid shift in events between life and death. Several days later a little fun was had with two "exciting chases" of buffalo that resulted in meat for everyone. They were becoming men of the prairie, as illustrated by Arms' comment, "We have had no timber since Saturday morning. Buffalo chips [dried buffalo dung] do first rate as a substitute."[31] Venturists must continually adapt to the resources available around them.

By June 25 the group had been together long enough for Arms to know who to trust. He wrote, "I am very well pleased with that part of the company which are from Michigan. They are quite gentlemen in their intercourse and intelligent men."[32] The Jonesvilleites had made a good impression with their good sense, positive attitudes, self-reliance, and ability to problem solve. The ability to hold together a group while weathering nearly daily life and death struggle marked him as a man upon whom others could rely. Baxter's company was the only one that Arms praised.

Mail delivery being what it was—with the uncertainties of weather, Native American threat, and just plain bad luck—it is amazing that regular correspondence existed at all. Rarer still are occasions when we know why the mail was disrupted. In August 1849 the *Hillsdale Whig Standard* published a letter from Henry Baxter to his father. The letter arrived in a charred envelope providentially saved from the wreck of the "steamer *Algoma*, burned at the wharf, at St. Lois [sic], on the morning of the 29th July 1849.—Said Boat had a large California Mail,—a large portion of which was entirely destroyed."[33] The article included "extracts" of Baxter's letter:

2. Rush for Gold, 1849–1851

Fort Laramie, June 25, 1849

I am now in advance of our train about two days—having came on ahead to look for cattle that we have lost, and I have thus an opportunity of writing and sending by the mail that will leave to-morrow morning....

We left Missouri as I wrote you, on the 23^d of May, and have got along finely with the exception of loosing our cattle.—We had driven three weeks without any trouble, and on Saturday night we camped in order to remain over the Sabbath—about 9 o'clock in the evening our cattle took fright (a Stampede, as it is here termed) and ran as I never saw cattle run before. They were all quietly in the correll, and in an instant, quick as a flash of lightning, they were every one on their feet, and on the full run, so quick even that men on guard standing in the correll could not make their escape, but were knocked down, and trampled under foot—though none were killed—two ... were severely injured, but have now nearly recovered.... The Fayette Rovers have lost ten head, but the balance of the train are well teamed, and by dividing up we shall all be enabled to proceed without difficulty, even should we find no more of our cattle. We may dispose of one of our wagons here, and go on with four, though I cannot tell until our train arrives.

I have never enjoyed better health in my life than since I started on the trip. It is the same with nearly all the members of our Company....

The feed on the hills and over the mountains, is said to be better than it has been before for years, and I think very likely this is so, as this has been a very wet Spring. I find the trip quite as laborious as I expected—though not so much so as to prevent my enjoying it very much.—[Adonijah] Welch is in good health and spirits and is a first rate man for the expedition—as indeed are all of our men.

I think the prospect now is, that we shall get through to the Sacrimento [sic] this fall. This however, we cannot say with any degree of assurance, as it will depend entirely upon luck, and many contingencies upon which we cannot calculate with accuracy.

The Indians, thus far, have not troubled or molested us, in the least—indeed we have seen but very few; and the reason assigned by those who are conversant with them is, that they dare not come among the emigrants for fear of the Cholera.... The cholera ... has been continually on the decrease since we left the river, and it is now seldom that we hear of a case in any of the trains—my opinion is that it may generally be avoided by proper precaution.[34]

That Baxter was sent ahead to Fort Laramie to look for lost cattle shows that he had won the trust of Ames and other group leaders after only a month on the trail. His letter reveals a realist, self-assured and confident in his ability to apply his extended local knowledge, but sanguine about the role of providence in success. As in later correspondence, Baxter is optimistic about the future and quick to acknowledge the good qualities of those around him. These were qualities liked by his companions.

The remainder of Baxter's group arrived in Fort Laramie about noon on June 28. They ferried across the Platte River on a small flat boat owned by the American Fur Company at $1.50 per wagon. Arms recorded that the fort itself did "not present a very imposing appearance."[35] Supplies were limited and therefore expensive. On the other hand, heavy items were in ready supply. "Wagons can be had for almost nothing. Rifles are thrown by the dozen into the river and worthless white beans almost cover the ground, old stoves are almost without number thrown away. We shall leave one wagon at least from our train, perhaps more."[36]

Arms felt that the group had been "favored in regard to health," but the stock was in trouble.[37] "We find grass very scarce indeed to-night, and we had to drive our cattle six miles from the road and expect it to get worse as we advance, as all [four] roads converge into one.... Where we now are there are several trains camping. I feel they are getting too thick, and whether we shall be able to reach California this fall is quite uncertain."[38] The lack of sufficient grass created counterproductive competition. Faster wagon trains passed in an attempt to grab the best pasturage before others could claim it. This logistical problem weighed heavily upon the slow-moving group as it neared Salt Lake.

Henry Gregory of Kalamazoo was also with the party, but ahead of the rest. He wrote from the Summit of South Pass, Rocky Mountains, that since leaving Fort Laramie they had had to drive their cattle up to ten miles from the road in order to find grass to feed them. Clearly, transiting country where so many wagon trains had passed had challenges:

> The road is lined with shovels, picks, crowbars, wagons, dead oxen, etc., and in fact, every thing that was not necessary to sustain life, has been left by the wayside, in order to get along a little faster. We have passed fifty dead Oxen in one day. Two yoke of our cattle have died within the last week, and the prospect for getting to California this fall begins to look rather discouraging.[39]

Though the progress was slow, the daily challenges they faced were not enough to dull the wonder of the changing topography. Whenever stopped near a prominent elevation, they climbed it to see "scenery the most beautiful and grand I ever saw" and gauge what lay ahead.[40] This fascination with learning the intricacies of the big country—large both in elevation and in breadth—was an ongoing theme of the venturists. Overcoming environmental impediments was ever present, but their sense of what constituted real struggle was stretched as ever greater challenges were met and matched.

A tenser political situation was posed by a growing difference of opinion within the group. One faction felt that they should stay together. A minority believed that the only way to insure proper feed for their oxen was to drive them ahead as quickly as possible, leaving the slower wagons to make their way forward as best they could.

On Sunday, July 8, the group had a meeting to discuss dividing the company. Baxter supported maintaining the existing order with Arms in charge. Captain Cephas Arms "took no part in it. The object failed, though four teams drove off and more will."[41] From this point onward, they found little grass. With no food available and left unattended at night, 34 cattle started for home, or the last place they remembered having food. A contingent from the company retraced the trail to recover them. Enough oxen were lost that they could not move all the wagons at once, instead using teams to haul some ahead, then returning for the others. On July 13 they only made six miles. Arms wrote, "The road is full of teams, some with oxen, some with mules, some with horses, some on carts, and some on foot with their packs on their backs," creating a disappointing rate of progress.[42]

Then there was another stampede. This time the oxen ran through the encampment stirring up such dust and commotion that no one could see or hear where the cattle were or which direction they were running. Members of the company had little cover and feared that they might be run down. Several people were injured. By then, because of the lack of good pasturage the "cattle are very much reduced in strength," creating the possibility that the group might be stranded or have to abandon its wagons.[43] Arms reported, "The road is strewn with dead cattle. Eight lay dead in one pile…. They are said to die from bad water."[44]

On July 15 the party passed the aptly-named Devil's Gate. They discovered a little valley that had been untouched by previous emigrant trains and the rich grass helped to restore strength to the stock. There were other issues. "The mountains rising far to the west and north are covered with snow and though the days are warm, the nights are quite cold."[45] Cold, tired, and reduced by hunger, the group continued through the mountains toward the Great Salt Lake.

Starting on July 19 stampedes further slowed the company. They spent July 20–22 camped while they retrieved their cattle. On Sunday, July 22, "five teams drew off this morning for fear of stampedes and went on."[46] In the mountains on July 24, they cut grass for the cattle because snow impeded pasturage for the next 24 miles.

On July 25 they made the South Pass summit (elevation 7,500 feet) about mid-day, and started down the west slope. That night they camped at Pacific Springs. "I think if we have no more misfortunes we will get through to California this fall," Arms wrote. "Our train is now reduced to our original number of wagons. All that joined us have again left us. We find that small companies get along better than large ones. Ours is too large now, but we do not like to divide." A Mormon from Salt Lake camped with the group, providing a positive impression of both California gold and the community at Salt Lake:

> We have determined to go by Salt Lake. By so doing we shall get better feed to the Lake and from there to the old road two hundred miles west of Fort Hall. When we arrive at the Lake if we find it impossible to go on, we must submit to stay there, and do the best we can.... Most of the boys are well and in good spirits, but very much afraid of stampedes, and it is no wonder. An earthquake is scarcely more to be dreaded, or more terrible.[47]

On August 1, they arrived at Fort Bridger and camped nearby. Arms was surprised that

> several Indians met us to-day, begging food and presents. There are three or four hundred of them at the fort, who thronged around us as soon as we camped, begging food and trying to get the advantage in some petty trade. They are much shrewder than I expected to find them. They abound in good horses, but are so much under the influence of the trade that they would not part with any of them to the emigrants. Mr. Bridger is a man 39 years old; and has been with the Indians 28 years. He appears much older, and is a kind hearted and affable man. He showed us a lump of pure gold found in the creek near him; and he is strong in the belief that it abounds here in the mountains.[48]

Bridger's post was 114 miles from Salt Lake. On August 4 they crossed the "highest ridge between the South pass and Salt Lake, being 7314 feet above the level of the sea."[49] On August 7 they made it up Kanyon Creek:

> From the top of the mountain was one of the most splendid views I ever beheld. It was a wilderness of mountains imposing and indescribable. One could hardly suppose so many could be crowded into so small a space. The Salt Lake valley was visible at the distance of 15 miles. I could have lingered long gazing on the magnificent scene before me, but time did not permit more than a hasty glance. The sun was sinking behind the far distant mountains, and a dangerous descent was before us.[50]

The main body of the group arrived at Salt Lake mid-afternoon on August 8. One can sense Arms' relief:

> It was truly pleasant after so long and tiresome a journey, being exposed to every hardship and danger and covered with dust, once more to look on the abodes of civilization, and to approach a spot where, however we might feel in other respects, we might hope to enjoy again for a short time a few of the comforts of life. The city is located at the foot of the Bluffs; and has the appearance, somewhat, of a very large farm. The little one story sunburnt brick [adobe] cabins being almost hid by the corn, and the land is so level that almost every foot in the city, and for a good distance around can be irrigated. This is done by turning water from the Kanyon and conducting it in every direction by means of little ditches.[51]

The Rovers had lost 14 of 32 cattle during the three month journey, but they had not lost a single man.

Time in Salt Lake was spent exploring. Some of the emigrants were recognized, singled out, and ostracized for having opposed the Mormons back east. Others, like Arms, attended services of which he said, "Such a meeting for religious worship I never attended."[52] There were bands, public notices, a variety of speakers, and sermons that were not traditionally experienced in more established faiths.

The group rested and discussed their next step. The northern route did not seem feasible. There were persistent rumors of trouble with tribes based on murders committed by a group of "packers" who were also rumored to have set fire to the grasslands. Claims of multiple roads impassable because of dead oxen and abandoned wagons abounded. They could go forward, presuming that they could choose a route and find a guide. The lateness of the season was of serious concern. They might not make it over the mountains before they were snowed in, and no one wanted to face a situation like the Donner Party had, stranded in the mountains and forced into cannibalism to survive. They could remain the coming winter, presuming they could collect enough resources to live on, and depart in the spring. However, the Mormons warned that they could not supply the group through the winter.

The company was of two minds. Arms led a faction who believed they should continue via the usual emigrant route despite the lack of pasturage. From Salt Lake stock feed was sparse and the second group led by Baxter felt they were better off waiting until October 1 to take the "more difficult route far to the south."[53] The route to the south was considered to be of about the same distance—roughly 800 miles—but safer given the reported situation to the north. They would have to raise the resources—in this case dozens of additional emigrant wagons in order to reach the 100 minimum needed to afford a guide. "So another long and tedious road is before me, or rather the sequel to a most toilsome one," Arms complained. "It is the prevailing opinion here that not one ox in fifty that leaves here at this season will ever reach California."[54]

C.J. Collins of Adrian left the group, took the northern route, and reached California on September 26. He later indicated that

> the Jonesville boys got as far as the Mormon settlements, and their Captain was afraid to go any further on account of the Indians. So about half of them stayed with him, and the rest have come along.[55]

This comment that Baxter was "afraid" seems oddly out of place for a man who is repeatedly mentioned by those close to him as leading difficult, uncertain incursions into the wilderness. A little over a decade later this same man went boldly into battle, was wounded many times, and was repeatedly promoted for bravery in the face of enemy fire. Baxter proved indefatigable in his efforts to keep the company moving forward. Perhaps this caution on behalf of the entire group, a sure sign of mature responsibility, put off the self-centered Collins. Ultimately the rumored perils of the northern route convinced Arms and a majority of the others to vote for the southern trail. On August 13 Arms wrote, "If we go this fall we shall go that route."[56]

On August 17 the Rovers and their companions moved south to a new camp located in "Utah Valley," 60 miles south near present-day Provo. They stayed for three weeks. Welch and others became acquainted with prominent members of the Mormon community while they planned a route that would strike the coast at San Francisco 600 miles south of the mines. They would traverse the southwest that had been acquired from Mexico via the Treaty of Guadalupe Hidalgo (1848). Through this country horses travelled better than oxen, and so they traded. Their preparedness for the last stage of the journey was savvy of the expected hardships:

> Our provisions will carry us to Sacrimento. [*sic*] All our clothing, except a pair of extra pants, three extra shirts, a coat, hat, and one pair of boots, apiece, is to be left in lieu of horses. Many emigrants have given as high as $200 for a good horse—others give two yoke of oxen and a wagon.[57]

Welch indicated that he could not "regret leaving Michigan … for I have entirely recovered my health."[58] Despite the hardships he had experienced, he lauded "the pleasure of the jaunt" as worth the privations[59]:

> Our long journey has wrought amusing changes in our personal appearance. If you saw me, as I now sit on the ground with my portfolio before me, you would hardly recognize me; and if you did, would be unwilling, I fear, to acknowledge your *quondam* acquaintance. A slouched hat, the worse for the wear, and a pair of moccasins set off the extremities of "*caput et calces*," and in addition, a red flannel shirt, and a pair of sheep's gray's complete your friends toilet. His face shows none of the pallor of the student or the sickliness of lean disease, but is full and sunburnt, and covered with a beard of three months' growth, in which tinges of pale yellow and white struggle for the mastery, the yellow on the whole predominating. But the change is in his person alone. His feelings, attachments, principles and prejudices remain unchanged.[60]

Baxter presided as the Fayette Rovers voted to become part of the larger group, then entrusted themselves to the hands of a Mormon guide named Jefferson Hunt who charged $10 per wagon to traverse the southern route, roughly from present-day Provo to Las Vegas and Los Angeles. Hunt's trail was one he had traveled with pack mules, but not with wagons.

At the encampment they enjoyed "excellent feed for our cattle … [and] … plenty of speckled trout."[61] Reports of local gold finds intrigued them, though the Mormons would not share where the gold came from. They viewed hot springs and observed the departure of local Indians for Santa Fe near which there were reportedly fights with "the Americans."[62]

Preparations for the trip continued. On September 25 Arms wrote, "I am opposed to leaving our wagons, and packing through, as we shall be far less comfortable on the way, and must leave our clothing, bedding here. We shall not reach the mines before December, or January."[63] The inaction in camp got to Arms, who was "heartily tired of laying here with nothing to do."[64] Lack of activity bred discontent.

Just before departure, a company of Mormons returned with two million dollars of gold dust from California. Arms reported, "The mines are becoming richer and richer, and what encourages us is that the richest mines are on the road we are going, nearer than the Sacramento."[65] Enthusiasm about their prospects was mounting.

The reconstituted train included families also leery of the dangerous northern route. Families were not the best traveling companions for the 49ers because they moved with less haste, slowing the entire train.[66] This would pose serious problems for a group that needed to move quickly and reach their destination before the supplies they carried were exhausted.

Welch helped draft a constitution, the third that the Rovers created during the trip. The constitution created seven divisions composed of ten or more wagons, each headed by a Captain. A Colonel and Adjutant were elected to overall authority. Together the nine officers made up a "council" that decided all major issues. As the foremost advocate for the southern route, Henry Baxter was elected Colonel. Dr. William McCormick was made Adjutant and Cephus Arms was elected Captain of the "Buckskin" division. Other divisions were named the San Joaquin (Sand Walkers), Bug Smashers, Hawkeyes, Jayhawks, and Wolverines. Arms was unfazed by being supplanted by Baxter as leader of this reconstituted group, indicating that he trusted that the train was in good hands. Baxter was elected by a group composed both of people who had traveled with him and knew him well, and people who had just met him and had little firsthand knowledge of his experience and leadership capabilities. To inspire the trust that he was the best leader to make good decisions, problem solve, and look out for the order and welfare of all among a group largely composed of virtual strangers illustrates how far he had come as a venturist. From this moment on, he was the key figure who made life and death decisions that impacted everyone.

One hundred four wagons started off on October 1, 1849. Three companies were sent ahead to mark the road, which worked well until they made Beaver Creek, 20 miles north of Little Salt Lake. They followed valleys that ran on a roughly northeast/southwest axis between mountain ranges, shifting periodically to the next major valley in order to make westerly progress. About October 18 their guide advised them to leave the main trail for a short cut along Beaver Creek, which traversed one of these mountain ranges and moved to the next valley. Hunt assured them this would save them 40 to 50 miles.[67]

Arms' band, including the Fayette Rovers, took the trail on the untried short cut. By October 22 the group found themselves in a "desert" without water. Arms reported for the first time "our guide is off the direct route and there is no disguising the fact that we are lost. With a further drive of twenty-five miles, at least, and no one knows how much further, before we come to water."[68] While the guide was off on foot looking for water, 30 or 40 wagons decided to return to the main route. When the guide and his party returned "nearly exhausted with hunger and thirst" early on October 24, the remainder of the group realized that retracing their route was all that could be done.[69]

Distrust grew into a serious morale issue. They needed to rely on Hunt, but his experimentation led the group to question not only the sensibility of their $1,000 retainer, but more importantly whether he was competent to get them to their destination alive. Since a quick passage was fundamental to success, the loss of time in unproductive travels compounded by the waste of essential provisions could prove fatal. Gradually the group began to splinter under the tension wrought by mistrust.

They lost several days backtracking to the Old Spanish Trail. On the way, they ran into a contingent of packers who told them of a shorter route that avoided the deserts of the Spanish Trail all together. After their recent failure, some were in favor of following this route. The more conservative—including Baxter, Arms and his group—continued on the main trail.

On October 26 they crossed in "much confusion" the mountain they had tried to avoid.[70] They arrived at Little Salt Lake on October 27. On the 28th the council heard complaints. Arms wrote, "Many are getting dissatisfied with so large a train, and are determined to leave it and find their own way to California, among them Capt. Doty's division [the Jay-Hawks], containing the Knox county boys and our division [the Buckskins]."[71] On October 30, the Jayhawks started off alone and the Buckskins determined to follow the next day. With the group splintering quickly in their mistrust of the guide, Baxter was unable to hold the group together. He remained with the group he had the most faith in. "Colonel [Baxter], who is a member of our division, resigned his office, producing quite a sensation in camp."[72] This was the final blow to morale.

The Buckskins followed the Jay-Hawks and arrived at the cut off for the new trail on

November 3. The two groups did not travel together since the Jayhawks wanted to remain independent of slow-moving families. All went well for two days, then on the third Arms caught up with the Jay-Hawks who seemed stymied by an impassable route. Arms pushed forward and found a way through to a small valley with grass, but no water. They camped on November 6 and searched for Captain Orson K. Smith's pack trail. At daylight Arms went off with Calvin Ralph of Jonesville and found Smith's trail, but after a 40-mile trek, they had to return to the Buckskins with the intelligence that the trail was impassable to ox-teams. Additional explorations were not positive, bringing the realization that the only "alternative [was] to retrace our steps, unless we conclude to throw away our wagons, pack our cattle and move on to California. The latter I am in favor of, as are many others. Captain Taylor and most of the families will return to the trail."[73] Morale sank even lower.

The group was coming apart. Arms reported, "The mind not being occupied with its accustomed daily duties, has dwelt upon the difficulties before and around us, at home, California and every other place until none know what to do, no two think alike. Truly we are in a multitude of counselors, but I fear the proverb will not prove true in our case, if we could but move forward all discontent would soon cease."[74] When the last of the scouts returned with reports that indicated even pack oxen might not be feasible, the decision became clear.

At this important juncture and when his leadership skills were most needed, Henry Baxter was incapacitated by "Mountain Fever" and for "three weeks afterward his life was despaired of."[75] The lack of a strong leader with practical problem solving and excellent people skills acerbated an already difficult situation. How much he was able to contribute at this point is unknown, but both Welch and Arms indicate that his loss was significant. Welch attributed Baxter's survival to "a good constitution and the kind attention of Doct. [Caleb] Ormsby of Ann Arbor."[76] By "the constant watching that his illness required," Welch too came down with the fever, though apparently not as severely.[77]

The inability to find an alternate route through the mountains forced most of the wagons back to the Old Spanish Trail. Arms led his division back to the trail on November 13. The ill-fated short cut cost ten days of travel and the associated provisions. Arms commented that they had "gained another lesson on the folly of exploring with ox-teams."[78]

Arms was made of strong stuff. He kept his sense of humor and positive perspective. He wrote that once they were back on the Spanish Trail "we got along very well."[79] On November 14 they got six to eight inches of snow. They reached the Virgin River on the 20th. Baxter was still ill, but was beginning to convalesce.

Companies that passed this way "had been molested by Indians," but the Buckskins kept a close guard and escaped unscathed warned by an encounter with a live ox they found pierced by seven arrows.[80] Such sights reminded them of their vulnerability and strengthened their vigilance.

Water along the trail was scarce and in order to reach it they had to overcome

> the hardest road we had as yet found, six miles of deep heavy sand and up hill, where many cattle gave out at the head of the train. We had to ascend a most tremendous hill, half a mile long with the sand deep until within 150 or 200 feet of the top, which was so steep that cattle could not draw, and we had to draw our wagons up with ropes. By midnight they were all up safe.[81]

By traveling all night they reached the Big Muddy about an hour after sunrise. At this point they were one valley east of present-day Las Vegas. They rested until December 3, allowing the oxen to eat what little grass and scanty shrubs were available in preparation for "the desert of fifty miles before us."[82] While in camp, a group they had not seen since the box canyons came in badly depleted from their trip over the mountains. They had eaten their horses to survive. There were 12 from the Sand Walkers and four of Smith's pack company. They were welcomed and their needs satisfied.

On the 3rd they crossed the desert, arriving at Cash Spring early on December 5. They were desperately short of supplies. Some of the Buckskins went ahead to send back help from the settlements. The company had difficulty finding water and snow covered what little grass for the oxen could be found.

On December 10 they began to ascend again, finding the snow getting deeper the higher they went. Wagons were abandoned and teams consolidated. They helped each other carry items of importance. Arms remained behind to help the stragglers. The pass held snow 15 to 18 inches deep and the ascent was steep. When Arms caught up with the main body that evening, they were stalled about two miles from the summit. Frozen feet and lack of food had paralyzed the group. Arms was able to get them moving, cresting the summit that night. The next day they had made it far enough down the western slope to find pasturage for their oxen.

They reached first Willow Spring, then Hernandez Spring on December 16. Two hundred eighty-four pounds of flour and beans had been left for them by Captain Charles Dallas. Arms relates, "We had to pay fifty cents per pound, but were glad of it at any price, as our mess had but ten pounds of flour left" and others were entirely out.[83]

Their next obstacle was the Mohave Desert. They crossed at night, using rain water to hydrate the stock, but found no grass at Bitter Spring. There was no choice but to push on. Continuing, they found only a dry river bed where there was supposed to be water. By then, the Buckskins were in terrible shape:

> Our teams were parched with thirst, not having drank for sixty hours, as they would not drink at the Bitter Spring. We continued to travel on until midnight, when many cattle gave out, yet we still expected every moment to get water, and continued to urge our exhausted teams until 3 o'clock a.m., when many more dropped down, among the rest two in our team. Finding it impossible to go on, we determined to stop until morning. Most of the teams kept on and reached the river at 5 o'clock a.m. I was nearly as much exhausted as the cattle, having taken nothing for supper except a small piece of bread, all we had, and drank half a cup of coffee, having no water to make more. About midnight, one of our Ladies gave me a piece of new bread, which was one of the sweetest morsels I ever [ate]. I … got an hour's sleep, and the next morning we reached the river, five miles distant, when I felt our troubles in regard to our teams were over; but could not but feel anxious in regard to ourselves. Our flour and meat were all gone…. I succeeded in the course of the day in killing a hare, which furnished our Christmas breakfast, and a rather sorrowful one it was too.[84]

On December 27 a messenger told them that food was on the way. The relief was palpable: "We all felt that God had not forsaken us."[85] The journey resumed and the following day they met "Spaniards" carrying flour and beans plus some sugar and salt, "enough to last us through."[86]

On New Year's Day they transited Calhoun Pass (Cajon Pass), arriving in rainy Lower California determined to finish their harrowing journey. They arrived in California with little more than the clothes on their backs. Arms reports,

> I suffered some from hunger and fatigue toward the close of our journey, as our provisions became exhausted and we had to subsist mostly upon our cattle, killing those that had become too weak to travel, and eating the beef with little or no salt, and this in crossing deserts over which we had to cross in the night time. In consequence, we all became very weak and thin. Many have lost all

their cattle and have been compelled to leave their wagons filled with goods upon the desert; but we came through with all ours and was thus able to render some assistance to others less fortunate.[87]

On January 4, 1850, they arrived at the Spanish Rancho after a ten month journey. They paid $12 to have a cow butchered and ate. Prices were high (pumpkins $1 each, onions $1.25 each, potatoes $5 per bushel), but they accepted the expense as good-humoredly as they could, knowing that the volume of emigrants created a high demand.

Cattle and horse ranches abounded, but farming was still small scale. The hills were virtually covered with cattle, "which are almost as wild as deer."[88] Californians used sharpened blocks of wood to till the soil, steel-bladed "American" plows being in short supply. The land was rich, but the "Spaniards and Indians" Welch rated as living in "a state of semi-barbarism, and consequently [California's] resources are to a certain extent undeveloped."[89] "They are too indolent to raise much grain," he complained, "though the soil will yield, I am told, eighty bushels of wheat to the acre."[90] Some ranchos were abandoned because everyone had gone to the gold fields. Arms marveled at the availability of oranges, figs, and bananas and declared the climate "delightful."[91]

The tired group finally arrived at Colonel Isaac William's Ranch in southern California near present-day Chino Hills, in February 1850. The Rovers found that "a joint stock company is not the 'thing' for this country." They took a short rest and amiably divided their few remaining resources before setting off on separate paths.[92]

Arms declared that he would never repeat the journey for any amount of California gold, but he had learned "a lesson in regard to the providence of God, which I shall never forget."[93] Despite this, Arms professed himself "perfectly satisfied with the decision of coming through the Spanish trail, and also that there has been far less suffering amongst us than there would have been had we gone through the northern route, though we might have got safely through."[94] Welch described the experiment of the southern desert route with so large a group of wagons as having "terminated disastrously."[95]

In late February Welch served as mineralogist on an expedition funded by Colonel Williams. The object was to reach a spot 150 miles inside the desert where gold had supposedly been found. If the expedition was successful, Welch expected his "fortune is made."[96] Baxter was recuperating at the Gabriel Mission, resting until Welch returned or sent for him. Welch was involved in this speculation for about three weeks, but the ore found was not sufficiently valuable to pay for the expense of mining it. He saved a specimen to donate to the University of Michigan.

When Welch returned, he and Baxter struck off together. They found little gold, a disappointing haul after taking almost a year to cross the continent. Welch, Baxter, and three others started north for the Mariposa digs (about 400 miles away) via the Tulare Valley. High rivers and exploration delayed their arrival in Mariposa, and once again they were disappointed by what they found. They continued on to Stockton. From there on June 20, Welch wrote home telling of their adventures in California. Baxter and Welch finally split up. Welch went on alone to the Merced River later that summer, but soon returned to Michigan.[97]

Few of the Rovers stayed in California long. Calvin Ralph and A.S. Welch returned via water, arriving back in Jonesville in early February 1851. Welch again became principal of the Jonesville Union School for the spring term and was feature speaker at the village July 4 celebration that year.[98] Baxter was not far behind. Most of the Rovers were back in Jonesville by 1852 without gaining the quick wealth they had hoped for, but strengthened by a test of character and a set of experiences that were to have a significant impact on their later lives.

⇒ ⇐

    Through his experience with the Rovers Henry acquired new depth to his leadership, organizational, and problem solving skills. The experience greatly extended his realm of local knowledge. He traveled easily among men, being elected by virtual strangers to exercise leadership where life itself was at risk. He picked very able companions, but was unafraid of striking out alone into the gold fields, which speaks to his confidence. He demonstrated the skills of an outdoorsman and indicated that the lifestyle agreed with him. He was, in short, the kind of man that would excel at whatever he did in a world where practical leadership was essential. The things that he learned on the trail to California prepared him for even greater levels of responsibility to come.

3

Building Family and Community, 1853–1860

By 1852 Henry Baxter had returned to Jonesville wiser and more experienced. Like his fellow Rovers, he traveled via ship from San Francisco, across Panama by pack mule, and by ship back to the eastern states. After the amazing heights and the tremendous lows that he had experienced, one might imagine that Baxter was ready to get back to work, which is exactly what he did. In 1852 he was again "engaged in milling and other business."[1] But he returned to his previous life with a significantly broader perspective of the world and its possibilities. The disappointment of not coming home gold-wealthy was superseded by his exhilarating encounters with the Indians, the mountains and valleys he traversed, and the Spanish culture he experienced in California and Central America. He had been elected to lead virtual strangers across alien deserts and mountains. Altogether, he came back an even more confident man, seasoned with a profound and extended local knowledge.

The seasoning was important. Henry was the only Baxter to follow the example of his grandfathers and father, traveling westward to seek his fortune in true venturist style. His limited education, practical business experience, leadership, and adventurous spirit more closely aligned him with the traditional expansionist emigrant than the focus on education, the law, and politics that fit his older brothers. With his extended local knowledge, ability to solve problems, and capability to lead people from divergent backgrounds, he had become the confirmed venturist, a broadly experienced and valuable man. Henry was the transitional figure that, based upon his own energy, experience, and cunning, was poised to advance onto the national stage.

Much had happened in Michigan while the Rovers were away. The massive expansion of potential slave territory of the Southwestern United States, a national constitutional crisis, and over a decade of Democratic dominance in state government led to significant changes.

In 1850 Michigan's economy was concentrated in the southern Lower Peninsula where Levi Baxter had carefully cultivated his economic and political power. Fully two-thirds of the 397,654 citizens of Michigan lived in the lower two tiers of counties, one third in the southeastern counties of Macomb, Monroe, Oakland, Washtenaw, and Wayne. This disparity in population was resented further north where railroads were non-existent and good roads hard to come by. The Great Lakes offered an ideal avenue for reaching western and eastern markets—including the eastern seaboard via the Erie Canal or St. Lawrence River—but only if one was able to get the product to a lake port. This problem was particularly acute in the northern Upper Peninsula where Lake Superior was not yet adequately connected to the other parts of the Great Lakes system because of the St. Mary's Rapids at Sault Ste. Marie. A state rich in resources, but lacking the infrastructure to transport them to market made a frustrating combination.[2]

From June 3 through August 15, 1850, a constitutional convention in Lansing altered the power structure. Many of the northern counties were not yet organized, but they would be eventually and their interests would differ from the southern counties. In the south, the Chicago Road and cross state railroads kept the area firmly on the trail of emigrants heading west and the flow of products to market. The northern counties received little, if any, of this trade. There was clear evidence of animosity between towns that had railroads and those that did not.[3]

The resulting Democrat-dominated Michigan State Constitution of 1850 focused on limited government in an attempt to pull power away from the control of a few politicians seated during the territorial and early statehood period. The intent was to invest control in the wider electorate. Underlying this move were pressures and anxieties acerbated by the shift from frontier subsistence to a market economy more closely tied to the east. In short, Michigan was experiencing growing pains in its transition from territory to mature state. Those anxieties manifested themselves amid significant economic fluctuations and increasing sensitivity to the national issue of slavery. The 1850 Constitution reflected this, providing limited biennial legislative sessions instead of the annual session, and replacing representation based on the number of organized counties and population with representation by single districts. Not surprisingly, delegates from Detroit resisted the change since it reduced the power that the metropolis would have in the legislature. The new constitution overwhelmingly passed by voters on November 5 limited government and attempted to offset sectionalism.[4]

None of the Baxters took part in the 1850 Convention because the Whig party was not in favor with Michigan voters. One of the representatives for Hillsdale County was Jonathan B. Graham of Jonesville. Graham held multiple elected offices, mostly in Fayette Township, but was a novice in state legislative matters. A prevailing influence—though not a delegate—was George C. Munro, who led the local Democratic Party.

Lack of participation in the convention did not imply lethargy. Levi was busy with state government and domestic matters. In February 1850 he represented the concerns of Hillsdale County citizens who objected to the county borrowing money to build a new court house without first putting it to a public vote. In May 1850 the *Jonesville Telegraph* recognized the existence of this enmity between Jonesville and Hillsdale in its exchanges with its Democratic adversary, the *Hillsdale Gazette*:

> It is well known that there has and still exist among local feeling and jealousy between the different local interests of this county, and however much any attempt may be made to disguise the fact the result of the present election speaks too plainly to be misunderstood.[5]

Bemoaning the switch of the *Gazette* from Whig to Democratic allegiance, the *Telegraph* echoed the belief of the Baxter faction that the world—or in this case Hillsdale County—was rapidly and indisputably going straight to hell.[6] In any case, Levi Baxter was firmly aligned with anti-slavery activity in the Michigan legislature.

He was also busy with an extended family. In June 1850 Levi was the head of a 12- person

3. Building Family and Community, 1852–1860

household. Levi and wife Elizabeth were joined by children Witter, Helen, Lois, Antoinette, Elizabeth, Susan, Clara, Charles, and Florence, and hired man Jacob Lafr. Levi's real estate was valued in the 1850 census at $30,000, a large sum in those days.

As the result of Levi's influence in the Senate, the Michigan Southern Railroad reached Jonesville in 1850. A subscription was opened for the Homer and Jonesville Plank Road Company. Homer was a growing town 15 miles northwest where the citizens were lobbying for a cross peninsula canal linking the Detroit River and Lake Michigan. In 1851 the population of Jonesville reached 565. The population of Hillsdale—now the county seat—was 1,067, indicating that Jonesville was firmly established as the second city of Hillsdale County. The community rivalry continued, the *Telegraph* reporting on October 21, 1851,

> Hillsdale is going ahead slowly, but not so fast as its persevering rival Jonesville. The latter village contains the most energetic, enterprising business men who will push themselves into notoriety somehow, and push their village along with them. If business will not come of its own accord, they will pull it there by the heels.[7]

Certainly the construction of a new railroad freight depot, burgeoning business blocks, and the new Presbyterian Church illustrated that Jonesville was making progress.

Henry's brother Witter—since early 1848 partner in a thriving Jonesville law practice with William Walton "Walt" Murphy (1816–1886)—married his law partner's sister-in-law. Through Murphy's wife Ellen, Witter became acquainted with her sister Alice Beaumont (1831–1872), daughter of Abram Lovett Beaumont and Clarissa Gregg Holley, and married her at Hillsdale on July 28, 1852. They shared an interest in education. Alice was a teacher at the Fayette Union School in 1851 and Witter—a former teacher himself—was soon elected to the local school board as well as the Michigan Board of Education. Other Beaumont sisters would eventually marry A.S. Welch and I.B. Sill, both educators at the Fayette Union School. The Beaumont girls were granddaughters of New York abolitionist and co-founder of the Liberty Party Myron Holly (1779–1841).

The association with Walt Murphy was to be one of the most important partnerships the Baxters were to form. From a politically-connected Monroe family, Murphy was active in county politics from his arrival in Jonesville in 1837. He was involved in a number of important firsts, including opening the first law office in the

The second son of Levi Baxter, Witter Baxter was an attorney, entrepreneur, and staunch Republican who frequently drafted the state party election platform. The influence Witter wielded with business partner W.W. Murphy was critical in building a strong power base in the county and the state.

county in partnership with William T. Howland (1838), proprietor of the first printing press (1839), publisher of the first newspaper (the *Jonesville Telegraph* 1839), and, for one term, county prosecutor. Late in life Murphy was described as "a rough diamond; one of the most uncouth mortals that ever lived; but bighearted, shrewd, a general favorite, and prized even by those who smiled at his oddities."[8]

Murphy's anti-slavery proclivities led to a small victory for abolitionists in 1839. Slave catchers representing a Maysville, Kentucky, slave owner found and attempted to return a runaway calling himself George Branegan. He was a well-known cook at the Jonesville Exchange (later the Fayette House), the primary hotel and restaurant in Jonesville. The case went before justice of the peace Henry Packer. The slave catchers argued that under federal law they had the right to return Branegan to Kentucky, a slave state. Murphy cleverly demanded that the court be shown written "authenticated laws" as proof that Kentucky was a slave state. Packer gave the slave catchers an hour to procure verification. Unable to produce written evidence, the plaintiffs withdrew their suit. Branegan left town, defeating the attempt to capture him. This tactic received national attention, was cited as a precedent in a Philadelphia case, and cemented the reputation of Jonesville as firmly anti-slavery.[9]

⸺

The Baxter family was reaching maturity. On June 15, 1853, 19-year-old Lois Francis married 31-year-old Robert Oliver Selfridge in Tecumseh. They moved to Jackson and then to Ripon, Wisconsin, where Selfridge owned a general store and became a founder of the local Republican Party.

Murphy's *Telegraph* burst with pride in the maturing town:

> Situated as it is, in one of the best wheat growing sections of the State, surrounded by heavily timbered land, rolling oak openings and burr oak plains beautifully interspersed, each giving the farm assurance of a fair, if not an abundant crop to renumerate him for his labor, it possesses advantages over those portions of the State which have only one of the above kinds of land.... Owing to the undulating surface, this section is more healthy than the lower portions which alone should be an inducement to emigrants to settle here, and when they can have good land, good schools and good markets in addition, the advantages are unequalled by any other part of the State....
>
> The St. Joseph River at this point furnishes a good water power, which is improved by the Hon. L. Baxter for his flouring mill. This mill has three run of stone, and is one of the best of equal capacity in the State. About one and a half miles down the River another water power is afforded and is occupied by the flouring and saw mill of Mr. John G. Gardner.[10]

By 1854 Fayette Township—home to both the "thriving and comely village" of Jonesville and its rival Hillsdale—had 1,427 males, 459 of them married, which indicated that the township had 14.3 percent of the total male population of Hillsdale County. There were 21 African Americans in the entire county, 23.8 percent of them in Fayette Township. Fayette had 44.4 percent of the flour mills in the County, and 66.7 percent of the total value of said properties, indicating that these mills were larger than those in other townships.[11]

The Baxters continued to advance. In 1853 former store clerk Ebenezer Oliver Grosvenor joined with Witter Baxter and Walt Murphy to found the Exchange Bank, also known as Grosvenor and Company, the primary local bank until 1887.

In 1854 the *Michigan Farmer* listed Henry Baxter as a primary purveyor of "Grain, Flour, &c."[12] He was working hard to recoup the resources he had expended during his western jaunt. With siblings settling down and his own fortunes again on the upswing, Henry began to turn his attention to other concerns. At the annual meeting chaired by his brother Witter, on February 10, 1854, Henry was elected a Trustee of the First Presbyterian Church. Though he had been active in the church for nearly a decade, this acceptance of official responsibility signaled that he was ready to settle down.

By early 1854, the political elements in the north were disenchanted by the Congressional logjam and its domination by the "Slave Power" which thwarted all efforts to limit involuntary servitude.[13] But it was Stephen Douglas' introduction of the Kansas-Nebraska Act in January 1854 that triggered the most aggressive opposition. The Kansas-Nebraska Act repealed the Missouri Compromise of 1820 and its prohibition against slavery north of latitude 36 degrees 30 minutes in the old Louisiana Territory. This aggressive expansionist move pushed divided party ideologies to unite in opposition to the greater threat, the spread of slavery into the northwest and the possibility that the free/slave state balance could shift in favor of the south.

The Democrats held authority on the national stage as long as their opponents remained fractured. The Kansas-Nebraska Act was the catalyst that finally united the opposition under a new party flag. The first informal meeting of what became the Republican Party included Baxter in-law Robert Selfridge at Ripon, Wisconsin, on March 20, 1854. The first official meeting of the named "Republican Party" occurred at Jackson, Michigan, on July 6. The Ripon convention covered a county-wide audience, while the Jackson convention included the first statewide audience. Michigan Whigs, Free Soilers, and free Democrats saw the need for change before the fall elections. Isaac P. Christiancy, a leading Free Soiler, prosecutor, and legislator from Monroe, called for a statewide convention independent of party affiliation, thereby allowing those of like opinions to discuss their areas of agreement without being held hostage to party dogma. Within two weeks over ten thousand people had added their support.[14] A written appeal for widespread convention attendance was symbolically timed for publication in the *Hillsdale Whig Standard* and other Michigan newspapers on July 4. The appeal declared that a "great wrong has been perpetrated. The Slave power of the country as triumphed.—Liberty is trampled under foot. The Missouri Compromise, a solemn compact entered into by our fathers, has been violated, and a vast territory dedicated to freedom has been opened to Slavery."[15]

On July 6 more than 1,500 people descended on Jackson, including Levi Baxter and his sons. The honor of opening the meeting went to M.A. McNaughton who called the meeting to order. Levi Baxter was elected temporary chairman because he "was one of the pioneer settlers of Southern Michigan, a business man of great energy and large capacity, and the founder of the family which has since attained distinction in Michigan."[16]

When Levi Baxter took the podium in Bronson Hall at 10:30 a.m., it was clear that a fundamental problem existed. The convention had grown too large to fit into the hall or into any existing building in Jackson. Men crowded in, filling the hall past capacity, while many more waited outside unable to hear the proceedings. Limited participation offered no reasonable chance of building consensus among those representing substantial divergence of opinion, so Baxter made an executive decision. Rather than lose momentum, he quickly opened and adjourned the meeting, setting 1:00 p.m. as the time to reconvene in an oak grove on Morgan's Forty, now the northwest corner of Second and Franklin Streets. Hence, Baxter found a solution that would be most appropriate to the development of consensus and camaraderie.[17]

When Levi reconvened the meeting outside "under the oaks" on that humid afternoon, the first agenda item was the selection of a permanent chairman. He presided through the process, during which Kalamazoo conservative Whig David Walbridge was elected and took over the dais. Walbridge was chosen to unite conservative and radical factions. Jacob Howard, a prominent Detroit attorney, Whig, and former United States Congressman, was elected chairman of the committee on resolutions. Howard was also a conductor on the underground railroad.

The appointed committee of 12 men adjourned to the edge of the grove to act on resolutions. In addition to those elected to the committee, "an additional name was added to each committee on resolutions: John McKieney, 3rd district; John G. Hilseudingen, county of Wayne; Judge Baxter, of Hillsdale; Z.B. Knight, of Oakland."[18] Vice Presidents were appointed to represent the counties. Walt Murphy represented Hillsdale County.

Several platforms were put forward and discussed, but the one presented by Howard himself was the one adopted. This platform called for the repeal of the Kansas-Nebraska Act, repeal of the Fugitive Slave Rendition Law, and the abolition of slavery in the District of Columbia. The change in platform united the participants with an ideology that led to the creation of a new party. The following resolution was passed:

> That in view of the necessity of battling for the first principles of republican government, and against the schemes of aristocracy, the most revolting and oppressive with which the earth was ever cursed, or man debased, we will cooperate and be known as *Republican* until the contest be terminated.[19]

Christiancy withdrew the Free Democrats' ticket and a new Republican ticket was substituted behind Kinsley Bingham (Livingston County Free Democrat) for Governor. A new alliance was formed with the nomination of four Free Democrats, four Whigs, and two Democrats.

The Republican State Committee urged local units to put together mass meetings and develop tickets for local elections. On September 15, the Hillsdale County meeting seated township representatives, including E.O. Grosvenor and Witter Baxter from Fayette, signaling the latter's ascendency in "almost every republican state convention, ... [where he was] generally on the committee on resolutions, [and] almost invariably formulated the platform of the party."[20] Witter and four others were appointed to draft resolutions that supported the statewide convention and its national goal. A slate of county officers was developed and presented. While infighting among the Whigs, Free Soilers, and Abolitionists had kept them out of power for over a decade, in 1854 the new Republican Party gained control of both Michigan legislative houses and the governor's office.

The Baxters' prominent participation in this and other political endeavors clearly demonstrate that they were very influential in state politics. Witter Baxter was a delegate representing Michigan at the 1856 Republican National Convention in Philadelphia. Murphy participated in the 1860 National Convention in Chicago. All the Baxters continued their involvement in politics, civic and economic organizations, their participation described as "partisan" and "outspoken and extreme" members of the Republic Party.[21] In less than three decades, a strong political power base in Michigan had been firmly established.

3. Building Family and Community, 1852–1860

Eighteen fifty-four was memorable for another reason. Thirty-two-year-old Henry Baxter finally married. On the evening of May 2 he wed Elvira Ellen "Vi" George (1830–1915) in a ceremony officiated by Rev. H.S. Stanley, pastor of the Presbyterian Church.

Elvira was born to Austin George (1807–1850) and Roxanna Smith George (1806–1880) in Newberryport, Massachusetts, on December 22, 1830. Austin George was an early Hillsdale County land owner, having first purchased land in Litchfield Township in 1841. He was a businessman widely respected in the lower tier counties, and mourned when he died in an 1850 buggy accident.

Elvira first appears in Jonesville in 1851 as an assistant to A.S. Welch—recently returned from his journey to California—at the Fayette Union School. After his California adventure it is clear that Henry had found someone to settle down with. On April 3, 1853, Elvira was accepted as a member of the First Presbyterian Church. Together Elvira and Henry were destined to have five children: Jennie H. (April 1, 1855–May 1948); Henry Grange (April 27, 1856-unknown); Carrie L. (1858–November 8, 1894); Lois "Lottie" Francis (February 11, 1866–February 10, 1949); and Edwin Warren (1867–1868).

The growing family required lodgings to match. On October 10, 1856, Henry purchased lot #14 of Lytles Plat (Jonesville) from Mr. and Mrs. Thomas Doney for $1,000. The land included a house then occupied by Dr. Allen Hobby. The next day Henry bought neighboring lot #15 of Lytles Plat from Nathan Brand for $500. The lots were located near the top of the hill on the east side of East Street, two blocks south of the Chicago Road. The neighborhood was one of the most fashionable in town and the "low cottage" owned by Baxter was actually a one-and-a-half-story home set well back from East Street.[22] This house was to be the base of operations for the Baxter family for the next two decades.

Jonesville was coming of age. The *State of Michigan Gazetteer & Business Directory* of 1856–57 described the community as having grown to a population of 1,000 with

> excellent mills, manufacturing of flour, woolens, coarse cottons, and all kinds of machinery. It has a considerable amount of trade. The Michigan Southern Railroad passes through the village 75 miles from Monroe. The "Jonesville Independent" is published weekly. It contains 5 dry goods stores, 3 taverns, 2 hardware stores, 2 drug stores, 3 groceries and 4 churches."[23]

Among the businesses listed were Wright and Levi Baxter, "machinists," William Murphy and Witter Baxter, "attorneys at law," and Henry Baxter, Aldrich & Company, "furniture manufacturers and dealers."[24] Quaker Amos Aldrich sold his Adrian farm in 1854 so that he and his sons could pursue their interest in cabinetmaking with Henry providing both capital and management experience.[25]

Jonesville was incorporated as a village via act of February 10, 1855, formalizing local government. Later that year, Witter joined with Murphy and A.J. Baker to create the northwestern addition to the town, including property along Murphy Street and north of Chicago Street. This addition included streets named for each of the three partners.

Henry Baxter was involved in a number of important firsts. On April 10, 1855, the first election of Jonesville village officers took place. Under newly-elected President George C. Munro several officers were appointed, including Henry Baxter as Street Commissioner. The appointment confirmed confidence in Henry's leadership and engineering skills, but he declined to serve. Either he found the position unsuitable or he was too busy to accept. In 1856 Levi was elected to the council, as was Witter in 1857 and Henry in 1859. The Baxters took turns sitting on village council for over a decade. On March 4, 1857, Henry became a founding member of the Jonesville Volunteer Fire Department. Prominent among the group were friends E.O. Grosvenor and Walt Murphy. The company was named "Protection Company No. 1" and purchased its first fire engine and hose cart at a cost of $1,339.82.[26]

Expansion of the mill was on Henry's mind in 1859. Hillsdale County deeds show that on November 23 he purchased land from his brother Witter for $1,000. Less than a month later the property was sold to Alexander Beach for $11,000. By the end of the decade Levi and Henry were partners in both the flouring mill and furniture business with a factory and store on Water Street. Henry was the proprietor of the "Sash & Blind Factory."[27]

During the 1850s all of the Baxter boys from Levi's first marriage were consolidating their political power. Notary public in those days was an important position, particularly for an attorney who frequently handled land transactions, wills, and business agreements. First Witter, then Benjamin became gubernatorial appointees in their respective counties.

Levi, Witter, and Henry became fixtures on the Jonesville School Board. Starting in 1847 Levi served as moderator, roughly equivalent to superintendent. In 1849 he was replaced by Witter who alternately served as a moderator, director, or trustee. Henry served as moderator 1857–59 during one of the rare periods when Witter was not on the board. W.W. Murphy served as a trustee from 1854 through 1858. Other regular board members of the period included George C. Munro and E.O. Grosvenor, indicating that those prominent in the community were closely associated with the school system. However, the Baxter family was the only group to have a continuous seat on the board from 1847 through the 1880s.[28]

The Hillsdale County Republican Convention was held at the Hillsdale County Court House on September 27, 1856. Henry Baxter, E.M. Hale, William Sinclair, and S. Leavens represented North Fayette (Jonesville). The Republican ticket for county offices was established and unanimous support for the state and federal tickets was expressed. The state convention included the Baxters and their friends. Murphy assisted chairman Zachariah Chandler and Benjamin represented Lenawee County. Murphy, Benjamin, and Witter were on the Second District committee to nominate state delegates. Witter was elected a Second District delegate.[29]

In an agricultural community, one avenue to notoriety and influence was through the county fair. The tradition of the fair as a means to test and highlight the productivity of agriculture was well-established in America by the mid-nineteenth century. The Hillsdale County Fair was started in 1851 by the Hillsdale County Agricultural Society, in which Witter was heavily involved. Most of the Baxters played some role on October 15–16, 1856, when the fair was held in Jonesville. Henry represented Fayette Township as a judge for flour and grain. Murphy judged poultry. Wives were suitably part of this effort as well, with Witter and his wife Alice judging needlework and embroidery. Not everyone was on the judging side. Levi Baxter won seven awards for his furniture. Witter won for best tomatoes, best currant wine, and best sculpture. H.B. Rowlson, editor of the *Hillsdale Whig Standard*, called it "the largest [fair] ever held in the County, surpassing anything of the kind in Southern Michigan. This

3. Building Family and Community, 1852–1860

… shows the progress and prosperity of the county. No county in the State has a more thriving farming population than Hillsdale."[30] Witter was on the Executive Committee of the Hillsdale County Agricultural Society in 1860 when a permanent fair site was established. He remained a leader in the state agricultural society for decades.

Witter was a Michigan delegate to the 1856 National Republican Convention. More than any other, this meeting set the platform for the new party, focusing on opposition to the repeal of the Missouri Compromise, resistance to the extension of slavery into free territory, and support for admission of Kansas as a free state. The convention brought together Free Soilers, Whigs, Abolitionists, and anti-slavery Democrats in a bid for the White House. Witter's colleagues from Michigan included people who were playing a significant role in state politics:

> Of this comparatively small delegation, [Kingsley] Bingham was either before or after this a member of Congress, Governor, and United States Senator; [Zachariah] Chandler was United States Senator and Secretary of the Interior; [Isaac P.] Christiancy was State Supreme Court Justice, United States Senator, and Minister to Peru; Fernando C. Beaman was member of Congress five terms and was appointed United States Senator; E.J. Penniman and Randolph Strickland were members of Congress; George A Coe was Lieutenant Governor, and most of the others held elective official positions at some time during their lifetime. It is doubtful if any other State sent a delegation of as high an average order of ability and distinction.[31]

Witter was appointed to the Michigan Board of Education by Governor Bingham—Michigan's first Republican Governor—in 1857 and would run successfully for a regular seat on the 1858 Republican ticket. He was elected to four six-year terms, serving 12 years as president.

The Election of 1856 brought a Republican majority to office in Hillsdale County. While acknowledging the loss of the national election, the *Whig Standard* celebrated the local gains and the bright future of the party, stating, "It was a glorious time for the Republicans of Hillsdale County."[32] The Baxters and their associates helped set and supported the Republican ticket for the Presidential election of 1860. Walt Murphy was a prominent Michigan delegate to the Republican National Convention in Chicago, May 16–18. He played an active role in the proceedings alongside Austin Blair, U.S. Senator Zachariah Chandler, and the like.[33]

The growing level of participation in political activities on the village, township, county, and state levels and the active support of the national Republican Party marked a significant growth in influence for the Baxters and their extended network. On the eve of the Civil War they had firmly established themselves as "unswerving" in their "political affiliations."[34]

In 1858 the rivalry between Jonesville and Hillsdale led the Board of Supervisors to split Fayette Township into two nearly equal townships. Fayette contained Jonesville to the north and Hillsdale became the primary community in the new Hillsdale Township to the south. Fayette received a sliver of southern Scipio Township as part of the arrangement. County seat since 1843, Hillsdale was finally free of direct political competition with its neighbor. The status quo thus achieved remains largely unchanged to the present day.

4

Off to War, 1861

North-south tensions intensified following the Presidential election of 1860, the first national victory for the Republican Party Henry Baxter and his family helped found. President Buchanan did little to thwart the secession of southern states prior to Lincoln's inauguration on March 4, 1861. Following the lead of South Carolina on December 20, 1860, 11 southern states abandoned the Union. In 1860–61 22 southern Senators and 58 Congressmen ceased to be a part of the 37th Congress. Through 1862, 14 legislators were expelled for disloyalty to the Union, further increasing the relative power of those that remained. Both the Senate and House left these seats vacant rather than acknowledge secession, thus making each northern legislator correspondingly more powerful and giving the Old Northwest Territory more clout.[1] This influence would increase as calls for volunteers and recruiting quotas mobilized men and resources. By the time Fort Sumter was fired upon on April 12, 1861, most northerners were prepared, even anxious, to enter the fray in order to maintain the union and/or end slavery.

In January 1861 the United States Army was composed of just over 16,000 officers and men. Secession brought the defection of many southerners, further weakening the ability of the federal government to respond forcefully.[2] The reaction to Lincoln's April 15 call for 75,000 militiamen for three months service brought volunteers from all walks of life.

On the night of April 25, prominent Jonesville citizens raised $1,500 to support "Grosvenor's Union Guard," Hillsdale County's first volunteer company composed largely of those connected with the militia. This unit became Company H in the 4th Michigan Volunteer Infantry. After the April 25 event, prominent Jonesville citizens Ebenezer Grosvenor, William Murphy, Witter Baxter, and George Monroe subscribed an additional $100 each. The delayed contributions were tied to politics surrounding an additional company being formed under the leadership of Henry Baxter. Grosvenor wanted the Baxter company to be absorbed by a regiment being formed under the command of his older brother, Ira R. Grosvenor of Monroe. Ebenezer was then a Republican state senator (1858–1864), later president of the state military board, and member of the financial committee in 1862. Ira had been involved in southern tier politics since the 1840s in connection with his law practice, and was active in the pre-war Michigan militia. Ebenezer and Ira Grosvenor were therefore extremely influential and were able to bring the Baxter company under Ira's command.

Henry Baxter's prominence as a capable and successful businessman, popularity among the young men of the area, political connections, and reputation as a leader of the Fayette

Rovers helped win his election as Captain of the "Jonesville Light Guards." Unlike the first company formed in Jonesville, this one was not primarily composed of local militia. Baxter's own friends and supporters formed the core. Baxter knew the local political landscape well and used his influence to the utmost. This method of gaining election to a captaincy was common.

Companies later incorporated into the 7th Michigan Volunteer Infantry were lobbying for mobilization within days of the attack on Fort Sumter. Units from Lapeer, Burr Oak, and Port Huron petitioned for acceptance immediately. The 1st through the 6th Michigan Volunteer Infantries were all forming more-or-less simultaneously, creating an administrative jumble as enthusiastic Michiganders tried to get into action as quickly as possible.

John Robertson, Adjutant General of the State of Michigan, received dozens of letters begging that companies be accepted immediately. An excellent example was one written on April 26, by John Waterman of Burr Oak:

> I have 40 Mens names on my list[,] all large athletic Men anxious to Serve under Me. I have helped Captain Abbott form & drill his Company. My Men want me to get some assurance from head Quarters that when the time comes that we Shall be enrolled as a company of Minute Men for any emergency—we don't ask for any Pay, expenses, or assistance until Mustered into Service. We Pledge you our honors[,] our lives & fortunes in defense of our Country and our Countries [sic] Flag. All is asked of you is Some authority to enroll My Men legally with proper Papers to hold them and drill them at our own expense until called into Service. Send Me enlisting Papers and I will give you 78 as good Sized Men and as brave as any in the State able to bear there [sic] own expenses if needs be. Men are comeing [sic] to Me from 20 Miles around. If I go into the Street I am beseth [sic] with anxious fighting Men to enlist under Me. Anything from you will do even as a prospect that if wanted that we May Stand a chance with the others—if I don't get some authority to enlist Men I Shall have to leave them in doubt as to whether a Company of Minute Men here would Stand a Chance if wanted.[3]

The group recruited by Waterman was mustered in as Company K of the 7th Michigan.

Formation of new regiments became highly political as the well-placed attempted to gain high ranking field commissions and ambitious local gentry tried to raise a company that would propel them to notoriety. Yet, in the midst of convoluted politics, regiments had to be established administratively and logistically furnished with the necessary equipment and supplies. The well-established militia organization of Michigan and other states suffered under the strain of so many people vying for prominent positions, making the process more trial and error than systematic for the first months of the conflict.

State governors had their own problems. The relatively small population-based quotas placed upon them by the federal government left each state with more applicants than there were slots to fill. Michigan's first quota was one regiment (approximately 1,000 men). Governor Blair was in good company with the governors of Indiana, Maine, New Jersey, Connecticut, New Hampshire, and Ohio in persistently admonishing the federal government that they should accept more of their enthusiastic volunteers. In response, on May 3, President Lincoln called for 42,034 volunteers (40 regiments), 22,714 regulars (ten regiments), and 18,000 seamen to serve three years or until discharge, whichever came first.[4]

Governor Blair used donated money to fit out the 1st Michigan Volunteer Infantry quickly, getting it to Washington on May 16, 1861. This was the first regiment from a western state to arrive and the timing could not have been better. Washington was in a panic as the result of repeated rumors of southern invasion. On hearing of the 1st Michigan's arrival to help defend the capital, legend has it that Lincoln exclaimed, "Thank God for Michigan!"

Enthusiasm for enlistment ran high and local newspapers did their best to keep the fire stoked. Inter-state rivalries proved a good mechanism to motivate recruits:

> The brave and loyal people of Michigan are determined not to be outdone in aiding the Government to sustain its supremacy and power. Up to this time, aside from the Regiments formed in this State, Michigan has furnished Regiments forming in other States, upward of 400 men.... So the aid Michigan will render in putting down the Southern rebellion, will not be confined to the Regiments which are formed entirely within her own borders. She will have a hand in the warfare on the Mississippi, as well as that in the Old Dominion.[5]

Some impatient Michiganders marched off to join regiments forming in more populous states. On June 20, 1861, the *Jonesville Telegraph* reported,

> The officers and non-commissioned officers of the "Jonesville Light Guards" left this place yesterday on the 1:30 p.m. train, for the "Camp of Instruction" for the 5th, 6th, & 7th Regiments of the State, at Fort Wayne near Detroit. The Company is assigned to the Seventh Regiment, Col. I.R. Grosvenor. The officers are to be placed under thorough military instruction at Fort Wayne.[6]

The commissioned officers were housed aboard a Great Lakes passenger steamer, ironically named *Mississippi*.

The Union defeat at the Battle of Bull Run (Manassas Junction) on July 21, 1861, made it clear that the rebellion was not going to end swiftly and decisively. With the Union army in retreat and the fate of the capital in doubt, determined action was needed. Recurrent rumors and alarms warned that a Confederate attack might be imminent. Congress passed and President Lincoln signed a bill calling for the enlistment of 500,000 troops for terms up to three years. Michigan's share of these recruits was 21,337.

The commander of the 7th Michigan was intent on preparing his men quickly. Ira Grosvenor was a Brigadier General in the Michigan State Militia, which made him an unusually practiced military administrator among those appointed to regimental commands. Most state governors chose from among those of influence and presumed ability for officer commissions. States controlled the appointment of volunteer officers at the rank of colonel and below. This situation became an irritant to general officers as some appointees proved unsuited for command in the field. Yet governors had the right to make appointments, sometimes putting one incompetent in the place of another. In July 1861 this system was legalized by Congress.[7]

Grosvenor was commissioned Colonel on June 19 to lead the 7th Michigan. At 44, his age was comparable to his subordinates. Of the field officers and regimental captains in the 7th Michigan, seven of 15 were older than 40. At 39 Henry Baxter was nearly one of them. Only three were in their twenties.

⇒ ⇐

The units integrated into the 7th Michigan Volunteer Infantry represented a cross section of the populated regions of the state.

Company A	Union Guard	Port Huron
Company B	Curtenius Guard	Mason
Company C	Jonesville Light Guard	Jonesville
Company D	Monroe Light Guard	Monroe

Company E	Tuscola Volunteers	Tuscola
Company F	Blair Guard	Farmington
Company G	"Rough and Ready" Lapeer Guard	Lapeer
Company H		Pontiac / Flint
Company I	Prairieville Rangers	Prairieville
Company K	Burr Oak Rangers	Burr Oak[8]

The Jonesville Light Guards (Company C) were led by Captain Baxter, First Lieutenant Sidney R. Vrooman, and Second Lieutenant William W. Wade, all residents of Jonesville. A total of 1,020 officers and men mustered at Monroe on August 22.

Lieutenant William Shafter of Company I recalled the training at Fort Wayne:

> Each company had its three officers, five sergeants, eight corporals and two musicians, making three commissioned and fifteen enlisted men.... To carry out this idea on guard duty, all enlisted men acted as privates, the Second Lieutenants as Corporals, First Lieutenants as Sergeants and Captains as Lieutenants of the guards, with field officers as officers of the day. In the company organization I was First Lieutenant.... But such exalted rank had its burdens, as ... I was detailed as Sergeant of the guard. I had never seen a guard mount and knew absolutely nothing of drill. I got through the guard mount somehow and put in all my time during the day in trying to comprehend grand rounds, which I was told would appear between twelve o'clock and daylight. They did appear as scheduled and after a fashion I got through with my part of receiving them, and was then told to take a guard and escort the rounds on its visit to the sentries. By personal direction to each member of the escort I secured a Corporal and three men and started. The officer of the day was Captain Tom Hunt of the Seventh, who had served with the First Michigan in the war with Mexico and who was supposed to know it all. His fierce examination of the sentries astonished us. He acted as though he thought the Fort might be attacked before morning. The culmination of his rounds took place however at the entrance to the magazine where a man from the Tuscola Company from the North Woods was posted. He challenged us as we approached and then the officer of the day opened on him.
>
> Q. What is your principal charge here sir?
> A. To guard this magazine sir.
> Q. Well sir, supposing the enemy should approach what would you do?
> A. Halt them sir.
> Q. But suppose they would not stop, what would you do?
> A. Halt them again sir.
> Q. But still suppose they came on, what would you do?
> A. I would halt them for the third time sir.
> Q. But, said the Captain, if they still persisted and were about to enter the magazine what would you do then?
>
> The man stood for a moment in silence and then with a wave of disgust toward his piece said, "well Captain I think I would snap this damned old gun at them." That reply broke us all up, and the Captain retired satisfied that one sentinel, proposed in case of danger to exhaust all his means of defense.[9]

Since they had yet to be issued ammunition, the man's reply was bravado indeed.

Sergeant Samuel Hodgman in Company I remembered the routine of the camp of instruction at Fort Wayne:

4:30 a.m.	Awakened by morning gun
5:00–6:00 a.m.	Roll Call and Drill
6:00–7:00 a.m.	Breakfast
8:00–11:00 a.m.	Regimental Parade
12:00 p.m.	Dinner

1:00–3:00 p.m.	Break
3:00–4:00 p.m.	Company Drill
4:00–5:30 p.m.	Battalion Drill
5:30–6:30 p.m.	Supper
6:30–7:00 p.m.	Dress Parade
9:00 p.m.	Taps[10]

Between Dress Parade and lights out, soldiers were at liberty to stroll outside the fort, but late return meant being thrown into the guardhouse. They had "plenty to eat and it is well cooked and of good quality." Hodgman reported, "Our Regimental officers are a very gentlemanly set of men and are very much liked by their subordinates."[11]

On Sunday, June 30, Henry Baxter wrote to Elvira:

> You cannot realize my desire to see and be with you and the darling little ones at home....
> I went up to the City this morning but did not go to church for the reason that I had not suitable clothes and I do not Know but you had better bring my black suit if you can conveniently do so—Now My darling wife do not censure me for not coming home for I do assure you it was a sore disappointment to me as well as to yourself and the little ones. What do they say?—I should think you could come and if you can do. I know a few weeks away from home will do you good.... You can come to the Fort almost every evening.[12]

Throughout his correspondence both during and after the war Henry expressed his desire to be with his family, swearing that only duty to his country could keep him away.

The officers were sworn into service on July 2. The training camp broke up at the end of July, though a few officers did not depart until early August.

Sergeant Charles Curtis used a rainy July 16 to tell his mother that he liked Fort Wayne:

> Mother
> I continue to enjoy Camp Life and all I wait for now is Orders to try the Southern Climate. You know I always had a strong desire to go South but never supposed I would be lucky enough to get the ride out of [the] Government.... Most of our Men are in perfect health although there are three in the "Hospital" I am now in our own room, the Ladies Cabin in a Steam Boat [*Mississippi*] that is too Large to be of any other use. The Lieut. Col. (Winans) and Maj. (Ex Gov Fenton) have come in to make a visit and write a Letter. They are both very fine men. I have no particular news to write. All is war!!... We now hope to Know very soon if we are called into service or not. Some think about the 1st Sept will be moving time.... If we have pleasant weather all winter it will be quite pleasant to be a "volunteer" but when it rains 8 or 9 days in a week it may in a measure cool the ardor of some of us....[13]

Anxious to get involved before the war was over, yet realistic enough to admit that no one wanted to drill in the rain, Curtis probably came closest to illustrating the limits of enthusiasm and human nature. He also provided a description of the regimental uniform as a "Gray Jacket with black braid on the collar & cuff and jogered [*sic*] up in the Sleeve ... [with sargeants stripes and] with brass Buttons. Pant same color as Jacket. Big Shoes and Gray Wool Shirts complete the present outfit."[14]

The enlisted men were to be trained at a new camp near Monroe, a place uniquely suited to facilitate the regiment's movement to the eastern front via the ports of Detroit, Monroe, or Toledo. Monroe was also home to Company D and the regimental commander, insuring that it received good coverage by the local newspaper. By early August the *Monroe Commercial* reported that preparations to receive the regiment were well underway:

> It has been determined to bring the Seventh Regiment, Col. I.R. Grosvenor's, to Monroe to form an encampment for drill and military instruction. The drill grounds have been selected, being the meadow fields on Water street, on the farm occupied by David Ebersol and that of T.G. Cole, adjoining, and containing together, some forty to fifty acres. The grounds are beautifully level and unobstructed and will make the best drill grounds that could any where be found.
>
> We learn that a contract has been made for tents for the Regiment, and that they will be furnished with all possible dispatch. Army rations will be furnished, the soldiers doing their own cooking. Thus the men will at once be gaining knowledge in all the routine of a soldier's duties, so that when they leave the State they will be much better prepared to subsist comfortably upon the soldiers fare than any who have thus far gone from the State, besides being more thoroughly instructed in every respect.[15]

Sergeant Curtis arrived at Monroe on August 12, to lay out the camp. Recruits began arriving on August 14.

The officers of Baxter's Company C returned to Hillsdale County on August 2, to recruit. Baxter opened an office in Hillsdale's Lucius A. Bostwick Building. The *Standard* lauded his efforts:

> Capt. Baxter, Liet. S. B. Vrooman and the other officers of the Company, are residents of this County and are well known to be gentlemen qualified for the positions assigned them, and we would advise volunteers in the vicinity to enlist in their Company in preference to those of other States.[16]

Baxter's notoriety, sense of the local culture and politics made him quickly successful. On August 13, he escorted 40 recruits to Monroe, returning for 40 more the next day.

The men of the 7th were in high spirits as training began. Their enthusiasm was fired by the fact that "ladies begin to Show themselves in good number and this independent City sustains reputation well. The ladies are beautiful."[17]

The camp at Monroe took shape quickly:

> The encampment of the Seventh Michigan, on the County Fair Grounds in the City, which is to be designated as Camp Monroe, now presents quite a lively appearance.... Considerable activity has prevailed today in putting up tents, and other necessary preparations. We understand all the tents have been received and will be pitched immediately, and that it is probable that the regiment will be in camp as soon as the fore part of next week. The tents are quite large and roomy, and will accommodate twenty men each.[18]

The best description of life in Camp Monroe was published by the *Monroe Commercial*:

> Dress parade was always an interesting event, and every evening crowds of people—ladies predominating—were present to witness it. The ten full companies took their positions upon the parade ground. Col. Grosvenor in front, at a little distance facing the regiment. Lt. Col. Winans and Maj. Henry Landon on the extreme right saw that the alignment was perfect before his clear resonant voice called—"At-ten-tion Battalion!"
>
> Then the usual formula was gone through with, the orderly sergeant's going to the center to report—"all present or accounted for." Orders were read by the adjutant, the band played as they marched in front and back, the officers all advanced to salute the colonel, the evening gun was fired, the flag descended gracefully and dress parade was over. The sergeants took the companies back and the commissioned officers joined the groups of civilians for an hour's enjoyment.
>
> Regimental services were held Sunday afternoons in Cole's grove, a locality our older citizens will remember.... It is safe to say that all churches and denominations had a much larger representation at those services than in their houses of worship.
>
> A great many events, like the presentation of colors, and swords marked the weeks while the regiment was in camp, and sorrow mingled with patriotism when they were ordered to the front.[19]

Through the formulaic drilling and routine established at Camp Monroe, Henry Baxter was not only developing extended local knowledge associated with military procedures and traditions, he was strengthening his authority over the men and applying his leadership skills in a new environment where civilian lassitude was replaced with military precision.

Curtis noted on August 21 "the Regiment is filling rapidly" as recruiting efforts brought new men from all over the state[20] By late August the enlisted men had received shirts and caps, but were still awaiting uniforms. When fully fitted out, the unit was to depart for Washington. Dr. Bolivar Barnum of Schoolcraft was appointed Surgeon and Dr. Syrus Bacon of Edwardsburg Assistant Surgeon. The Reverend A.K. Strong, Pastor of the Presbyterian Church in Monroe, was appointed Chaplain. On August 22 the 7th Michigan Volunteer Infantry was officially mustered in as a unit of the Union Army and assigned to the Army of the Potomac.

Whether glory and adventure, humiliation and death awaited them, the knowledge that they were soon to leave home for an uncertain future made enjoying their last few days a priority. Some shopped for items that they thought would be difficult to find close to the front. Others looked for the delights that a large city held. Sgt. Curtis "bid farewell to Detroit and the loved ones there who are known only to myself. And I tonight Stand before the world 'non-committed' ... if I never more return none will be the wiser."[21] "All is excitement preparing to leave" during the week before departure.[22] The packing of regimental, company, and personal gear for the field by green troops made the camp one of great confusion, especially since they had yet to receive essential items like knapsacks.

Elvira, Jennie, Harry, and Carrie were in Monroe to see Henry off on the morning of September 5. Farewells said, the regiment marched to the train station, departing by rail for Toledo with honors presented by the ladies of Monroe. This "pleasant ride" was followed by embarkation aboard the lake steamers *May Queen* and *Ocean* for the trip across Lake Erie to Cleveland.[23] The boats got underway about 9:00 p.m. and the regiment was happy to enjoy "a nice smooth trip on the water, and several hours of sleep."[24]

The 7th Michigan suffered its first casualty during the early morning hours of September 6. Twenty-six-year-old Private William Thirds of Company K was lost overboard while *May Queen* was underway. The boat stopped, but efforts to recover him were unsuccessful. His body washed ashore west of Cleveland. An inquest on September 12 ruled his death accidental.

The men had breakfast aboard the boats before they disembarked early on September 6. They were "transported to comfortable quarters on the cars of the Cleveland and Pittsburgh Rail Road."[25] The ride was described as "one of interest and great enjoyment."[26] Blessed with comfortable passenger coaches and a "good supply of ice water, a luxury that is seldom furnished to a whole Regiment," the men were quite content.[27] The "people of the 'Buckeye State' along the whole route gave evidence of their patriotism and hospitality by generous donations to the soldiers. At nearly every station where we stopped the citizens met us with baskets loaded with the good things of life and distributed them freely among the men."[28] "Girls with boquets [sic] of flowers" thrilled the soldiers.[29] M.S. Rice of Company I surmised, "They could not do enough for us [since] we were [off] to Slaughter."[30]

When the regiment arrived at Pittsburgh at 9:00 p.m. they marched into a large pavilion adjacent to the depot. There they found "ample tables ... spread and a warm supper served up to every man ... waited upon by the young men and ladies of Pittsburgh who volunteered their services for the occasion."[31] They were done by 11:00 p.m. and were settling aboard the cars of the Pennsylvania Central Railroad when it was learned that not enough coaches had been supplied to transport the entire unit. Colonel Grosvenor eventually solved the problem. At 1:00 a.m. Saturday, September 8, they at last got underway with a proper number of coaches.

As the men slept, the train made its way slowly through the Alleghany Mountains to Altoona. The late departure from Pittsburgh created an additional three hour delay, the unit arriving in Altoona at 9:00 a.m. The breakfast of steak, potatoes, and coffee was a good one. The scenery in this stretch of the trip was described as "grand, and in some places sublime."[32] Of particular interest was the winding mountain railroad:

> A few miles beyond [the mountain summit] the road passes through a tunel [sic] of about a mile in length. Shooting out of the depths of the earth you glide down the mountain side, on a grade of 130 feet to the mile, hanging for a moment over a horrid chasm, then rushing through the leafy grove, till by innumerable windings, by short and abrupt turnings, you reach the banks of "The Blue Junietta," gliding quietly through grassy plains to its ocean home.
>
> The very scenery seemed to inspire the soldiers with enthusiasm of patriotism and when, as occassionally [sic] was the case, a flag was seen waving on the hill side, or the inhabitants were congregated to witness the passage of the troops. Our ears would be greeted with redoubled shouts, and we would witness such exhibitions of patriotic feeling from our own men as they never would perform in other situations.[33]

Nine locomotives were needed to pull their 40 car train slowly through the mountains. Delayed by slow cattle trains, the 7th Michigan did not arrive at Harrisburg until 9:00 p.m. Two men missed the train at Altoona and had to hop the express in order to rejoin the regiment. They got underway again in cattle cars at 3:00 a.m. on Sunday, reaching Baltimore about noon. They found Maryland as welcoming as Ohio and Pennsylvania had been, surprising because of the lingering resentment many harbored after the Baltimore draft riots of April 19.

They transferred to the Baltimore and Washington Railroad, marching a distance of two miles between stations. Some took time to see the city while waiting for their train. Others met members of the 6th Michigan Volunteer Infantry, who—though having departed Michigan a week previously—had been detailed to guard a Baltimore magazine. Unsympathetic to the assignment given their fellow Michiganders, the members of the 7th Michigan promised that "while the 6th were employed in guarding the powder[,] the 7th would go forward and help burn it."[34] A spirited verbal exchange followed.

By 4:00 p.m. they were underway again, arriving five hours later in Washington where the "cheers were almost deafening."[35] They were served a good supper at the "Soldiers Rest," then turned in. Those in charge of equipment, slept near it to provide security. They were assigned wagons, loaded baggage, and marched through Washington and out to their camp at Meridian Hill (about two miles away) on September 10. Firearms and additional uniforms were issued there. The old Belgian rifles they were given were inadequate, even dangerous. The regiment expected to get new Sharps rifles when they became available. The Sharps rifles were given to flanking companies, but the rest received the Belgians until better arms could be obtained. Like all who received the inferior European cast-offs, the 7th Michigan was handicapped by senior army officials suspicious of the new technology and reluctant to place multiple types of ammunition on the battlefield. Instead, the 7th accepted Belgians of uneven caliber, with bent or brittle barrels and malfunctioning locks. The soldiers could not wait to be rid of them.[36]

The camp was so close to Washington that the partially constructed capitol dome was visible. Robert Knaggs may have spoken for more than himself when he said, "I shall never forget the feelings I had when I first saw it. The sun was shining for the first time that day and the dome was beautiful."[37] Their presence meant they were helping to guard the nation's most important city, the symbol of the Union. They finally felt like they were serving their country.

The days spent so close to Washington were both inspirational and recreational. Some saw a military observation balloon over the Potomac. Others ignored the heat and explored the city as they waited to learn their destination and assignment.

One of Washington's less endearing characteristics showed itself. The brigade commanders in Washington were scrambling to fill their commands, and the 7th Michigan became the subject of a dispute among Generals. Four generals wanted the regiment. The primary protagonists were Israel Richardson and Frederick Lander. Richardson was a Michigander, but Lander won because of better connections at headquarters. The 7th Michigan was assigned to the 2nd Brigade (Lander) in the Division of Brigadier General Charles Stone.

On September 9, they marched 26 miles, six miles the next day, 12 miles the next, and ten miles the morning of the final day. Their camp was halfway between Poolesville and Edward's Ferry, almost across the Potomac River from Leesburg. They were on cleared high ground surrounded by woods about a mile from the Potomac and two miles southwest of Poolesville, where General Stone's headquarters were located. To the north was camped the 1st Minnesota, to the northeast was the 10th Massachusetts, and to the east the 19th Massachusetts. Other regiments from New York and California were nearby. The main army signaling station on Logan Loop Mountain—the highest promontory in that part of Maryland—was about ten miles north.

Their initial quarters were Sibley 16-man tents with only straw on the damp ground. They quickly became used to the unwelcome onslaught of wind-triggered cold drafts and dampness from the leaky canvas fed by rain or heavy dew. They professed to have plenty of food and good appetites to eat it, aided no-doubt by their constant drill.

The regiment had many men with construction skills who built officers' quarters and barracks that stood up to the worst Maryland winter. Some of the lumber was shipped all the way from Michigan. The camp was laid out in a square with barracks on three sides, the headquarters and officers' quarters on one side, and the parade ground in the middle. Knaggs later remembered this camp as "the best one we had."[38] General Lander named the place "Camp Benton" in honor of Colonel William P. Benton of Indiana.[39]

The new camp was tantalizingly near to the enemy and the first sojourn in the south brought new experiences. M.S. Rice reported that he "saw a Slave owner Breeding pen where Blacks were raised for the market to be sold as Cattle" and confessed that he "thought Slavery to be a cursed institution."[40]

Baxter had learned on his trip to California that small comforts created cohesiveness among men in the field. He knew that one of the most significant challenges was the quality of meals, so he recruited a Black cook for Company C at a cost of $10 per month.

His men reported "all sound" was a favorite saying of Henry Baxter, a quirk that endeared him to his men. The term "sound" meant a structure that was safe, functional, and solid, so it was a natural phrase for a man who spent most of his life processing flour and lumber.[41] Since many of them had similar experiences with wood and grain themselves, they identified with their leader.

That Baxter held wide esteem was shown by the presentation of a sword and sash by the people of Jonesville:

> Camp Benton
> September 30, 1861
>
> Editor of the *Standard*—Allow me thorough your paper to express my heartfelt thanks to my friends of Jonesville for their presentation through Colonel Ira R. Grosvenor, of a very fine sword and sash. To the donations let me say, I do assure you that it is with deep felt gratitude and pride that I accept the token of rememberance [sic] and friendship at your hands, and God helping me it shall be my every endeavor to so use it in the common cause of our country, that I may return, if return I may, with it unsullied and unstained by any act of mine that may not reflect credit upon you as my friends and donors, and also upon myself.
>
> James Baxter
> Capt. Co. C, 7th Regiment Michigan Infantry[42]

The authenticity of the note was challenged by the editor of the *Jonesville Independent* because Henry Baxter never used the name "James," though his full name was "James Henry Baxter." Ultimately, the editor of the *Standard* pronounced the note genuine.

The brigade drilled most of the time. The focus on company, battalion, regimental, and brigade level drills sharpened cooperative skills and cohesiveness. There were frequent inspections. They also took turns on picket duty and guarding Edwards Ferry with Battery B, 1st Rhode Island Light Artillery, a unit attached to the brigade.

In the absence of fulfilling activity, anyone will find something to complain about. Soldiers in camp are no different. They had good shoes, stockings, and clothes, but poor caps. They lacked a full range of cooking equipment. The water was not clear and had a bitter taste. Their pay was late. Their boots did not keep the mud off their pants.

For the officers, the complaints had a more political bent. General Lander took a strong dislike to Colonel Grosvenor because he seemed to pay little attention to details, yet the earlier date of Grosvenor's commission meant that he outranked Colonel Raymond Lee of the 20th Massachusetts, a West Point graduate. Lander tried to bypass Grosvenor in the chain of command so that the more experienced man would be in charge when he was away. Some of Grosvenor's officers responded with negativity that was acerbated by an alleged Lander comment that the reason that the regiment had lost 11 men to the measles was that they were so dirty. While drinking, some of the regiment's officers plotted revenge for Lander's remark. While officer of the guard Lieutenant Shafter stumbled upon "three old grey-headed captains, all of them old enough to be my father, and my own captain sitting around a pitcher of whisky" as they discussed who should kill the general. Shafter joined the group, became drunk, passed out, and could have lost his commission had he been discovered. Fortunately, they never followed through on their imprudent threats.[43] Clearly the professionalism of the regiment's officers had a lot of room for improvement.

The nature of camp life may be extrapolated from a September 29 letter from Corporal Chester Bangs (Company B), addressed to a young lady friend back home:

> The boys from N— [Napoleon] are all well except Alonzo Palmer[.] [H]e will be all right in a day or two[.] I was surprised to hear that so many of our boys had enlisted, but unless their Spunk is renewed you will see them coming back soon[.] The life of a soldier is a hard Life[,] I assure you[,] but it is no worse than I expected[.] I came prepared for it. Nothing would of enduced [sic] me to take this Position in life had it not been for the honor of our Country[.] I

am not sorry I enlisted[.] [N]either have I been homesick, though I am deprived of many things that I considered valueless when at Home.... See nothing but nigers and Soldiers. I can give no idea of the number of troops in and around W— [Washington] but its nothing but tents as far as the eye can extend.... We are the advance Brigade and so situated that we can hear every little skirmish that takes place between the opposing force[s] across the River, and in some instances see the smoke as it rises after a heavy discharge, and in a short time we expect to be right there doing our share of the glorious work necessary in the behalf of the union.

Augusta we see some good times here and some hard times. We don't have to drill very hard only about 6 hours a day and go on guard once a week[.] I was on last night. I guess you would laugh if you should happen in here and see me washing my Clothes and Dishes and to see us gather around the tent to eat our rations[,] four crackers and a piece of meat, perhaps a little coffee[.] [W]ho wouldn't be a Soldier—They say the artist from Monro[e] will be here next week, if so we will get some Pictures....

Truly Yours CH Bangs

[P.S.] [W]e shall all be Home next New Years and then we will have a time[.][44]

The overconfidence aside, the troops were in good spirits and itching for a fight.

Despite the machismo, there was a reality that was hard to get around. The people on both sides of the conflict were Americans with much in common, so it is not surprising that Union and Confederate pickets exchanged information while they traded coffee for tobacco. Robert Knaggs named several Michiganders that crossed the Potomac to visit friends who were fighting on the other side. One of them was George Armstrong Custer.[45]

Not all the entertainment available to the men was considered appropriate by their leaders. In early October two news vendors from Virginia came into camp with papers and immoral books. This was reported to Colonel Grosvenor, who had them arrested on pretense that their accounts were not correct. The men played checkers and cards, but the Colonel outlawed gambling, a move that probably reduced friction.

In late October Colonel Grosvenor as ranking regimental commander filled in as head of the Brigade for General Lander who had received a special assignment to rebuild the 120-mile Baltimore and Ohio Railroad between Harpers Ferry and Cumberland. There was a rumor that Grosvenor would be promoted to General.

Another storm was brewing on the home front. Henry's volatile father crossed swords with H.N.F. Lewis, editor and owner of the *Jonesville Telegraph*, over local politics.[46] The *Jonesville Telegraph* was founded by Walt Murphy in May 1839. In the early 1850s it was a Free Soil newspaper, evolving into a Republican paper as the owner's politics matured.[47] Levi was therefore used to support from the editor and was not pleased by criticism from Lewis when he purchased the paper in 1859.[48]

During his dispute with Levi, Lewis published an unsubstantiated statement attributed to Henry Baxter that Company C could rid Jonesville of traitors, in other words shut down the *Jonesville Telegraph* over a difference of opinion.[49] The only evidence that this might be true was the word of Lewis. By November, Levi Baxter had had enough. He sued Lewis for libel. As Jonesville's postmaster, Levi Baxter wielded considerable clout when it came to newspaper delivery, a threat that put Lewis at a disadvantage. This kind of tumult in a small town could cause problems for everyone and the resulting uneasy truce was a god-send.

Lewis' troubles were not over. His brand of journalism was unwelcome in Hillsdale

4. Off to War, 1861

County, advertising and subscriptions declined, and in 1863 he sold the paper and purchased the *Western Rural*. He moved to Illinois.[50]

One of the areas of increased Michigan influence lay in the field of diplomacy. Through his support of William H. Seward during the 1860 Republican National Convention and the considerable efforts of powerful Michigan Senator Zachariah Chandler, in July 1861 Walt Murphy was appointed by President Lincoln to be Consul General Resident at Frankfort-on-the-Main, a free city among the German republics. Murphy assumed his duties on November 7, replacing southerner Samuel Ricker who had tried to gain financial and political support for the south. Murphy built good relationships, using his background as attorney, banker, and newspaper man to focus investment on the anti-slavery Union. By paying for articles favorable to the Union in German and French language newspapers, he was able to turn the tide of public opinion. He was credited with having secured the support of Baron Rothschild and other prominent Germans for the Union cause, an accomplishment of significance.[51]

Fall settled upon the countryside with little prospect that the stalemate along the Potomac would be broken. Action was sparse after the Battle of Bull Run in July sent the Union army back to its lines around Washington. Major General George McClellan became head of the Army of the Potomac on July 26, extolling the belief that the loss had been as much a failure of training as a failure of leadership. He began rectifying both deficiencies through a regimen of repetitive drill and resupply. Above all, he called for more men, a message that came to dominate his tenure.

The receipt of new supplies and equipment, the constant training and review built confidence among the troops, while the avoidance of battle built both anticipation and a sense that McClellan really cared about his men. At the same time, the troops expected a short war, and the longer the rebellion wore on the more their optimism waned. They wanted to fight, to prove that they could put an end to the war that kept them from home and family. They imagined a glorious return and were anxious to reach it. Mounting deaths from disease in camp highlighted the costly futility of avoiding a fight.

With all of these forces at work, ambitious officers lost patience with McClellan's slow approach to prosecution of the war. They were hungry for decisive action that would bring victory to the army and glory to themselves. After all, what post-war voter would deny an office to a man who had played a prominent role in quelling the rebellion? In this environment some leaders chose to exceed their orders. One such case occurred at the Battle of Balls Bluff near the town of Leesburg, Virginia, where the 7th Michigan had its first experience with action.

On October 20 McClellan telegraphed divisional commander General Charles P. Stone ordering him to make a reconnaissance of Confederate-held ground across the Potomac River in the area of Leesburg. Late that night a small force crossed the river at Harrison's Island. The next morning General Stone gave Colonel Edward Baker—an ambitious Senator from Oregon—discretionary authority to either reconnoiter in force or retire from the area. Baker ordered his brigade to cross the river. Stone ordered Willis Gorman's Brigade to support him by crossing at Edwards Ferry. Baker's poor reconnaissance identified little opposition. He took up a defensive position atop Ball's Bluff, an eminence that allowed his men to face any potential enemy from the wooded heights inland, but that had nearly a 100-foot bluff and the Potomac River at its back. Baker left his men vulnerable to an attack from a well-covered position in his front and with no escape route to the rear. He was caught there by Confederate Brigadier General Nathan Evans, whose three infantry and one cavalry regiment quickly enveloped and pushed the Union troops back over the precipice. Of the 921 federals engaged, more than 207 casualties were suffered, including Baker. Of the total, 714 were captured or missing.[52]

The 7th Michigan was involved in the battle, but not as combatants. They were detailed to a supporting role at Harrison's Island, spending the night helping others cross in boats, digging rifle pits, and standing guard. They were ordered to cross the river the morning of October 22, but were delayed by the rush of higher-priority troops. They moved upstream one half mile and camped without tents. The night was a cold one, so when the regiment was awakened two hours later and "ordered to retreat in the most profound silence" some men had caught cold.[53] Their coughs brought rebukes from the officers, including an ironic threat from Colonel Grosvenor that he would shoot them if they did not remain quiet. They moved quietly to the ferry and embarked. Colonel Grosvenor remained behind to facilitate crossing by the last of the federal forces.

Rain the next day brought an end to hostilities, but not an end to looting. Union troops took cattle, hogs, sheep, cabbage, turnips, corn, and wheat. They burned a brand new reaper, just for spite, since it reportedly belonged to a "Confederate General."[54] Later pickets exchanged fire with rebels. The 7th Michigan was drawn up to attack, but artillery dislodged the Confederates before an advance occurred.

Blame for the loss of so many Union soldiers had to land somewhere. Colonel Baker had many friends in Congress intent on shielding him from responsibility for exceeding his orders, so the blame fell on General Charles Stone, his division commander, for allegedly not providing support. Sergeant Curtis wrote a long account vindicating General Stone in his journal, stating that Colonel Baker's motivation was to "enter Leesburgh and carve his name among the heroes of the times … but the [enemy] force was too much for him and he fell a prey to his own ambition."[55]

Though the regiment did not serve under fire, it was not without losses. Their brigade commander—the "Poet General" William Lander—returned from his special assignment after the disaster at Balls Bluff and tried to extricate his regiments from enemy territory. In the process, he was shot in the leg and later died because "his wounds were not properly dressed."[56]

Knaggs quipped that the only thing that Union forces won at Balls Bluff was the "chance to go back to camp."[57] For the men of the 7th Michigan who spent their time in Camp Benton enduring the cold, rainy weather, it was not a very promising start to what they dreamed of as a short, glorious military affair. Baxter and his comrades were beginning to learn that boldness needed to be tempered with intelligence and discretion. Failure to have properly functional weapons made the unit virtually useless. Morale plummeted. In the wake of Balls Bluff, Frederick Oesterle reported, "We certainly didn't think ourselves great soldiers."[58]

The regiment delayed going into winter quarters in case they might yet still see action. Wild rumors of probable marching orders, victories and defeats ran through the army, alternately raising and lowering morale. Their blankets were too thin to keep them warm during the freezing nights and on the drizzly days. By November reports reached home that measles had appeared in the camp and that Colonel Grosvenor had converted a tobacco barn into a regimental hospital. By late December a cemetery had been established in a nearby grove. Despite the apparent nearness of death from disease, accident, or battle, Chaplain Strong was perplexed that officers and men used profanity and failed to observe the Sabbath. Yet, the 7th Michigan seemed to be less prone to these faults than regiments quartered in the vicinity. In fact, as the regiment closed each day with dress parade, it formed into a square with the officers in the center and the chaplain held a brief service, the only unit in the area to do so. Strong concluded that rough behavior seemed "to be necessarily incident to a life in the army."[59]

McClellan never delivered on his assertion that the army might yet be mobilized. In Washington there was growing disenchantment with him. The general was preoccupied with obtaining more troops, more supplies, more weapons, but appeared to have no definite plan to use them. President Lincoln, the Cabinet, and Congress were deeply concerned and disappointed by his inaction.[60] Even among the men of the 7th Michigan, there was growing disgust with the immobility. Chaplain Strong wrote in early December,

> The Army is impatient for an onward movement of some kind. It seems as though it would have a bad effect if these scores of thousands of men in arms on the Potomac shall be constrained to lie inactive until spring. But the Powers that be in Washington know their own counsels, and we would have, in lively and cheerful exercise, that faith which believes their counsels to be wiser than our own judgment.[61]

By late December the 7th Michigan was in winter quarters. The log barracks with fire places were a boon to morale. Yet, the war seemed no closer to conclusion, and this point had begun to wear upon them. The original enthusiasm that had carried so many off to war waned as they realized that this Civil War would not be of short duration.

For Henry Baxter, the end of the year brought acknowledgement that his performance might lead to promotion. On New Year's Eve 1861 he wrote Elvira:

> The promotion you speak of does not trouble me nor do I feel particularly anxious for it—I should feel proud to be considered by our Colonel worthy and fitted to fill the position but I am proud of and love my company and think I could lead them on to battle and then would do honor to themselves and their Commander. Our regiment I think is acknowledged to be one of the best in the field and our Colonel I Know to be the best and if we are ever placed in position to be tried much will be Expected of us and I hope we shall prove ourselves not over Estimated.... How soon I can come home now my dearest wife I cannot tell but ... something seems to be coming up continually that renders it very difficult for me to leave and be doing as I consider my duty demands. I did not join the army for pastime, but because my country called and stern duty looks me in the face continually and her demands must not be neglected. I hope before long however My dearest one to be permitted to see you and our darling little ones.[62]

Henry's mixed feelings—pride in his unit and his own accomplishments, yet desire to be with friends and family—were common among soldiers far from home. His growing confidence in his abilities and his increasing local knowledge of military practice showed that he had settled in as a regimental officer.

Back home, Michiganders had much to be proud of. Still in many ways a frontier state, Michigan had mobilized for war quickly and effectively. The *New York Herald-Tribune* editorialized,

> The quiet and unobtrusive State of Michigan has already sent nine full regiments of infantry and two of cavalrys into the field, and has six or eight more regiments nearly completed and ready

for service; beside which she has furnished two companies for the Lincoln Cavalry, two companies for the Sharpshooters, and numerous squads of men for different organizations in other States.... Gov. Blair enters into the business with a true patriotic spirit, and has done and is still doing all in his power for the credit of the State he so ably represents.[63]

Michigan units had seen some action, but the primary contest lay ahead and the people of Michigan felt sure that their men were up to the challenge.

⸻

The first year of the Civil War was a dynamic learning experience for Henry Baxter. He adeptly applied his knowledge of local and state politics to recruit, fund, and ensure that the company he formed entered service under the well-connected Ira Grosvenor. He embarked with his regiment upon long months of training, first in Michigan and then in Virginia. He applied his knowledge of human nature to build unity and discipline while he acquired proficiency with military procedures, discipline, and politics. He was loyal to Colonel Grosvenor and was in turn well-liked and respected by his men. Through the frustrations and adversities of 1861 he had solidified his leadership, inspiring the confidence of his superiors and the men he led. These qualities would prove critically important in meeting the challenges of 1862.

5

Action at Last, Early 1862

From the Union perspective, the crusade had come to naught, the short war had turned into a long one, and many had fallen without definitive result. Yet the commitment to reunite the nation was still strong, resolve maturing from an early fervor to a promise that the bloodshed not be in vain. And so the military preparations continued, the troops grew increasingly stoic as their boots showed the wear of forced marches, and the generals became more experienced amid the thrust and parry of strategy, both military and political.

The Commander-in-Chief was not happy. The Lincoln administration needed to move quickly to maintain political support at home and to discourage foreign intervention on behalf of the south. Lincoln's only acceptable options for Union success were predicated upon military victory. But the President had serious doubts about George McClellan's ability to win. Of particular concern was McClellan's lethargy. Decisive action was essential. So in January Lincoln mobilized Secretary of the Treasury Salmon Chase and Secretary of State William Seward to meet with Generals Irvin McDowell and William Franklin—senior generals, but subordinate to McClellan—to push an aggressive strategy.

McClellan reacted badly. He refused to provide details of his plan of attack to the Commander and Chief. Though Lincoln continued to support him, McClellan's behavior alienated more people in the highest political circles. With little indication that a plan existed, Lincoln issued General War Order No. 1 on January 27, 1862, stating that Union forces on land and sea were to be ready to engage the enemy on February 22. Special War Oder No. 1 dated January 31, ordered the Army of the Potomac to move on or before February 22 to take the Orange and Alexandria Railroad southwest of Manassas Junction. McClellan needed to unveil his stratagem for the campaign of 1862 or accept a strategy imposed upon him. Lincoln eventually withdrew his orders, allowing McClellan to initiate what became known as the Peninsula Campaign. Over time the places of embarkation and debarkation were altered to fit changing circumstances, but the essential strategy remained the same. McClellan intended to use Chesapeake Bay to circumvent the Confederates by water and capture Richmond from the east. With Richmond in Union hands, he expected the south to capitulate.

Senior strategy aside, the work of the army went on. With the growing losses through disease, accident, and skirmish, recruiting became an ever more important exercise that allowed regiments to survive slow attrition. The War Department recruiting system was designed to keep regiments operational by sending commissioned officers and men on recruiting tours. Under this authority, Captain Baxter sent Lieutenant Vrooman to Jonesville where he signed up nine new recruits for the 7th Michigan.

The veterans of 7th Michigan spent the winter of 1861–62 in Camp Benton with as much comfort as they could manage. The regiment had enough to eat as the temperature and the winter snow steadily fell. For the common soldier, the world settled into tedium.

The winter had its moments. On Saturday, January 11, two Lieutenants came into camp in great haste, mobilizing the regiment with the news that Professor Thaddeus Lowe's observation balloon was under attack. Four companies of the 7th Michigan turned out to protect the important reconnaissance craft from a Confederate raid that never came. They "had been fooled into a march of a mile in a dark, foggy night through the mud."[1]

On February 7 word was received of a "brilliant victory," the capture by General U.S. Grant of Fort Henry in Tennessee. The regiment gave three rousing cheers, and the band played Yankee Doodle, Hail Columbia, and even Dixie. Further celebrations occurred on February 12 when news came of General Ambrose Burnside's victory at the Battle of Roanoke Island, North Carolina. The regiment had a "great time" riding Jeff Davis' effigy on a rail before burning it. They also gave three groans for their former corps commander Brigadier General Charles Stone, who was arrested on February 8 under suspicion of treason for his actions at the Battle of Balls Bluff.[2]

They continued to drill, improving marksmanship and skill with bayonets. They reacquainted their feet with marching, a skill under-appreciated today. Armies of the Civil War primarily traveled on foot, marching and counter-marching with unremitting frequency based on the unfolding of events and—all too often—the poor navigation of their officers. Arguably, the war was not won by fire power or strategy as much as by the ability to march armies from place to place quickly. In this, the Army of the Potomac was becoming proficient—though as Confederate General "Stonewall" Jackson's foot cavalry were to prove—they needed much improvement. The officer corps got better all the time. Politicians without talent for military leadership or administration faced gradual attrition. More proficient officers were rising in the ranks. One of them was Henry Baxter.

In March Henry learned of the death of his father at age 73 on February 28, of an inflammation of the lungs. The *Hillsdale Standard* grieved that the illness was something that a "younger man might, perhaps, have easily resisted."[3] Henry wrote to Vi on March 20, telling her how "very sad that I could not have been at home during fathers sickness."[4] His rival at the *Jonesville Independent* wrote a predictably sparse obituary, in which he skipped Levi's political achievements to concentrate on his role as a pioneer miller and as a father who sired via two wives 17 children, 11 of whom outlived him. The Republican *Standard* extolled his political achievements.

Levi's funeral was held at the Presbyterian Church in Jonesville, an edifice he helped fund and govern. The Reverend H.C. Harvey of Coldwater conducted the service. On Sunday, the first chairman of the Republican Party was buried in a plot appropriately situated under the oaks in Jonesville's Sunset Cemetery. The substantial marble marker erected in his memory faced west, the direction that his ambition had drawn him.

Levi left a sizeable estate. Probate records showed that he owned a house on Chicago Street valued at $2,500, lots and a shop on West Street (including steam engine and machinery) valued at $1,250, and a warehouse and lot on Chicago Street valued at $200. Witter slowly moved Levi's estate through the probate process. Levi's second wife Elizabeth, age 56, retained of all but $450 worth of the household property on Chicago Street. On December 15, 1864, the surviving children were listed as Helen Smith, Mary Jane Kellogg, Lois F. Selfridge, Antoinette Baxter, Elizabeth Baxter, Charles Baxter, Clara Case Baxter, and Florence Baxter. Benjamin, Witter, and Henry, sons by his first wife, had already received their inheritance from their father.

Levi's legacy was inestimable. He built a small commercial empire, mentoring his sons in both business and politics. He left his older sons propertied and prosperous. All were involved in his political designs, including the growth of the Republican Party. They were among their communities' elite and were well-placed for continued success.

Henry was making progress. The promotion hinted at in December manifested itself when he assumed more responsibility during the winter and spring, acting as Lieutenant Colonel. Such opportunities came to those that were both politically savvy and militarily competent, and that he was both was demonstrated by Colonel Grosvenor's faith in him. One observer quipped, "He seems to be the Colonel's favorite officer."[5]

On the home front, Elvira Baxter was helping the war effort in her own way. The flood of support for military action from men in northern communities was "paralleled by a similar uprising among women. The patriotic speech and song ... nourished the self-sacrifice of women, and stimulated them to the collection of hospital supplies, and to brave the horrors and hardships of hospital life."[6] Much was done through voluntary aid societies. As early as April 1862 Elvira hosted meetings of the Soldier's Aid Society in her Jonesville home.[7] Such gatherings were not only a means of aiding the soldiers at the front, the social interaction helped reinforce the ascendancy of the military leader's wife among her peers. No matter that the blankets, uniforms, socks, stationery, and food supplied by these societies were often of inferior or inconsistent quality. These things represented home and the support of those who lived there. The impact on soldiers' morale was higher than the needs satisfied.

Early in the war, articles from local aid associations were either sent directly to the regiments or forwarded via the Michigan Soldiers' Relief Association, a group headquartered in Washington that marshaled packages in the Patent Office warehouse, then delivered direct to Michigan units via the donated services of Adams and Company Express. Later in the war the United States Sanitary Commission served as the primary conduit, collecting donations in its Chicago office from Michigan and the other Old Northwest Territory states. The Sanitary Commission helped to sort, cull, and route supplies in a manner that reduced waste, while increasing quality and efficiency. With more than 10,000 aid societies in the north contributing one box of medical supplies per month, the organization was desperately needed.[8]

The Army of the Potomac command structure was reorganized during the winter. The 7th Michigan was in 2nd Corps under Brigadier General Edwin Sumner, 2nd Division under Brigadier General John Sedgwick, the 3rd Brigade led by Brigadier General Napoleon Dana. Sedgwick's Division included three brigades, five batteries, and one regiment of cavalry. Dana's Brigade was composed of the 7th Michigan, 19th and 20th Massachusetts, and the 42nd New York.

The late winter of 1862 was a peculiar time. The army dealt with intermittent snow and rain that made the roads difficult and brought sickness. The men hoped for action as they waited for their pay, reluctantly borrowing to stay ahead of expenses. In March a change in southern policy led to the observation that "hundreds of Virginia Citizens are hurrying to this state [of Maryland] for safety as the C.S.A. commences drafting."[9]

As regimental commander, Colonel Grosvenor was feeling the stress of administering a frustrated regiment anxious to face the enemy. He asked permission to cross the river near Leesburg where on March 8–9 the Confederates had abandoned their works, burning crops, buildings, and railroad depots as they withdrew. At the time, it was not known whether or not this was a general withdrawal from the Confederate position around Manassas. McClellan and his staff were developing bigger plans and these did not include the kind of small, local operation that Grosvenor had in mind. Permission to occupy the area was denied and the following day another unit raised the American flag over Leesburg. Not knowledgeable of the larger strategic picture and tired of inactivity, the disenchanted Grosvenor posted a card in his office that read "Head Quarters of Grin & Bearit."[10]

At 3:00 a.m. on March 10 the regiment was awakened with orders to be ready to march with four days rations. The men were vaccinated against smallpox and told they would depart the following morning for Harpers Ferry. Their mission was to counter an anticipated invasion by Confederate General Stonewall Jackson up the Shenandoah Valley.

The regiment's gear was packed, placed on canal boats, and taken up the Baltimore and Ohio Canal, leaving on March 11 and arriving at Harper's Ferry the morning of March 12. They passed beautiful scenery, particularly the lofty summits between Point of Rocks and Harpers Ferry. But it was hot, and they quickly learned what a real march was like. Some discarded "bullet proof" vests with steel lining that they purchased for protection.[11]

They marched to Charlestown and bivouacked for the night in a grove about half a mile east of the town. They resumed their march down the Shenandoah Valley the following day, arriving outside Berryville by evening. They were foot sore, but soothed themselves with the idea that the other regiments were somehow worse off. They never fired a shot. On Friday they were ordered to return to Harpers Ferry. On the way Lieutenant William Shafter of Company I learned from a runaway slave that an officer in the Confederate Quartermaster Corps was visiting his nearby home. Shafter sought and received permission from Colonel Grosvenor to go after the rebel, and captured Major E.B. Pendleton as he was about to sit down to breakfast with his family. Pendleton graciously invited Shafter and his men to breakfast before they took him into custody. That night they bivouacked in Charlestown. Saturday morning they started again, this time stopping at Bolivar Heights where some were quartered in the homes of departed Secessionists and Union sympathizers.[12]

Henry Baxter recorded his shock at the terrible destruction that the war had wrought upon Harpers Ferry:

> Such a perfect destruction of property you can hardly image. Fine houses marble finished in the most costly style are very many of them used for stabling horses. The marble, which is of the finest Italian, broken and destroyed, the columns and door casings and inside works cut in pieces for firewood. It is enough to make one heart sick to see the destruction and desolation but such is the fate of war and especially Civil War. We may be thankful that it is not carried into the North.[13]

The time in historic Harpers Ferry had an impact on Baxter. He wrote,

We are achieving victory upon victory and it would seem that this war must soon be brought to a close, but a civil war of all others is clung to with the most tenacity and the hardest to put down. We will hope that this rebellion may soon be brought to a termination.[14]

Included in his letter home was a sample of Virginia money, a piece of Jefferson's Rock, and "a piece of the stump on which John Brown made his last speech."[15] Baxter was aware that history surrounded him and that he and his men were playing important roles in the American pantheon.

The men wanted more than anything to be tried in battle. Reflecting their mood, on March 20 Chaplain Strong wrote:

> And yet, strong and able as it is to cope with the enemy, it looks as though both the Regiment and Division would never be permitted to see the enemy. Nothing would so much gratify both the officers and men as to be placed where they could make a record for themselves and reflect credit upon the State which sent them here to fight, and not remain month after month in inglorious activity.[16]

The 7th Michigan was close to more action than anyone would ever want to experience.

⇒ ⇐

The issue of the Belgian rifles was finally concluded in the spring of 1862. At Balls Bluff outdated firearms had kept the unit out of the action. Everyone longed to shed them for new Springfield rifles. They discussed upgrading to the highly prized Sharps repeating rifles that had the advantage of better accuracy, firepower, and rapid reloading. Had the unit purchased the Sharps rifles themselves, each man would have had to pay $42. Higher authority kept this from occurring, so the 7th Michigan carried Springfield rifles.

Accounts differ as to when the Springfields were actually received, but they arrived in an unexpected manner.[17]

> One morning the quarter master handed me [Robert Knaggs] an order to take two four[-] horse teams to go to the freight house at Washington, where we were to exchange our Belgian guns for Springfields, the best guns that were to be had at that time....
>
> The Quarter Master described to me the doors of the freight house. He said that on the left side of the door were cases which I would find to take the place of the ones I was returning. I presented my orders to the sentry for the muskets and we unloaded our Belgian muskets as rapidly as we could. Then we loaded the others in the wagons. We went out to Meridian Hill where we remained until the next morning when we started for Edward's Ferry.... The boys cheered me on my arrival. The Quarter Master was glad to see me and called me a d— Thief. I was mortified. He said I had no legal right to [the guns].
>
> The Springfields were intended for a New York regiment, and when they went for them they had to take the Belgians or nothing. At that time in Washington, if you wanted anything and wanted it in a hurry, you had to steal it, for there was so much red tape. The boys had the laugh on me, but.... I distributed the arms among them.
>
> A few days later, a Colonel of a New York regiment came riding into Camp and went in our Colonel's tent. He said we'd stolen his rifles and he wanted them. Our Colonel [Grosvenor] said "We have those rifles. If you want them [go] get them!" Needless to say, he did not get them for it would have taken more than one regiment to retake them.[18]

The new Springfield rifles were not only a boost to the unit's firepower, but to their morale as well. Finally they felt like part of the army.

⇒ ⇐

By late March the regiment was outside Washington, making preparations to move yet again. McClellan's strategy was to circumvent General Joseph Johnston's army at Manassas Junction by loading the 120,000 strong Army of the Potomac aboard ships and transporting it behind Confederate lines, between the rebel army and Richmond. With the withdraw of Johnston's Confederates and other changes to the strategic alignment, McClellan altered the plan to take his army down the Potomac River using approximately 400 chartered steamers, sailing ships, and barges. He intended to deliver them to Fortress Monroe, a stalwart northern outpost located at the entrance to Chesapeake Bay just outside Hampton and across Hampton Roads from Norfolk. The ships could move only 25,000 men per trip, so at a cost of $24,300 per day the flotilla was kept busy for over three weeks ferrying men, horses, equipment, and supplies. With the addition of escorting naval vessels, this effort became the largest combined naval and military movement in North American history up to that time.

The first army units began to embark at Alexandria on the evening of March 16, starting with Major General Samuel Heintzelman's 3rd Corps. By March 22 McClellan ordered Heintzelman to move his troops toward Yorktown, preparing for the arrival of additional units.

The 7th Michigan was assigned to a steamer, but when they arrived at the landing on March 25 Colonel Grosvenor refused to allow them to board what he judged to be an overcrowded vessel. The steamer *T.V. Arrowsmith* was substituted and they "had a fine ride down the Potomac and Chesapeake Bay" until a storm forced them to anchor overnight.[19] On March 27 they arrived off Fortress Monroe amid hundreds of ships, including the *USS Monitor*, which was at the height of its fame having engaged the *CSS Virginia* on March 9. The masts of the *USS Congress* and *USS Cumberland* were visible above the water, after being sunk by the *Virginia* on March 8. However, Knaggs had to return to Washington for the regimental stores that had not made it aboard the transport. He found the supplies and returned aboard a small steamer with a hold full of horses. The trip was rough enough that both horses and men struggled with footing, eating, and resting. Through a mistake in intelligence, they nearly landed at Ship Point, which was in Confederate hands. Fortunately the mistake was realized in time, the steamer sheered off and they landed safely.

The 7th Michigan landed baggage at Fortress Monroe on March 29 and camped at Hampton. Members of the regiment took a look at the fort and were suitably impressed with its massive artillery. The town of Hampton lay in ruins, burned to the ground by Confederates to keep it from falling into Federal hands.

On April 4 the leading elements of the army moved inland. Heintzelman took the Great Bethel Road toward Yorktown. Citizens of Richmond heard cannon fire. On April 5 the 7th Michigan marched from Little Bethel, bivouacking five miles from Yorktown. The congestion on the roads made progress slow:

> Made but one mile because of the Artillery. One hundred and twenty three pieces and cassions. And the entire baggage train about 20 miles in length—This Army of the Potomac now contains one hundred and twenty five thousand Infantry, 300 pieces Artillery, and 8000 Cavalry.[20]

To make matters worse, they were soaked by a cold northeast rain. Short of rations, wet, and cold, they built some huts in the pine woods and started fires in an attempted to dry themselves. The regiment would have had no food had they not found Confederate provisions. The men were anxious to start foraging, something they were allowed to begin on April 7. Companies I and K were able to find molasses, bacon, and hard bread to keep everyone fed.

Local people showed the Union soldiers no kindness. Curtis recorded, "Of the people there is no opportunity to judge there being but a few scattering Ladies or Women ... and though they pretend to be union now, their doors are bared against us."[21] The soldiers knew for the first time what it felt like to be outside their country.

At Yorktown McClellan was convinced he faced a much larger enemy force than actually existed. Inflated reports of Confederate troop strength from intelligence chief Allan Pinkerton helped to buttress this idea. Instead of a frontal assault, he decided upon a siege. Earthworks parallel to the Confederate entrenchments were thrown up as siege guns were laboriously brought up despite the heat, the mud, and the intermittent rain. At the time, McClellan's available troops vastly outnumbered the Yorktown defenders.

The Michiganders were ready to be tried in combat. Colonel Grosvenor wrote to Michigan Adjutant General Robertson from Yorktown on April 15, "We are and have been in line of battle for a week momentarily expecting an engagement. The regiment is in fine health and spirits and anxious to be led to the fight.... Our Michigan troops, I am proud to say, stand in the first rank in the estimation of our General Officers. I trust we may not prove unworthy our good name and State."[22] Baxter and his comrades were excited by the prospect of their first real action.

The discomfort did little to distract from the historic nature of their situation. The Union troops used some of the same lines held by Washington during the American Revolution. On April 20 the 7th Michigan was on the spot where Lafayette's troops were in 1781 and only ½ mile from Washington's headquarters. For Union troops, the sense of a righteous cause was heightened by the historic spot on which they fought.

The brigades took turns on 24-hour picket duty, starting at noon. The 7th Michigan took its turn on April 18 and 21. They got little rest even when not on picket duty. The fighting was close and the regiment was awakened by repeated alarms. With frequent orders to assemble, followed by hours spent standing in the rain waiting to go into action, only to be dismissed again, one would assume that the troops would become discouraged, especially since they felt keenly the deprivation of pay since December 31. But Hodgman at least expressed confidence in Gen-

Henry and Elvira "Vi" Baxter were married in 1854 and had four children who reached adulthood. This image was taken while Henry was serving in the Army of the Potomac. Courtesy Charles Henderson.

eral McClellan and the army of which he was a part. Not all agreed with him. Curtis recorded on April 8 that it just occurred to the generals that an impassable eight-mile wide swamp was in their front and noted "our hope now is in the gun boats upon the James."[23]

By April 29 the 7th Michigan had encamped near Cheeseman's Creek. They were on good ground, with sandy soil that supported dense yellow pines 40 to 50 feet tall. Three miles away from Ship Point, their part in the siege of Yorktown entered a new phase. The sandy soil became like quick sand in the recurring rain so 80 rods of corduroy road per day was built to keep the highways passable. They were on picket duty directly behind an area where signaling stations were constructed. This drew enemy fire, but though they were frequently fired upon, no one was hurt.

While besieging Yorktown Henry wrote to Elvira one of his most expressive letters:

My own darling and dearly loved Wife—

The Second day of May

I let my thoughts fly back over the past and on the evening of the second day of May eight years ago they rest, and with the heartfelt pleasure do they continue to rest, for on the evening of this day the loved Vi George became my own loved and loving wife. Would that I could be with my own loved Vi tonight to clasp you to my heart and implant the longed for Kiss upon your lips and receive one in return which I know full well would be given as it would be received with pleasure. Well darling, this cannot be and we will await patiently the time when we will be again united the happy family. Eight years have passed since our pledged Vows and as they pass we have one, two, three, darling little ones that fill our hearts with love for them, and still there is none the less room left for my loved and loving, Wife....

Well, my dear, here we are before Yorktown still and still the preparation for the battle goes on. I sometimes think the rebels will evacuate the town before the artillery commences its work of destruction and again sometimes make up my mind that they will not give up their stronghold until driven from it. That the armies of the Union will be Victorious, and the Flag of the best government on Earth, again float over the entire country unmolested and that too at no very distant day I do not have a doubt. The thunder and roar of Cannon and the iron storm that will be hurled forth when the work does commence in earnest will be terrific indeed. It will probably be sometime yet before all preparations are completed and ready—

This has been a very pleasant day and this afternoon in company with some of our officers I took a stroll to York river passing over a field where one of our batteries is placed and at which the rebels fired twenty-three shots this Morning doing them no damage however. Don't think dearest I am carelessly exposing myself for there was no danger here at this time and I do not put myself in harms way unless duty calls me. This country is full of the rebel works fortifications trenches &c which they have deserted for their present situation. The labor they have expended has been immense and all for their wicked unholy cause but this passes for naught when we think of the many lives that have been sacrificed by their unrighteous rebellion... .

Good night
Your affectionate husband
Henry[24]

The letter was quintessential Baxter. Love for his family was expressed fully, reinforcing that only the war and his duty could keep them apart. He articulated a realistic assessment of the military situation while minimizing the potential danger to himself to avoid worrying his family. Upbeat like all his letters, he reaffirmed his devotion to the sacred cause and expressed his unshakeable conviction that the Union would eventually prevail.

5. Action at Last, Early 1862

Suddenly the rebel position went quiet late on May 3. Baxter had correctly posited that the Confederates might withdraw before an assault was made. This was confirmed the next morning when Brigadier General Heintzelman spied on the enemy works using a military reconnaissance balloon and found the Confederates had retreated. He had over-estimated the number of Confederate defenders and could not believe that they had abandoned their strong position. McClellan had missed his opportunity to cut them off.

The men of the 7th Michigan made their feelings clear. Curtis remarked sarcastically, "So much for the immense preparation that has been made to subdue this town."[25] The rebels abandoned plenty of equipment, though little of use to the Union Army. Curtis wrote, "Should have brot. [sic] Home trophies but have concluded all the trophy I want is to get back myself—Are now on the way to West Point to pursue the flying foe."[26]

They pursued the Confederates up the peninsula, clashing at Williamsburg on May 5. There federal troops met a determined resistance, but made progress in a hard rain. By 3:30 a.m. on May 6 Union pickets reported the Confederate withdrawal, and at first light northern forces moved into the abandoned southern works. The Confederates effectively slowed the Union advance, gradually evacuating the peninsula. Union forces held the ground after the battle, clearing the way for continued advance. McClellan delayed consolidating his forces while he dealt with the wounded and waited for his supply train to catch up.

Neither the 7th Michigan nor Henry Baxter played a role in the Battle of Williamsburg. When Yorktown was evacuated, they marched all day through rain and ankle deep mud to reach the steamer that carried them to West Point. No one dared move off the path because the Confederates had planted "torpedoes" (land mines). Since there were not enough shallow draft craft to take more than one at a time, Franklin's Division was loaded on May 5 and disembarked at Etham's Landing the following day. Their landing was lightly opposed by enemy artillery. The boats brought up Sedgwick's division—including the 7th Michigan—the following day.

By comparison to the march, the trip to West Point via steamer *Augusta* was a "pleasant ride" up the York River.[27] They disembarked at Etham's Landing with Dana's Brigade in the early morning of May 7 and found Union forces fighting for the ground. They were in the line of battle and were charged seven times that day, suffering 60 men killed and wounded. Confederate General John Bell Hood's men delayed their advance and then withdrew before sunset.

The Union leadership was unsure of enemy intent, so on May 8 the army was called out at 3:00 a.m. to repel an anticipated dawn counterattack. At daybreak "news came today of the Glorious victory at Williamsburg and rumors of the fall or evacuation of Norfolk and the destroying of the *Merrimac*."[28] Confederate forces reached the defenses around Richmond on May 9. Franklin's force from Etham's Landing did not pursue the enemy, moving instead over to the main road to await the march north with the main body of federals.

The 7th Michigan continued to move toward Richmond, but did not see immediate action. They routinely moved up seven or eight miles, then camped about two days as the army shuffled forward. By May 23 they were 16 miles from Richmond. Confederate citizens were apprehensive of being "at their mercy" as the federals approached.[29]

Arrival outside Richmond did not make McClellan more aggressive. He set about consolidating his position, delaying offensive action, thereby handing the initiative to the Confederates. By May 30, the Confederate army had 94,813 men present for duty, while McClellan had 103,382. When McClellan divided his forces, sending the 3rd and 4th Corps south of the Chickahominy River while keeping the other three corps north, Johnston saw his chance to attack the federals with superior numbers before they could be supported from across the river.

Johnston planned to launch his attack on the Union 3rd and 4th Corps on May 31, concentrating at Seven Pines, located at the intersection of Nine Mile and Williamsburg Road. If he was successful, he might turn McClellan's left flank and force him to realign his position. The coming battle would be better known to Union troops as Fair Oaks Station (a station on the Richmond and York River Railroad to the northwest of Seven Pines) because federal troops were heavily engaged there.

The attack was set to begin at dawn, but confusion among the Confederates slowed the advance. Another setback was caused by heavy nighttime thunderstorms that left roads muddy, fields flooded, and streams overflowing. The latter problem actually worked to the Confederate advantage, threatening the connection of the Union 3rd and 4th Corps south of the Chickahominy River as makeshift bridges were strained by a rising torrent of water. Finally at 1:00 p.m. Confederate General D.H. Hill attacked troops commanded by Brigadier General Silas Casey. The fighting concentrated around the Williamsburg Road was marked by confusion as Casey's inexperienced regiments were pushed back and supporting units were committed piecemeal. By the time the firing ended at nightfall, Union forces had been severely mauled. But support was on the way.

McClellan ordered Sumner's 2nd Corps across the Chickahominy River with General Sedgwick's Division leading sometime between 1:30 and 3:00 p.m. Major John Richardson rushed a 7th Michigan fatigue party of 200 men to rejoin the regiment, which was already marching for the river. Though sick with cholera, Colonel Grosvenor lead the regiment. Only through a direct order from General Dana was he induced to leave his men. Richardson assumed command. The bridge they crossed had been jury-rigged and was tottering amidst the surging storm water, but it got them across. The 7th Michigan marched up the flooded, splintered corduroy approach and crossed the bridge at mid-afternoon. Dana continued with the 20th Massachusetts and the 7th Michigan. The 19th Massachusetts was on picket duty and did not accompany the brigade.

After crossing, Dana heard no firing in front, so he stopped for his men to load their weapons, then restarted at the double-quick. When about a mile from Fair Oaks Station, General Sumner directed Dana's Brigade to a position on the left wing of the division, extending the line to the south. The 7th Michigan went from a forced double-quick march through thick mud directly into the line on the extreme left of the middle Union front. They were heavily engaged, suffering casualties even as they formed up. Dana reported,

> I may be pardoned a feeling of pride when I can report that the [20th] Massachusetts men, the veterans of Ball's Bluff, and the Western men of Michigan, as yet unscathed [by] fire, came into action with a bearing of which their States may well be proud, and before the movement was fully executed received a withering volley from the enemy's right at short range with steadiness.[30]

They received conflicting orders simultaneously, causing confusion as they entered the line under Confederate fire. As a result, "Co. C by mistaking the order came near leaving us."[31] Major Richardson reportedly told them,

5. Action at Last, Early 1862

Men of the Seventh, Michigan expects every man of you to do his duty to day, let no one flinch; the issue depends on you; forward now and drive them before you.[32]

Before them in a shallow valley Dana saw the enemy trying to extend their lines right to outflank his brigade. He ordered a charge that drove them back about 150 yards to a wood, the 7th advancing with fixed bayonets. During this action the "enemys balls came thick and fast."[33] They charged the rebel lines twice at Fair Oaks and many of the men had narrow escapes. The result was the repulse of the Confederate advance and the capture of several artillery pieces. The 7th remained in the field that night, squatting in the rain at the last line of advance.

Both the 20th Massachusetts and the 7th Michigan suffered, Richardson's command experiencing 95–100 estimated casualties, 14 of whom were killed. Many of the wounded fought until they either fainted or expired from loss of blood. Curtis reported, "By Flag of truce the Rebels worked all night within Fifty yards carrying away their dead and wounded. Still many hundreds of the dead were left where they fell and there was no counting the wounded."[34] Curtis helped the "wounded friend and foe all upon the same terms."[35] By 3:00 a.m. all of Sumner's 2nd Corps had arrived. Their position to the north of the railroad and east of Fair Oaks Station was a strong one.

They expected to reengage in the morning, but the fighting shifted and the regiment moved about two miles to Seven Pines. Grosvenor reported that the regiment held the brigade flank and worked with the 20th Massachusetts and a battery of artillery to "check the left wing of the enemy during the entire day."[36] They held against an early June 1 counterattack initiated by General Hill. The 7th Michigan was hotly engaged and sustained the majority of the casualties, 16 killed and 113 wounded. The regiment captured the battle flag of the 7th Mississippi during the two day battle.

In editorializing on the 7th Michigan's first combat experience, a *Detroit Tribune* correspondent wrote that after so long performing menial tasks and awaiting an opportunity to show their metal, the men of the regiment

> can say with pride: "this is the 7th Michigan," for we have been in battle, where every man stood his ground and performed his whole duty, and every officer showed himself cool and collected.[37]

The evening of June 1 Curtis wrote, "We have a very important position to hold" adjacent to the railroad at Fair Oaks, near the geographic center of the skirmish line south of the Chickahominy River.[38]

There was Confederate cavalry nearby on June 2. Curtis went forward with a party of pickets, and then was sent by General Dana south to establish contact with General Hooker's pickets, only to learn they had withdrawn. For days afterward the men on the line were edgy about the prospect of another attack.

Regimental casualties were 180 killed, wounded, and missing. Adjutant Henry B. Landon was mortally wounded at Fair Oaks and his successor Lieutenant William R. Shafter—later awarded the Medal of Honor for his exploits—was wounded at Malvern Hill, so Robert Knaggs was appointed Adjutant.

Northern forces held the ground when the fighting was over. The Confederates withdrew and the 7th Michigan helped build earth works along a defensive line that followed the Richmond and York River Railroad. The men settled into the works but got no rest. Frequent alarms roused them day and night. Many men were sick, some with scurvy, yet hope kept their spirits high. Their proximity to the Confederate capital made them confident that Richmond would soon be captured and the war over. The rumor spread that they would be discharged in six weeks.

But those fantasies were short-lived. Confederate General Joseph Johnston was hit in his right shoulder and chest during the first day of the Battle of Seven Pines. Unable to continue, Johnston's second in command General G.W. Smith carried the battle into its second day. Confederate President Jefferson Davis selected his chief military advisor to succeed Johnston on June 1, while the battle raged. Davis' new head of the recently rechristened Army of Northern Virginia was General Robert E. Lee, a far more aggressive and imaginative leader.

By sunset on June 1 neither side was in a position to renew the battle. Hill still held Seven Pines and McClellan moved his forces to face him. But Hill was ordered to withdraw so June 2 did not bring a renewal of the engagement. On the night of June 3, General Hooker's federals reoccupied much of the Seven Pines battlefield.

McClellan prepared for his own attack, calling for siege guns to be brought up while moving the 2nd and 6th Corps south of the Chickahominy River. Porter's Corps was the only one left north of the river, and was therefore open to attack. General Lee dispatched General Jeb Stuart to reconnoiter the Union right to establish its exact position and level of exposure. Stuart's cavalry became famous for their three day ride around McClellan's army, during which they determined that Porter's Corps was indeed vulnerable. As a result, Lee summoned General Stonewall Jackson's army from the Shenandoah to support an attack on McClellan's right. McClellan's men prepared better roads and stronger defensive works. Curtis expected that McClellan's siege meant "we Shall probably be here some time."[39]

On June 25 McClellan attempted to push his line forward to reach Old Tavern, at the intersection of Nine Mile Road and New Bridge Road, to secure a position closer to Richmond for the siege guns. Though the Union attack at Oak Grove fell short, it moved federal forces 600 yards closer to their objective.

Ironically, both Lee and McClellan planned major attacks for June 26. McClellan intended to attack near Fair Oaks (south of the river) to capitalize on ground taken the day before, while Lee's attack would hit the Union right (north of the river). McClellan wanted to secure a position closer to Richmond for his siege guns, while Lee hoped to pull Union forces out of their works and fight in the open field where he could turn their flank. Lee felt that this approach would be less costly and more effective than the traditional frontal assault. In the end, McClellan never launched his attack and Lee's advance—delayed and erratic—made McClellan realize that Porter's 5th Corps was in an indefensible position with General Stonewall Jackson approaching from the northwest. McClellan was forced to react, effectively losing the initiative.

McClellan decided that the logistics of moving enough troops north to support Porter were too much. He cancelled his attack on Lee's thinned lines south of the river. Instead, he chose to pull Porter back to a more defensible position closer to the Chickahominy River and shift the army's supply base from White House Landing on the Pamunkey River to Harrison's Landing on the James River. He sent part of Franklin's 6th Corps north to help Porter fight a rear guard action while the change of base occurred.[40]

On the morning of June 27 Union and Confederate forces met north of the river near Gaines Mill. Porter fell back under fire to a new defensive line south of Boatswain's Swamp. He awaited the Confederate attack in a superior defensive position. Confederate General

5. Action at Last, Early 1862

John Magruder used artillery and skirmishes to keep the corps south of the river from decamping and heading to Porter's aid. The ruse convinced McClellan that he was in a precarious position. Thus, McClellan delayed reinforcing Porter. So the afternoon was spent with Porter picking up reinforcements as they became available and holding a larger force at bay. Porter's 34,000 men faced 57,000 Confederates for five hours before giving up ground. Losing the fight at Gaines Mill pushed the federals south of the river, continuing the Union retreat.[41]

On June 27 Confederate Generals John Magruder and Richard Garnett staged small, isolated attacks in the vicinity of Garnett's Hill. Starting about 4:00 p.m. these probes allowed Confederates to ascertain enemy strength and kept Union units from assisting north of the river. The 7th Michigan entered the line just before dusk. A reconnaissance in force by the Confederates the following day did little to open up the battlefield.

Early on the morning of June 29, General Magruder found that Union troops were leaving their positions in his front. The men of the 7th Michigan were not happy to give up the "strong hold" gained and held at such great cost.[42]

Lee was determined to engage the federal army before it could settle into a strong defensive position. To do so, he had to get his men across the river and push southward quickly. Generals Magruder and Huger left their works around Richmond and set off eastward toward Fair Oaks Station, hoping to catch McClellan's rear guard before it reached the covering fire of Union gunboats on the James River or retreated down the peninsula toward Yorktown. Lee hoped he might corner McClellan, allowing the Army of Northern Virginia to concentrate and destroy the Army of the Potomac before it could be reinforced.[43]

The 7th Michigan was "among the last to leave" the Union works around Fair Oaks Station.[44] They departed about 7:00 a.m., stopping at Allen's Farm to regroup. The Union rear guard stopped at the crucial crossroads of Savage Station, about five miles east of Fair Oaks around 2:00 p.m. Several corps congregated there; Smith to the north, Sumner oriented north and south, and Heintzelman to the south of town. They depended upon Brigadier General Henry Naglee to shield them from the northeast. Dana's Brigade was west of Savage Station, just north of the Richmond and York River Railroad with Burn's Brigade on their right flank to the north. Heintzelman's Corps was to the south of the railroad. McClellan's orders were to hold the ground until after sunset, then retreat across White Oak Swamp to take up defensive positions.

First at Allen farm (Peach Orchard) east of Savage Station, and then again closer to the crossroads, the rear guard exchanged a lively fire. Both Heintzelman's 3rd Corps and Smith's 6th Corps made their escape during the afternoon, leaving only Sumner's 2nd Corps to make a stand. General Magruder pressed his 14,500 men against 16,000 federals. The engagement built in intensity through the afternoon heat. General Burns' Brigade took the brunt of the early attack, but as the afternoon wore on multiple regiments on both sides were committed. The 7th Michigan entered action at dusk. Estimated casualties for the Confederates were 375, for the Union 600, not counting the estimated 2,500–3,000 Union wounded captured when the hospital at Savage Station was overrun. These casualties bought time for Union forces to withdraw.

Curtis reported that the regiment supported

> General Burns [when he] had a brush and we helped him through, then made good our retreat nearly five miles and was again attacked upon our right. Here had a desperate conflict and Genl.

Dana moved in at dark ¾ mile at run & charged but we did not get sight of the enemy. Still Colonel G[rosvenor] was determined we should fire and fire we did. Soon as darkness of the night settled in and drenching shower and wind we plodded our way until day break[45]

Massive stores of supplies, ammunition, and equipment were staged at Fair Oaks and Savage Station. At the latter, Company H was detached to unload supplies brought up via railroad. When the retreat toward Harrison's Landing occurred on June 29, the army could not take the mountain of stores with them. They emptied barrels of whiskey over the stacks and set them on fire. The hard tack, coffee, and sugar burned with vigor. The whiskey trickled all the way down to the ground and pooled in the road ruts, where soldiers "lapped up what they could."[46] The drunks drinking from mud puddles, the flames and the exploding ordnance created a "perfect hell" that Knaggs remembered his entire life.[47] One Union soldier reported seeing "more government supplies burned and destroyed than I had ever seen before. Millions of dollars worth of provisions and forage were burned and whole train loads run off the bridge into the river, cars, locomotives, and all."[48] Such acts of destruction showed the Confederates that the federals were in full retreat. Troops guarding against a northern counter-attack were released to pursue their foe.

The 7th Michigan retreated, marching and fighting during the day and suffering cavalry attack at night. The recurrent cycle of daytime fighting and a marching retreat at night became a nightmare. Summer heat and intermittent rain did little to improve the situation. Baxter and his men were uncomfortable, hungry, exhausted, and harried, but they continued to do their duty. Baxter was learning valuable lessons about how the war would be prosecuted, and how much stress his men could withstand.

Most of the army crossed White Oak Swamp the night of June 29–30. But Sumner resisted leaving Savage Station with his Corps, claiming its defense as a victory. Finally a written order to withdraw from McClellan and an order to arrest Sumner if he did not comply reached him. He finally started his tired men down the road.

On June 30 the rear guard reached White Oak Swamp and Glendale, but not without considerable confusion. Richardson's 2nd Corps was the last to leave Savage Station at 1:00 a.m. Skirmishers of the 20th Massachusetts were not notified of the withdrawal and came close to capture. Hazard's batteries A & C of the 4th United States Artillery got underway at first light, finding that they had slept behind enemy lines. These batteries made it across the White Oak Swamp Bridge just before it was burned at 10:00 a.m.

Early on the morning of June 30, the pursuing Confederates were joined by Stonewall Jackson. He continued along roads close to the Chickahominy while Longstreet moved southeast on the Darbytown Road. They expected to intersect at Glendale, where they hoped to cut off the retreat. Glendale was surrounded by Union troops, many of whom had marched all night in the rain and mud only to find little sleep without tents or cover. McClellan's design for their preservation had them falling back to a new base on the James River. The place was named Berkeley Plantation, southeast of Glendale, and its port on the James River known as Harrison's Landing. Here was a spot close to Richmond, but out of range of Confederate river batteries so that Union gunboats would be free from bombardment. He placed 55,000 of his troops in a defensive perimeter around Glendale and at the White Oak Swamp Bridge, holding Sedgwick's Division in close reserve. The rest of his troops were located at Malvern Hill. The Confederates converged from the west, north, and southwest with 70,000 men. Federal troops felled trees across roads, slowing the Confederates who had to clear obstructions, construct new roads around the obstacles, or leave their artillery behind. The fire of Union pickets slowed the advance.

As Confederate forces took up positions around the Union perimeter, a hole a mile wide was discovered north of Glendale between Richardson's and Slocum's Divisions and General Sumner sent two brigades to plug it. The men of Sully's Brigade formed up on the left of Richardson's, while Dana's Brigade—including the 7th Michigan—was held in reserve.

The Confederates attacked Glendale from the west and southwest on the afternoon of June 30, advancing far enough to threaten to sever north-south communications via the Willis Church Road, the primary artery of retreat to the Union fallback position at Malvern Hill. Another hole in the Union lines developed between the Whitlock House and Willis Church. Sumner ordered Dana to return with his and Sully's Brigades. Marching through the heat and dust with little water to drink under frequent exhortations to hurry, many men were overcome and fell out along the way. That afternoon the two brigades went into the line west of the Willis Church Road. As it turned out, the 20th Massachusetts, 19th Massachusetts, 7th Michigan, and 42nd New York were placed in the center of the gap. The Confederates of Branches' brigade hit the gap a short time later and a bitter firefight ensued during which Federal muskets fouled and overheated. The unit on the left flank of the 7th Michigan broke, dumping the strain onto the Michiganders, who also broke, followed by the 42nd New York. The 19th Massachusetts and 71st Pennsylvania were able to fill the gap. The 20th Massachusetts fell back in good order as Sedgwick's Division reformed just west of the Willis Church Road. Though federal troops fell back, the arrival of Sedgwick's Division plugged the gap at just the right moment, the Confederate advance stalled, and the Willis Church Road was saved. Most of the night was spent collecting the widely dispersed men of the 7th Michigan.

The Battle of Glendale began about 4:00 p.m. and concluded in the gathering darkness. The engagement involved about 23,500 Federals and 19,500 Confederates and cost approximately 2,853 northern and 3,615 southern casualties. Yet, for the battle's ferocity, relatively little ground changed hands. At the end of the day the Union line of retreat was safe and the Confederate attempt to cut off the retreat was stymied. Further, much of the federal wagon trains, artillery, and troops had made their escape to the safety of the James River where the cannon of Union gunboats dominated. Had Jackson and Huger engaged the enemy more forcefully, the outcome of the battle might have been different.[49]

After nightfall, General Franklin withdrew his corps, having accomplished his mission of delaying Jackson's advance. The other corps followed, moving southward toward Malvern Hill. Once again, exhausted men who had fought during the day were ordered to march through the night. The remnants of the 7th Michigan began to withdraw at 3:00 a.m., arriving at Malvern Hill in the morning. General Hooker was left to hold the Willis Church Road to cover the retreat, which he did until he withdrew at daylight on July 1.

Generals Lee and McClellan had other problems. Lee regrouped his army overnight to attack the following day. McClellan's job was easier. Having already set Malvern Hill as his next position and begun its fortification, he need only organize the defense to let him extricate his army with the fewest losses.

At Malvern Hill the federal units went into defensive lines. The 7th Michigan arrived at Malvern Hill after seven days of battle and

> rested about one hour for coffee and were ordered out to the left and to this time have been under heavy fire which has proven unpleasant to many of the troops. But not this Reg[iment].

Men and Officers are about used up. Having had fighting days and marching nights since Saturday last with nothing but bread & water for subsistence are now upon Picket which gives us a trifle rest.[50]

Throughout the morning units of the battered army marched to Malvern Hill and were assigned positions. Porter's Corps had been there for a day and had made progress in preparing the position. Heintzelman's Corps was placed to the northeast, Sumner's Corps went to the southeast, Warren's Brigade was put in the southwest quadrant, Sykes' Corps covered the western approach, and a division of Couch's Corps with Morell's Division defended the northern approach. Seymour's brigade was in reserve just north of the Malvern House. Other units, including part of Couch's Corps and Slocum's Corps, were positioned in the rear near Haxall's Landing. In total, the Union position formed a large "U" with the open end facing south, the expected direction of withdraw to Harrison's Landing. They held the high ground, had well-positioned artillery, enjoyed interior lines, and had defensive works prepared. McClellan could field 54,000 men, Lee 55,000.[51]

At 11:00 a.m. the Battle of Malvern Hill started as an artillery duel. The first Confederate infantry assault took place at the northwest corner of the Union position, where the determined attack sought to exploit a perceived weakness between Brigadier General George Morell's 1st Division and Major General Darius Couch's Corps. There another group of Michiganders, the 4th Michigan Volunteer Infantry, were credited by General Porter as having saved the Army of the Potomac.[52] Overall, the Confederate frontal assault was best characterized by one participant: "It was not war—it was murder."[53] Additional assaults on Malvern Hill were similar in outcome, no significant gain at the cost of many lives. Confederate casualties were 5,650, Union were 3,214. McClellan had won a victory and still held a defensible position. Yet he withdrew to Harrison's Landing. Sumner's 2nd Corps—including the 7th Michigan—left the hill about midnight and retreated in a driving rain over crowded muddy roads.

Most of the federals were off the hill by dawn on July 2, but the rear guard remained in a heavy fog until 10:00 a.m., when they too received orders to depart. Confederate forces—exhausted from a week of fighting culminating in the near suicidal assault on Malvern Hill—were not eager to pursue the retreating federal troops through sporadic rain. The men of Sedgwick's Division marched through the night, arriving at Harrison's Landing between 10:00 a.m. and 2:00 p.m. The 7th Michigan arrived about noon to find stakes with flags marking their new camp on the muddy wheat fields.

Harrison's Landing was a relative oasis for the men of the 7th Michigan. They had been fighting days and marching nights for nearly a week. At the Landing—their "last resort" described as "one grand mud hole of nineteen hundred acres"—the river gunboats provided cover and security.[54] By July 4 the "men are feeling quite themselves again," a quick recovery after all they had been through.[55]

They remained at Harrison's Landing for several weeks, suffering oppressive heat and back-breaking work as fortifications were thrown up. Lee chose not to attack.

As early as July 4 there were signs that the 7th Michigan was having trouble with its command structure. During the Seven Days battles several men recorded instances of questionable conduct by Colonel Grosvenor, included leaving the field of battle, being out of touch with his men, and taking the cased regimental colors with him as he left the field. Twice

5. Action at Last, Early 1862

during the retreat from Richmond Grosvenor was relieved by subordinate officers because of illness.[56] Curtis recorded on July 4, "There is some chance & probabilities of trouble with the commander of the Regiment—He [Grosvenor] did not stand fire very well."[57] How much Grosvenor's behavior was influenced by having cholera and scurvy is unknown. The *Monroe Commercial* indicated that when Grosvenor requested a furlough due to ill health, he was refused it because of "a difference in opinion with Gen. McClellan."[58] Grosvenor—unable to obtain a furlough—was forced to resign to deal with his deteriorating health. On Monday, July 14, Curtis reported two bits of remarkable news:

> Yesterday eve be it known all the troops were allowed to rest from extra labor, which is the first instance of the kind to my knowledge since we came upon the Peninsula. Colonel Grosvenor resigned about the 8th inst and has gone home. Col. Baxter is by General Sedgwick appointed Lt. Colonel commanding. All else has been as usual since last date. Lieut. Hall U.S. is said to be our Colonel hereafter.[59]

Acting Colonel Norman Hall had been appointed to command by General McClellan. Henry Baxter served in temporary command until Hall took up his new duties.

Hall was an excellent choice. A regular army officer from London, Michigan, Hall had graduated from West Point in 1859, serving initially with the 1st U.S. Artillery. He was stationed in South Carolina before evacuated to Fort Sumter after secession. During the standoff between federal forces under Major Robert Anderson and Confederate forces that occupied the abandoned forts around the harbor, Hall served as an emissary. Fort Sumter came under artillery assault on April 12, 1861, and Hall earned fame for retrieving the national flag when its pole was toppled during the bombardment. Passing through fire and crossing the parade ground to get the flag, he was assisted by two artillerists to raise it again. As a result, he received burns that left him permanently devoid of eye brows. When Major Anderson surrendered the fort on April 13, Hall became a prisoner of war. He was paroled and returned to Michigan, where he aided recruitment efforts in Monroe. In May 1861 he was promoted to first lieutenant and assigned to the 5th U.S. Artillery, playing a key role in the Peninsular Campaign as the commander of Hooker's divisional artillery and temporarily on the staff of the chief engineer. In mid–July he assumed command of the 7th Michigan and was to prove a steady and indefatigable commander through the war's harshest engagements. General Sedgwick assured Michigan Governor Blair that the regiment would be "under good and competent leadership," recommending Hall be commissioned Colonel of volunteers immediately.[60]

Though logical to appoint a regular army officer from Michigan to head the unit, the act was unusual because "the persistence of the War Department in maintaining both a regular and volunteer army made it very difficult for a regular-army officer to be transferred to the volunteers."[61] Officers of volunteer regiments were normally voted in by the officers, usually from within their own ranks, and then confirmed by the state governor. In this case, McClellan made battlefield appointments and then asked for gubernatorial confirmation. Appointing a regular army veteran to lead a volunteer unit probably indicated a corrective action intended to stiffen the sagging morale and discipline of a troubled regiment.

The removal of Grosvenor uncovered regimental politics. Captain Henry Baxter was a favorite of the Colonel and a competent, energetic, and courageous officer. He was ambitious, well connected politically, and got along with both superiors and subordinates. Being favored by Grosvenor created internal jealousies. A complaint filed with Michigan Adjutant General Robertson in October 1862 indicates that Grosvenor broke tradition, promoting Baxter over others in the regiment regardless of seniority. Grosvenor was accused of "not being just in his dealings with his officers," instead instituting "Col. G's plan" by appointing Captain Baxter as his second in command after Lieutenant Colonel Frazey Winans resigned and before Major John Richardson resigned.[62] Captain Thomas Hunt of Company A thought he deserved promotion based upon service during the Mexican War.

The appointment of a career United States Army officer from Michigan to lead with one of the veteran captains promoted as second in command implies that this opportunity was used to solve a leadership problem by simply refusing Grosvenor furlough, waiting for his resignation, and then appointing two individuals capable of bringing stability. This explains Grosvenor's issue with McClellan, and also explains why Hall and Baxter were delayed in confirmation of their appointments by the Governor of Michigan until after they had proven themselves at the Battle of Antietam.

Additional evidence comes from Oliver Wendell Homes, Jr., who fought in the Seven Days battle as a Lieutenant in the 20th Massachusetts and who wrote a letter dated July 5, 1862, that on June 30,

> The Mich. 7th on our left breaks & runs disgracefully (private) *they lay it to Col. Grosvenor who they say showed the white feather*—[63]

Published biographies of Colonel Ira Grosvenor point to sickness as the cause of his departure:

> May 31st found the regiment in sight of Richmond at Fair Oaks Station, and Colonel Grosvenor suffering from an attack of cholera morbus. Lying under a tree, under the influence of opiates, while the regiment went forward to take its place in the line, he was shortly aroused by the sound of infantry firing in the advance. Hastily climbing on his horse he started for the battle. He soon came up with his regiment, and was at its head in the charge described in glowing terms by the historian Lossing. For a month after the battle of Fair Oaks the regiment remained encamped on the Chickahominy. The sultry southern sun beating down upon the swamps bred disease, and was more fatal to the unacclimated [sic] northern troops than the rebel bullets.
>
> During this time Colonel Grosvenor began to suffer seriously from scurvy. His teeth became loosened, and the external manifestations of the disease increased in violence. When the movement across the peninsula to the new base upon the James River began, he was scarcely able to sit upon his horse; but in this condition he led his regiment through the battles of Peach Orchard and Savage Station on June 29th; White Oak Swamp and Glendale on June 30th; Malvern Hill on July 1st, and then accompanied the army to Harrison's Landing. The exposure and fighting of the seven days before going into camp at Harrison's had seriously told upon him in his exhausted condition, and he was informed by the surgeon that he must make a speedy choice between a change of climate and a coffin. He applied for leave of absence, but, under Halleck's orders a furlough was denied. This left the alternative between resignation of his command or a death from the scurvy, which had now attacked his bowels. On July 7th he resigned his commission and started for Fortress Monroe.

A difficult journey home further weakened him so that when having recuperated he was offered another command:

> The colonel of the Fourth regiment had fallen in battle, and Colonel Grosvenor was offered a commission as its commander. He accepted the offer, hoping to speedily be able to go to the front. But as the time passed he became convinced that the effects of his disease were incurable, that further campaigning was a simple impossibility, that a month's exposure in the field or on the march would be undoubtedly fatal, and he was compelled to decline the proffered position.[64]

Such a long explanation suggests a sensitivity to the subject of his resignation even 28 years after the event occurred. In 1897 a briefer biographical sketch states, "He resigned ... with health greatly shattered and returned to his home soon afterwards."[65] After the war Grosvenor was elected President of the Seventh Michigan Volunteer Infantry Association, illustrating that the men he led held no qualms about his behavior.

Baxter was confirmed in his field commission as Lieutenant Colonel of the 7th Michigan by order of Brigadier General John Sedgwick at Harrisons Landing on July 8.[66] When Governor Blair confirmed Baxter's July 8 battlefield commission as Lieutenant Colonel he dated the permanent commission May 22, recognizing that Baxter had actually been in charge of the 7th Michigan during Grosvenor's illness, which corresponds to that date. The facts may never be known. But as events would show, Baxter would excel in this new position.

6

An Authentic Piece of Human Heroism, Late 1862

On July 8 Lincoln discussed the situation on the Peninsula with General McClellan. Lincoln could get no definite plan from McClellan and returned to Washington convinced that a change in leadership was needed. General Henry Halleck was appointed general-in-chief of the Union Army effective July 11. McClellan was not notified until Halleck himself arrived for a conference on July 25 and still found no plan to renew the attack on Richmond or withdraw from enemy territory. McClellan argued that he needed a total of 300,000 men to attack Richmond. Halleck gave him the ultimatum of pushing on with minimal reinforcement or of withdrawal. When no action was forthcoming, Halleck ordered the sick evacuated from the Peninsula.[1]

The presence of 90,000 inactive Union troops was intolerable and Lincoln authorized Halleck to take action. On August 2 McClellan finally showed some initiative, advancing a small force that clashed with the Confederates at Malvern Hill. But Halleck had already made the decision to evacuate. On August 3 the order to withdraw was telegraphed to McClellan. Still, McClellan persisted, sending out at dusk on August 4 Hooker's Corps and Sedgwick's Division of Sumner's Corps, including the 7th Michigan. They took Malvern Hill, but "did not capture 4,000 Rebs because they did not go the right way."[2] The 7th Michigan was back in camp at daylight on August 7.

By the time they returned to Harrison's Landing, plans for the evacuation were well underway. On August 14 the 7th Michigan was on picket duty and then joined the retreat. Most units marched eastward through Charles City Courthouse, crossing the Chickahominy on a 2,000 foot pontoon bridge before proceeding to Fortress Monroe. By mid-day on August 18 the army had crossed.[3]

The Army of the Potomac began its departure on August 19. Loading ships took time, fostering the concern that Lee would threaten Washington before reinforcements for Pope's 50,000-strong Army of Virginia could arrive. The first federal troops arrived in Alexandria on August 22. Sumner's 2nd Corps left on August 26 and arrived in Alexandria on August 28. When they arrived, they found that their gear had not made the trip with them and that rations on the other end were unavailable, further delaying their return to combat readiness.[4]

Halleck's concerns were well founded. As soon as he was sure that McClellan's army was leaving the Peninsula, Lee attempted to exploit a temporary superiority in numbers by sending the Army of Northern Virginia to reinforce Stonewall Jackson in the Shenandoah.

6. An Authentic Piece of Human Heroism, Late 1862

This put Pope on the defensive. McClellan came ashore at Alexandria on August 24 expecting to be in command of both Pope's Army of Virginia and the Army of the Potomac. Instead, Pope remained independent and most of the Army of the Potomac was transferred to him.[5]

Jackson faced Pope on the old Bull Run battlefield on August 29. Pope expected an easy victory, but found "Stonewall" living up to his nickname. Pope did not bring his whole army into the fight, allowing Lee to commit his entire force and push him from the field. McClellan contributed to the problem by failing to release Sumner's 2nd Corps and Franklin's 6th Corps because their artillery had not arrived from the Peninsula yet. The 7th Michigan arrived too late to do more than cover the retreat.[6]

The defeat at Second Bull Run demoralized Union forces. The days of marching and counter-marching interspersed with picket duty and rear guard action resonated with the troops. Rumors persisted that Jackson was everywhere. The 7th Michigan never spent two nights in one place. An exasperated Curtis wrote, "No knowing where the Rebs won't be next."[7]

The 7th Michigan arrived in Taneytown, Maryland, on the afternoon of September 4. Of the Company C that originally numbered 100, only 30 were left. Lt. Sidney Vrooman wrote,

> Since I rejoined the regiment at Harrison's Landing August 4th, the 7th regiment has been constantly on the march almost day and night, or else on picket duty. Since we landed at Alexandria, August 28th, our route has twice led us through that place, once through Georgetown, twice in sight of the latter place, twice across Chain Bridge, and once to Centerville, Va. We were the last pickets at Harrison's Landing, and our Brigade the last before Centerville, and the rear guard of one column of the army, as it moved towards Washington on the retreat.[8]

After Pope's defeat, the army was demoralized. Much as Lincoln distrusted McClellan, he needed help to rebuild. Hence, McClellan was retained, the army was again concentrated around Washington, and the retraining and reequipping began anew. Pope was unceremoniously relieved of duty on September 12. McClellan's ego hit a new high.

Fate then dealt Union forces the greatest of good fortune. General Lee decided to invade the north via Maryland and Pennsylvania, sensing the low morale of the northern army and civilian population in the crucial months before fall elections. He had the opportunity to initiate a crippling blow that would force the Union to sue for peace and/or bring European nations to the aid of the south. Lee's invasion orders fell into the hands of Union forces a few days later. McClellan held an outline of Lee's invasion plan, but when McClellan moved to counter Lee's thrust into Union territory he failed to act decisively, squandering his advantage.

Jackson captured Harpers Ferry on the morning of September 15, consolidating the army near Sharpsburg, Maryland. The Union Army was converging. Hemmed in with the Potomac at his back, Lee was in a difficult position where withdrawal was problematic.

The 7th Michigan was on the road early on September 16, but did not go far before encountering the enemy. The brigade moved several times in support of other units and came under fire on the second day of the Battle of Antietam. The neighboring 42nd New York Infantry was hotly engaged, eventually breaking in the face of enemy fire.

Colonel Hall led the 7th Michigan into battle on September 17. The brigade was moving to its third position on the Sharpsburg Turnpike that afternoon when Hall noted General Dana riding to the rear ahead of him. Dana was wounded and one of his staff officers intercepted Hall, telling him that Dana had given him command of the brigade. Baxter assumed command of the 7th Michigan, but Hall remained with the regiment as it was the only regiment within sight.

The 7th Michigan gave way slowly before the Confederate assault. Hall set up a fall back position at the edge of the woods one-quarter mile behind their starting point and determined to make a stand. Momentary confusion occurred when Hall found the regiment 150 yards in front of and covering a small part of General Gibbon's Division, but eventually the 7th was reformed and reunited with the 20th Massachusetts, under the command of Colonel Lee, which still had "very full ranks."[9] More confusion reigned as Colonel Hall tried to turn over command to Lee, the senior officer. But General Howard confirmed Colonel Hall in command. Hall ordered the scattered regiments to rejoin, but sent the 20th Massachusetts to support a battery. Other regiments were ordered forward to support batteries in the corn field. Hall reported that the men of his brigade "were subjected to an annoying fire from the enemy's artillery for several hours during the afternoon of the 17th, during which time their conduct was unexceptionable."[10] At the close of the battle, the 106th Pennsylvania Infantry reported again to its own brigade.

Antietam was a horrendous fight. Charles Curtis wrote that the "17th inst. was the most brutal battle of the war."[11] Of the extant descriptions, Lieutenant Knagg's account of 7th Michigan's role in the action at Antietam on September 17 is the most spirited:

> We held the line until the brigade of each of our flanks broke and made for the rear leaving us to fight fire from our front and on both flanks. My horse was shot, a ball hit him in the head and killed him instantly. A sergeant in my company had said he thought I could make a cigarette under fire. When my horse was shot from under me I said "Andy this is a good place to make a cigarette. I believe I'll try," but just then the third colors bearer was shot.
>
> I took the colors from him as he went down and advanced a few steps toward the enemy calling on the boys to stay with me as the colors of the Michigan Seventh had never left the field and we never wanted it said that they had. There were only two that could get up to me. They stood one on each side, and taking their caps and raising them said they would stand by me as long as any man stood on the field. They were soon wounded and went down leaving me alone. During the few moments that I held the flag, I was hit five times without having the skin broken. Then the Colonel rode in and I was relieved of the flag. I went at once for the rear walking backwards for I never wanted to be shot in the back. I was out in the open forming a good heavy skirmish line[,] but the enemy couldn't run and neither could I. They kept up an incessant fire hoping to get me. When I got nearly across the field Captain S.N. Smith hailed me and requested me to assist him to a barn where the wounded were being carried. He put his arm around my neck and we got to the barn. I gave him my handkerchief to stuff into the wound to stop the blood. I thought I'd see where the Johnnies were before stopping long[,] so I went to the corner of the barn and found the Johnnies at the other corner. I had to run. I got into a lane with a stake and rider fence on both sides. By running in and out of the corners of the fence, I managed to escape.
>
> The enemy never got any further than that barn for our artillery opened on the field in our rear and soon sent the enemy back to the woods. What few of us were left were ordered to lie down. I, as Adjutant, pick[ed] up the boys who kept on going when ordered to the rear. I found quite a few and ordered them back to where their comrades were lying down. I took the names of all the boys. There were one hundred thirty eight. When we went into that fight there were three hundred fifty-two. Not one man or horse came out of that fight without a wound or bullet hole in his clothes.[12]

Tremendous casualties were suffered on both sides. Henry Baxter was hit in the stomach, but stayed in the saddle directing his men until loss of blood incapacitated him and he was carried to the field hospital.[13] Union forces overall suffered 2,108 killed, 9,550 wounded, and 760 missing in the two day battle. The Confederates lost 2,700 killed, 9,025 wounded, and 2,000 missing. The total of those who died in the War of 1812, Mexican War, Spanish-

6. An Authentic Piece of Human Heroism, Late 1862

American War, and the Indian Wars was less than those killed at Antietam.[14] Melvin Rice simply concluded, "We have lost a lot of good men."[15] Such a shocking loss was difficult to justify.

Yet, for all the lives lost, the victory was incomplete. The battle blunted the Confederate momentum toward victory, but McClellan again failed to aggressively pursue the retreating Lee. To Lincoln's chagrin a great opportunity to destroy the Confederate Army was lost to McClellan's over-caution and failure to appreciate the comparative strength of his army. Back on the battlefield, the casualties were dealt with and the army regrouped. In Richmond on September 21 the news of Lee's withdraw had civilians suffering a "day of gloom."[16]

For Henry Baxter, his wound occupied his sole attention. The ball had entered "near his right femoral region and passed posteriorly to the right and back of the ileum."[17] The best contemporary description of his wound was

> He was mounted when struck in the abdomen by a Minnie ball. He thought his case hopeless, so he stayed in the saddle until he was exhausted, then was carried off the field, expecting to die. However, the bullet had not struck any vitals and instead lodged in his hip, where it remained for the rest of his life.[18]

As news of the great battle filtered into the north, there was much consternation for loved ones, and for good reason. The news about Baxter that reached home was not good:

> There has been great anxiety and suspense in this place for the past few days relative to a report that Lt. Colonel Henry Baxter (of this village) of the 7th Mich., had been killed. The *New York Herald* of the 23d. inst., reports him "severely wounded." By a letter from Dr. Chadlock we learn that he is doing well. On going to press, we learn of the arrival of Lt. Col. Henry Baxter, in town.[19]

A full description of the Battle of Antietam gave substantial attention to Baxter and Hall. The surviving officers were pressing hard to have their commissions made permanent:

> ... Acting Lt. Col. Baxter had his horse shot, his revolver struck by a ball, his sword belt-plate torn off by another, and while rallying the men around the colors, was struck by another in the abdomen, inflicting a dangerous wound.
>
> We cannot here understand how it is that such men as acting Colonel Hall and acting Lt. Col. Baxter, whose appointment to those positions have been asked for by every officer in the regiment who was present with it, should not receive their appointment. They have won them where such honors should be won—on the battle-field, and are doing the duties of those positions for the pay of lesser ranks. This is of lesser consciousness that they may at any moment be displaced to make room for some new appointees unasked for by their commands. Surely, we of the regiment best know whom we want to lead us, and our wish should be the controlling influence.[20]

Every officer in the 7th Michigan except Colonel Hall and Captain Hunt were wounded.

On behalf of the officers in the regiment, Quartermaster Charles Walker wrote Michigan Governor Blair from Bolivar, Virginia, on September 30, that they had learned that the Governor had received neither McClellan's recommendation for permanent commissions nor a unanimous petition from the regiment's officers requesting that Hall's appointment be confirmed. Walker asked again that Hall's commission be made permanent, requesting that it be dated from Colonel Grosvenor's resignation so that Colonel Hall would outrank regimental commander of the 42nd New York in their brigade.[21] Walker extolled Hall's "magnificent behavior at Antietam, and covering with the Seventh the retreat of its Division, holding the Entire force of the rebels in check until the Division had re-formed in [the] rear."[22] The article concluded with a tribute to the bravery of the men of the 7th Michigan:

Our colors were the last of the division to leave the field and our regiment was ordered to receive three cheers from the rest of the division, for this fact so creditable to them.[23]

Baxter was still at home recuperating under the care of his friend and brother-in-law Dr. Edwin M. Hale. Though there continued to be "some pain in the right hip and knee and walking was painful," on November 5, he left Jonesville to return to his unit.[24] His wife and children accompanied him as far as Ypsilanti where they intended to stay the winter to be close to Vi's family.[25]

What followed was one of the strangest incidents of Baxter's career. Baxter was actually dismissed from the service despite having an excellent service record:

> While he was at home wounded [at the Battle of Antietam], an order was made requiring all officers who visited Washington to have a pass. On his return, to report to his officers, he passed through Washington, and, being without a pass, was directed to report to the proper officer, which he did; but from some oversight on the part of that officer or his subordinate Col. Baxter was reported in Washington without a pass, contrary to orders, and he was actually dismissed dishonorably from the service, the papers being sent on to Michigan. He, however, did not get the notice, and in the meantime the battle of Fredericksburg was fought.
> Either the mistake was detected and the error corrected or his later conduct at Fredericksburg erased the black mark, in either case the order was revoked and Baxter himself did not learn of it until long afterward.[26]

An order had indeed been issued to counter a problem that had developed among the officers of the Army of the Potomac, who were spending too much time enjoying themselves in Washington and too little time with their commands. The order simply required a pass from a superior officer that verified that they were in Washington on official business. Those caught without such a pass were to be dismissed from the service.[27]

The same order might have caused the loss of others with bright futures. First Lieutenant William Shafter of the 7th Michigan was wounded at the Battle of Fair Oaks on May 31, 1862, but concealed his wound so that he could continue to fight. After the battle he was unable to "sit, stand, or lie," but was afraid to leave the regiment to recuperate for fear of losing his commission and being dismissed from the service.[28] Shafter was later awarded the Medal of Honor for his actions at Fair Oaks, became a Brigadier General, transferred to the regular army, and went on to lead the American invasion of Cuba during the Spanish-American War. Imagine what loss the Union might have suffered with the discharge of those who repeatedly proved themselves such valuable combat officers.

The 7th Michigan kept moving under Colonel Lee, who replaced the wounded brigade commander Dana. Two captains and ten sergeants were dispatched to Michigan on October 28 on recruiting duty. McClellan made another foray into northern Virginia along the route of the Orange and Alexandria Railroad (O&A RR), but did not spark a decisive battle. General Lee eventually blocked McClellan's slow move southward at Culpeper Courthouse.

Late on November 7 McClellan received word that he had been relieved of command, the news of which "fell on the country like a thunderbolt, and a fierce partisan discussion sprang up concerning the wisdom of the removal and the merits of the retired commander, which created great bitterness."²⁹ Curtis reported on November 10 "General McLelland [*sic*] took the last review this day and a gloomy parting it was."³⁰ The depression of an uncertain future continued the following day when "the genial sun of this our Indian summer would almost make us happy if we could forget that our days are numbered. This day marks the 25th year of my stay upon earth and so short seems the past.... What the future may be none but <u>God</u> knows."³¹

Henry Baxter received a pass dated November 21 that allowed him to transit Union lines returning to his unit. Vrooman wrote on November 28, "We all are rejoiced to see him return looking so well."³² Colonel Norman Hall had been in charge of the brigade since the middle of October and was "very popular with the 7th as also in the Brigade."³³ They were now camped near the "secesh" town of Falmouth, Virginia, and spent most of their time building corduroy roads and log bridges. Vrooman lamented, "Had the President's call for troops [in 1861] been promptly answered, this thing would not have been."³⁴

⇒ ⇐

As the men of the Army of the Potomac approached another long winter having fought more, harder, and with higher casualties than they first anticipated, they were doubly uncertain what a new general commander would mean for their future. The new chief of the Army of the Potomac was Major General Ambrose Burnside, who, under pressure from Lincoln, quickly unveiled a new offensive.

Burnside owed his promotion to his early success in North Carolina and the fact that the Republicans had taken a beating in the fall 1862 elections. Lincoln could not afford the plodding, over-cautious approach of McClellan if he was to maintain control of the government. He was also concerned about foreign intervention on behalf of the south. Issuing the Emancipation Proclamation on September 22, 1862, and challenging the southern states to return to the Union by January 1, 1863, was in part an effort to neutralize potential overseas interference using the victory at Antietam to illustrate northern power.

In late 1862 Lincoln pushed all Union armies forward, hoping that a coordinated attack on all fronts would deny the south the benefit of its interior lines that had allowed the rapid shifting of troops to meet superior Union numbers in each theater of operations. Lincoln desperately needed Burnside to make a significant thrust into Virginia, just as Jefferson Davis needed Lee to frustrate any such offensive. The Confederates needed time to rest, resupply, and rebuild, having spent the early summer facing McClellan outside Richmond, and the late summer in the abortive invasion of Maryland. Hence, Lincoln forced a campaign during a season when armies rarely embarked upon major adventures. He believed that he had a good chance of destroying the rebel army at its nadir.³⁵

The Union Army was expanding. Between those volunteering to avoid conscription and those inspired by the emancipation of slaves, the army gained nearly 80,000 men that fall. The Confederate Army was growing as well, though not as fast. Both armies were preparing for winter with no prospect of intense fighting.

General Burnside inherited an army that had established a forward base at Warrenton, Virginia. However, McClellan had been stymied in his southern push at Culpeper Courthouse. Trying to find another route to Richmond, Burnside looked south to Fredericksburg where the Richmond, Fredericksburg and Potomac Railroad could be used for resupply. Initial reconnaissance showed that this route was feasible, leading Burnside to make the decision to shift the Union advance in that direction. He telegraphed General-in-Chief Halleck in Washington on November 10, asking for approval of the plan.

Fredericksburg was a good objective. A direct link in the railroad and road transportation systems between Washington and Richmond, the town was also on the fall line, a set of rapids that interrupted transportation by water. Above the town, the river was not directly navigable, but below the Rappahannock allowed supply via the Union-controlled waters of Chesapeake Bay. Hence, there was no naval threat from above and Union forces could use the navigable portion opposed only by Confederate batteries.[36]

Burnside had to deal with an army demoralized by the removal of a leader who seemed to have shielded them against the politics of Washington. There was a real fear that the army would not give its best for anyone but McClellan. Burnside had inherited an extremely uncomfortable position.

But he set about making the command his own through reorganization. He created three new Grand Divisions, one for the left, center, and right. Major General Edwin Sumner was given the right, which was composed of 2nd Corps and 9th Corps, as well as the cavalry division led by Brigadier General Alfred Pleasonton. The Left Grand Division, including the 1st and 6th Corps, was commanded by Major General William Franklin. The Center Grand Division, including the 3rd and 5th Corps, under Major General Joseph Hooker. He also created a Reserve Grand Division from the 11th and 7th Corps under Major General Franz Sigel.[37]

On November 14 Halleck wired Lincoln's reluctant approval of what became known as the Fredericksburg Campaign. Lincoln felt that only quick action would allow the plan to succeed and Halleck made this opinion clear to Burnside. Quickness of action was something that the Army of the Potomac was not used to and Burnside had trouble from the outset. Pontoons for temporary bridges across the Rappahannock were ordered even before approval of the plan, but the necessary resources took much longer than expected to arrive. Burnside pushed forward with dispatch—a clear difference from his predecessor—to beat winter weather, but he did so without all the necessary resources.[38]

On November 15 Burnside sent some of his forces against Lee in his front, forcing him to fall back. Then Burnside sent the balance of his army toward Fredericksburg, an action that Lee had not foreseen. Sumner's Right Grand Division led the way, the 2nd Corps in the lead, putting the 7th Michigan among the first regiments on the road from Warrenton to Falmouth. Rain slowed the march and raised the level of the river, making it harder to ford. The vanguard reached the north shore of the Rappahannock opposite Fredericksburg the afternoon of November 17, only to find that the necessary pontoons had not arrived. The pontoons were just then arriving in Washington and would not be on site for several more days. Lee could only be deceived for so long. As early as November 12 he had sensed Burnside's true objective and had ordered Fredericksburg's commander Colonel Ball to destroy the Richmond, Fredericksburg and Potomac Railroad north of the city and the bridges across the river as a precaution. Lee himself only sent token reinforcements until he was sure that Burnside was moving away from him.[39]

Suddenly Fredericksburg—a town of 5,000 inhabitants—was center stage in what promised to be one of the war's largest battles. Colonel Ball spread his force of less than 1,500 Confederates along the river in front of the town, hoping to slow the anticipated Federal crossing. But no such crossing was attempted. Instead, Burnside awaited the pontoon boats so that floating bridges could be put in place. For five days the beleaguered Confederates opposed the coming assault. Civilians began to flee Fredericksburg.[40]

Lee assumed that Burnside would quickly cross the river and march on Richmond before the Confederates could stop him. On November 18 he sent Longstreet to fight a delaying action on the south side of the Rappahannock, while Lee marshaled his forces in a defensive position at North Anna 35 miles to the south. Later learning that Burnside had *not* crossed the Rappahannock, Lee redirected all his available forces to Fredericksburg. North Anna therefore became the second line of defense should the Federals not be stopped at the river. Lee knew that drawing Burnside across the river toward North Anna might allow him to sever Union supply lines, trap and destroy the northern army.[41]

Longstreet's men began to arrive at Fredericksburg on the evening of November 20. Most had consolidated around the city by November 23, but Longstreet left Ball's tired men on the front to delay letting the Union troops know that reinforcements were present. Burnside tried to bluff Fredericksburg into surrendering, but by November 21 his ultimatum rang hollow with Confederate forces arriving in ever greater numbers. While Burnside waited for his boats, the Confederates quietly fortified the community, creating breastworks on the heights behind the city, sniper perches within the town, and additional rifle pits along the river. Hence, 40,000 Confederates prepared to receive a Union army of more than 120,000. Stonewall Jackson was not far behind. The first of his men arrived on December 1.[42]

The situation at Fredericksburg had become extremely difficult. Had they moved immediately upon their arrival on November 17, the Army of the Potomac would have been able to cross before Confederate reinforcements arrived, presuming that the pontoons were available for temporary bridges. But failing that, the army sat waiting while the Confederate numbers grew and the sophistication of their defenses was heightened.[43]

Forty pontoons on wagons with associated gear had started overland with the 50th New York Engineers on November 19, a full two days after General Sumner's Corps arrived and began to shell Fredericksburg. They made poor time negotiating muddy roads and fording swollen rivers, despite Burnsides' constant exhortations to hurry. The boats were taken to the Potomac River town of Dumfries (about 23 miles overland from Fredericksburg), where they were floated and made into rafts to be towed down the Potomac and then up the Rappahannock by steamer. The men went overland with the empty wagons, arriving late on November 25. The pontoons completed the nearly 230 mile trip by water, reaching Belle Plain before the wagons did.[44]

With his surprise attack thwarted, Burnside was unsure how to proceed. Ultimately he pushed the construction of the pontoon bridges, even though they would have to be built under enemy fire. General Sumner—whose troops carried the burden of the first crossing—warned Burnside that a direct assault across the river would be monumentally costly in human life. President Lincoln met Burnside on November 27–28, and it was decided to attempt a surprise crossing at the unguarded Skinker's Neck, about 15 miles downstream. On December 5, Union forces marched to the landing in a cold rain, sleet and snow, only to find the position now heavily guarded. No attempt to cross was made and six inches of snow accumulated before the army returned to its camps the following day. By now 30 miles of the south shore was well defended.[45]

Burnside finally decided that the greatest surprise would be achieved by crossing where the Confederates would least expect it, in front of Fredericksburg itself. Despite predictions of a bloodbath, Burnside held a council of war on December 9 and put forward the plan to his generals. He argued that Fredericksburg marked the seam between Longstreet's and Jackson's Corps, was at one of the narrowest parts of the river, and was the place where an attack was least anticipated. Once established on the other side, Union forces would quickly divide the two enemy corps and cause irreparable damage, perhaps creating the opportunity to destroy the rebel army piecemeal. The meeting adjourned at 5:00 p.m. with less than an optimistic view of the outcome. A public berating by Burnside himself on December 10 was necessary to quell the grumbling of the Corps and Division commanders.[46]

General Daniel Woodbury—commander of the engineering troops working on the bridges—was in charge of putting the pontoon bridges in place. The plan was to complete five plank and frame bridges laid across pontoon boats at three different places. These three locations were (1) the old pontoon crossing a few rods above the Lacy House used by General McDowell; (2) the old ferry landing below the damaged railroad bridge; and (3) a place about one and a half miles south of the railroad. The two most distant bridges were about two miles apart.[47] A reconnaissance by the bridge engineers concluded that the work of building bridges in the face of the enemy at and below Fredericksburg was suicidal. As one bridge commander remarked, "We all came to the conclusion that we might now return to our quarters and with great propriety execute our last Wills & Testaments."[48]

Several feints by the army and navy were instituted along the 30-mile front as the 50th and 15th New York Engineers and the United States Engineer Battalion began their preparations. The engineers began to move at 8:00 p.m. using darkness as cover. Each of the three pontoon trains was composed of 34 boats and 29 support vehicles. The crew for the southernmost bridge continued south, the others paused at the Lacy House where they rested until the moon set at 1:00 a.m., making detection of their work more difficult. The pontoon boats were brought to the bridge heads about 3:00 a.m. on December 11. Six of the teams broke down on the road, forcing some boats to be left behind. But the others arrived, were manhandled down the embankment, and floated about 4:30 a.m. amid a dense fog and unremitting chill.[49]

Several regiments were sent to cover the crossings. The 57th and 66th New York assembled on the bank to cover the upper crossing, as did the 46th and 89th New York for the middle crossing, and the 2nd United States Sharpshooters and the 10th Pennsylvania Reserves for the lower crossing. Burnsides' chief of artillery Brigadier General Henry Hunt set his batteries to provide covering fire to mitigate direct sniper and infantry fire on the bridge heads, engage enemy artillery, and interdict any attempt to reinforce the areas under assault. He had 147 guns ready before 2:00 a.m.[50]

The engineers began moving the pontoon boats into position in sequence, anchoring them in place 13 feet apart, and then laying the bridge frames and deck across each on the way to the rebel-held shore. The bridge builders were hampered by river ice, which in some places was more than an inch thick. They worked as quietly as they could, trying to maintain the element of surprise.[51]

The bridges began to take shape. The upper bridge progressed most quickly, the middle bridge lagged behind, and the lower bridge did not take immediate shape at all. The Confederates had a sense that the crossing would take place that night, but the troops were ordered to allow the builders to continue their work until within easy range. After all, an unfinished bridge close to the Confederate position was as usable as an unfinished one at a distance, but the closer one presented better targets for the Confederates and temptations for the Union.

6. An Authentic Piece of Human Heroism, Late 1862

Both options tied up scarce Union resources. The Confederates notified the remaining civilians in Fredericksburg to quietly vacate their homes. General William Barksdale was ordered to remain in place and hold back the enemy until ordered to withdraw.[52]

Captain Wesley Brainard of the 50th New York Volunteer Engineers superintended construction of one of the two upper bridges. Through a break in the fog at dawn he saw the Confederates massing on the other side opposite him. He informed General Woodbury, who instructed him to keep going, but retire if necessitated by enemy fire. This order would have important consequences. Woodbury did not ask for artillery support. Union forces therefore lost an opportunity to dislodge or demoralize the enemy quickly, while Woodbury's order encouraged reluctant engineers not to work under fire. This was counter to the training of veteran infantry who were used to facing the fire in line, sometimes at point blank range. Hence, as the work progressed, the infantry began to malign the engineers for not standing to their work.[53]

At 5:00 a.m. when the upper bridge was nearing completion and the final pontoons were being moved into place, two Confederate signal guns sounded. Ten minutes later enemy troops at the upper and middle bridge sites began firing, driving the bridge builders from their work. Men and officers alike fled toward the safety of the shore without orders, panicked by a murderous fire. Work on the upper two bridges halted.[54]

Enemy fire checked the progress of the engineers with their bridges heartbreakingly close to completion. The upper bridge was only 80 feet from shore. The middle bridge was two-thirds complete. The lower bridge was barely underway and remained undiscovered. The engineers on the upper bridges did not intend to resume their work.[55]

Federal batteries opened on the Confederates, concentrating their fire on the upper and middle bridge heads, as well as structures along the Fredericksburg shore where enemy troops had been observed. At 9:00 a.m. more artillery was activated, gradually increasing Hunt's command to an impressive 183 guns. As the morning wore on, Fredericksburg crumbled under the cannonade. Yet the entrenched Confederates held their ground.[56]

The Third Brigade, 2nd Division (Howard), 2nd Corps (Couch), was sent to support the engineers and to take the lead in crossing once the bridges were completed on the morning of December 11. Colonel Norman Hall reported at the Lacy House to Brigadier General Daniel Woodbury and learned that the work on the bridges could not advance because of the "deadly fire of the enemy's sharpshooters."[57] At the time, Colonel Hall's brigade was badly under strength because of casualties suffered at Antietam. The 7th Michigan Henry Baxter now commanded originally numbered over a thousand men, but now had only 143 effectives.[58]

Confederate sharpshooters were dug into rifle pits, in cellars and behind brick buildings on the opposite shore. At 6:30 a.m. Hall broke camp and deployed the 7th Michigan and 19th Massachusetts along the shore in the vicinity of the Lacy House, intending to cover the work of the bridge builders by neutralizing the Confederate sharpshooters. At 8:00 a.m. Colonel Hall's Brigade was detached to General Woodbury in order to more directly support the engineers. This arrangement proved no more satisfactory. Camouflaged sharpshooters repeatedly drove the engineers from their work despite the ongoing artillery support.[59]

The cannonade proved ineffective and the gunners rested in the early afternoon. The bombardment left the city on fire in several places, "causing a dense smoke, which, together with the explosion of so large a quantity of powder, almost hid the city from view."[60] An estimated 8,000 to 9,000 rounds were expended in the bombardment without dislodging the

Confederates. From the "vast thunder of cannonading.... Chimneys toppled, bricks and timbers flew, and great gaps opened in the walls of the buildings by the river," yet the sharpshooters remained.[61] Burnside had lost the element of surprise and the momentum of assault he counted upon to carry the day. He appeared once again to be at a stalemate, but with growing losses as his men received the fire of Confederate sharpshooters. The dire predictions of Sumner and others seemed to be coming true.

Meanwhile, the lower bridges were delayed because of the challenges in getting the 1,300 pound pontoons from Stafford Heights to the river at the prescribed spot opposite Deep Run. The area had not been properly reconnoitered, so the 15th New York Engineers worked out their own methods. The resulting delays meant that construction did not begin until 7:00 a.m.. The engineers solved their problems by unloading boats upstream of the actual bridge site, then floating as quietly as they could 250 yards down river. The Confederates heard the boats and materials being unloaded through the fog, and the 18th Mississippi prepared for an assault from a bridge that they perceived being built in their front. In fact, only the materials were being unloaded across the river, the bridge was actually built further downstream. The Mississippians did not alert Confederate units downstream from them. The noise created by the construction was masked by the firing at the upper bridges. The bridge was actually completed even after the Confederates detected them. No rebel opposition blocked the initial party of Union engineers that finished the landing abutment on the south side of the river. By 11:00 a.m. the bridges in front of Franklin's Left Grand Division had been completed with only minor Confederate resistance, but General Franklin was not allowed to cross until the upper and middle bridges at Fredericksburg had been finished. General Burnside wanted multiple bridges to allow the army to flood across the river in force and have several escape routes as necessary. Union forces amassed artillery on the north side to defend the bridges and then awaited orders to cross.[62]

That left the middle and upper bridges at issue. The Union's supporting infantry shot at the Confederates from the opposite river bank with little more impact than the artillery. The Confederates were dug in and their fire began to tell on the Union regiments. The 57th New York took the worst beating and was relieved by the 7th Michigan at 8:00 a.m..[63]

The engineers thought the bridge construction hopeless. But with his bridge in the south complete, Burnside was not to be deterred. He ordered General Woodbury to complete the upper and middle bridges "whatever the cost."[64] Several heroic attempts were made to restart work on both bridges, but enemy fire sent the engineers running. By 10:00 a.m. not enough trained engineers were left to do the job. Woodbury even brandished a pistol to force the remaining engineers back to work in the face of enemy fire, without satisfactory results.[65]

After several hours of sniping across the Rappahannock with the lower bridge completed, an idea suggested earlier resurfaced. Why not have the engineers ferry infantry across in boats to secure the bridge head so that the sharpshooters could be neutralized, allowing the engineers to finish their work? Brigadier General Hunt presented the idea to the commanding general. Burnside liked it. He saw this method as a way to break the deadlock, but refused to order any unit to cross under such conditions. However, if an infantry unit would volunteer, he would support them.[66]

Hunt and Woodbury met with Colonel Hall at the Lacy House and discussed the practicality of crossing the river in boats, then storming the Confederate strongholds that impeded the progress on the middle bridge. The artillery was to pound the city so that the engineers could place boats at intervals along the river bank and—at the right moment—clamber into them, load an infantry unit, and row across in the face of enemy fire.[67]

As Colonel Hall later reported, "Lieutenant-Colonel Baxter, commanding the Seventh Michigan Volunteers, was informed of the plan, and his regiment volunteered to be crossed and storm the town as proposed. Captain Weymouth of the 19th Massachusetts also volunteered to support the Seventh Michigan, if required, to cross in the same way."[68] The 7th Michigan was already at the river bank and was soon prepared to board the boats. The 19th Massachusetts was deployed along the bank along with Captain Plummer's independent company of sharpshooters under Colonel Hall's direction.[69]

They faced a conglomerate of entrenched Confederate detachments made up of the 17th, 18th, and 21st Mississippi, and the 8th Florida. They were engaged by the 46th New York and the 89th New York without much success at the middle crossing. General Burnside ordered four officers and 100 men of the 89th New York to cross in boats also. Not all of the 89th New York felt this was a good idea, and so their commanding officer—Colonel Harrison Fairchild—had difficulty pulling the prescribed force together. The 15th New York Engineers would man four pontoons for them to cross in.[70]

General Hunt ordered the batteries to bombard the riverfront aggressively. He wanted the Confederates driven underground so they could not concentrate fire on the boats or the landing site. General Woodbury ordered the engineers to set and man the boats. At a prescribed time the artillery was to cease and the crossing was to occur. The batteries opened up at 3:00 p.m. with a heavy, rapid fire that continued for more than half an hour and concentrated on the brick buildings close to the upper bridge landing site. This barrage left Fredericksburg a crumbling, smoking wreck. Viewing the bombardment safely from Marye's Heights south of Fredericksburg, Confederate Colonel Edward Alexander described it as

> the most impressive exhibition of military force, by all odds, which I ever witnessed ... in front, was the three mile line of angry blazing guns firing through white clouds of smoke & almost shaking the earth with their roar. Over & in the town the white winkings of the bursting shells reminded one of a countless swarm of fire-flies. Several buildings were set on fire, & their black smoke rose in remarkably slender, straight, & tall columns for two hundred feet, perhaps, before they began to spread horizontally & unite in a great black canopy. And over the whole scene there hung, high in the air, above the rear of the Federal lines, two immense black, captive balloons, like two great spirits of the air attendant on the coming struggle.[71]

The 7th Michigan prepared to depart, resting until needed in a ravine north of the Lacy House. Baxter instructed his men to concentrate on propelling the boats across as quickly as possible. They were not to waste time returning fire. When on the other side they were to gather and then charge the enemy rifle pits without reforming ranks.[72]

Hall and Baxter moved the regiment down to the river bank, where they lay among the willow trees and bushes, trying to remain concealed. The 15th New York Engineers were reluctant to get into the pontoons, seeing the new method of crossing as just as likely to lead to their slaughter as the prior method. When the bombardment stopped, the engineers approached the pontoons, but the fire from Confederate sharpshooters sent them "running away from the boats ... and seeking shelter." While not all the engineers ran, enough did to change the situation significantly.[73]

Hall saw little chance for success if the operation relied upon the demoralized engineers. Improvisation with the resources at hand was essential. The only way for the plan to work would be if Baxter's men could themselves position the boats, clamber into them, row across, and then disembark and storm the river bank when they got to the other side. All would have to take place in the face of a withering fire from the enemy. Hall later admitted in his "apprehensions of disaster in this attempt, as, without experience in the management of boats, the shore might not be reached promptly, if at all, and the party lost."[74] General Marsena Patrick, Provost Marshall of the Army of the Potomac,

> swore it was folly and madness to send ever so small a number in boats to be butchered by the rebels, and predicted that not a soul of them would come out alive, but Gen. Sumner said the 7th Michigan boys were brought up under him and he knew them never to flinch when called upon in case of danger, and he was sure they would prove themselves victors.[75]

Many believed that the direct frontal assault by water would end in disaster. Even before it started, it began to be described as the "Forlorn Hope" at headquarters.

Baxter used his experience with ferries and river crossings in 1849–50 to manage the boats, a few of which needed to be carried to the water. The heavy artillery fire covered the arrangements and Lieutenant C. B. Comstock—the Army of the Potomac's chief engineer—personally supervised the embarkation. Then a new challenge arose. The artillery abruptly stopped before all the boats were loaded. Confederate sharpshooters renewed their fire and General Oliver Howard reported,

There are a number of contemporary engravings of the "Forlorn Hope," the crossing of the Rappahannock by the 7th Michigan under fire from sharpshooters in Fredericksburg. This one published in *Frank Leslie's Illustrated Newspaper* is arguably the best, although the pontoons were actually bigger, more unwieldy, and Baxter had the men not rowing lie flat to create fewer targets for the Confederates. This order undoubtedly saved lives.

Poor workmen [engineers], unused to soldiering, made only abortive attempts. Two or three would get hold of a boat to move it, but as soon as a bullet struck it in any part they would run back. Finally, Baxter said that his men would put the boats into the water. His soldiers did that at command, filled them with men and shoved off so quickly that the enemy's fire became fitful and uncertain.[76]

Baxter pushed them across fearing that a delay would give the Confederates a chance to reestablish themselves and—with the nature of the Union operation now unveiled—make preparations to oppose both the crossing and the landing.[77]

Across from the upper landing, the Confederate defenders suffered under the cannonade. Badly shaken by progressively heavier pounding, their nerves were raw. Yet, when the barrage ended and they saw the boats being manned, they leapt into action, doing their best to slow the advancing blue coats.[78] Clara Barton at the Lacy House remembered soldiers near her lamenting that the Confederates sharpshooters had not been put out of action.[79] The operation appeared doomed.

Ten boats pushed off about 3:30 on the afternoon of December 11, in the first frontal daylight amphibious assault on an entrenched enemy in American history.[80] The 7th Michigan began receiving fire from the Confederates as soon as they touched the boats. Baxter attempted to minimize casualties by having all those not engaged in rowing lie down flat, an action that undoubtedly saved lives.[81] Moving across a 400-foot-wide river in ungainly open boats within clear view of an entrenched, elevated enemy was bad enough. Taking fire from sharpshooters while wrestling with currents and ice was even worse.[82] Having to disembark and storm up the steep embankment was seen as impossible, as it would more than 80 years later to Allied troops landing on the beaches of Normandy.

The crossing that Baxter led included significant leadership challenges. Not only did Baxter have to adjust the plan at the last moment to convert his men from passengers to boat crew, he also had to force the men to think about the landing and assault that lay ahead of them, while withholding their own fire under a hail of enemy bullets.

The 7th Michigan crossed the Rappahannock quickly. The men chanted "Row, Row" to keep time as they tried to minimize their vulnerable time in the direct enemy line of fire.[83] Baxter and many of his men were hit on the way across. Fortunately, as the boats approached the opposite shore, the projection of the steep bank caused the Confederates to lose a clear view of them and the firing slackened. The embankment between the river and parallel Sophia Street provided enough protection for the 7th Michigan to tumble out without being under a harsh fire. They splashed ashore through the cold water accompanied by deafening cheers of the Union troops watching from Stafford Heights. The men assembled and under the leadership of Major Thomas Hunt—who took over for the paralyzed Baxter—stormed up the embankment and crossed the intersection of Sophia and Hawk Streets. They took the waterfront building by building. Though ordered by Hunt to give "no quarter," not all the Michiganders obeyed. In 20 minutes Hunt reported 35 prisoners were taken and the immediate waterfront was cleared. Five men were killed and 16 wounded during the crossing and the assault of the river bank, a far lighter cost than was anticipated.[84]

Of the action, Colonel Hall wrote,

> The boats pushed gallantly across under a sharp fire. While in the boats, 1 man was killed and Lieutenant-Colonel Baxter and several men were wounded. The party, which numbered from 60 to 70 men, formed under the bank and rushed upon the first street, attacked the enemy, and,

in the space of a few minutes, 31 prisoners were captured and a secure lodgment effected. Several men were here also wounded, and Lieutenant Emory and 1 man killed. The remainder of the regiment meanwhile crossed, and I directed the Nineteenth Massachusetts to follow and gain ground to the right, while the Seventh was ordered to push to the left. Seeing no preparations for advancing the bridge, which, according to the plan, was to have been under construction when the crossing commenced, I went to the engineer battalion and asked the commanding officer to send down parties at once. He replied that General Woodbury was in command, and was away. I entreated that men should be instantly sent, nevertheless, but could obtain no satisfaction.

The firing in the street had now become general and quite rapid, and, as I had been informed that a brigade of the enemy had been seen moving toward the bridge head, I requested General Hunt to reopen fire upon the flanks and in advance of the party which had crossed....

All firing upon the bridge had been now silenced, and the bridge was rapidly completed. I reported to General Burnside directly the conduct of the engineer troops. An order for the Twentieth Massachusetts Volunteers to move across the bridge the instant it was down was incorrectly transmitted, so as to cause Acting Major Macy, its commanding officer, to throw it across in boats. This regiment was held in line along the bank to resist any attempts of the enemy to recover this point by an exposed movement, and the Seventh Michigan Volunteers and the Nineteenth Massachusetts Volunteers could hold against any advance through buildings.

The moment the bridge was ready, the Forty-second and Fifty-ninth New York Volunteers and the One hundred and twenty-seventh Pennsylvania Volunteers moved across, and the Twentieth Massachusetts was formed in column in the street. The guide, a citizen, was killed at the head of the column. Upon attempting to cross the second street, it became evident that the enemy was in considerable force, and could only be dislodged by desperate fighting. It was fast growing dark, the troops were being crowded near the bridge head in a compact and unmanageable mass, and I was informed that the whole division was to cross to hold the city. It was impracticable, in my opinion, to attempt to relieve the press by throwing troops into the streets, where

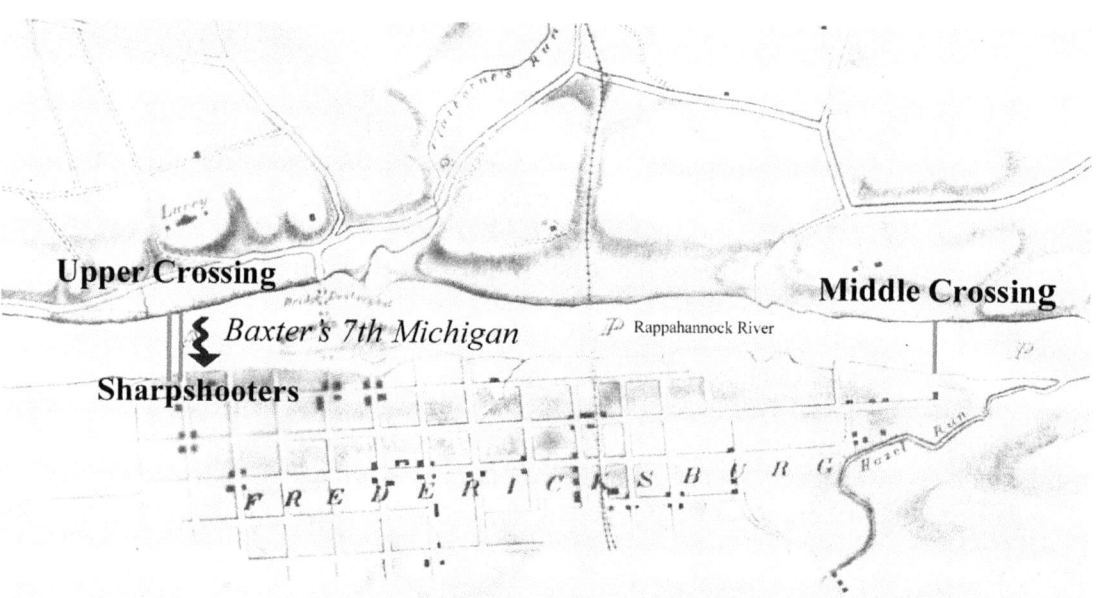

On the afternoon of December 11, 1862, Lieutenant Colonel Henry Baxter led the 7th Michigan Volunteer Infantry across the Rappahannock River in bridge pontoons to assault Fredericksburg. Despite a horrific fire from Confederate sharpshooters on the opposite shore, the 7th Michigan completed the crossing and established a bridgehead on the other side. Adapted from an 1862 U.S. Army map of Fredericksburg.

they could only be shot down, unable to return fire. To give time to fight the enemy in his own way, I sent urgent requests to the rear to have the column halted on the other side of the river, but was ordered to push ahead. The Seventh and Nineteenth had been brought to a stand, and I ordered Acting Major Macy, commanding the Twentieth Massachusetts, to clear the street leading from the bridge at all hazards.

I cannot presume to express all that is due the officers and men of this regiment for the unflinching bravery and splendid discipline shown in the execution of the order. Platoon after platoon was swept away, but the head of the column did not falter. Ninety-seven officers and men were killed or wounded in a space of about 50 yards. When the edge of town was reached, the Fifty-ninth New York was sent to relieve the portion of the Twentieth engaged in the street leading to the left, and lost a number of officers and men.[85]

At least one source indicates that the engineers never returned to complete the bridge, the work being done without orders by the 87th Pennsylvania under heavy fire as their best expedient to support the 7th Michigan. Two bridges were completed by 4:30 p.m.

Ironically, the best succinct account of the action came from Confederate General James Longstreet who admitted grudging admiration for Baxter and his men:

Colonel Norman J. Hall, of the Seventh Mich. Regiment, commanded the troops, worked for a foothold on the west bank. After the several attempts to have the bridge built, he accepted Gen. Hunt's proposition to load the boats and have the men push across. Lieutenant-Colonel Baxter, commanding the regiment, volunteered to lead the party. Capt. Weymouth, of the Nineteenth Mass., proposed to support the move. Under signal for artillery fire to cease, the command of Lieutenant-Colonel Baxter pushed across. Under the best fire the pickets could bring to bear only one man was killed and Lieutenant-Colonel Baxter and several men were wounded. The party of seventy were rushed up the bank, gained position, captured some prisoners, and were soon reinforced. The enemys fire over the west bank was so sweeping that Barksdale could not reinforce at the point of landing.[86]

General Thomas Meagher wrote in his report that his men moved forward once the bridge was completed thanks to

a body of daring volunteers [who] had crossed the river in boats, and taken possession of the city of Fredericksburg. The State of Michigan will fairly reserve to herself the largest measure of pride justified by this achievement.[87]

The crossing received significant attention nationally. The *New York Times* on December 14 included a full description.[88] *Harpers* and *Leslie's* carried articles with full page illustrations of the crossing.[89] But a significant part of the Army of the Potomac witnessed the event as well:

The moment the boats touched the shore a shout went up from the cannoneers at our guns, from the soldiers drawn out in line of battle, from line and staff officers gathered by the hundreds to witness the crossing, and from all spectators of whatever rank or class, that almost drowned the roar of artillery.[90]

On December 12, brigade after brigade of Union forces were pushed across the pontoon bridges while the Confederates pulled back to the hills that ringed the city to the south. Several minor skirmishes occurred, but the Confederates concentrated on strengthening their prepared positions on the ridges south of town while northern troops crossed the river and took up positions outside the city.[91] Some believed Burnside a fool if he thought he could carry the well fortified elevated position of Lee's well-seasoned troops:

Burnside must have greatly superior numbers, or else he is a great fool to precipitate his men into a plain, where every Southern soldier is prepared to die, in the event of failure to conquer! There is no trepidation here; on the contrary, a settled calm on the faces of people, which might be mistaken for indifference. They are confident of the success of Lee, and really seem apprehensive that Burnside will not come over and fight him in a decisive battle. We shall soon see, now, of what stuff Burnside and his army are made. I feel some anxiety; because the destruction of our little army on the Rappahannock might be the fall of Richmond.[92]

An onlooker predicted that Burnsides' army "will cross the river, and there will be a battle, which must result in a great mortality."[93]

Saturday, December 13, dawned cold with frost on the ground and fog cloaking Fredericksburg and environs. Below freezing that morning, it gradually warmed into the 60s by mid-afternoon, making it surprisingly mild for the season. General Franklin wanted to attack the well-prepared elevated Confederate position before dawn to give his men some cover, but Burnside did not get orders out quickly. By the time the orders arrived around 7:30 a.m., the opportunity to launch an attack under cover of darkness had passed. Now irritated beyond consolation, Franklin prepared the Left Grand Division to attack but the vague orders he received left him without definitive insight into Burnside's strategy. Burnside intended Franklin to cut his way through the Confederate lines, both cutting Lee off from retreat and also forcing him back upon Sumner's Right Grand Division to the north. But Franklin felt his orders only called for a demonstration of force. Hence, the battle began badly because of poor planning and miscommunication. Franklin's men fell under artillery attack as they advanced about 10:00 a.m. With a frontal assault impossible because of the Confederate guns, an artillery duel took place until about 1:00 p.m. when Major General George Meade's Division charged the Confederate works at Prospect Hill. The blue coats had remarkable success, finding a gap and exploiting it to displace many of the Confederate forward units. They were eventually stalled, and the attack came to naught despite a hard day of fighting.[94]

At about 2:00 p.m. Hall's Brigade was called upon to support Brigadier General William French's attack upon the Confederate works in the vicinity of Marye's Heights. French's attack was part of Sumner's Right Grand Division that was supposed to attack at the same time as Franklin's Left Grand Division. Hall's brigade made several attacks on Confederate lines moving up the slope on open ground with Hanover Street on their left. The brigade made some progress, the 19th and 20th Massachusetts taking the brunt of enemy fire as the 42nd and 59th New York, followed by the decimated 7th Michigan, broke under a galling fire. The brigade took shelter in an old mill race at the outskirts of the city. They held what ground they took until being relieved by Sykes' Brigade just after midnight on December 14. Some felt that this battle was worse than Antietam.[95]

Late on December 13, Burnside still felt that the Confederate position could be carried by assault and ordered an attack the following morning. But on December 14 his generals stood united against such a move. The Confederate works were just too strong. Burnside wasted all of the 14th and most of the day following before he realized that his assault was a failure and renewal of the battle would be futile. By 5:00 p.m. on December 15 a dejected Burnside ordered his generals to pull from its forward positions, but to retain defensive works around the bridgeheads. Early on the morning of December 16 Burnside decided to withdraw from the bridgeheads as well. The engineers were summoned to dismantle the bridges that had been assembled at such cost of human life only five days earlier.[96]

6. An Authentic Piece of Human Heroism, Late 1862

By dawn on December 16 the troops were safely across the river. The Confederates reoccupied the town and river front by mid-morning. One Union officer wrote, "We stand now precisely where we did before we crossed the river minus the killed & wounded."[97] In Richmond, this victory left the population of "the city exalted to the skies!"[98]

Most Unionists saw the Fredericksburg Campaign as "useless."[99] The Army of the Potomac lost 12,653 killed, wounded, captured or missing, while the Army of Northern Virginia lost 5,315. The 7th Michigan suffered 7 killed, 27 wounded, and 2 missing. The victory went to the Confederates for stopping the thrust toward Richmond. The only salvageable part of the Union effort was the story of the valiant effort that went into it. As 7th Michigan Private Melvin Rice wrote, "I am not much pleased with such bad Generalship."[100]

The novelty of the crossing of the Rappahannock, as well as its pivotal importance to the progress of the campaign, meant that it was well-watched, being within sight of a parameter ridge to the north that provided great views from almost 180 degrees. This visibility in part accounted for the widespread reports of what the *New York Times* called an "authentic piece of human heroism, which moves men as nothing else can."[101] Major General Couch, commanding the 2nd Army Corps, called it "a gallant affair."[102] The *New York Times* opined that those of the 7th Michigan who made the crossing were men who "merited the recognition of their country."[103] Some members of the press advocated Medals of Honor for the 7th Michigan, but predicted that "we fear that all the recognition and reward these men will ever receive for their day's service, will be to be kept waiting half a year or more for the forty cents they earned by it," a prediction that almost literally came true.[104]

Baxter's was not the only reputation enhanced on this day. General Howard gave Colonel Hall "the most unqualified recommendation to the post of general officer. For gallantry and good service he is not excelled."[105]

The Fredericksburg Campaign proved a failure, but the crossing of the Rappahannock became—for a time—a symbol of northern courage and resolve as very few feats up to this time had. After Colonel Hall's famous act of saving the flag at Fort Sumter, his participation in this further act of heroism seemed to mark him for a great future. Yet, though Hall was recommended for promotion to general, it was Baxter who was promoted. Leading the troops in the suicidal "forlorn hope" was an act that caught the public imagination, and once momentum had built there was no stopping it. The courage of his act in the face of a deadly fire inspired the troops, including one who wrote on December 12, 1862,

> At dark the last round of musketry had died away, and only the occasional shot of some picket was heard, and when we learned that the gallant Nineteenth Massachusetts and Seventh Michigan had crossed in the pontoon boats, and were even now in the streets of the city, our enthusiasm broke forth in ringing cheers:
> Cheer after Cheer we sent them,
> As only armies can,
> Cheers for Old Massachusetts,
> Cheers for Young Michigan.[106]

Fellow Michigander D.G. Crotty witnessed the crossing and wrote a decade later, "Those few who crossed in those open boats have earned for themselves a crown of glory, and that little party will be remembered as long as their country will last, for performing one of the most daring feats of the war."[107]

Others outside the army were equally affected by the bravery displayed at Fredericksburg. When the battle inspired Winifred Lee Brent of Detroit to create a state song to the tune of "Maryland, my Maryland," the 8th stanza commemorated the crossing of the 7th Michigan.

But the highest official pronouncement on the action was delivered by the Commander-in-Chief in an open letter to the troops dated December 28, 1862:

> The courage, with which you on an open field maintained the contest against an entrenched foe, and the consummate skill and success with which you crossed and recrossed the river in the face of the enemy, shows that you possess all the qualities of a great army, which will yet give victory to the cause of the country and of Popular Government.... I tender to you—officers and soldiers—the thanks of the nation.
>
> Abraham Lincoln[108]

Baxter's star was clearly on the rise, presuming that his robust body would recover.

⇒ ⇐

Henry Baxter's wound immediately disabled him, as the *Jonesville Independent* reported:

> The ball was no doubt, aimed at his heart, but he was at that moment stooping to hand an oar to one of the men, and thus his life was saved.[109]

The ball that struck him in the left shoulder exited the body near the spinal column, leaving him paralyzed for several days. He had to be carried ashore while his men stormed the embankment. Yet, he "cared not for the wound but was vexed that he could not lead the men to their work."[110] Ironically, the man who led the amphibious assault that opened Fredericksburg to Union attack and occupancy did not set foot upon its streets. Instead he was transported back to the north shore aboard the pontoon that took the Confederate prisoners across. At the Lacy House a dressing station had been established and Clara Barton was among those that received the wounded. Baxter remained in care of military physicians until he was well enough to travel and then went home on sick leave to Ypsilanti where his family was then residing.

While he was convalescing, the *Independent* reported that his field commission as Lieutenant Colonel had been confirmed by Michigan Governor Blair with the retroactive date of May 22, 1862, which coincides with when Colonel Grosvenor first showed the signs of illness. Baxter's officers had only asked that his commission be confirmed to July 8, the date of Grosvenor's resignation. This is an indication that Baxter had really been in charge of the regiment because of Grosvenor's disability.

For taking charge of the boats crossing the Rappahannock his men gave him the nickname "Commodore."[111] Though not an official title, the nickname was a sign of respect from the men who served with him. He was soon to receive a more lasting honor.

⇒ ⇐

In late December General John Geary of the 2nd Division, 12th Corps, wrote, "Everything is quiet in the army since the battle at Fredericksburg," but his experience told him "the probabilities are something will be up before long."[112]

Soldiers in the Army of the Potomac retired into their frigid winter camps wondering what disasters awaited them, but happy for a few months of monotonous freedom from battle and forced marches. Direct from an unparalleled demonstration of their bravery, followed by the morale-crushing retreat from Fredericksburg, the men of the 7th Michigan were in an understandably foul mood. Too great a price had been paid to experience another winter separated from friends and family.

7

Stalemate, 1863

Eighteen sixty-three dawned with the Union at its lowest point. The Army of the Potomac had withdrawn defeated to its camps. The northern public was beginning to doubt the eastern army's loyalty, leadership, and ability to bring the war to a satisfactory conclusion. The army too had concerns about its leadership, one officer writing, "We had lost all confidence in the man behind the whiskers."[1] Yet they had faith in themselves and that was something.

Ambrose Burnside pursued the enemy aggressively as Lincoln desired, attempting a mid–January winter campaign, but the weather was against him. Instead of the glorious thrust into the south he planned, the cold rains produced the "Mud March" so vile and unproductive that it was halted after a few days. The men of the 7th Michigan returned grumbling to their camp at Falmouth with an even greater contempt for their leaders.

In this atmosphere, Lincoln felt he had little choice. On January 26 he replaced Burnside with Major General Joseph "Fighting Joe" Hooker, a man whose ambitions and impetuosity left Lincoln with lingering concerns. But he needed a general who would press the enemy and press him hard, and Hooker seemed just the man. When the troops received the news of Burnsides' replacement on the 27th, the "rank and file were pleased, but the officers were not all of one opinion; some felt that we should be less gratified to be commanded by Hooker than happy to be rid of Burnside."[2]

Hooker was a Massachusetts native and an 1837 graduate of West Point. He had distinguished himself in the Seminole and Mexican Wars, but became bored with the army and left in the 1850s to pursue private interests. His return in 1861 as a Brigadier General put him in the midst of the action, allowing him to rise quickly to prominence.

Hooker inherited an "unhappy army" and tried to make something of it.[3] His soldiers were "defeated, despondent, ravaged by desertion, unpaid, and stuck in the mud without hope of moving forward before spring."[4] So troubled was one junior officer that he could not conjure anything positive to say about the army to his family and friends when he returned home on leave that February. His only confidence was in his regiment. That spring Hooker began to rebuild the army as he developed his strategy. New clothes appeared, a liberal leave policy was instituted, fresh rations were distributed, and regular drills reinstated. The army was reorganized and leadership reinvigorated.

One of the changes that Hooker put in place that April was a series of uniform insignia that differentiated between Corps and Divisions. For Baxter's brigade, the sphere insignia worn on the fatigue cap was white. How much these insignia promoted cohesiveness remains unmeasured.

Henry Baxter took no part in maneuvers early in 1863. He was still convalescing from the wounds he received at Fredericksburg. Dr. A. K. Kinnie of Ypsilanti provided two notarized statements that Baxter was under his care for a "severe" Minnie ball wound in his left shoulder and abdomen.[5] He was back with the 7th Michigan by the second week of February and wrote to Elvira,

> Yesterday and this Morning I was Corps officer and had to ride a six mile line of pickets. I found my shoulder gave me notice that it had at one time had a ball hole through it. However, I am hoping it is improving and will improve with use.[6]

On March 19 the *Independent* reported that Henry Baxter was to be promoted Brigadier General of Volunteers for gallantry and meritorious service at Fredericksburg.[7] The reaction at home was delivered with characteristic Midwestern straightforwardness:

> Hillsdale County is proud, and especially does Jonesville rejoice in the honor shown her distinguished son.[8]

Once claimed principally by Jonesville, Baxter was now a county-wide celebrity.

On March 11 President Lincoln recommended to the Senate that Baxter be promoted because of his "gallant conduct at the crossing of the Rappahannock, Va."[9] The Senate ratified the recommendation by unanimous vote. Jonesville could boast its first combat general.

Baxter wrote to Elvira on March 29 expressing his thoughts about the promotion:

> I have received no notice up to this time from the War Department altho [sic] this is not strange. Probably shall within a few days and until I do can write no particulars. I made no huge ejaculations on receiving the news of my promotion altho [sic] it was certainly entirely unexpected as I have never said one word with reference to such a probability and we all know these positions are generally worked for when given. I cannot help but feel, dearest, it is a very heavy responsibility for me to assume and I am letting time move along while I am considering for it does come as you know entirely unexpected. It is very gratifying to receive it in this manner and I fully appreciate this, I do assure you.[10]

He also sent along a small piece of the flag of the 7th Michigan "which we have carried from the beginning, and through every battle, which are not a few (seventeen in all) and many of them fierce and hotly contested. We have made it known and feared by the traitors who have dared to oppose it. It is our glorious National Flag that must and shall be sustained and may just chastisement be meted to all opposers."[11]

Confirmation of Baxter's promotion was reported in the *New York Times* on April 5.[12]

The soldiers of the Union Army were weary of sacrifice without success. Spring 1863 was depressing, following a long winter, the not so distant memory of the defeat at Fredericksburg, and the despised mud march. Thomas Jones could have spoken for the entire Union army when he wrote of the coming campaign season, "I hope to see a great victory and not a Fredericksburg retreat."[13]

By 1863 there were few optimists left among the veterans of the Army of the Potomac.

Half way through his three year enlistment Lieutenant Charles Curtis of Company E commented that "it really seems impossible the time has passed so quickly."

> ... The Regiment has been in Eighteen Battles besides the thirty days fighting before Richmond and have lost all but 476 Enlisted men. Have had 770 men in action and 461 have been Killed or wounded beside 23 Officers wounded and 7 killed.... I have been with the Regt in all its trials save Antietam & Fredericksburg[.] [I]f we continue on as in the past before the three years have gone we will all be dead or wounded.[14]

Given the difference between the quick, glorious victory that had been expected and the reality they experienced, Curtis' pessimistic expectation is not surprising. He was just 25 years old. A week later he wrote to his mother, complaining,

> It is supposed by all that General Hooker will fight every man to please the people and the army had rather not trust Him, believing he would sacrifice twenty thousand lives to save his own Reputation And theres [sic] too. A member of the U.S. Senate in a public speech before that honorable body declares every Officer and Soldier of the Army of the Potomac "Cowards and traitors and advises them all shot in cold blood." Which makes us love the country and respect the Lawmakers. You probably have heard of the collision between those darling attributes of Deity? "the Negro"; and the white man. There is trouble brewing and a revolution I fear will soon show itself in the West And our last two years of war will be like Silence in Heaven compared to the next five years. And I fear it will be rather expensive completing the pet Idea of some abolitionists, to wit, taking from a State of perfect happiness three millions of Ignorant blacks and making their ... time on Earth worse than the rebel imaginations of Milton have pictured the tortures of the fallen angels.[15]

At the end of the letter his mother penciled the postscript:

> This letter makes me provoked[.] I believe there are some soldiers in that army who would not be pleased if the angel Gabriel should take the place of Geo B McClellan.[16]

Clearly the men of the army were out of step with the folks back home. The two perspectives—one facing death in combat, the other weary of hardship—made more than an interesting contrast. The differences threatened to tear the Union apart.

Hooker intended to move with superior force upon Lee's army at Fredericksburg. He planned a pinchers movement around Lee's left flank to get into the Confederate rear. As his men set out in late April, Hooker sent an army-wide circular illustrating both his confidence and vanity: "With heartfelt satisfaction the commanding general announces to the army that the operations of the last three days have determined that our enemy must either ingloriously fly, or come out from behind his defenses and give us battle on our own ground, where certain destruction awaits him."[17]

Lee was not fooled by Hooker's feint. He divided his army, sending part west to meet Hooker at Chancellorsville on May 1–3. Lee outmaneuvered Hooker easily, sending Stonewall Jackson around Hooker's right flank to surprise and rout him. The battle was later described by one Union general as one of "the greatest of bunglings in this war."[18] Union forces withdrew across the Rappahannock on May 6 to maintain a defensive position while recovering. Confidence in Hooker plummeted. Melvin Rice of the 7th Michigan wrote "our Army has suffered another defeat all because we have not a General big enough to meet the requirements."[19] Lincoln agreed. He began looking for a general, considering a stable of candidates with the ability and the necessary political backing, including George G. Meade, Winfield S. Hancock, John Sedgwick, Darius N. Couch, and John F. Reynolds.

The Confederate situation was only slightly improved by the quick defeat of Hooker at Chancellorsville. The death of Stonewall Jackson was a loss of extraordinary leadership that the Confederacy never recovered from. Many realists in the government and military believed that a narrow margin of time remained to prove the South's resolve. This could only come from shattering the northern army and forcing a negotiated peace. With available men and material dwindling and Major General U.S. Grant's western army taking the initiative in the Mississippi River Valley, something had to be done with dispatch. Hence there arose a plan for a new offensive to strike at the very heart of Union territory where the Yankees were most vulnerable.

Before officially advanced to his new rank, Henry was performing his duties on an acting basis. On April 11 he served as General Officer of the Day, supervising the Division's pickets. He wrote to Elvira, "We have the Rappahannock between us and the rebel pickets making it a very safe line on which to do duty putting one in mind of the Potomac of a year ago."[20]

Before his departure from the 7th Michigan, he helped surprise Colonel Hall with a new sword and belt. On April 12 he himself was surprised when Colonel Hall called him before the regiment, made a speech testifying to his accomplishments and surprised him with a new sword. He confessed in a letter to Vi his emotion at the honor from men with whom he served so long: "I fancy my knees trembled fully as much as they would to meet the enemy in battle."[21]

The mud was drying and the roads were quickly improving, providing the prospects for a good campaign season. Henry hoped that the insurrection was coming to a close:

> I look forward with great hopes for our spring campaign.... The blow when it is struck I trust will fall heavily and with telling effect upon the rebels traitors and treasonists. The prospect is that we are to have quite a march for we are ordered to take in Haversack and Knapsack eight days rations which is five days more than we have ever carried before though five days of meat is to be driven on the hoof. We shall have to wait however and see what we shall see. We are not moving yet and doubtful things are very uncertain.... I had hoped ere this to have heard of the fall of Charleston, that hotbed of treason, and hope now ere long to know it has met it's just doom.[22]

On April 18 Hooker ordered, "Brig. Gen. Henry Baxter, volunteer service, will report in person to the major-general commanding the First Army Corps for assignment to a brigade in that corps."[23] Baxter was mustered out of the 7th Michigan as Lieutenant Colonel on April 19 so that he could accept his new commission as Brigadier General. Captain Amos Steele of Mason—commander of Company B—took command of the regiment on April 20. In making this transition, at 41 years of age and with almost two years of military experience, Baxter passed from the influence of politicos in Michigan. His fate now lay in federal hands, which is to say that the command staff of the Army of the Potomac, Congress, and the President of the United States superseded the hierarchy of Michigan government. Since the members of the command staff were overwhelmingly West Point graduates, he had his work cut out for him.

With him he took officers he knew to be trustworthy, loyal, and energetic. First Lieutenant Robert Knaggs of Monroe was Baxter's Aid-de-Camp. The ability to retain aides he had faith in was the last bit of good news he had during his transition to general officer.

Baxter's 2nd Brigade was in Brigadier General John Robinson's 2nd Division, of Major General John Reynolds' 1st Army Corps. The Brigade was composed of the 12th Massachusetts (Colonel James L. Bates), 26th New York (Colonel Gilbert S. Jennings), 90th Pennsylvania (Colonel Peter Lyle), and 136th Pennsylvania (Colonel Thomas M. Bayne). This appointment was fortunate for Baxter. General Reynolds was a West Point graduate who maintained good rapport with volunteer units. He also ran a tight ship and was even suggested as a replacement for Hooker, but declined because he felt he would not receive the free hand he needed to make the army perform to its potential.

Baxter's brigade had its problems. The two year enlistment of the 26th New York was nearly over, and the regiment was close to mutiny because of the apparent intent to retain them in service. Fact-finding on April 26 focused on determining whose enlistment was up and when. When on April 28 the regiment received orders from General Baxter to move out, about one third of the men refused. Neither Brigade Commander Baxter nor Division Commander Robinson tolerated this insubordination. Robinson already had experience with a near mutiny of the regiment's junior officers three months prior and he was not interested in going through the same experience with its enlisted men. There were other regiments that had two year enlistments coming due, so how this situation was handled would set an important precedent when enlistments expired in the field. The generals dealt with the situation promptly. Baxter formed the men on the parade ground and asked who among them refused to fight. More than 100 men stepped forward, were stripped of their arms, and sent off as a heavy fatigue party. This example had limited impact. The following day another 20–30 men refused to fight.[24]

Expiring enlistments created problems throughout the army in spring 1863. Some soldiers might have reenlisted, but the bounty system paid substitutes for conscripts $300 or more if he returned home and then agreed to substitute for a draftee. Expired enlistments cost the Army of the Potomac about 20 percent of its men in May and June 1863. Since these men were experienced, the loss was particularly irksome and could not be immediately offset by recruiting replacements.[25]

The war would go on with or without the men of the 26th New York. General Hooker's plan was to use the 1st, 3rd, and 6th Corps near Fredericksburg to maintain General Lee's attention in front of his entrenchments. The 5th, 11th, and 12th Corps were to move up the Rappahannock River, then hook south behind Lee's army, hopefully catching him in the open field between his present position and Richmond.[26]

Baxter's brigade left its encampment near Fletcher Chapel about 1:00 p.m. on April 28. That night the division bivouacked in the rear of the Fitzhugh mansion near the edge of the woods. The following day the division began its diversionary mission, moving up to cross the Rappahannock River at the mouth of Pollack's Creek, about three miles south of Fredericksburg. But fire from Confederate artillery forced them to seek cover along the river.

Hooker's strategy did not work as planned. Lee divided his army, leaving Jubal Early in command at Fredericksburg, while he took the larger part west to meet the Union end-around. When the two forces met, Hooker consolidated his position at the Chancellorsville crossroads, expecting to force Lee to attack through the tangled brush of the Wilderness. Lee instead learned from Stuart's cavalry that the Union right wing was unprotected, and attacked it. On May 2, the Union 11th Corps was surprised, causing a general withdraw.

Robinson received orders on the morning of May 2 to head for the United States Ford, which the division crossed at sunset in an attempt to shore up the northern line. The division headed for Chancellorsville, "driving back hundreds of the fugitives of the Eleventh Corps."[27] Ordered to take up a position on the Hunting Creek Road, the division made a 22-mile march and arrived at 1:00 p.m. on May 3. Bringing up the rear, Baxter's and Leonard's brigades were both deployed in line of battle to the left of the road, while Root's First Brigade formed between the road and the creek on their right. Robinson ordered breastworks thrown up, his men creating "a formidable line of rifle pits" as the day wore on.[28] Batteries came up to support the infantry and action between pickets brought in about 100 prisoners taken by Robinson's Division. The 1st Corps was now on the extreme right of the reformed Union line.

Union forces made progress at Fredericksburg, breaking through Early's small force, but Hooker was pushed out of Chancellorsville. Lee was then able to throw back the Union advance from Fredericksburg.

Hooker worried that the Confederates would make a flanking move and ordered a reconnaissance in that direction. On May 4 Robinson led the 12th and 13th Massachusetts and a section of Hall's battery on a reconnaissance of the road leading to Ely's Ford. About three miles in their front, they found the Confederate skirmishers and fire was exchanged. Robinson believed that the enemy was in greater force to his left (toward Chancellorsville), but his orders dictated that he not start a general engagement and so Robinson returned to his former position. The force that Robinson actually faced was a small detachment of Confederate cavalry who were convincing enough to keep Robinson's Division in place.

Most of Hooker's officers were in favor of attacking, but the commander was hesitant. Lee's position was fortified and Hooker's army was short of rations. Though they were in a solid defensive position and outnumbered their opponents, Hooker made the decision to withdraw. On May 5 Robinson's Division was ordered back across the Rappahannock River, arriving near Pollock's Mill on May 8. Officers and men alike were dispirited by the withdrawal since their position seemed strong and their forces intact. Members of the 1st Corps felt "that if our corps had been used" the outcome might have been different.[29]

The casualties among Union forces were 18,000 to 13,000 for the Confederates. Since they had done little more than skirmish, Robison's Division suffered only 75 casualties during the Chancellorsville Campaign.

In the wake of the campaign, the investigation of the 26th New York resumed. Robinson and Baxter concluded that hanging more than a hundred men was not in anyone's best interest. On May 10 the regiment was ordered to return to Falmouth for rail transport home. They reached Elmira on May 11.[30] No doubt Baxter missed the man power, but was relieved to be rid of the rebellious unit.

The officers and men of the 1st Corps settled back into camp. According to Lieutenant Abner Small,

> Our bitter chagrin at the outcome of the battle was soon abated. We were pleasantly sheltered; our mail came almost regularly; our duties were performed with a reasonable regard for comfort. We drilled early in the morning or late in the afternoon, avoiding the heat; it was soon very hot at midday.[31]

Baxter missed his old regiment. He saw them occasionally as they marched from place to place, and he endeavored to keep up with regimental happenings. In September 1863 in a letter to his wife he noted, "You have probably seen that the 7th is in New York and I hope they are having a nice time. They deserve it."[32]

Though away from the regiment, the politics of Michigan were still on his mind. He wrote to Elvira on May 28 that he

> had the pleasure to day of meeting Gov Blair, Mrs Blair, Mrs Gorham, and.... Also Mr. Barns of Detroit[,] the Asst Adjt Genl of the State [Lt. Colonel Frederick Morley], [and] also Dr. [Joseph] Tunnicliff of Jackson, which was quite a Michigan delegation. Especially the ladies. Senator Chandler has been in our vicinity two different times and I endeavored to see him but failed. I rode over to the 24th to see Gov Blair with Genls Williams and Robinson and we found him making a speech to the regt.... I met Col [Henry] Morrow [of the 24th Michigan Volunteer Infantry] today for the first time. His regt is in the 1st Div of our Corps.[33]

Morley was a Detroit newspaper man and Tunnicliff was a Jackson physician. Both were staunch Republicans. Henry was moving up in the world and seeking out those in the state hierarchy that would be vital contacts after the war concluded.

⇒ ⇐

The Confederate strategy in the summer of 1863 was simple. President Davis needed a decisive victory and Lee had to deliver it. A victory would force the Union to sue for a peace that included recognizing the Confederacy as a sovereign power that would share the North American continent. This was distasteful to the Union because it could no longer abide the scourge of states rights and slavery, nor forgive the terrible bloodshed that had already occurred. To recognize the Confederacy was to accept the potential for continuing conflict over territory, natural resources, and strategic points with a country diametrically opposed in almost every philosophy. Most northerners believed that peace under these conditions was intolerable. Davis recognized that the tightening strangle hold of Union forces and the limited resources of the south would inevitably mean defeat if the war was not won soon. A bold stroke was needed.

The plan developed by Lee would take the war to the north. In conference with Davis on May 14–17, Lee asked for more troops for a massive thrust northward. By moving past Washington to the west he would force the Army of the Potomac to follow. He believed this would force Grant to abandon the Mississippi River Valley and respond to an invasion of the north, a campaign that—based on the recent performance of Hooker—seemed guaranteed to succeed. Even if the plan was not successful, it would draw the fighting away from northern Virginia, allowing farmers to harvest their crops unmolested. At the same time, his army would live off the produce of Maryland and Pennsylvania as it threatened Washington, Baltimore, Philadelphia, and other northern cities.[34]

While Davis approved the plan, he vetoed Lee's intent to strip coastal defenses of troops to supplement his own for the northward thrust. Lee would have to push deep into enemy territory with the resources at hand, taking on the Union army piecemeal while avoiding a general engagement.

Lee began to concentrate his forces around Culpepper Court House. A collision at Brandy Station between an expeditionary force led by Alfred Pleasonton and J.E.B. Stuart's division on June 9 did little to slow preparations. What it did was show Lee's hand, mobilizing northern forces in pursuit.

7. Stalemate, 1863

Using the intelligence provided by Pleasonton, Hooker shifted several Corps northwestward, including Reynold's 1st Corps which moved to the vicinity of Berea Church to act as a reserve. Hooker put Reynolds in charge of the army's right wing, including the 1st, 3rd, and 5th Corps. Lee raced north, with pursuing Union troops attempting to stay between the Confederates and Washington.

After Chancellorsville more changes awaited the Army of the Potomac. Many units were discharged as their period of service came to an end, thus reducing the size of the army. In 1st Corps the three brigades were consolidated into two. One brigade was eliminated and its units distributed among Henry Baxter's 2nd Brigade and Colonel Adrian Root's 1st Brigade. Root was soon replaced by Colonel Samuel Leonard of the 13th Massachusetts and Root's regiment was transferred elsewhere. Leonard was superseded in a few days by General Gabriel Paul, whose brigade in the 1st Corps, 1st Division was consolidated out of existence. Paul was a regular army officer—West Point Class of 1834—and Missourian.[35]

On the eve of the Battle of Gettysburg, Baxter's Brigade was in the Army of the Potomac (Major General Joseph Hooker), 1st Army Corps (Major General John F. Reynolds), 2nd Division (Brigadier General John C. Robinson), as 2nd Brigade. Baxter's Brigade included the 12th Massachusetts, (Colonel James L. Bates), the 83rd New York (Lieutenant-Colonel Joseph A. Moesch), the 97th New York (Colonel Charles Wheelock), the 11th Pennsylvania (Colonel Richard Coulter), the 88th Pennsylvania (Major Benezet R. Foust), and the 90th Pennsylvania (Colonel Peter Lyle).

Hooker was removed following a series of disputes with his superiors after the debacle at Chancellorsville. Instead of pursuing Lee northward, Hooker wanted to seize Richmond, a move vetoed by Lincoln because it left Washington and other northern cities vulnerable. When he finally started after Lee, Hooker offered his resignation due to a difference of opinion over troop disposition at Harpers Ferry. The resignation was promptly accepted. On June 28 he was replaced by Major General George Meade, an 1835 West Point graduate then serving as 5th Army Corps commander. One member of the 1st Corps wrote, "The change was almost a surprise, and was not altogether to our liking. We should have chosen [our Corps commander] Reynolds."[36] Unbeknownst to his men, Reynolds had been offered the command and rejected it out of fear that he would not have a free hand in army operations.

Meade was not universally beloved. A perfectionist with a quick temper and zero tolerance for incompetence, many of his subordinates fell victim to his tongue. Yet he was a competent and dedicated career army officer, and the kind of leader that the army needed badly at this juncture. With a crisis developing, he had to pick up the reins of power quickly and decisively. As a Pennsylvanian he could be expected to defend his homeland.

Federal troops marched northward in pursuit of Lee's invading army without the knowledge that on June 25 Lee had detached Major General Jeb Stuart for another of his rides around the Union Army. This turned out to be a fateful error for Lee.

The Union army headed northward, marching "all day in dust and burning heat. The water was scarce; we drank from occasional muddy pools by the roadside."[37] Supplies were more plentiful in Pennsylvania.

First Lieutenant George W. Grant of the 88th Pennsylvania Volunteer Infantry (of Baxter's Brigade) recorded that the 1st Army Corps crossed the Potomac River on June 25, passed through Stanleyville on June 26, reached Middletown and occupied the passes of South Mountain on June 27. On June 28 "we passed through the loyal city of Frederick, meeting with a hearty reception."[38] On June 29 they halted north of Emmitsburg a few hours before dark, "but the march was resumed early the next morning, crossing into Pennsylvania we bivouaced [sic] near Marsh creek, on the Emmitsburg pike, within five miles of Gettysburg."[39]

The two armies converged on the commercial town of Gettysburg, population 2,400. The Confederates under Brigadier General J. Johnston Pettigrew entered this crossroads community seeking supplies, having heard that a shoe factory existed there. Union 1st Division cavalry under Brigadier General John Buford were attempting to shadow the larger Confederate movement and were already at the crossroads. Buford realized the importance of the ground north and west of Gettysburg and occupied Herr, McPherson, and Seminary Ridges in hope that Union infantry would arrive in time to defend them. He fought a delaying action starting around 7:30 a.m. on Wednesday, July 1.[40]

On that day, General Reynolds—commanding the infantry vanguard—was with the 1st Corps as they had breakfast and got underway between 8:30 and 9:30 a.m., marching at a good pace up the Emmitsburg Road. The day was hot and humid. The 1st Division led, followed by the 2nd and the 3rd.[41] The lead units of Reynolds' 1st Corps arrived at Gettysburg about 10:00 a.m. Reynolds received a message from Buford indicating that he was engaged with the enemy on the Chambersburg Pike (the Cashtown Road). He gave orders to hurry the men along and rode ahead, finding Buford on McPherson Ridge where his men were already being pressed by the Confederates. Reynolds told Buford to hold the position and then rode back to order his men to cut across open country to reach Buford's position, thus saving precious time. He also alerted Meade and exhorted Howard's 11th Corps to hurry. Howard moved up and took a position north of Gettysburg to control the roads radiating out in that direction.[42]

The 1st Division led by Brigadier General Lysander Cutler's 1st Brigade and Captain James Hall's 2nd Maine Battery were double-timed onto McPherson Ridge and positioned by Reynolds himself. The 2nd Division cut through lanes and fields heading in the general direction of the firing. They met a black servant at the side of the road with General Reynolds' horse. He told them that the general had been killed in the battle, shot down as he placed the Iron Brigade along the ridge. Command fell to Major General Abner Doubleday, commander of the 3rd Division.[43]

There was a lull in the fighting just as the 2nd Division hurried onto Seminary Ridge west of town around noon. The ridge sported a few trees and houses, but was dominated by a large brick Lutheran Theological Seminary. The men were detailed to throw up a protective barricade of fence rails along the western face of the building. They could see and hear firing along McPherson Ridge to the west. The general officers collected in the upper floor of the Seminary and saw that the fighting was extending off to their right, to the northwest of their position.

Doubleday was superseded as ranking commander on the battlefield when Howard arrived at 11:30 a.m. Howard established his headquarters on Seminary Ridge and then supervised the placement of his corps north of town. In doing so, a hole was left between Doubleday's 1st Corps position to the west and northwest and Howard's 11th Corps position to the north and northeast.

The Confederates were rapidly converging. Hill moved in along the Chambersburg

7. Stalemate, 1863

Road, Major General Robert Rodes from the north on the Middletown Road, and General Jubal Early from the northeast via the Heidlersburg (Harrisburg) Road. Lieutenant General Richard Ewell accompanied Rodes' division. Hill was well established facing 1st Corps west of town between the Fairfield and Cashtown Roads and was bringing more troops into the line as Reynolds was killed. Ewell brought Rodes into action from the northwest as the 11th Corps was taking up position north of town.[44]

The real object of the first day became a race to occupy and hold the high ground. The

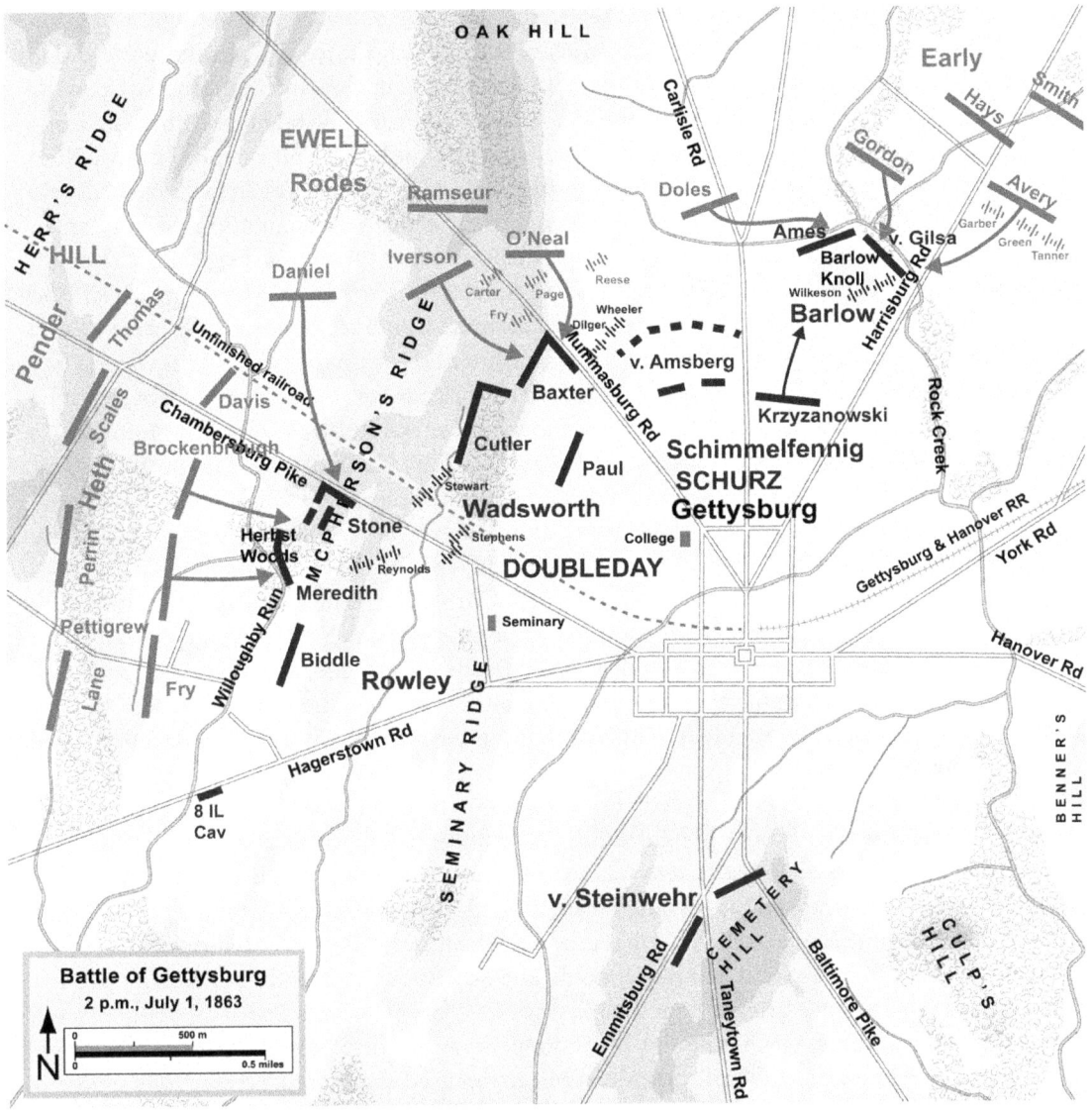

On the first day of the Battle of Gettysburg Baxter's Brigade was placed athwart the Mummasburg Road northwest of town and held a triangular position that was among the most exposed and hotly contested pieced of ground on July 1. Between Baxter's position and Howard's 11th Corps to the east there was a gap of approximately half a mile which enticed repeated assaults by Rodes' Division. Map by Hal Jespersen, www.cwmaps.com.

Union initially won by arriving first and occupying in force. But Rodes grabbed Oak Hill north of Seminary and McPherson Ridge, placing the batteries in his front where they had a clear field of fire. An artillery duel followed.[45]

Early afternoon found the bulk of the 1st Division, 1st Army Corps west of Gettysburg between the Fairfield and Cashtown Roads, flanked on its distant right by 11th Corps. Howard met with Doubleday at McPherson's Ridge about 2:00 p.m. and confirmed the disposition of troops there. Howard ordered Doubleday to hold the position as long as he could and then fall back. Doubleday later wrote that the gap between the two corps was brought to his attention by Lieutenant Colonel Henry C. Bankhead of his staff.[46] Doubleday sent General Robinson with the 11th Pennsylvania and 97th New York of Baxter's Brigade to fill it, moving into position between Culter's 2nd Brigade (1st Corps, 1st Division) on the left and the 11th Corps on the far right. The balance of the brigade was dispatched "in a very few moments," forming along Oak Ridge on the right of the regiments already sent into the line.[47] This extended the McPherson Ridge line onto Oak Ridge. Since he knew that he held a vulnerable position, Baxter adroitly chose a generally northwest-facing "V" shaped formation that was about 400 yards forward of any other Union brigades, but was not actually connected to them on either flank.[48] The 11th Pennsylvania and 97th New York joined a short time later, forming up on the brigade's left and completing its compliment of 1200 men. Troublesome Confederate skirmishers were nearby and Baxter sent out a company of the 12th Massachusetts that ran them off.[49] This was the first major engagement for Baxter, still inexperienced as a brigade commander. He did not have long to wait to be tested by the 8,000 officers and men of General Robert Rodes' Division.[50]

Before Baxter's Brigade could completely form up, Confederate Colonel Edward A. O'Neil's Alabama Brigade of Rodes Division attacked. The assault fell first on the exposed right flank. But it was not well coordinated and Baxter wheeled his line to face it, covering his right flank which had a gap of "at least 400 yards" between his extreme right and the 45th New York, the western most regiment of the 11th Corps. Skirmishers were sent forward after the attack, but the brigade was quickly assailed on the left flank by Brigadier General Alfred Iverson's Brigade who aimed for the gap between Baxter's and Cutler's Brigades. Baxter shifted his regiments again to adjust his line, swinging on an axis that allowed him to hold the top of the hill and meet the enemy face to face, making sure that all his men's guns were trained on the advancing enemy.[51]

Clearly exposed in an advanced position beyond the point held by 11th Corps and facing superior numbers with rapidly diminishing ammunition, Baxter needed a way to hold his ground and he needed it fast. There was a stone fence along the Mummasburg Road on his right flank. Baxter moved his brigade forward to take shelter behind it. The brigade's front was covered by an angle in the wall that ran to the southwest. Baxter ordered the men to lay down behind this barrier. The ruse worked. The 5th, 20th, 23rd, and 12th North Carolina regiments of Iverson's Brigade approached from the Forney farm house at an oblique angle without skirmishers, reaching point blank range unaware that Baxter's Brigade was close. They did not know that O'Neal's brigade had been repulsed and retired.[52] At the right moment General Baxter gave the order and his

> men sprang to their feet and delivered a most deadly volley at very short range, which left 500 of Iverson's men dead and wounded, and so demoralized them, that all gave themselves up as prisoners. One regiment, however, after stopping our firing by putting up a white flag, slipped away and escaped.[53]

Baxter's men "furiously assaulted" Iverson's command with fire that, with the aid of supporting Union positions, was so heavy that whole lines of Confederates dropped dead still in formation, making it look from afar as if they had simply stopped and laid down.[54]

The shattered remains of Iverson's North Carolinians were caught in a deadly crossfire. Their only shelter was a shallow gully barely deep enough to provide cover. All escape routes were within range of Union forces and so the Confederates maintained what return fire they could. An attempt by the 23rd North Carolina to charge the wall again was cut short by deadly fire from Baxter's Brigade. Union soldiers continued to shoot at the prone men in an uneven contest that lasted about an hour.

Suddenly, Baxter shouted, "Up boys, and give them steel" and led the 97th New York, 83rd New York, and 88th Pennsylvania, in a charge that captured almost 400 rebels in the gully.[55] Three battle flags were taken, the regimental colors of the 23rd North Carolina and the 26th Alabama by the 88th Pennsylvania and that of the 20th North Carolina by the 97th New York.[56] Colonel Charles Wheelock reported his 97th New York captured 213 members of the 20th North Carolina, "more prisoners than we had men in our regiment at the time."[57] General Doubleday later recalled that Baxter "drove the rebels before him in handsome style, but was constantly outflanked and enfiladed. Nevertheless, the brigade behaved nobly."[58] Though Baxter's men were the primary catalyst for this event, many others contributed. At the time of Iverson's advance, the men of Culter's Brigade had been thrown forward, forming an enfilade of devastating effect. In addition, artillery fire and distant fire from Colonel Roy Stone's 2nd Brigade, 3rd Division, 1st Army Corps, on Baxter's left also contributed.[59]

No sooner had this threat disappeared, than the enemy reformed in his front and attacked simultaneously. Baxter ordered Colonel Lyle to swing backward hinged on the right end of the line so that the 19th Pennsylvania could face the threat to the right flank. This was accomplished in "perfect order," but the Pennsylvanians faced a "very severe fire."[60]

Paul's Brigade had been held in reserve at Seminary Ridge but the threat to Baxter's Brigade and the hole between that point and Howard's Corps forced Doubleday to commit him. Paul's men took enemy fire as they came into line with Baxter's Brigade.[61] According to General George Meade, the situation at this juncture became "more and more desperate."[62]

Baxter's and Paul's Brigades were holding the extreme right of Oak Ridge and the two units joined together behind the stone wall at the crest of the ridge. Together they staved off an attack. Years later, Lieutenant Abner Small remembered

> the still trees in the heat, and the bullets whistling over us, and the stone wall bristling with muskets, and the line of our men, sweating and grimy, firing and loading and firing again, and here a man suddenly lying still, and there another rising all bloody and cursing and starting for the surgeon.[63]

In the midst of these attacks, General Paul was hit by a bullet that entered just behind his right eye and exited through his left eye socket, taking the left eye with it. The wound put him permanently out of action.[64]

The regiments of Baxter's Brigade were heavily engaged, but held their ground as the ammunition ran out. This was reported to 2nd Division Commander Robinson, who gave orders to hold the critical position by bayonet if necessary. Baxter's men scrounged ammunition from the cartridge boxes of the dead and wounded. The 90th Pennsylvania and 12th Massachusetts were pushed north across the Mummasburg Road and were caught in a "galling fire on the flank" by Iverson's sharpshooters.[65]

Baxter's Brigade was out of ammunition after two hours of close combat and was pulled from the line. Paul's Brigade filled the gap along the ridge, holding the extreme right. There remained a gap between Paul's Brigade and Howard's 11th Corps which was off to the east crossing the Carlisle and Harrisburg Roads, anchoring the right wing. Small later wrote that the position of Baxter's and Paul's Brigades was "a hard place to hold, the rebels half surrounding it."[66]

Baxter's Brigade was ordered to support Lieutenant James Stewart's Battery B, Fourth U.S. Artillery, at the railroad cut on the eastern slope of Seminary Ridge north of the Chambersburg Road.[67] By mid-afternoon the situation had become dire in the face of overwhelming numbers and retreat became inevitable. Doubleday wrote,

> As the enemy were closing in upon us and crashes of musketry came from my right and left I had little hope of saving my guns, but I threw my headquarters guard, under Capt. Glenn of the One Hundred and Forty-ninth Pennsylvania, into the Seminary and kept the right of Scale's brigade back twenty minutes longer, while their left was held by Baxter's brigade of Robinson's division, enabling the few remaining troops, ambulances, and artillery to retreat to comparative safety.[68]

Baxter's Brigade remained there until outflanked on both the right and left and ordered by General Robinson to withdraw. They retired to Cemetery Hill under heavy fire.

The Union brigades set up defensive positions. By nightfall, Robinson's Division with Baxter's Brigade had been repositioned atop Cemetery Ridge as part of the reserve. About 5:00 p.m. Baxter's Brigade moved with the Division "to the left and forward, near and parallel with the Emmitsburg road" where they threw up breastworks and remained for the night.[69] Baxter lost roughly half his men that afternoon.

The confusion of the first day at Gettysburg is best described by Knaggs, Baxter's adjutant:

> When we passed through the town of Gettysburg the general [Baxter] asked me to go into the town[,] find a blacksmith[,] and get his horse and mine shod. The enemy began to shell the town. Quite a number of shells burst over the shop and pieces came through the roof. The smith wanted to stop before he came to our horses. I drew my six shooter and told him he'd shoe my horses or I'd kill him. He shod both horses but it got very hot before he was through.
>
> I then started up the street toward our brigade.... Our command was placed in an open field and across a road that was stake and ridered on either side. The entire ninetieth Pennsylvania regiment was placed on the extreme right. With nothing in fighting distance on their right they were obliged to reverse and fall back to the other side of the road as the enemy was crowding them heavily. Colonel Lyle reported they were out of ammunition and I reported the same to the Brigade Commander [Baxter] and then to the Divisional Commander [Robinson]. I was authorized by the Division Commander to say to each Colonel in our brigade to hold that line even if by the bayonet alone for it was the key to the situation. I rode back and reported to all the Colonels, and in riding up to the Colonel of the Twelveth Massachusetts, my orderly rode in ahead of me and received a bullet through his chest. I saw the blood spurt from the wound. I directed him where to go to get to a barn that we were using as a hospital and told him that if he could raise his horse over a four foot stone wall it would save him at least a quarter of a mile travel. He made the attempt and just as his horse rose over the wall a six pounder cannon ball went through the horse. My orderly lay there until we retook possession.... I continued down the line until I came to within about fifty yards of the fence on the other side of which I supposed the ninetieth [Pennsylvania] regiment was. But they had been withdrawn during my absence and the fence was full of enemy. They shouted at me to come in. I wheeled my horse and laid down as close to his neck as I could get and dashed away. The enemy all seemed to shoot at me. My horse was hit but he carried me at least an hour longer. When I reached Brig. Gen. H. Bax-

ter.... I was notified that we were ordered to withdraw from the line of battle and rendezvous on Cemetery Hill. I was ordered to go back and bring those who might be separated from the command, up to the rendezvous. I started off to obey and thought it would be a good idea to head off the boys that might make for the town instead of going around it for that would make quite a difference in the distance to be traveling. I rode into the town about two blocks when I was halted by two soldiers in partly blue uniforms. I supposed they were a part of the Provost Guard that we had thrown around the town as usual. But when I got up to them I found that they were a part of General [John D.] Imboden's Cavalry, who had cut around in our rear and had the town in their possession without our knowing it. The only thing left for me to do was get off my horse and give up my sword and sidearms.[70]

Knaggs was sent to Andersonville Prison before being paroled and returned to Baxter's command in 1864. Though Baxter was not wounded, several of the regimental commanders were. His staff was decimated. Baxter commended the men of his brigade whom he reported "behaved nobly."[71]

One historian has indicated that Baxter's defense of the center of the Union position on the first day was "magnificent." But the best comment came from Colonel Charles Wheelock of the 97th New York, who wrote in his action report that Generals Baxter and Robinson "were on every part of the field, encouraging and stimulating the men by their presence and bravery."[72]

Through the night and early the next day reinforcements arrived. General Lee was on the field by the evening of July 1, General Meade arrived before dawn on July 2. Meade expected to hold the strong position he had at all costs and force the Confederates to push him off it. Lee was confident that his army would do just that.

The next day Baxter and his men learned that Major General John Newton was the new 1st Corps commander. Doubleday felt he "had earned the command," but was instead sent back to his division.[73] Newton was a Virginian and 1842 West Point graduate unknown to his new corps.

July 2 dawned hot and sticky, with early fog in the low lying areas of the battlefield. The battered 2nd and 3rd Divisions of the 1st Corps were replaced by the recently arrived 2nd Corps led by Major General Winfield S. Hancock. Baxter's Brigade held its place on Cemetery Ridge near the Emmitsburg Road with the Taneytown Road at its back until it was relieved about 10:00 a.m. by General Brigadier General Alexander S. Webb's 2nd Brigade.[74]

Baxter briefed Webb, then moved his men to the rear and north of their former position to be held in reserve. Meade made the best of his interior lines. Units already in the fishhook-shaped position did not have to march more than two and a half miles to reach another section of the Union defenses. For the remainder of the battle, tired veterans of Doubleday's and Robinson's Divisions were used where needed, arriving in time to throw back Confederate attacks or fill gaps unexpectedly opened along the line.

These units of 1st Corps remained near the federal center, just behind Howard's 11th Corps on Cemetery Hill, until about 4:00 p.m. when they were moved to the right to support the Union batteries which were now amassed on East Cemetery Hill. While there, the Brigade was exposed to enemy sharpshooters and "a heavy and remarkably accurate cannonade" by 16 guns of General Ewell's Corps.[75] Baxter's Brigade lost "some men" to the artillery.[76] The Confederates were preparing to attack Cemetery and Culp's Hills.

About 6:00 p.m. Baxter's Brigade moved to the left to assist Major General Dan Sickles' 3rd Corps, which—having been positioned to the west of the other corps out in front of Cemetery Ridge and Little Round Top—caught the brunt of the Confederate attack that day. Though supported by Major General George Sykes' 5th Corps and Hancock's 2nd Corps, Sickles units were "hard pressed" by the Confederate Corps of Generals James Longstreet and A.P. Hill.[77] General Meade himself waited with his staff in the breach as Doubleday's and Robinson's Divisions were thrown cheering toward the collapsing lines of Sickles' Corps. "At the right moment [the veterans of 1st Corps] ... came dashing up the ridge," sent the southerners flying back toward their lines and held the ground in anticipation of a renewal of the Confederate attack.[78] Baxter's brigade was exposed to enemy artillery, losing more men. They deployed skirmishers, but no enemy was encountered before dark.

Meanwhile over on the left, Ewell finally launched his attack from the north and east, striking Cemetery Hill and Culp's Hill. The attack at sunset had early and unsettling success. With the 3rd and 2nd Divisions of the 1st Corps, Baxter's Brigade was moved from the line they had just secured and sent to the right to support the 11th Corps at Cemetery Hill, occupying very nearly the position that they had held earlier in the day. They played no active role in this part of the engagement, but they were positioned where action was anticipated for the third day of battle.

After two challenging days in the heat and humidity, continually shifting positions, and alternating between being targets for enemy artillery and the reserve force that plunged into retard Confederate advances, the men of Baxter's Brigade were exhausted. They slept in the moonlight with the expectations that the coming light would bring a renewal of the battle.

In the early morning hours of July 3rd the engagement was renewed in the area of Culp's Hill on the Union right. Dawn came with a general call to prepare for an early morning attack. The remnants of 1st Corps had been broken up by division. Wadsworth held Culp's Hill. Doubleday had moved left along Cemetery Ridge, about halfway between 11th Corps' northern position and Little Round Top. Robinson remained in reserve behind Cemetery Hill, available to support either 11th or 2nd Corps.

Baxter's Brigade was once again ordered to support the batteries of the 11th Corps, where they had been located the previous evening. By 9:00 a.m. they were on the move again, "ordered to the right and rear of Cemetery Hill" to support the hotly engaged 12th Corps at Culp's Hill through late-morning.[79] By then Longstreet and Hill were advancing preparations for an assault on Cemetery Ridge on the Union left. At 1:00 p.m. the attack began with an artillery barrage involving more than 150 guns with concentrated fire on a one mile front. Few Union veterans would ever forget it.[80]

About 1:00 p.m. Baxter's Brigade was ordered to move again, this time to the right and front of Cemetery Hill. They had just formed line of battle when they were ordered to move again, this time to the left where they took their place on the right side of Brigadier General Alexander Hays 3rd Division, 2nd Corps, to again form the line and throw up earthworks. They did this "under one of the most galling fires of artillery ever witnessed."[81] The main Confederate attack culminated in Pickett's Charge, which Baxter's men helped repulse, but the brigade continued to be bothered by fire from Confederate sharpshooters and skirmishers.

The 12th Massachusetts and a detachment of the 19th Pennsylvania were sent forward to push the enemy back, which they did, holding the crest of a small slope.

Around 1:00 a.m. on July 4 Major Charles Northrup of the 57th New York relieved the pickets along the slope. For reasons unknown he moved the line back from the crest of the slope about 15 rods (247.5 feet) closer to the main line held by the brigade without orders and without being forced to do so by the enemy. Baxter was not pleased. He ordered Northrup to move the line back to the point designated before he would relieve his men.[82]

The new day brought a respite, such as it was:

> July 4th the armies kept their opposing lines all day without attacking or being attacked. Skirmishing continued. The morning was lowery, and some rain fell, and shortly after noon there came a drenching downpour and a wild wind. The wounded lying on the ground, and protected only by trees, were in a sorry plight.[83]

On the morning of July 5 the withdrawal of the enemy was discovered and Baxter's Brigade abandoned the entrenchments in favor of encampment. Baxter's 1200 man brigade had been reduced by 645.

Baxter's unit fought against a force eight times its strength on day one, was moved 13 times in three days, and fought in multiple places along the central lines. He shifted to meet many new circumstances, repeatedly built breastworks, and used all the cover available. To say that it was a difficult three days demanding of both stamina and combat skills is an understatement. Yet the ordeal was still not over. The pursuit of Lee's army began on July 7 and lasted most of the month. The forced marches south from Gettysburg toward Frederick, Maryland, kept Union forces between Lee's army and Washington, but it did not closely press the Confederates as Lincoln wanted, nor did it offer much opportunity to trap and crush the enemy before they made it back across the Potomac.

Some conclusions about Baxter's performance can be drawn from the reports of Doubleday and Robinson. He had already shown courage leading his men in combat. On the first day at Gettysburg he anchored a key position in the Union lines in the face of intense pressure from multiple sides and a vastly superior force. Yet the report shows something else of significance. He asked much of his subordinates and he expected it to be done. He did not tolerate subordinates whom he felt did not carry out his orders competently. Fellow officers trusted Baxter. Gabriel Paul even trusted Baxter with his son Augustus, who served as Baxter's aid-de-camp until captured in 1864.[84]

The human toll of Gettysburg was staggering. The Union suffered 3,063 killed, 14,492 wounded, and 5,435 captured or missing. By comparison, the Confederates lost 2,592 killed, 12,706 wounded, and 5,150 missing or captured. While the total Union losses were nearly equal to the Confederate number, more telling is the fact that these losses represented 24.5 percent of the Union forces engaged and 32.4 percent of the Confederate. The south could not sustain this level of loss.

According to General Robinson's action report, the 2nd Division of 1st Corps went into battle with less than 2,500 officers and men. The division sustained a loss of 1,667, including 124 commissioned officers, a casualty rate of 66 percent. Most were lost on the first day. Though the 2nd Division made up only 2.7 percent of the total Union forces engaged over the three day battle, it sustained over seven percent of the total Union casualties.

Baxter's performance at Gettysburg was outstanding.[85] Doubleday himself reported, "My thanks are due to Brigadier-Generals Paul and Baxter for the able and zealous manner in which they handled their brigades."[86] He moved his troops where they were needed quickly and efficiently, and he rapidly readjusted his lines to meet new threats in one of the most exposed positions on the field during the first day. He motivated his men to fight against growing odds by leading from the front and taking advantage of any cover he could find or make. And he answered the call in succeeding days as reinforcements were needed along the Union line.

If Baxter is poorly remembered for his role in the battle now, it is a product of a larger failure of 1st Corps to receive commendation from General Meade for the role it played on July 1. Meade treated the withdraw from the original position held on the first day as a failure of 1st Corps durability rather than as a controlled response to a practical reality in the face of enormous odds. Second Division commander Robinson complained to Meade

> of the intense mortification and disappointment felt by my division in reading your report of the battle of Gettysburg.
>
> For nearly four hours on July 1 we were hotly engaged against overwhelming numbers, repulsed repeated attacks of the enemy, captured three flags and a very large number of prisoners, and were the last to leave the field.
>
> The division formed the right of the line of battle of the First Corps, and during the whole time had to fight the enemy in front and protect our right flank (the division of the Eleventh Corps being at no time less than half a mile in rear). We went into action with less than 2,500 men and lost considerably more than half our number.
>
> We have been proud of our efforts on that day, and hoped that they would be recognized. It is but natural we should feel disappointed that we are not once referred to in the report of the commanding general.
>
> Trusting that you will investigate this matter and give us due credit.[87]

The men of 1st Corps deserved the credit that Robinson expected. They fought long and bravely on July 1, suffering serious casualties. Yet they were reconstituted and maintained their discipline despite a difficult retreat in the face of a determined enemy, and lived to fight again on both July 2 and July 3 when they changed positions multiple times to plug holes in the Union line. In the eyes of Robinson, his men were owed the primary credit for a victory, not the dismal silence of a commander who was not present to witness what they had achieved.

In the north, the reaction to the repulse of Lee's invasion at Gettysburg was inseparable from the surrender of Vicksburg:

> The battles fought and won in the East and in the West, at the beginning of July ... [meant that] everything military looked bright and hopeful. Rebel armies defeated, strongholds captured, territory occupied, rebel lines contracted, rebel forces demoralized, and the rebel Confederacy apparently in the throes of dissolution. Our armies all strong, well planted, well led, filled with the spirit of victory, and needing only to deal a few more blows upon the enemy, and then fold up their battle-flags and contemplate the glories of the triumph achieved.... Public confidence has never been as high during the war as in July, August and September of the current year; and there never was such good ground for it. It seemed as if we could almost descry the dawning of the morning of peace over a Union reconstructed, and a nation braced up and made stronger by the bloody hurricane under which it had passed.... As things stood a fortnight ago, we certainly considered that, if only our good fortune were maintained, the Confederacy must speedily totter to its fall.[88]

7. Stalemate, 1863

In the south, the reaction was different. Just after the "unexpected announcement" that Vicksburg had surrendered on Independence Day, reports from Gettysburg were treated lightly. The press called for General Joseph E. Johnston, the man "responsible" for the surrender of Vicksburg, to "be hung, shot, cashiered."[89] On July 15 the *Richmond Examiner* bristled over the "exaggeration" of the results of the battle wherein "a great many people were shot within a space of six miles, near Gettysburg":

> It was a battle in which the Confederates had their own way during two days, and were repulsed in an attack made during the third on certain powerful positions. They remained a day unmolested on the ground, and then retired in complete condition and order. So far as the fighting went, all that the Federal army did was to prevent its own annihilation. The Confederates were repulsed, but cannot, at present, with justice or candor be said to have suffered defeat.... We are not worse off than before it began, nor is the North a whit stronger.[90]

Union soldiers finally felt vindicated. They had met the Confederacy on northern soil and defeated it. As one soldier wrote,

> The war cant [*sic*] last much longer; with news of such victories as Vicksburg, Gettysburg, Port Hudson, Tullahoma, & Helena all coming in one weeks time. In my mind it will strike the death blow to Rebellion.[91]

As strong and decisive as victories at Gettysburg and Vicksburg were, they did not destroy the primary Confederate armies nor the southern will to fight. Much more would have to occur before this was accomplished.

The reaction abroad was equally important. With the Confederate army no longer the invulnerable entity it once seemed, support in Europe waned. Baxter's old friend Walt Murphy received the good news in a carriage on one of the busiest streets in Frankfort. His assistant handed him a newspaper that described the twin Union victories at Vicksburg and Gettysburg, after which Murphy "instantly jumped out into the middle of the street, waved his hat and began to shout. The public in general thought him mad, a crowd assembled; but as soon as he could get his breath he pointed out the headlines of the newspaper."[92] Since many in the city had followed Murphy's advice to invest in Union war bonds, the northern victories were widely celebrated in Frankfort that night. Altogether, Murphy was the catalyst for six war loans from Frankfort-based investors. The sale of Union bonds accelerated in 1863 and 1864. Even Karl Marx—the father of Marxism—bought them.[93]

The expiration of terms of enlistment continued to annoy Baxter and his fellow commanders. By July 31 the 2nd Division of 1st Corps had lost all except the 39th Massachusetts and gained the 8th, 39th, 46th, and 51st Massachusetts (Brigg's Brigade), and the 12th, 13th, 14th, 15th, and 16th Vermont (Stannard's Brigade). The regiments that composed Baxter's Brigade remained the 12th Massachusetts, 83rd and 97th New York, and 11th, 88th, and 90th Pennsylvania.

Despite his problems, Henry was thankful for his deliverance from the ultimate sacrifice of war. On September 5 he wrote to Vi:

> Two years ago today I left my darling wife and little ones in Monroe and launched out into this sea of war and strife—How little did either of us realize, or for a moment contemplate how much our country would be brought to suffer and how rent, and torn asunder, ere peace and quietness would again reign supreme. But so it is and the end is not yet. Many … have been called to give their dearest ones on earth, laid in a distant land with naught but a dear memory to console them and again others far away, engaged in the din and clash of battle have been called to mourn loved ones taken from them by foul diseases…. How have we been blest my darling one and we may indeed render thanks to a Kind Providence that we have been thus blest.[94]

In August Meade prepared for a thrust southward. Henry reported on August 4 that the Union had a strong position on the south side of the Rappahannock and could have done great destruction to the enemy, had the Confederates just attacked them. But this was not to be, and Baxter complained:

> I am glad [Brigadier General John] Morgan is captured and I should be willing to see him hanging from the limb of a tree as I should very many others who are leaders of this dastardly rebellion. Since the first of July the so called Confederacy has been Kicked and Cuffed Kocked and Thumped, in every direction but still they will have to be whipped yet again, and the first opportunity we get we will endeavor to give them the finishing touch.[95]

Lee was too sharp to attack Meade on ground of his own choosing, and little progress was made until Meade attempted to regain the initiative in what became known as the Bristoe Campaign. Under pressure from Lincoln, Meade looked for opportunities to strike Lee's Army of Northern Virginia. His chance came in September when Lee took advantage of his interior lines, detaching two divisions of Longstreet's Corps to reinforce Confederate forces in the Western Theater.

Meade's plan was to advance on Lee, forcing him into battle with greatly inferior numbers. The effort in mid–October proved a fiasco as Lee's forces met sections of Meade's army in small battles that goaded him into retreating with little gain. This campaign with many marches and countermarches became "known generally among our soldiers as the 'Culpeper-Centreville Express.'"[96]

Determined to succeed, Meade planned another movement south. On November 7 his army crossed the Rappahannock and forced Lee south of the Rapidan River. Meade planned what became known as the Mine Run Campaign.

On November 25, Meade initiated a rapid movement to envelop Lee's army around Clark's Mountain. However, delays in fording the Rapidan and the slow movement of his units gave Lee time to react. He held off the attack and fortified a position at Mine Run. A planned assault on the Confederate position was cancelled because the fortifications seemed too strong. Meade withdrew his force on December 1–2. Baxter's Brigade lost two men wounded and 33 captured or missing during the campaign.

Meade put the Army of Potomac into winter quarters near Brandy Station and Culpepper, Virginia. Lee's army wintered near Fredericksburg. The campaign season in the east ended in stalemate once again.

8

Pushing South, 1864

The Union was in a good position in January 1864. Though the victory at Gettysburg had not resulted in the destruction of the Army of Northern Virginia, it had shown that Lee was beatable. Gettysburg and the resulting campaigns also illustrated Union persistence and commitment to ending the rebellion on its terms. Together, these facts eroded European support for the south, foreshadowing the defeat of the Confederacy unless some significant incident dampened the northern will to fight.

Politics had come to mean little but aggravation to soldiers on both sides. The Confederate winter encampment was just across the Rapidan River from the Union camp, in some places only three miles apart. Soldiers awaited the latest strategy their leaders developed. On the Union side, March brought anxiety over a potential movement of Lee's army, triggering multiple alarms.

That month Lincoln brought Lieutenant General Ulysses S. Grant from the west and gave him command of all Union armies. Grant stayed with the Army of the Potomac, which was still commanded by George Meade. The promotion of Grant led Captain Abner Small to remark, "We thought he would do; yet we were inclined to wait and see."[1] The officers and men of the Army of the Potomac had learned to be cautious about new leadership.

Grant advocated a strategy to use up Confederate resources rapidly. The Union would mobilize completely, sending forward multiple armies in different theaters of operation to press the south to the limits while negating the value of their interior lines, an advantage that the south had used well. No longer would the primary Union objective be the capture of the Confederate capital at Richmond. Instead it would be the destruction of the South's most effective fighting force. Barring a Confederate surrender or major defeat on the battlefield, Grant's strategy would create a war of attrition where superior Union resources bled the south of the men, the material, and the will to fight.

In mid–March 1864 General Order #7 reorganized the Army of the Potomac, reducing it from five to three corps. Not all "relished" the amalgamation of the 1st Corps with the 5th Corps, which some felt diminished the glory earned in combat. The changes altered familiar relationships and transferred general officers that many had become used to. General Newton was removed from command of the new 5th Corps in favor of Major General Gouverneur K. Warren, who had held the Roundtops at Gettysburg. Warren was younger than the other Corps commanders. He liked big horses and wore full uniform when he rode into battle, cutting "a rather odd figure" as compared to his contemporaries.[2] During the reorganization, the 2nd Division was briefly commanded by Baxter until General John Robinson returned.[3]

The regiments that composed Baxter's 2nd Brigade, 2nd Division, 5th Corps, were 90th Pennsylvania (Col. Peter Lyle); 11th Pennsylvania (Col. Richard Coulter); 97th New York (Col. Charles Wheelock); 83rd New York (Col. Joseph A. Moesch); 88th Pennsylvania (Capt. George B. Rhoades); and 12th Massachusetts (Col. James L. Bates).

March and April were wet months punctuated by lovely spring days. Grant reviewed several regiments each day, riding "past our regiment so rapidly that we hardly saw him."[4] Grant was of "common size and build," wore a plain general's uniform, sat squarely on his horse, and was overall neither "impressive" nor "inspiring."[5] Small later wrote, "It would be easy now to say that we all perceived in the square and bluntly bearded jaw the force of relentless persistence; but I doubt we more than glimpsed a quiet solidarity."[6]

Grant had decided upon a strategy that would maintain pressure on the eastern Confederate army, and by extension, the government and western armies as well, until they collapsed. This escalation of the war became the Overland Campaign, an extended series of savage battles that traded the elegance of strategic maneuver and counter maneuver for a straight forward pugilistic fight to the finish. The bloodshed was enormous, but so were the stakes. In Grant, Lincoln had finally found a general that would pursue victory at any cost.

Grant would strike Lee's army head on, then press him with a series of flanking moves. This resulted in Lee's retreat to keep his army between Grant and Richmond. In multiple battles spread over more than a month, Grant pushed the mental and physical limits of his men. More importantly, he did the same to his opponents whose smaller numbers and weaker supply chain gave them fewer reserves. Meade would later call the campaign "one unparalleled in military history for its duration, the character of the operations, and the number of battles fought."[7]

Starting at 2:00 a.m. on May 4, Meade moved the 2nd, 5th, and 6th Corps plus artillery, cavalry, and supply train against Lee's army at Fredericksburg. The 5th Corps was in the vanguard, crossing unopposed at Germania Ford with its objective the Old Wilderness Tavern on the Orange and Fredericksburg Turnpike. The 2nd Corps crossed at Ely's Ford, about six miles further east. Assigned positions were reached by early afternoon. Warren's 5th Corps camped in order of battle near Wilderness Tavern.

Grant wanted to push quickly past the old Wilderness battlefield where low shrubs and ground clutter made it difficult for large armies to maneuver. Unfortunately, Meade was unable to move quickly. The available Union forces numbered 120,000, while Lee's Confederates included about 65,000 effectives. Lee needed to offset Union superiority and rushed his armies to the Wilderness where the terrain had slowed Federal forces before. Without a clear view of the field, the Yankees did not know what they were up against.

The following morning Grant was again on the march, attempting to turn Lee's right flank in order to avoid his entrenchments at Mine Run. The 2nd Division—including Baxter's Brigade—was "on a country road toward Robertson's Tavern."[8] By 7:00 a.m. reports were received that enemy forces were on Orange Pike. Warren was ordered to halt, reform, and attack any enemy force in his front, which he did with Griffin's and Wadsworth's divisions. They at first pushed Lieutenant General Richard Ewell's Corps backwards.

On the first day of the Wilderness, the balance of Robinson's Division, Leonard's 1st and Baxter's 2nd Brigade, were held in reserve near the Lacy house, where General Warren had his headquarters. They waited, watching the general and his orderlies come and go. Colonel Andrew Denison's 3rd Maryland Brigade was committed in the fore-noon. About noon

Leonard's and Baxter's Brigades were brought up to relieve Colonel William S. Tilton's demi-brigade. The 5th Corps was put in to aid Brigadier General G.W. Getty's 2nd Division of 6th Corps. These units forced back the divisions of Confederate Generals Henry Heth and Cadmus Wilcox.

As Private R.E. McBride of the 11th Pennsylvania reported, Baxter's Brigade ended up in a dreadful situation:

> Soon it was discovered that the division was flanked. Our line was at right angles with the position in which the subsequent fighting took place. To crown it all, the woods took fire, and soon the only problem that remained was to withdraw as quickly and safely as possible.[9]

Small reported that Leonard's and Baxter's Brigades

> hurried across bushy fields into the forest and along the turnpike a mile. A scattering of men was running in, some of them crying disaster, and ahead of us there was an uproar of yelling and firing. We came to a clearing and filed off to the right of the turnpike and went into line along the edge of an old field. The field, ragged with bushes, sloped down to a hollow and then up to the forest beyond. The fight had swept across it and back again, and now the hollow was filled with wounded, and out where the pike went over it were two fieldpieces, abandoned, the dead horses lying near by. The rebels wanted those guns and tried to get them, but our brigade, and the reserve of the troops that were in action before we came up, were now in line, and sent so hot a fire from our side of the field that the rebels drew back to their side and stayed there. The wounded in the hollow called vainly for water. The guns on the pike stood lonely in the sun.[10]

That night 5th Corps threw up temporary breastworks. The following day the engagement resumed.

Baxter's men were in the midst of it. He was leading the brigade when a bullet struck the front of his left leg above the knee, emerging "on the inside of the middle third of the femur," passing the bone without breaking it.[11] The ball went through his saddle and killed his horse, the second horse killed from under him during this engagement. But this time the loss of blood was severe. He could not continue, passed command to Colonel Richard Coulter, and was carried from the field, one of 18 officers and 394 men wounded that day. Three officers and 55 men were killed, while three officers and 63 men were captured or missing.

The Army of the Potomac had been obstructed in its advance, something Union soldiers had become accustomed to during years of facing Lee. On May 7, the army waited to see what its new commander was made of. Would he withdraw? Would he remain? When at 8:00 p.m. the army began to move toward the enemy rather than away, "Grant was seen, and a great burst of cheering greeted him as he rode swiftly and silently by."[12] The army finally had leadership that would persistently pursue and engage the enemy. Grant started around Lee's right flank, hoping to get between him and Richmond.

Baxter was carried to the field hospital. Since the bullet missed the bone and there was no sign of infection, he did not lose the leg like so many of his contemporaries did. In less than a week he was transferred to the Corps hospital in Washington. He eventually went home on sick leave, not returning to his command until August.

As a convalescent, Henry returned to Ypsilanti on May 13 to be with his wife and children. Of him the *Telegraph* said,

By sterling worth and military merit, he has won his way to a distinguished position. He is a man of indomitable pluck and splendid fighting qualities. He will yet live to be in at the death of the rebellion.[13]

During Baxter's absence, the brigade was commanded by Colonel Richard Coulter of the 11th Pennsylvania until he himself was wounded on May 18. He was succeeded by Colonel James Bates of the 12th Massachusetts.

While Baxter was mending, the pursuit continued. Facing an enemy who sought the destruction, rather than the capture, of his army, Lee moved his smaller, nimbler force as rapidly as he could. The Army of the Potomac had fought one of its most difficult battles at the Wilderness. Yet to cut off Lee, Grant pushed his army with forced marches on May 7 and May 8, attempting to reach the crucial crossroads at Spotsylvania Court House first. The Confederates barely beat them, and began to throw up fortifications to hold off the anticipated Union attack.

The battle at Spotsylvania Court House was really a series of engagements spread from the initial meeting on May 8 through the Confederate withdrawal to counter Grant's flanking movement on May 20. The battle included some of the most brutal hand to hand combat in the war, accruing 18,399 Union and 13,421 Confederate casualties. Among them was General Robinson who was wounded the first day and carried from the field. On the following day 6th Corps commander Major General John Sedgwick was shot through the head by a sharpshooter. Still, the federal troops responded with spirit:

> Grant had grappled with his enemy, intending to hold on "all Summer." The same spirit seemed to animate his army, from General Meade down to the latest recruit in the ranks. The lines of blue came out from the smoking underbrush of the Wilderness, their ranks torn and decimated, and closed in around the bristling batteries and rifle-pits of Spottsylvania [sic] with a relentless courage that was sublime.[14]

Small but hotly contested battles occurred at Jericho Mill on May 23 and at Bethesda Church on May 30, the two armies remaining in virtually continuous contact. Union forces crossed the Pamunkey River on May 28 and reached Cold Harbor on June 1 where a small engagement was fought over the next few days.

On June 9, Grant began to move his army south with the intention of crossing the James River. On June 15 the leading units reached the Petersburg defenses and undertook preliminary assaults. The Overland Campaign had effectively concluded and the siege of Petersburg had begun.

The Overland Campaign had kept the pressure on Lee. The forces at his disposal had suffered an estimated 31,700 casualties in a month and a half, men he could hardly afford to lose. Grant's army had suffered a larger number (54,926) of casualties, but he could better afford to lose them and was not distracted by the loss in the way that his predecessors had been.[15]

On August 18 5th Corps was ordered to move west from their position about three miles south of Petersburg to take the Weldon and Petersburg Railroad and disrupt the flow of supplies from the south via Wilmington, North Carolina, the South's primary entrée point for blockade runners. General Warren advanced, taking the railroad near Globe Tavern. His men tore up the tracks and burned the ties. In the afternoon, Confederate Major General Henry Heth counterattacked, attempting unsuccessfully to retake it. Confederate attacks on August 19 and August 21 were also unsuccessful. But the determination with which the attacks were made went far toward illustrating how important the railroad was to southern supply efforts.

Loss of the railroad was a serious inconvenience, but not a complete failure. The line was still usable from Wilmington to Stony Creek Depot, so supplies were shipped to that point—south of the position that Baxter held—and then carried to the west on wagons around the Union obstruction. To break this supply line and capture the critical Southside Railroad and the Danville Railroad, Grant needed to move further westward. Such a move would make Richmond impossible to supply, dealing the Confederates a blow both strategic and symbolic.

When Baxter resumed command of his brigade on August 29 it was in a far different situation than when he left it. Entombed in the earthworks outside of Petersburg "in some respects unprecedented in war," his men had become used to the life of moles.[16] The siege would last for eight months, but there were only short breaks in combat as Grant inched his men forward and to the left, always trying to encircle and cut off Lee within his defensive works. Union forces solidified their gains with new fortifications. The trenches at least offered some shelter.[17]

The men under Baxter's command were different now. The sustained violence, forced marches, lack of sleep and sustenance, intense summer heat, and the shift to fortifications and trench warfare had raised the stress upon everyone. The horrors of this protracted conflict began to desensitize soldiers. Morale was increasingly an issue.[18]

There was an unusual break on September 13, 1864, when Major General Meade visited 5th Corps. The men of Crawford's Division and all the general officers of the Corps—including Henry Baxter—attended an assembly during which Meade presented the Medal of Honor to men from the 3rd Delaware, 18th Massachusetts, and 11th Pennsylvania. After the ceremony, General Warren led the men in offering three cheers for the general before treating the officers to a brief social.[19]

By September Baxter found himself building and managing fortifications, gradually creating a salient that pushed ever westward around Petersburg.[20] Several units were sent out from these forts to reconnoiter the area to the west. This was 5th Corps territory and Baxter participated in these efforts. It was during one such operation on September 15 that 1st Lieutenant Samuel Cormany of the 16th Pennsylvania Cavalry met Baxter, spending a day as part of an action to drive in enemy pickets near Poplar Springs Church, also known as Peeble's Farm. As the day came to an end, Cormany "had the honor to become acquainted and have some talk with both Generals Warren and Baxter. Both were very affable, especially the latter."[21]

Reconnaissance showed that the "country west of the Halifax Road and south of Petersburg was virtually a military vacuum."[22] Yet, the area was important for staging any movement west, and so the Confederates could field reinforcements. Strengthening the Union defensive line in this area made sense.

Baxter was exhausted by these maneuvers. He wrote Elvira,

> I put the heading to this [letter] last evening thinking I would write a few lines, but having been up for two nights and in the saddle most of the time both day and night I found myself very dull and instead of writing I dropped myself into my bed sleeping finely until this morning—On the 15th I started on a reconnaissance at 4 o'clock in the morning with my own brigade and 800 Cavalry going some three miles beyond our picket lines. I met both rebel cavalry and Infantry but succeeded in driving them out of our way and Keeping them out of the way until we had succeeded and accomplished the object for which I was sent out—I lost but two Killed and 8 or 10 wounded. My brigade is now in two forts on our line 5 regiments in one and 4 in another and my own HD QRS between the two. The forts are something over a mile apart.[23]

Baxter's exhaustion came in part with the stress of being entrusted with an important and exposed position at the extreme southwestern end of the Union line. His men garrisoned three forts south of Petersburg. They held Fort Davison on the line of the salient a mile and a half east of the Weldon Railroad with the 94th New York and the 5th Massachusetts Battery. Fort Wadsworth was located in the northwest part of the salient facing the Confederate lines and was held by the 16th Maine, the 97th New York, and the 107th Pennsylvania under administrative control of Colonel Thomas McCoy of the latter regiment. They were supported by the 1st New York Light Artillery and Company B of the 4th U.S. Artillery. They also completed and garrisoned Fort Dushane, located on the Halifax Road near the intersection with Flank Road, just to the west of Weldon Railroad. The dirt and timber fort was a "magnificent piece of work ... in the form of a square with bastions at each corner for three guns."[24] Railroad iron was added for armor. It was manned by the 39th Massachusetts, 104th New York, and the 11th, 88th, and 90th Pennsylvania, supported by the 9th Massachusetts Battery and Company D of the 5th U.S. Artillery. Colonel Richard Coulter of the 11th Pennsylvania exercised immediate command. The incomplete fortification was an active military outpost, with the occupants alternating between construction and exploratory attacks on the adjacent enemy lines.

The most singular comment about life in Fort Dushane came from artilleryman Charles Reed who noted in September,

> [I] have been wet to the skin for days, have slept in the mud, stood in the mud, kneeled in the mud to avoid shells, worked in the mud, rode in the mud, been splattered with the mud from head to foot with mud by shot and shell and drank muddy water. Altogether we have had a nasty time of it.[25]

Generals Grant, Meade, Warren, Grant's Chief of Staff Major General Andrew Humphrey, as well as Secretary of State William H. Seward and Illinois Congressman Elihu B. Washburne visited Fort Dushane on Sunday, September 25. The visit included a briefing by General Baxter.[26] His personal interaction with the commanding generals, as well as highly placed government officials, further increased his personal contacts and no doubt his reputation.

The inspection tour was organized in advance of a planned offensive. Grant intended to send Major General Benjamin Butler against the Richmond defenses in the center, then launch units on the left—including two reserve divisions of Major General John Parke's 9th Corps, two divisions from Warren's 5th Corps (including Baxter's brigade), and most of Brigadier General David Gregg's cavalry—against the southern Petersburg defenses. They were to be ready to move at 4:00 a.m. on September 29. The objective was the railroad and important roads, but Grant was ready to exploit a break through, should it occur.

The garrison of Fort Dushane was called out just after midnight on September 29. The troops were paid two months back wages at 3:00 a.m. and fed a breakfast of baked beans. They packed up to march, but only part of the corps was sent out with cavalry toward Reams Station.

The attack was delayed until September 30. There was some doubt about the size and composition of the opposing Confederate force. As a result, Warren sent Baxter and his brigade out the Poplar Springs Road on this reconnaissance in force, basically repeating what had been done on September 15. The 39th Massachusetts encountered Confederate pickets and drove them back a mile. When they passed Poplar Spring Church and were approaching Peebles Farm, Confederate artillery opened fire. Both skirmishers and a line of battle advanced on Baxter's right flank. Having exposed the Confederate positions and strength, Baxter retired without loss by 5:00 p.m. The 5th and 9th Corps attacked, consuming a part of the Confederate line and capturing Fort Archer, located near Peebles' Farm. This moved the Union line closer to Petersburg and forced the Confederates to rework their defenses.

A series of actions in October had the 5th Corps and 9th Corps either initiating or repulsing attacks on the left flank. Grant was attempting to the push westward, expecting to build more fortifications as each advance tightened the noose. On October 27 Major General Benjamin Butler's Army of the James (the 10th and 18th Corps) struck north of the James River near the Williamsburg Road. General Parke took his 9th Corps and Warren took the 5th Corps to their left, seeking to push west through Confederate lines, cross Hatchers Run, reach the Boydton Plank Road, and then strike north to cut the South Side Railroad, the last rail connection.

Warren started forward early on October 27 from the camp near Fort Dushane. He was slowed by inclement weather and unexpected contact with enemy troops north of Armstrong's Mill. Warren led Crawford's Division forward toward Hatcher's Run. They were delayed by the dense brush and terrain, failing to connect with General Hancock's men, and were forced to retreat as a result.

The Election of November 1864 was critical in deciding the course of the war. Would the Union continue to fight to reunite the nation, or would it choose a negotiated settlement? The Republican ticket of Lincoln/Andrew Johnson argued that the continued prosecution of the war was paramount to America's future. The George McClellan/George Pendleton Democratic ticket campaigned with the opposing view that a negotiated peace was a reasonable alternative given the allusiveness of victory. Confederates understandably wanted McClellan to win since it meant securing their independence, or at least ending the war in a manner more favorable to them. On the eve of the election some even released captured Union prisoners on condition that they vote for McClellan.[27]

On November 8 Lincoln won with 55 percent of the vote, carrying all northern and western states except McClellan's home state of New Jersey, Delaware, and the border state of Kentucky. A staunch Republican, Baxter supported Lincoln. More than 75 percent of Union soldiers in the field voted for the administration. Lincoln even carried the Union-occupied Confederate states of Louisiana and Tennessee.[28]

Many northerners rejoiced at the outcome. Even with the privations of war, the horrendous loss of life, and the occasional threats of invasion, winning the war was the most important priority. As Walt Alexander wrote from upstate New York in November 1864,

> We have had some very exciting times here for the last few months what with stump seaking [*sic*] and fear of raids from Canada and mass meetings. But it is all over now and we never had a more quiet election than the last. good old Jeff. County gave a great majority for old Abe as did all the rest of New York State. I think she has done nobly this time and we can feel our hearts beat with pride once more and say I am a New York man… Hurrah for Abe[!][29]

The outcome of the Presidential election made clear what was expected of the army in the coming weeks and months. A political solution now seemed remote, crushing the morale of southerners.[30]

National politics were not the only issue. The politics of the Union army were a significant part of a general's purview. As the war was winding down it was clear that each unit would want to be credited with participation in as many important battles as possible. What battles a regiment was in would be a source of post-war pride, and could potentially make or break political careers. Regiments were already debating who did what, often times promoting their claims on their regimental colors.

To bring order to chaos, General Grant asked each corps to determine what regiments could be credited with action in specific engagements. From a rain-drenched encampment before Petersburg on November 2, Brigadier General Robert McAllister wrote,

> By order of Army Headquarters, I am on a committee of three from this Corps to decide what battles are to be placed on regimental flags. Genl. Miles, commanding the 1st Division, Capt. [R. Bruce] Ricketts, and myself are the three that are to decide for this Corps. Today we met with a similar committee from the 5th Corps to have an understanding as to what engagements are to be considered a battle. We met Genl. [Samuel W.] Crawford, Genl. [Henry] Baxter, Genl. [Edward] Ferrero, and others in counsel and decided…. It is a delicate matter; some will be disappointed and dissatisfied. But we will, by the help of God, do our duty.[31]

The decisions of Baxter, McAllister, and leaders like them would be emblazoned on hundreds of regimental flags, be lauded in regimental histories, and debated by veterans for years. As one of the decision makers, Henry Baxter's influence extended far beyond his own corps. As it became clearer that his future after the war involved the political realm, Baxter the venturist sought out opportunities to meet and impress the influential and the well-placed among both his base in Michigan and on the national level.

Baxter hoped to settle down in winter quarters, using the privileges of his rank to bring Elvira to live with him.

> I had made my arrangements for building a house to accommodate my wife dear when she gave me the pleasure of her company and should have commenced it on Monday morning when lo and behold the order came that we would be ready to leave at once which broke into my building arrangements most decidedly and leaves me all at sea again as to the probable time we may again get settled down with a show of permanency for the winter and as to the place that cannot be conjectured with an degree of assurance.[32]

Baxter misjudged Grant's intentions. Though Grant himself had quarters built for he and his wife, he had no intention of allowing his generals to settle peacefully into winter quarters. On December 7 Warren's 5th Corps was sent south along the Jerusalem Plank Road to disrupt Confederate supply lines. They marched to Hawksville, then moved to the southwest, crossing the Nottoway River and camping at Sussex Court House. On December 8 Crawford's men continued west, arriving around noon at the Weldon Railroad north of Jarratt's Station. They wrecked the line while cavalry harassed the enemy. On December 10–11 Warren withdrew, leaving the railroad in a shambles and the surrounding communities stripped of resources.

With Major General William T. Sherman's men marching south through Georgia, there were high hopes that the Confederacy's back would soon be broken. But the southern commitment remained strong in Virginia.

December 1864 closed with Baxter and 5th Corps still entrenched, gradually trying to close the noose around Richmond and Petersburg. There was a sense that the war was coming to a close, but there was no indication of exactly how or when that might occur. Still, there was confidence in a Union victory. Baxter had never strayed from his own conviction that the Union would inevitably win. Meanwhile, the people of Petersburg and Richmond suffered from the meager flow of supplies. Starvation and stress took a severe toll on the civilian population as well as the Confederate military.

9

Traitors Defeated, Home Regained, 1865–1868

General Grant had proven himself the type of man who pushed forward with energy, despite failures and disappointments. His victories were testaments to this characteristic and served the needs of Abraham Lincoln well. In 1864 he pursued a war of attrition to its logical end. Hit the enemy and keep hitting them, using superiority of numbers to keep pressure on. Using a series of assaults that allowed him to advance his fortifications south around Petersburg, Grant kept gaining ground on Lee. On March 4 Lee met with Davis and told him that defending Richmond was ruining his army. In order to fight on, the army needed to break out of the ever-shrinking perimeter and become mobile again. Lee formulated a plan for a retreat that would allow the army to reform 60 miles southwest near Burkeville.

Now desperate and after months of heated debate, on March 13, 1865, the Confederate Congress voted to accept African American soldiers into the Confederate army. Some were recruited and it appeared that the south might be willing to sacrifice the institution of slavery in order to achieve independence. But the move came too late to change the course of events.[1]

Lincoln could see the end. In his second inaugural address on March 4, he called for reunion and reconciliation with, rather than revenge against, the south.[2] Most Americans in both the north and the south agreed about one thing. They wanted the ghastly war to end.

The winter of 1864–1865 was brutal. Cold wind, freezing rain, and thick snow kept the men under cover when not forced out for military operations. Gone were the days when the winter meant relative inactivity, boredom, drill, and rest in more or less comfortable quarters. Now food was scarce and monotony and discomfort prevailed. The battle continued, with shelling, attacks and counterattacks.

Diversions were rare, but one came for Baxter January 2 when the officers of his brigade presented him with "a beautiful, a magnificent sword sash and belt."[3] To Vi he reported,

> I am proud and I feel that I have a just right to be proud, when they tell me that not an officer of my command but contributed toward the procuring of this present—I hope I may be found worthy of the feelings of respect this expressed. It has been one of the proudest days of my life and I feel that it well may have been when those with whom I have been associated for near two years in the deadly strife that has been ragging for sustaining the Honor and integrity of our country against a wicked and unjust rebellion when the whistling of the musket ball and the screech and

9. Traitors Defeated, Home Regained, 1865–1868

howl of shot and shell have laid low the stalwart forms of many,… I say when these officers say that I am worthy of this testimonial of their regard and esteem it well may have been a proud day for your husband, and it is a day that I shall remember with the deepest feeling of pleasure so long as time lasts with me.[4]

The sash was dark red and the leather sword belt was clasped by a gold buckle.

Baxter valued the admiration of the men he led, a theme recognizable in his reaction to his promotion to general officer and the gifts from the different groups of men he commanded. This characteristic connection between the recognition of his manly venturist achievements and his response to the plaudits he received from the men around him was a theme in his life. As a middle child and a boy who spent much of his life under the scrutiny of his overbearing father, this suggests that the admiration of other men replaced a level of unconditional acceptance that he lacked from his father as a child and young man.

Early in the new year Baxter served as acting Commander of the 3rd Division, 5th Corps. Division commander Major General Samuel Crawford had been temporarily appointed to command the Corps. When Warren returned on January 27, Crawford returned to command of the division, and Baxter to command of his brigade. The composition of Baxter's brigade was unchanged. The 107th Pennsylvania was briefly attached to the 3rd Brigade on February 5, but returned to Baxter's command early on March 29.

Supplies were still flowing into Confederates lines via the South Side Railroad and the Weldon Railroad via a circuitous route. Wagon trains linked the railroad, making the trek from the terminus of the severed railway line all the way around the extended left flank of Grant's army. In February Grant instructed Meade to do something about it. On February 5, General David Gregg's cavalry, supported by Warren's 5th Corps moved west. Warren's men broke ice while crossing Rowanty Creek and routed a small Confederate force. Crawford's Division held the intersection of Vaughan and State Roads. Major General Andrew Humphrey's 2nd Corps met stubborn resistance too as it shielded Warren's advance and held river crossings to ease Warren's retreat.

Baxter's 2nd Brigade was encamped on the Jerusalem Plank Road on February 5. At 7:00 a.m. the brigade moved out in "light marching order" with four days rations. The 3rd Division marched west to the Halifax Road, then south, crossing Rowanty Creek and bearing westward onto Vaughan Road, where it formed line of battle, encountered some resistance, and bivouacked for the night on Gravelly Run farm.[5]

At 4:00 a.m. on February 6 the brigade was again on the move, marching back to Hatcher's Run. There they massed on the north bank and waited. Warren was providing time for Humphreys to reconnoiter toward Dinwiddie Court House. However, Meade meant for Warren's Corps to reconnoiter also and arrived at Warren's headquarters and told him so. At 2:00 p.m. the division recrossed Hatcher's Run, the 2nd Brigade trailing, and advanced upon the Confederate works near Dabney's Mill. Baxter was ordered forward, moving the 39th Massachusetts and 16th Maine into line on the left. The 97th New York, 11th and 88th Pennsylvania were formed up behind as they advanced into heavy fire. General A.P. Hill's Confederates were driven back and the division occupied Dabney's Mill, described as "an elevated position formed from the debris of an old mill."[6]

The position was held until the Confederates reorganized and attacked with reinforcements, driving the Union line back 200 yards. The division counter-attacked, again retaking the mill. The reinforced Confederates attacked, driving the Union line backward again. The troops on Baxter's left were forced back, subjecting his brigade to a "galling flank fire." Baxter was able to check the slippage. He threw up a "slight protection of logs," and held on. The brigade was out of ammunition and awaiting resupply about dark when they were again attacked. The troops to the left gave way and his brigade "fell back in some disorder." Baxter retreated across Hatcher's Run, massed his people, bivouacked, and remained there until the following morning.[7] This fight was described by witnesses on both sides as one of the hottest of the war.[8]

The night was uncomfortable for friend and foe alike. The troops contended with rain and a cold wind that froze their clothes. Then it began to snow. Some Confederates "plundered" the dead for clothing. They slept as best they could on the frozen ground, the exhaustion eventually overcoming their discomfort.[9]

At 9:00 a.m. on February 7 Baxter received orders to move forward in the lead of the division and retake the ground around the mill. The brigade was formed amid a gale that blew all day. The 39th Massachusetts in the lead followed by the 11th Pennsylvania deployed as a double line of skirmishers, the balance of the brigade advancing in line of battle upon the enemy position to the right near Armstrong Mill. Crawford's Division drove the Confederates skirmishers in, retaking most of the battlefield and clearing the Confederates from their rifle pits back to the main line of breastworks. Baxter halted his advance about 300 yards from the enemy's works and was ordered to hold. The 57th Pennsylvania detached to serve as reserve. The entire day was spent in heavy skirmishing. At 6:00 p.m. the division attacked the enemy's works en masse, but were repulsed. The brigade returned to the skirmish line, holding it until 9:00 p.m. when it was relieved by a brigade from the 6th Corps. Baxter ordered his men to throw up a breastwork about 400 yards from the enemy's works, connecting up with units to the right and left, making this the new line of advance. At 1:00 a.m. on February 8 Baxter marched his men back to the north side of Hatcher's Run, where they bivouacked.[10] Baxter was to be recognized for his leadership in this engagement. The Union losses in this action totaled 1,539, comparable to Confederate loss of about 1,000 men.

On February 10 the brigade moved close to the Halifax Road, where it camped for the rest of the month. Major General Warren wrote that Baxter's "old and reliable brigade" numbered only 52 officers and 800 men.[11]

There was little doubt that the Confederacy had a short time to live. By March 7 Lee had issued plans for an evacuation of Richmond and Petersburg. Throughout March ideas of how to extricate the Army of Northern Virginia and regain some initiative were discussed. Peace with concessions to southern demands was elusive and abandonment of the capital without a fight was unthinkable to President Davis. That left only a concentrated attack upon the Union forces at their weakest point as the best option. The center of the Union position at Petersburg, just south of the Appomattox River near Fort Stedman, was selected because of the challenges the Union would have of moving reinforcements across the river. Major General John Gordon was chosen to lead the offensive and he developed plans to carry not only Fort Stedman, but also open a corridor into the Union rear where southern cavalry could exploit the confusion while infantry widened the gap. This plan would confuse the enemy, allowing the army to evacuate safely and unite with the forces of Major General Joseph Johnston in North Carolina. Confederate defenses were stripped to provide as much support as possible.

Union forces prepared in their own way for spring. Baxter's men were reviewed on March 14 by Meade, on March 15 by President Lincoln, and on March 16 by Secretary of War Edwin Stanton, General Meade, and General Warren.[12]

Late on March 24 and early the following morning Confederate troops were shifted to support the offensive. The attack was launched from Colquitt's Salient in the pre-dawn hours of March 25, sending 11,500 Confederates against the Union works. The attack was at first successful, the Confederates capturing three batteries, Fort Stedman, and surrounding trenches before first light. Surprise and panic slowed the concentration of Union forces, but by dawn northern reinforcements were rushing to the breech. Baxter's Brigade moved up to support the 9th Corps at Fort Stedman, but the attack had already been repelled. Gordon saved as many of his men as he could, returning them to Confederate lines. Southern casualties were about 4,000. Union casualties were about half that. No significant result was achieved.[13]

In late March Grant recalled Major General Philip Sheridan and his 5,000 cavalry from northwestern Virginia. Sheridan converged on the Richmond-Petersburg perimeter, following orders from Grant to pressure Lee at Dinwiddie Court House. Sheridan attempted to turn Lee's flank, territory held by Major General George Pickett at the Battle of Dinwiddie Court House on March 29.

At 6:00 a.m. on March 29 Baxter's brigade broke camp near Hatcher's Run with 5th Corps and moved southwest across Rowanty Creek, taking the Quaker Road to the intersection of Gravelly Run and the Boydton Plank Road before crossing Gravelly Run near the Spain House. The Confederates tried to outflank the division, but were out maneuvered. Baxter's brigade formed line of battle with the 1st Division to their right and the 3rd Brigade on their left, before deploying skirmishers. The Confederates retreated, leaving the brigade to bivouac in a field near the Boydton Plank Road, a highway of great strategic importance.

The following day in heavy rain, the brigade moved up to a position parallel to the plank road, where they threw up breast works and felled timber in front of their position to provide a clear field of fire. They stayed there through the day and the following night.

On March 31 Pickett learned that the opposing 5th Corps was anticipating reinforcements and tried to withdraw to a safer position on the other side of Hatcher's Run. However, Lee put a stop to this, ordering him instead to a position at the critical crossroads of White Oak Road, Scott's Road, Ford's (Church) Road, and the Dinwiddie Court House Road in order to save the Southside Railway, the major supply corridor to Richmond. This place, known as Five Forks was described as

> a magnificent strategic point. Five good roads meet in the edge of a dry, high, well-watered forest, three of them radiating to the railway, and their tributaries unlocking all the country.[14]

Lee's dispatch ordered Pickett to hold this crossroads whatever the cost. Pickett's men threw up basic fortifications.

On March 31 Baxter's brigade was called out early, forming line of battle about 6:30 a.m. They abandoned their works and Baxter led them down the Boydton Plank Road about two miles. The rain continued all night and forenoon, "rendering the roads deep with mud and water swelling the streams."[15] They filed off to the right, halted, and waited in a wood with Gravelly Run on their right. The 2nd Division on their left advanced, only to be pushed back beyond their original position by the Confederates. Baxter came under fire and took his brigade across Gravelly Run to keep it from being cut off and captured. There he reformed it and the advance of the enemy was stopped. At 3:00 p.m. he moved forward, recrossing the river and recovering the lost ground. He threw up breast works near White Oak Road and connected with the 2nd Division to hold the ground. The brigade bivouacked there for the night.[16]

Pickett's Confederates were consolidated behind works at the critical Five Forks junction. On the evening of April 1 Major General Philip Sheridan advanced on Pickett, planning to keep the Confederates in place by using his cavalry to demonstrate in front and on Pickett's right flank, while he sent General Warren's 5th Corps in a sweeping flanking maneuver on Pickett's left. Sheridan's combined force of 22,000 men pushed back Pickett's 10,600 men, who were left leaderless by Pickett's absence at a picnic.

Confusion was created by terrain "composed of woods, fields, thickets of underbrush, swamps, ditches, streams, &c" that threw Warren's attack into disarray.[17] While the 2nd Division under Brigadier General Romeyn Ayers struck Pickett's left flank, Brigadier General Samuel Crawford's 3rd Division—including Baxter's brigade, and Brigadier General Charles Griffin's 1st Division were staged near White Oak Road to the east of Five Forks. They marched to Gravelly Run Church at 3:00 p.m. Baxter formed the brigade on the right of the 3rd Division, between the 1st Brigade commanded by Colonel Kellogg and the 3rd Brigade commanded by General Coulter. The line was ordered to advance at 3:30, driving the enemy skirmishers in as they went. The brigade reached White Oak Road, wheeled to the left, moved parallel with the road, and flanked the Confederate works. They attacked the rebel position, forcing them to retreat in great confusion, followed closely by Baxter's men until dark. One stand of colors and several wagons and ambulances were captured. Baxter's brigade reached Ford's Road around 5:00 p.m. cutting the Confederates off from retreat to the north and forcing them to flee through forest and undergrowth to avoid capture.[18]

Writer George Townsend reported that General Crawford "fulfilled his full share of duties throughout the day, amply sustained by such splendid brigade commanders as Henry Baxter, Richard Coulter, and John A. Kellogg." He saved the highest praise for General Joshua Chamberlain and his sustained attack on the Confederate left which pinned down the enemy and created the opportunity for the others to advance.[19] In his report of the battle, Colonel Thomas McCoy leading the 117th Pennsylvania wrote,

> The movement and the fighting continued, we driving the enemy all the time, until dark ended the battle, being one of the most grand, complete, and important victories of the war. Indeed, it seems to have been the turning point in the great movements against Petersburg and Richmond and the destruction of Lee's army, as all of these important places and that great army that has confronted us for nearly four long, wearisome, bloody years soon after fell into our possession.[20]

Nearly a third of Pickett's men were casualties and the rest barely escaped.

Sheridan was a ruthless and zealous combat soldier who spared little patience for those that did not act as he felt necessary. Toward the end of the battle he removed General Warren, as he had dismissed others, because "the officer was simply not aggressive enough."[21] Ironically, he removed Warren from command just as he had achieved the objective set out for him. This action cast a pall over what was otherwise a great victory and ruined Warren's military career.

Pickett's defeat at Five Forks left Lee with little alternative but to abandoned his entrenched position around Petersburg and Richmond. He informed Jefferson Davis that he would need to withdraw. Grant had the opportunity to force Lee out of the Richmond-

Petersburg position and he knew it. On the evening of April 1, he ordered a general advance upon the Confederate lines.

Just after midnight on the morning of April 2 a general bombardment began. The exchange of artillery fire lasted three hours. An attack followed at 4:00 a.m., beginning 18 hours of continuous combat during which the Confederates were first pushed back, then counterattacked, and finally withdrew from their works toward an inner line of defense.

Lee informed Davis that Richmond would fall that day. Davis asked Lee to hold as long as he could while the capital was evacuated and valuable government stores were moved. Now facing a wave of advancing blue coats, Lee tore up the note, saying, "I am sure I gave him sufficient notice."[22]

Chaos spread as the evacuation began and discipline broke down. The burning of the Confederate arsenal and tobacco warehouses created uncontrolled fires that the wind spread throughout the city, damaging or destroying more than 900 buildings. Davis evacuated with his cabinet about 11:00 p.m. via railroad to Danville, Virginia. Under the cover of darkness Lee began to withdraw Confederate troops through Richmond. At midnight the Confederate evacuation of Petersburg began, the soldiers passing between lines of weeping civilians who knew now that they would be left to the mercy of the hated Yankees.

Grant was calm in the face of the Confederate evacuation. Setting up his headquarters in a private Petersburg residence, he shook off suggestions from subordinates that he should pursue Lee closely. He did not want to pursue Lee, he wanted to get ahead of him and trap his army. He quickly issued orders to this effect. This aggressiveness in the face of a general melee was exactly what the Union needed to bring the bloody war to a conclusion.

General Sheridan's cavalry and the 5th Corps raced to get ahead of Lee as he retreated westward. Baxter's brigade marched to Hatcher's Run and crossed the South Side Railroad, catching and attacking the retreating Confederate column at midnight after a 25-mile pursuit. The Confederates withdrew before daylight, leaving enough gear by the roadside to show that they were now retreating in greater than normal haste.

The first Union soldiers arrived in Richmond about 7:00 a.m. on the morning of April 3. By 8:00 the Confederate flag was lowered and Richmond was the capital of the southern states no more. Meanwhile, Baxter's men were marching west toward Jetersville when word reached the line that Petersburg and Richmond had fallen. "Great cheering and most hearty rejoicing" swept the ranks as the great rush westward continued.[23]

On April 4 Lee continued west, arriving at Amelia Court House. He hoped to link up with General Johnston in North Carolina and continue the fight. But his army had little food with it and attempts to forage met with limited success.

After a two day march interspersed with attacks on the retreating Confederates, Baxter's exhausted brigade followed the cavalry into Jetersville, about 45 miles from Richmond and Petersburg. There they were able to cut off the Richmond and Danville Railroad and throw up breastworks in anticipation of a Confederate attack.

April 5 found Baxter's brigade still holding those works. Units of the Union army were making a dash westward to stay with Lee and allow him no time to recover. Grant was afraid that Lee's army would escape, and ordered Sheridan to get his cavalry in front and stop the Confederates from turning south.

At Amelia Springs on April 6 Lee realized that he was cut off from reaching Danville for victuals he expected to come up by train. Blocked by Union cavalry to the south, early that morning Lee turned west toward Farmville, 19 miles away, hoping that he could be resupplied. The 5th Corps formed line of battle and advanced on the Confederates in their front, still presumed to be in Amelia Springs. The remaining Confederates withdrew and joined the rest of Lee's army moving west. Fifth Corps turned toward Farmville in pursuit on the Painesville Road. The 2nd and 6th Corps pursued via other roads.

Later that day multiple Union units caught up with Lee's rear guard at Saylors Creek. The attack that followed was a disaster for the Confederates, with nearly one-quarter of the army and eight general officers killed or captured. Artillery and supply trains were taken.

Lee continued west with the survivors, arriving at Farmville on the night of April 6–7. There he was briefly able to feed some of his men. An attempt to burn High Bridge on Antietam Creek failed, allowing Grant's men to cross the bridge and continue the pursuit unabated.

Grant sent a letter to Lee, requesting his surrender. Some of Lee's officers were for surrender, but Lee himself was not. Neither was Davis who urged Lee to continue the fight. Lee decided to continue moving to Appomattox Court House where he expected more food to be awaiting his soldiers. He sent a non-committal letter to Grant, asking about terms for surrender.

Baxter's brigade was in pursuit on April 7, and camped that night near Prince Edward Court House, three miles southwest of Farmville, having marched more than twenty miles that day.

On April 8 Grant sent surrender terms. The Confederate forces continued westward, massing at Appomattox Court House. Union forces were urged forward to trap the Confederates. Baxter's brigade began marching at 6:00 a.m. on April 8, covering 35 miles by 2:00 a.m. on April 9, further tightening the noose.

On the morning of April 9 (Palm Sunday) Union forces were converging. Baxter's brigade was only a few miles away and cannonading was audible. They marched—Baxter's brigade leading the division—and quickly reached the front lines. There, Colonel T.F. McCoy of the 107th Pennsylvania reported,

> We soon came near the spot where this last skirmish with the rebel army took place, and found that the cavalry under Sheridan, part of the Twenty-fourth Corps, and our own (Fifth Corps) were occupying the road leading through Appomattox Court-House toward Lynchburg, over which General Lee with his army must pass if he ever succeeded in reaching that point. At this time our columns were forming to advance upon the enemy, then a short distance east of the Court-House.[24]

Lee held a council of war in which both surrender and continuation of the war as a guerrilla campaign was discussed with depressingly little hope of success. Lee came through the lines for a 1:00 p.m. meeting with Grant at the McLean House. After a short discussion of terms, he formally surrendered the Army of Northern Virginia.

News of the surrender was announced at 4:00 p.m. Celebration broke out along the Union lines, but Grant quickly quashed this. On April 10 Jefferson Davis learned that Lee had surrendered. He vowed to continue the fight, fleeing with most of the Confederate government by train. On April 11 the news of Lee's surrender sparked celebrations in Washington. Baxter's brigade remained camped near Appomattox through April 14 as the surrender was consummated.

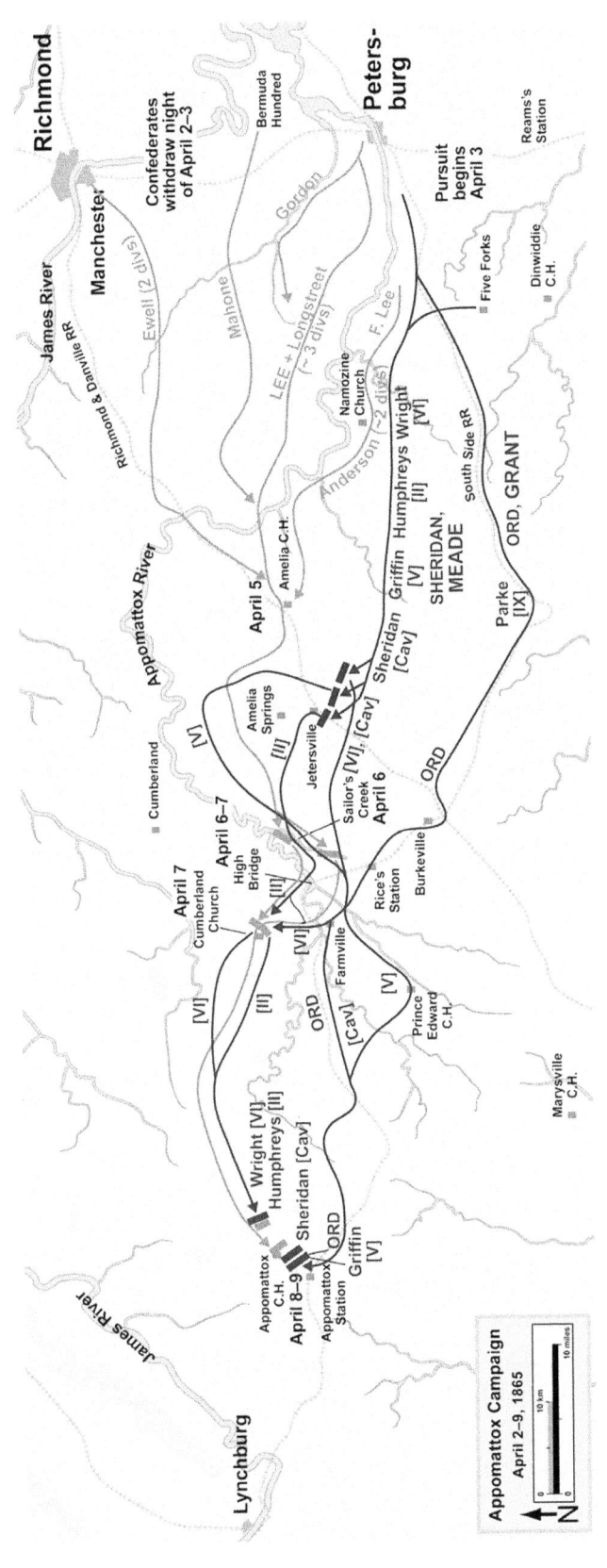

The Confederate defeat at Five Forks sent the Army of the Potomac—including Baxter's Brigade—on a headlong run to get ahead of Lee's retreating army. The pursuit ended with Lee's surrender at Appomattox. Map by Hal Jespersen, www.cwmaps.com.

The surrender of General Robert E. Lee's Army of Northern Virginia was a historic moment that no one in the Army of the Potomac would ever forget. Daniel Bentz of the 190th Pennsylvania wrote on April 26,

> I will let you know that us Soldiers have Easy times at Present. Our Regiment is Camped in a nice Woods, Alongside the Railroad about Four Miles from Nottoway Court House. It is most a Splendid neighborhood. Plenty of good Drinking Water. We Marched to this Place Since the surrender of Gen Lees Army[.] This Place is Fourty [sic] Miles from Appomatox Court, Where Gen Lee surrendered ... a place Which I shall never forget as long as I live, Friend Dave. I will now tell you the day that General Lee Surrendered His whole army to Gen Grant It was on Sunday the 9th Day of April at 10 O'Clock Forenoon[.] Our Regiment was on the Skirmish line, the hour that Gen Lee Presented his white Flag for a surrender General Sheridans Cavalry Force and the 5th Corps Formly [sic] commanded By Major Gen Warren Had Gen Lees army Entirely Surrounded. Lee had no way for to get out Whatever. He was Compelled to surrender[.] His Whole army was Paroled as a Prisoner of War and sent to their homes all free of Transportation[.] I suppose it was quite an Excitement in Manheim [Pennsylvania] when the news reached there about Gen Lees surrender. You cant imagine how it was out here in the army[.] It was one of the greatest Excitement I saw in my life time.[25]

Colonel Thomas McCoy of the 117th Pennsylvania closed his action report of April 14 with words that were reflective of the way the younger regiments saw the momentous events so recently unfolded:

> In closing this, which will doubtless be the last and final report of battles for this regiment, I would express my gratitude to a kind and ever merciful Providence that He has permitted us to pass through the many exposures, hardships, and great perils of this last great and closing campaign of an unprecedented war with comparatively so little sacrifice of life and blood, and that the lives and the health of so many brave officers and men of the regiment have been preserved, under the shield of His almighty power during the past three eventful years, to return to their homes to dwell in peace and rejoice over violated laws vindicated, a righteous Government preserved, the Union restored, and the old flag re-established with more than its original power, beauty, and significance, in some honorable degree through their instrumentality.[26]

For older units that had bled themselves to near extinction in the service of the cause, the joy was tempered by recognition of how many had been sacrificed. More than 752,000 lives were lost as a result of the Civil War.[27]

The news of Lee's surrender stunned many in the south who refused to believe "the cause" was lost. Catherine Edmondston's reaction may have been indicative of others on the home front when she wrote in her journal on April 16,

> How can I write it? How find words to tell what has befallen us? *Gen Lee has surrendered!* Surrendered the remnant of his noble Army to an overwhelming horde of mercenary Yankee knaves & foreigners....
>
> Since we heard of our disaster I ... I go about in a kind of *"drowsy dream."* I sleep, sleep, sleep endlessly; if I sit in my chair for ten minutes, I doze. I think of it, but I cannot grasp it or its future consequences. I sit benumbed.[28]

With complete faith in both the "cause" and the invincibility of Lee's army, southerners who had sacrificed so much faced the loss of the society and institutions they cherished.

⇒ ⇐

The joy of the surrender and dispersal of Confederate forces nationwide was tempered by the assassination of President Lincoln by John Wilkes Booth on April 14. Despite the

9. Traitors Defeated, Home Regained, 1865–1868

antipathy that many soldiers felt toward the political forces that sent them again and again into peril, the sudden death of their wartime leader at the moment of victory was too much to take. Many, including the new President Andrew Johnson, believed that the south should be punished for this act. Fortunately, cooler heads prevailed.[29]

Though the church bells in the south tolled Lincoln's passing illustrated a respectful sorrow, many southerners blamed Lincoln for the Civil War and privately rejoiced at his death. These feelings were rarely expressed in public for fear of reprisal by Union troops.[30]

On April 19 Lincoln's funeral procession down Pennsylvania Avenue allowed the capital to express grief and show respect. So too did the funeral train that made its way across the northern states release pent up tensions. Lincoln's assassination hardened northern determination to put the twin issues of states rights and slavery to an end forever.

Most southerners had no heart to reopen the conflict. One of the most defiant was Confederate President Jefferson Davis, who finally declared that the insurrection was at an end on May 9, a day before he was captured. On May 13 the final engagement of the war occurred at Palmetto Ranch about 12 miles east of Brownsville, Texas. On May 26 in New Orleans Confederate General Kirby Smith surrendered the last major Confederate army. By the end of May, the major elements of the southern political and military infrastructure had disintegrated. On June 23 the last Confederate force in the field surrendered.

There remained the capture and pacification of small Confederate military and militia units in the south and west. Much of the south was in chaos, demoralized with the destruction of property, the social upheaval caused by the end of slavery, and the poverty that followed the war and the post-war economic depression. With the breakdown of authority, the Union Army assumed a police function. The influx of northern politicians and opportunists—the "carpet baggers"—created even more need for military intervention. The occupation had begun.

⸺

The Union command was quick to recall its forces. On April 15 Baxter's Brigade was ordered to Burkeville Junction, which it reached on the 17th after "a leisurely march eastward."[31] On April 20 the brigade was ordered to relieve the 9th Corps "in performance of duty on line of the Richmond and Danville Railroad."[32] Brigade headquarters were established at Blacks and Whites Station on April 21. The brigade composed of 86 officers and 1,506 men covered the six miles between Nottaway Court House and Blacks and Whites Station until April 30.

On May 1 the men of the 5th Corps—now under the leadership of Major General Charles Griffin—decamped and began the march home. On May 2 they camped outside Petersburg, and marched in review through the city the following day. On May 4, they were at Manchester, just across the James River from Richmond, and camped within sight of the notorious Libby Prison. Henry wrote to Elvira:

> Here I am finally in Richmond, the former Head Quarters of rebellion.... I say in Richmond, but I am some ¾ of a mile out altho I have ridden through the city this afternoon on this 4th day of May. I went through Libby Prison with Lieut Knaggs who enjoyed this his second much more than his first visit. It now contains a few rebel prisoners but very few however. One who reigned there but a few weeks since (Dick Turner) is now confined in a cell and lives on bread and water. It has been a very handsome and pleasant city but the business portion is in ruins the

work of themselves, however. Yesterday we passed through Petersburg before which we have lain so long and around which we have fought so many battles. It was a fine town also, but has had to pay the penalty of war—We shall remain here but a short time.... Shall march to Washington which will take from 7 to 10 days and I should not be surprised if the Armies of the United States were there about the same time. Their work is done.[33]

He enclosed a "rose & bud" from Petersburg and a "sprig of trees" from the grounds of the Confederate capitol in Richmond. He bought a copy of the April 17, 1865, *Richmond Whig* as a souvenir.[34]

On May 6 Baxter led his men across the James River and marched in review through the ruins of Richmond. Far from cowering, the civilians of the Confederate capital rationalized their defeat:

> The vast armies of our conquerors, on their homeward march, now began to pour through the streets of Richmond. Day after day, as we witnessed the passage of the countless, and as they seemed to us interminable legions of the enemy, against which our comparatively little army had so obstinately, and all but successfully held out for four years, the question that arose in our minds, was not why we were conquered at last, but "how we could have so long resisted the mighty appliances which operated against us." Our pride, our glory in our countrymen was heightened, and we felt indeed, "the South is the land for soldiers," and though our enemies triumphed, it was at a price that was felt by them.[35]

Baxter and his men passed through Hanover Court House and Fredericksburg, crossing the battle ground that they had reason to remember so well. Many uncovered their heads in recognition of fallen comrades. They went on to Fairfax Court House and finally Arlington Heights, where the entire corps camped near Ball's Crossroads on May 12. Multiple corps camped there.[36]

By now the Corps, Division, and Brigade commanders were quite adept at keeping troops busy for extended periods in camp. So "drills were held daily, and camp duties were performed, to keep the men in hand, for all were impatient at the delay that postponed the supreme moment when we should end with being soldiers and become peaceful citizens of the restored Republic."[37]

⇒ ⇐

As April turned to May there was growing support for a celebration worthy of the enormity of the challenge met and the number of men lost. Only a month after Lincoln's spectacular funeral procession, a grand review of the army was scheduled for May 23.

Symbolic of the nation, Washington had changed significantly during the war. The Capitol Dome had been under construction when the war began. By mid–1865 the exterior was complete and the interior was nearing completion. Washington itself had better streets, with lighting, sidewalks, and crossings. Horse-drawn street cars were in wide use. In general, the place had a business-like bustle that had replaced the messy, dull feel of four years before.

And down these bustling streets the grand review was to march on May 23. Major Abner Small, commanding the 16th Maine, wrote,

> The line of march was bordered by a vast throng of spectators, and happy faces and gay colors contrasted strangely with the black draperies which everywhere proclaimed grief for the martyred President Lincoln. The gloom of the capital city could not modify the heartfelt joy of everyone that our days of fighting were done.

9. Traitors Defeated, Home Regained, 1865–1868

The review was indeed a magnificent spectacle. The vanity of Halleck, that prince of military humbugs, and of President Johnson, must have been fully gratified. I can't say one good word for it, in principle; yet I must admit that I enjoyed my part in the show. I was conscious of great honor and good fortune in riding at the head of my regiment; and because I was riding there, I was showered with flowers and bouquets. My colored servant, George, walked all the way beside my horse, and I handed the flowers down to him, when I had kissed them to acknowledge the kindness of the givers. He was fairly smothered in the fragrant blossoms. From their midst rose his contented and continual gurgling laugh; they made him forget his hunger.[38]

In this magnificent display of military force, Small rode some distance behind his brigade commander. Brigadier General Henry Baxter rode at the head of the 2nd Brigade, 3rd Division, 5th Corps, twelfth general from the front of the corps as the troops marched down Pennsylvania Avenue and past the White House reviewing stand.

The end of the war brought into focus for state politicians the power of the dispersed electorate that would soon be returning home. Men scheduled to be released from military service would be an important force at the polls, so steps were taken to help them see potential post-war leaders in a positive light.

Current and potential Michigan politicians took one last opportunity to be remembered in a positive way. The single most important topic was not hard to imagine. Most soldiers simply wanted to know when they would be released to go home. Andy Ewing of the 2nd Michigan wrote home on May 26,

> The goviner of mich and old Baxter of Jonesville and Colonel [C.J.] Dickison of hillsdale and 4 or 5 others was here yesterday and made us a speech[.] [T]he 1, 2–20, 17, 27 Mich Redge was all Marched to one place[.] [T]hey all that spoke and that was 8 or 10 of them all seamed to think that we all would soon get home but yet did not say how long they thaught it would be but I hope it wont be long[.][39]

With so many Michigan regiments in one place, Governor Henry H. Crapo, General Baxter, Colonel Dickinson, and others were able to give the men good news. The news would get better the following month when Michiganders learned that General Baxter would be one of those in charge of shrinking the army and sending home its soldiers quickly and efficiently.

Baxter must have considered himself well-situated politically in Michigan. Being able to have these Michigan veterans have their last memory of service be of the rapid discharge presided over by General Baxter meant that he could be remembered positively. The name recognition alone would be valuable at the polls. Even better, when Governor Crapo assumed his office on January 3 his Lieutenant Governor was his old friend and fellow Republican Ebenezer Grosvenor of Jonesville. The venturist had learned from community, business, and military establishments. Now he was ready to apply his extended local knowledge to post-war politics.

The administration of President Andrew Johnson focused on the rapid demobilization of the world's largest and most expensive army. Union demobilization was the hurried invention of Assistant Adjutant General Thomas Vincent, who provided an outline to Secretary of War Edwin Stanton in May. The plan was very basic. Regular army units were to serve out their enlistments. Volunteer troops were to be gathered at nine sites scattered around the country for processing. Once their service records were accurately compiled, they were to be sent on to their state where they would be mustered for discharge. The intent was to disperse the troops as quickly as possible, allowing federal back pay and state enlistment bounties to be paid closer to their point of origin with the hope that they would make it home with most of the money still in their pockets.[40]

On June 22 Assistant Adjutant General Colonel George D. Ruggles inquired of 5th Army Corps commander Griffin what "general officers of the Fifth Corps [are] 'most entitled to and best fitted for assignment to command.'"[41] Griffin ranked Henry Baxter third behind Romeyn B. Ayres and Joshua Lawrence Chamberlain. Ayres was an 1847 West Point Graduate and Division commander at the end of the war, while Chamberlain was a former college professor, hero of Little Round Top at Gettysburg, and a Division commander. Baxter was, at the time of this communication, commanding the 3rd Division.

Provisional commanders were to rapidly discharge volunteers, while providing a force to keep order. Regular troops were to be retained and used to occupy the south, provide national defense, and occupy territories in the west. General Griffin's recommendations led to the assignment of "Third Division, from Sixth Corps.—Brevet Maj.-Gen. B.B. Ayres, commanding division. First Brigade, Brig.-Gen. J.L. Chamberlain, commanding. Second Brigade, Brig.-Gen. Henry Baxter, commanding. Third Brigade, Brig.-Gen. Joseph Hayes, commanding" for the Provisional Corps on June 28 when the Army of the Potomac was officially disbanded.[42] All the volunteer regiments were to be staged at "some healthy location on the Baltimore and Ohio Railroad, west of the Monocacy" for discharge and transport home.[43]

Baxter remained in the service through the summer. He was promoted one step to Major General of Volunteers on May 31 for gallantry at the Wilderness, Dabney's Mills, and Five Forks. The promotion was made retroactive to April 1. Along with other Union general officers, he was presented by a grateful Congress with a beautiful commemorative sword that cost $1,500.[44]

———

Even before he returned home, it was clear that Baxter had made some decisions. In June Reeves & Selfridge leased the Baxter Planning Mill and Sash, Door, and Blind Factory. This move indicated that Henry did not expect to return to business as he knew it before the war.

The job of dispersing state volunteer regiments was over in late July and Major General Baxter started home, to be mustered out with the remaining volunteers via blanket order of the Adjutant General on August 24, 1865. Like the other military leaders of the Civil War, he had a reasonable expectation that the notoriety that he achieved during the conflict would propel him into a prosperous and prominent post-war career in politics and government service.

Baxter finally arrived back in Jonesville in early August to be "welcomed by friends and relatives."[45] With the war over, he and those like him understood that winning the war did not necessarily win the peace. As former Michigan Governor Austin Blair remarked at Hudson that Independence Day,

> The great question of reconstruction, we still have now to grapple. The people of the south are conquered and have been compelled to give up the struggle, but they are not cleansed. A con-

9. Traitors Defeated, Home Regained, 1865–1868

quered rebel is a rebel still, though he may swear a hundred oaths, and if he can gain by political chicanery what he has failed to win by battle, he will certainly do it.[46]

Baxter would come to experience the wisdom of these sentiments first hand.

Baxter wasted little time in applying for his pension. On August 25 he listed his services to the government in a petition. He declared that he was not presently working much, but when he did he "wrote in a lawyer's office," his brother Witter's law practice.[47] He was successful in his application.

The rapidly fading glory of their Civil War rank left most of the 1,100 generals from the north and south with a basic dilemma; what to do next? Those Union generals that had or sought careers in the military could—usually with significantly reduced rank to fit within the peace time establishment—continue in the service. They were dispersed to posts around the country, including the reconstruction districts of the south. Those that came from thriving pre-war careers in business, engineering, or politics often returned to them. But many sought a change that would maintain them within the footlights of a national stage.[48]

The future Baxter had in mind for himself was unveiled on September 14 when an extensive biography appeared in the *Jonesville Telegraph*. The majority of the article was dedicated to his exploits in the late war, but there was enough to remind readers that he had long been active and influential in Hillsdale County politically, commercially, and socially.[49] With all the connections that he made on the national level during the war, he knew that he could convert a county level public office into an elected or appointed federal post.

Henry did not completely abandon either his or his father's business interests. Witter delayed settling Levi's estate to give Henry time to capture properties of especial value to him. Two months after his return to Jonesville, Witter held a public auction of Levi's properties at his old machine shop on West Street. On October 13 Henry was the highest bidder on three parcels along the St. Joseph River and mill race in Jonesville for a total of $2,000.[50]

As the war years drew to a close, Jonesville, Hillsdale County, and the State of Michigan were at the height of their power and influence. The 1865 Michigan Census showed Fayette Township (Jonesville) with a population of 1,469 (8.8 percent of the county) and Hillsdale with a population of 3,117 (18.6 percent of the county). Fayette had fallen behind in all areas of manufacturing. Yet, an atypical percentage of the Hillsdale County men who had made their mark in the early statehood period and during the Civil War came from Jonesville. Now they were in positions to exert tremendous influence through the Republican Party.

The Baxters were the leaders. Witter was a successful attorney active in state and local education and agriculture. Benjamin in Tecumseh was also a successful attorney involved in education on the state level and contemplating a run for the Michigan legislature. Henry had achieved and maintained a high profile based on his recent military service.

Their friends and business associates in Jonesville were doing well. Ebenezer Oliver Grosvenor became Lieutenant Governor of Michigan (1865–1867), then moved on to become State Treasurer (1867–1871), president of the Board of State Building Commissioners (1871–1879) tasked with designing and building the new state capitol, and a member of the Board of Regents of the University of Michigan (1879–1888). He operated the local bank and several insurance companies, and was also Vice President of the Fort Wayne, Jackson, and Saginaw Railroad Company.

Adonijiah Welch went from founding President of what is now Eastern Michigan University, to serve a partial term as United States Senator from Florida during Reconstruction, and in 1869 the founding President of Iowa State University at Ames.

Shockingly few of the original members of the 7th Michigan that left Monroe four years before returned home in the summer of 1865. During the war the regiment was decimated by disease, combat, and fatigue. Of those mustered in August 1861, less than 11 percent reenlisted after their three year term of service and were in the regiment the entire war. Four percent were in other units by the time the war ended. Although a number joined regular army units, only one is known to have a career in the post-war army.[51]

Baxter could count himself lucky. Of the 1020 that mustered into service with the 7th Michigan in August 1861, 73 percent survived the war. Of the roughly 100 men of Baxter's original complement of Company C, only ten percent remained in the 7th Michigan at the end of the war. Approximately half did not reenlist, were retired upon a surgeon's certificate of disability, or were discharged and lived to return home.[52]

The 7th Michigan earned an inspirational epitaph from Norman Hall, who inherited the regiment at a difficult time. Upon his departure from command on July 9, 1864, he wrote an emotional farewell, asserting, "You have written your history high upon the column erected to commemorate the names of the men and their mighty deeds that are to be the ground work of the grand tragedy of the present age. Upon that stage of History glorious brighten with fames and honors than any other in the whole record of mans endurance and achievements your number is all glorious and your star suffers not in luster by comparison with any other."[53]

The war might be over, but the paperwork lived on. Early in 1866 Baxter was still completing paperwork for gear and ordinance used by the 7th Michigan and his brigade. In May of that year he was finally cleared of any responsibility for equipment used by men under his command. He was also corresponding with Major General Warren who was—given his own ill-usage at the hands of the military establishment—determined that Baxter and other men under his command received credit for their heroism and long service to their country.[54]

Henry Baxter came to grips with his own mortality. Though involved in the Presbyterian Church his entire life, like his father and siblings he exhibited an independence of spirit not entirely in keeping with the strictest faith. But his experiences on many bloody fields of battle and his own survival despite his frequent exposure to enemy fire lay heavy upon his mind. He wrote, "I see and feel my own strength is but weakness, but I have the assurances through the promises of God that I may come ask for all needed help and for the sake of our blessed Savior Jesus it will be given."[55] He determined to dedicate his life to God. On Sunday, May 6, 1866, he went forward with his daughter Jennie to be baptized at the First Presbyterian Church in Jonesville. He remained a devout member until his death.

Riding the wave of post-war notoriety, Baxter was elected to several offices. In March 1866 he was elected Trustee of the Village of Jonesville representing the Fourth Ward. Later in the spring he was chairman of a committee that met in Philadelphia to "erect a monument to the memory of the Late Gen. J[ohn] F. Reynolds [at Gettysburg]. Other committee members included Col. H.A. Morrow of Detroit, Michigan, General [Charles S.] Wainwright of

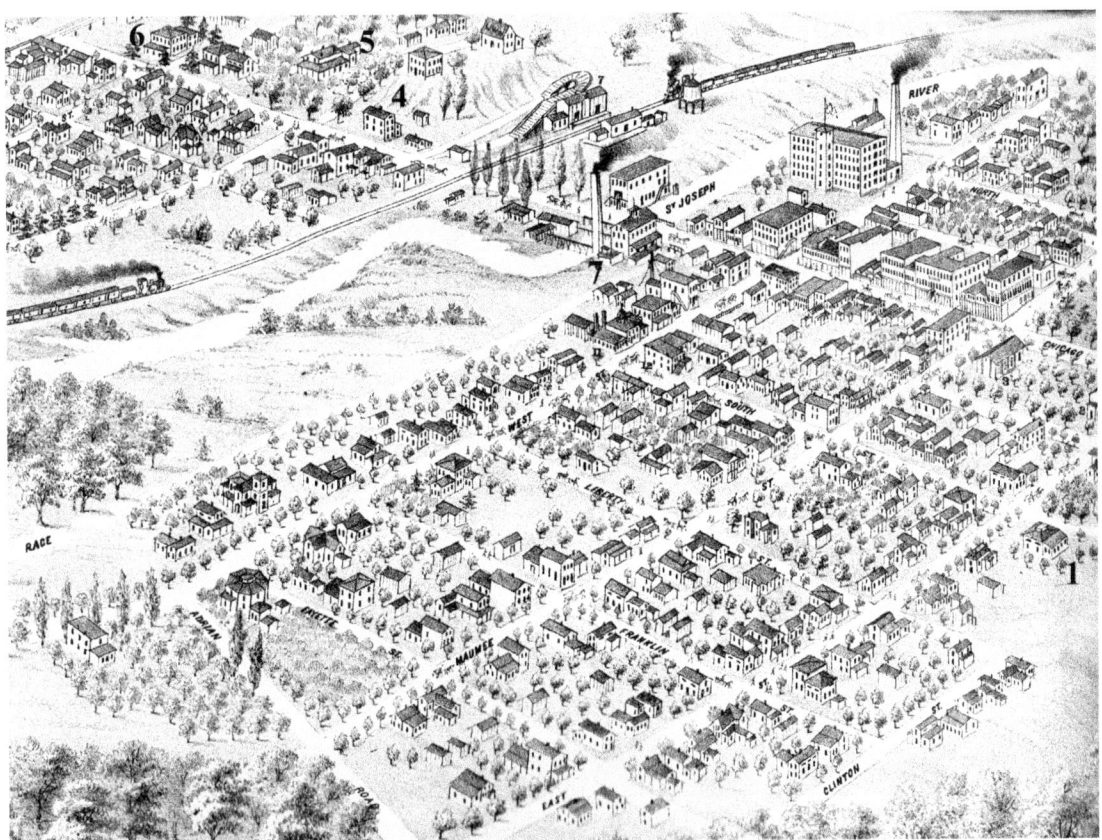

This 1872 bird's eye view of Jonesville shows the Henry Baxter home (1) in the foreground (far right) on East Street, one block east of the homes of former Michigan Lieutenant Governor/Republican Party leader E.O. Grosvenor (2) and Democratic Party leader George C. Munro (3). Levi Baxter (4), Witter Baxter (5) and W.W. Murphy (6) built homes on Chicago Street on the west side of town within one block of each other. The Baxter Fayette Mill (7) is at the intersection of the St. Joseph River Bridge and the Chicago Road (modern US12) at the center of town and close to the Lakeshore and Michigan Railroad. Adapted from a 1872 Strobridge lithograph.

New York, and General [John A.] Kellogg of Wisconsin."[56] Baxter served as Chief Marshall of the July 4th celebration in Hillsdale, a rare honor for a Jonesville resident.

Baxter's participation in this local event kept him from attending the presentation of Civil War flags to the State at Lansing on the same day. Major General Orlando B. Willcox of Detroit—the leader of the first Michigan regiment to enter enemy territory—lauded the efforts of Michigan men during the war. Ironically, the presentation of flags for display at the capitol was symbolic of Baxter's influence in two ways. First, it memorialized what he and his comrades had accomplished as soldiers. Second, it was literally a display of his work as a member of the 5th Corps committee that adjudicated what battle names each regiment was entitled to have on its regimental flag.

In 1866 Henry was also elected Hillsdale County Register of Deeds, a position he held starting January 1, 1867. The position was of great economic advantage in that it allowed him to keep his existing business, yet put the family right in the center of local knowledge regarding county land transfers. Many business advantages accrued as a result.

There were clear signs that the rift between Hillsdale and Jonesville had not healed. When the Detroit, Hillsdale, and Indiana Railroad was formed in 1869 with Henry Waldron as leading stockholder, not a single resident of Jonesville purchased stock. The prominent men of Jonesville instead invested in the competing Fort Wayne, Jackson, and Saginaw Railroad led by E.O. Grosvenor and closely backed by Witter Baxter. Henry Baxter's rise to county-wide office was therefore a sign that his popularity transcended sectional interests.

From his separation from the army on August 24, 1865, until his death, Baxter was provided with a $22.50 per month federal pension as a wounded Civil War veteran. This small pension, when combined with his income from his business and his position as Register of Deeds provided a comfortable living.

The spring of 1866 brought another homecoming. Walt Murphy returned on leave from his position as United States Consul General at Frankfort. Murphy caught up with his old acquaintances and imparted stories of his adventures in Europe. He talked enthusiastically about his position as Consul General, making it sound appealing. Baxter decided this was an avenue through which he could be of further service to his country.

By July Murphy was on his way back to Frankfort. Tensions between Austria and Prussia had reached a breaking point. War was declared on June 14 and Frankfort was occupied by Prussian troops on July 16, ending the city's independence. On July 18 Murphy was back on the job, but in a very different country, one now controlled by Prussians.

═══ ═══

With the Civil War concluded only 17 months before and his military service still a fresh memory, Baxter led the local effort to build a nationwide fraternal/political group of Union veterans. The group called the "Boys in Blue" was intended to have township, county, state, and national leadership. The new fraternal organization started on the East Coast in 1866. The platform that fall was support of the return of constitutional rights to citizens in all states of the restored Union, the spread of constitutional liberty worldwide, adherence to the Monroe Doctrine, and unity among Union veterans.[57] At issue was the seeming degeneration of the country into lawlessness as reconstruction became lost amid political maneuvers.

A September 27, 1866, article in the *Jonesville Independent* reported that a statewide convention held in Hillsdale decided "politically it is to be known as the 'Boys in Blue,' of Hillsdale County, and militarily as the 'Michigan Boys in Blue.'" Baxter was elected President and would lead a contingent to the first annual convention in Pittsburgh.[58]

The Boys in Blue was one of several fraternal-political organizations developed by Union veterans in the months following the war. These organizations sought to maintain the service of Union veterans in the forefront of popular memory, to address common veteran issues, and to build political power. Founded in Illinois, by the spring of 1866 the Grand Army of the Republic (GAR) became the predominant Union veterans organization. A strong political focus allowed it to displace the host of other veterans organizations, including the United States Soldiers and Sailors Protective Society, the Boys in Blue, and the Brotherhood of Soldiers.[59] Still, in the first decade after the Civil War the organization's membership never grew above 30,000. Only after the organization had matured and veteran issues raised their heads again in the 1880s did it begin to grow to meet its potential, eventually reaching a membership of more than 400,000 in 1890.[60] The GAR offered an alternative to the contemporary class structure that abounded in America, providing an opportunity to mix the classes and express a classless ideal, while maintaining much of the military structure that mimicked the service life of the men.[61]

Baxter was one of many Union veterans that saw such groups as a means of cultivating a power base. He was destined to reach beyond Hillsdale County, but making sure his local position was solid was a critical part of the post-war years. Baxter was of interest to the GAR given his influence in Michigan politics, but he did not live long enough to have a lasting impact. Still, his wartime leadership was recognized and his name was considered iconic a decade and a half after his death.

⇒ ⇐

To his family he and Elvira added a fifth child, Edwin Warren, in late 1867. The baby's middle name honored Henry's former commander, General Warren. But the new arrival was not with them long. He developed a "bowel complaint" just short of his first birthday, was baptized privately on September 7 and died on September 8, 1868, his father's 47th birthday. He was buried in Jonesville close to his grandfather Levi.

⇒ ⇐

The Baxters seemed to be on an upward trajectory in 1868. Witter was second in wealth only to E.O. Grosvenor in Jonesville, and third to Grosvenor and Henry Waldron in the county. Henry was not among the wealthiest, but solidly among the elite. While Grosvenor appeared to be a solid candidate for Treasurer, Witter positioned himself as "a man of ability" for a run for state representative and Henry assumed that he would be reelected Register of Deeds. But there was growing unrest in the county. The influence of the north county community of Jonesville and old families—particularly the Baxters—was resented by some. Seemingly Henry and Witter were unaware that the departure of their father Levi and friend W.W. Murphy had weakened their influence countywide. The influx of new settlers and the proliferation of existing families changed the county demographics, while the departure of slavery and states rights issues from center stage allowed the Republican Party to lose some of the moral authority it held since the 1850s.[62]

The storm that found them was unexpected. When the Republican Party held its countywide convention on August 15 to select nominees for local and state office, the Baxters and their supporters expected that Witter would quickly be held up for state office and that Henry as incumbent would easily be renominated for county office. Instead, Witter was nominated, but not elected. The former Register of Deeds William Montgomery arranged to flood the meeting with his supporters, unseating Henry from his nomination as Republican incumbent for the office with a 58–50 vote on the second ballot.[63] This surprise was strongly felt and brought unusual ferocity and violence to county politics, demonstrating the limits to which Baxter—the venturist—could expect his military service to carry him without careful and continuous cultivation.

Under the title "Injustice of Packed Conventions" *Jonesville Independent* editor James Dennis sermonized that a "great injustice" had been done General Baxter, a faithful public servant, a long time Republican, and a veteran drenched in the blood of the Union cause. Worse yet, William Montgomery was a party-changing opponent of the war effort who used cronyism and the allegation of poverty to convince others to turn a deserving fellow-Republican out of office. Montgomery responded through a letter to the *Independent* that his multiple terms as Hillsdale County Supervisor and sundry other levels of service indicated his suitability for the office.[64]

Now alerted to the dangerous shift in political power, the Baxters mobilized supporters. On Saturday, August 29, Adonijiah Welch, now a United States Senator from Florida and since winter Witter's brother-in-law, spoke at the Jonesville Village Hall at the corner of Chicago and Evans Streets to a "large audience" that included "many of our business men" who "were his pupils" when he was principal of the Jonesville Union School. Witter Baxter, President of the Republican Club, presided. Using his experience in Florida, Welch spoke about the importance of the Republican Party and the need to support it in the upcoming local, state, and national elections.[65]

More importantly, powerful United States Senator Zachariah Chandler joined Welch on the steps of the Hillsdale County Court House on the evening of Tuesday, September 1, 1868. Republican "tanners" from Hillsdale and Branch Counties were present to show support, but were assailed by "the drunken, low-lived, rioting copperheads of Hillsdale," the "traitors" who composed the Democratic Party. The demonstrators exchanged words with the Republicans, particularly those from Jonesville and Coldwater. The latter drew so much ire that while they were boarding the train for the trip back home, the Hillsdale men "went at them with brick-bats and stones, smashing in the cars and seriously injuring many."[66]

This event deepened the gulf between Jonesville and Hillsdale. Concerned that the Republican Party was threatened from within and without, John C. Robertson, President of the Village of Hillsdale, called a meeting of the trustees on September 2. The result was a resolution through which citizens of Hillsdale officially expressed their "grief and mortification at the unprovoked onslaught made last evening by a band of lawless rowdies on unoffending citizens of Coldwater and Jonesville."[67] As many as 15 rioters were arrested. Not all proved to be Democrats, a fact that illustrated that the division was along class and community, rather than political lines.[68]

Complicating these matters was competition between Jonesville—led by Witter Baxter—and Hillsdale for placement of the proposed Jackson, Fort Wayne, and Cincinnati Railroad through the respective communities.[69] Jonesville looked at this additional railroad as critical to community success. The *Independent* argued that if $180,000 in stock was not raised to pay for the cost of roadbed, the project "will fail, leaving Jonesville and vicinity dead beyond the hope of resurrection."[70] Ultimately, Jonesville won, claiming some impact on the "*prestige* of Hillsdale," but its citizens—including the Baxters—were oppressed by the stock debt for years.[71]

The Baxters used every opportunity to focus on the election. Witter was chair of the Fayette Republican group, which he mobilized. He also hosted a party for the Presbyterian Society, among others, to get the word out. They reached out to Republicans in the southern part of the county—most notably Henry Waldron—to stir party support across geographic lines.[72]

When the election concluded, Hillsdale County newspapers had expended nearly as much ink on the contest for Register of Deeds as for President of the United States. Republicans swept the election on all levels. But in an unexpected turn of events, Republicans countywide voted for their party consistently except in the Register of Deeds race. Many voted for George Munro, long the leader of the Democrats in Jonesville, instead of party turncoat William Montgomery. The few that could not bring themselves to vote for a Democrat wrote in Henry Baxter. Montgomery still won with 198 votes to Munro's 192, but had Baxter's 8 write-ins gone for Munro, Montgomery would have been bested. The scandal of this turn of events was too much for Montgomery, who accused Baxter of breaking party ranks. Speaking for the Baxter faction, the *Jonesville Independent* pointed out that this was a surprisingly high-handed accusation from a man who had actually changed parties *twice*! The *Independent* asserted that Henry Baxter "worked hard ... for the success of the whole Republican ticket; and, to our certain knowledge, General Baxter voted for every candidate, Mr. Montgomery not excepted."[73] The Republicans who voted for Munro

> preferred an out-and-out Democrat to a Republican whose past political record has been dishonorable, or, to say the least, very ungenerous; and those who simply crossed the name for Register of Deeds, did so from the fact that they wished neither to support a Democrat nor a man who was once a stump candidate against the regular Republican nominee, and who during the war ran for an important State office on a ticket whose principal support came from the "fire-in-the-rear" Democracy.
>
> Mr. Montgomery did not run behind his ticket 208 votes in Fayette because he is a resident of Hillsdale, nor simply because he was nominated instead of General Baxter; but it was owing in great measure to his past political record, and also the popularity of Mr. Munro. If our favorite candidate had been out of the field entirely at the Convention, and then Mr. Montgomery the nominee, the vote in this township would, perhaps, have been far different. But when the General with the loyal record he has made, was set aside for one with a record like Mr. M.'s, the contrast was too great, and hence the result which the latter thinks was not wise. Our people would have regretted very much had the General been defeated in the Convention by *any* man; but if his successful competitor had been a true Republican, he would, without doubt, have received the full party vote of Fayette, as did the other Republican candidates who are residents of Hillsdale.[74]

Montgomery's influence remained confined to Hillsdale County while Baxter's continued to grow beyond it.

Henry Baxter continued his work with veterans. He planned a reunion of the 7th Michigan Volunteer Infantry for June 1869 as he awaited his old commander Ulysses S. Grant's swearing in as the 18th President of the United States on March 4, 1869.

At its inception, the Grant Administration held promise. Americans assumed that the commander that had secured the surrender of Vicksburg and Lee's army would hold the reins of government firmly and fairly. But they were to be disappointed. Grant's military education and experience held very little practice in "the exercise of statecraft."[75] Indeed, Grant's ability to control his administration seemed from its earliest days to slip away as his old cronies from the military and political establishment inundated his cabinet and chief officers with requests for appointments. His only criteria for selecting appointees seemed to be focused on rewarding supporters rather than political advantage or astuteness.[76]

After losing the office of Hillsdale County Register of Deeds, Baxter made an attempt to land the position of United States Marshall of the Eastern District of Michigan. Toward this end he supported Republican Fernando C. Beaman for reelection as United States Representative for Michigan. Thwarted again when J.E. Bennet received the Marshall's post, Elvira Baxter wrote to President Grant asking for an appointment for her husband on April 15, 1869, stating,

A gross injustice has been done my husband[.] If you had ever seen the papers which ought to have been sent to you with the names of the prominent Michigan men in behalf of my husband we are just confident that Mr. J.E. Bennet would neve[r] have received the appointment.... Mr Beaman promised my husband he should surely have the position and it was by supporting Mr Beaman in our last election when there were other candidates that he lost his place as register of deeds in Hillsdale County. My husband was the Col[onel] that command[ed] the seventh Michigan or the little band of forlorn hope in the crossing to Fredericksburg and was wounded in the crossing.[77]

This plea was initially unheeded.

Then Baxter learned that family friend William Murphy would be losing his appointment as Consul General at Frankfort-on-the-Main. By then, the city had been annexed by Prussia and Murphy—never one to keep his opinion to himself—was accused of speaking up against Prussian dominance. A Prussian remonstrance was filed with the State Department. Murphy had supported his patron, the radical Michigan Senator Zach Chandler, in his antipathy toward President Andrew Johnson. Word of his intemperate comments against the leader of the administration reached Washington and Murphy was recalled on May 13, 1869.[78]

Baxter made an effort to gain the position. On April 12, 1869, a recommendation letter for Baxter's appointment as Consul General at Frankfort-on-the-Main was received by the State Department. The letter was signed by a number of influential Republicans, including Zachariah Chandler (powerful United States Senator from Michigan), William A. Howard (Former United States Representative from Michigan's 1st Congressional District and Chairman of the Michigan Republican Party), Fernando C. Beaman (United States Representative from Michigan's 1st Congressional District), and William L. Stoughton (former Union General and United States Representative from Michigan's 2nd Congressional District).[79] Baxter was informed that the position in Frankfort had been eliminated.

Disappointed, he returned to wood products manufacturing. On February 11, 1869, Henry and Elvira sold to John Selfridge for $1900 one quarter of lot #36 in Jones Platt and "one quarter part of the Sash, Door, and Blind Factory, Engine and Machinery."[80] The *Independent* reported in April 1869 that Baxter and Selfridge bought a new planning machine for their mill. John was brother of Henry's brother-in-law Robert, who in 1853 married his sister Lois. This mill continued to operate until at least 1879 under the name of Selfridge, Baxter & Company.

Baxter's failure to be appointed Consul General in Frankfort was not the end for him. His connections and persistence led to another, albeit less prominent, assignment. On April 22 the *Independent* reported that Baxter had been appointed United States Minister to Honduras. Though hardly a plum assignment, one can see why Central America was a good fit for Baxter. He was a courageous, rugged man with an adventurous spirit. Who better to send to a place with few roads, frequent civil wars, and a climate that had the reputation as a man killer?

His salary would be $7,500 per year. By comparison, President Grant was paid $25,000, Vice President Schuyler Colfax $8,000, and Secretary of State Hamilton Fish $8,000 annually.[81] Being a diplomat was therefore a lucrative assignment. Certainly with a low local cost of living and access to opportunities for commerce and investment, the appointment to Honduras might make a man's fortune.

10

Mission to Honduras, 1869–1873

One can never over estimate how far ability, persistence, and the right connections can take a person. For the son of a Michigan businessman, equipped with a limited education, a lot of extended local knowledge, and his own wits to become a player on the international scene was truly a sign of success that anyone could recognize.

On April 15 President Ulysses Grant sent Henry Baxter's diplomatic appointment to the Senate. The next day, the *Jackson Citizen Patriot* ran the headline "Henry Baxter, of Michigan, Nominated for Minister to Honduras."[1] Dozens of other papers across the United States carried the list of appointments, spreading Baxter's name nationwide. The appointment was reported favorably on by the Committee on Foreign Relations and on April 21 the Senate approved it.

The official offer of appointment was penned on April 29. Baxter accepted the appointment on May 14, 1869. In the same letter Baxter provided his oath, swearing that he would do his duty for his country in this new position, a declaration that must have seemed superfluous for a man who had spent nearly four years risking his life to save his country from the scourge of rebellion.[2]

Henry was disappointed not to be serving in the coveted appointment to a European nation that he sought, but instead with a position in a relatively small Central American republic. Yet these appointments to smaller countries were proving ground for those not experienced with international diplomacy. Baxter was about to enter a different type of apprenticeship.

The Honduras that Baxter knew had a population of about 360,000. The mountainous country spanned the Central American isthmus between Atlantic and Pacific, making it one of the key places to cross the continent. Honduras was bordered to the north by the Gulf of Honduras, to the west by Guatemala, to the southwest by San Salvador, to the south by the Bay of Fonseca, and to the east by Nicaragua.[3]

The State Department sent Baxter his official diplomatic instructions, a passport, and instructions for the management of the legation. He had 30 days to reach his post, where he was expected to find the papers of his predecessor, which were to guide his actions until other instructions were received.

In his new role, Baxter had as his superior Secretary of State Hamilton Fish. A New York blue blood descended from Peter Stuyvesant, the last Dutch Director-General of New Amsterdam, Fish was a former United States Congressman, Lieutenant Governor, Governor, and United States Senator from New York. According to his biographer Allan Nevins, Fish's record

With coasts that had potential to link both the Atlantic and Pacific oceans via railroad and canal, but with querulous neighbors on all other sides, Honduran affairs were of interest to European nations, the United States, and the other Central American republics. Map by Dakota Camarena.

before becoming Secretary of State was "able, though never conspicuously brilliant and never connected with dramatic events. To no office had he been reelected."[4]

But Hamilton Fish's ascendency to the office of Secretary of State was a happy circumstance. Fish set a high standard for honesty and hard work, a rarity in the scandal ridden Grant administration. He had a good sense of America's place in the world and was competent—and sometimes brilliant—in his management of foreign affairs. America's future looked bright, having "emerged from the war conscious of titan strength; it had placed in power a highly popular leader; industrially and agriculturally, it had made giant strides under the most adverse circumstances; the recent fears of financial convulsion had vanished; before it stretched a boundless future."[5]

But Fish first had to sort through the tidal wave of former Union soldiers and Republican spoilsmen seeking appointments. He was overwhelmed by four hundred men a day during his first six weeks in office. Of those interested in consulates, most wanted lucrative jobs in Europe where the world was genteel and the opportunities good. The Grant administration clearly intended to "make a general change of the Representatives of the United State abroad" to insert those loyal to the current administration.[6] Fish was responsible for separating those that were able from the purely ambitious.

10. Mission to Honduras, 1869–1873

For Baxter, whose closest previous experience in international diplomacy came from his interactions with Native Americans, Mormons, Mexicans, and Latin Americans on his way to and from California, Fish's directions were critical. Fish instructed him to maintain the current course, avoid entanglements, and look after American political, commercial, and individual interests.

The propensity for strife among Latin American nations was a concern. Such volatility gave the influence of foreign powers increased opportunities. The right people were needed on the spot, leaders who would be able to defend the Monroe Doctrine and deal with the intrigues of European powers as well as the frequent eruptions of passion that had created a series of wars and coups since the Spanish colonial authorizes were pushed out in the early nineteenth century. Baxter's military reputation, lead from the front philosophy, and cool detachment of thought under pressure were ideal for the place he was selected for. Honduras was a lightning rod for the rest of Central America and a man with experience in dealing with an unpredictable environment was essential. In other words, it required a venturist.

The role of Honduras in Latin American politics and conflict was critical because of the nation's central geographic position on the Isthmus. There had been continual interference in Honduras's internal affairs by stronger neighboring countries, while domestic jealousies and competition for power left the nation rife with discord. For much of the century, Guatemala, Salvador, and Nicaragua were involved in a nearly continual series of revolutions and civil wars in Honduras, started and participated in by all three.[7] Hondurans seemed content to waste "much of their energies in civil and military strife," as demonstrated by the 170 military conflicts the nation was engaged in between 1824 and 1876. The average endurance of a regime in power during the post–Spanish era was eight months.[8]

Yet, Honduras had much to recommend it to American interests. The fertile soil spawned plantations and the mineral wealth in gold and silver—its major high dollar exports followed distantly by indigo, horned cattle, timber, and hides—were a temptation to American entrepreneurs. The position of Honduras athwart the isthmus was even more important for a future canal between Atlantic and Pacific.

Baxter would be the 9th United States Minister appointed to Honduras since the Franklin Pierce administration opened a legation there in 1853. Three of those appointed declined to serve. For the first eight years, the Honduras legation was combined with those of other Central American nations. In April 1862 James Rudolph Partridge (1823–1884) became the first Minster to Honduras who actually presented his credentials in that country. He remained in Honduras for only seven months. Baxter was the first Michigander to accept the post and actually live in the turbulent country.[9]

The Honduras that Henry Baxter contended with was very much a product of the combined influence of Native Americans, conquering Spaniards, and imported slaves. This mix lacked sufficient cohesiveness to maintain long term stability. When combined with a tendency toward an emotional response to insult or injury, there was little chance that the country would pull together without strong leadership.

Problems in Honduras arose not long after the colonial authority of Spain was overthrown in 1821. At first Spanish Governor José Gregorio Tinoco de Contreras at Comayagua attempted to seize power. He was opposed by the people of Tegucigalpa, starting a civil war that lasted for years. The Federal Republic of Central America (La Unión) brought together the Central American states we know today as Guatemala, El Salvador, Honduras, Nicaragua, and Costa Rica in 1823, with its capital in Guatemala. But any promise of peace was dashed as factions divided the population. In Honduras, the largest city of Tegucigalpa became a Liberal stronghold, while the city of Comayagua was Conservative. An army from Tegucigalpa led by Francisco Morazán played an important role in defeating Salvador and in throwing out federal authority in 1829. Revolution in Guatemala led to a short-lived Liberal government in Honduras that disintegrated after the disruption of La Unión in 1839. President Rafael Carrera of Guatemala helped the Honduran Conservatives return to power in 1840. Carrera supported Francisco Ferrer as President and then Commander-in-Chief of the Army from 1840 to 1852. He was succeeded by the Liberal José Trinidad Cabañas. Three years later Carrera sent an army to replace Cabañas with José Santos Guardiola, who was assassinated January 11, 1862.[10] José Francisco Montes served as acting President, as did Victoriano Castellanos, José María Medina, and Francisco Inestroza. Finally on March 15, 1864, Medina was elected President.

José María Medina was a career soldier, born in 1826 in the Gracias a Dios Department of northeastern Honduras. He joined the army at age 18 and was engaged against William Walker's filibuster forces after the American attempted to overrun and unite all of Central America in the 1850s. A later attempt to invade Honduras was unsuccessful and Walker was ultimately caught and executed on September 12, 1860. The Walker Expeditions briefly united the Central American republics against a common invader. Once that enemy was eliminated, the same jealousies emerged again.

Medina was very ambitious. He watched the Austrian-born Ferdinand Maximilian Joseph (Maximilian I of the Habsburg line) establish himself in Mexico in 1864 and, with the support of Napoleon III of France, subvert the Monroe Doctrine while America was preoccupied with its Civil War. The reemergence of a European monarchy in the Americas under the protection of the French created apprehension among the American republics that self-rule would be undermined.

Medina maintained relations with both the Maximilian administration and the Lincoln-Johnson administrations in the United States. When Baxter's predecessor Richard Rousseau took his position in Honduras, his first private meeting with Medina in October 1866, revealed a man who saw in the mirror the reflection of greatness. He was ruthless in putting down opposition in his own country, earning the nickname of "Ahorcancina de Olancho" (Mass Hangman of Olancho) as a result of the terror he instilled in rebellious people.[11] There were persistent rumors that adventurers planned to take control of Honduras. By the fall of 1866, President Medina had made up his mind to go forward with a plan to reunite Honduras, San Salvador, Guatemala, Nicaragua, and perhaps Costa Rica under one constitution. He intimated to Rousseau that Maximilian had approached him to take charge of these republics and unite them as part of the "Mexican Empire," but that would not give up his republican principles for near dictatorial control. However, with the United States warned of the ambitions of both Mexico's European monarch and a shadowy group of displaced Confederate freebooters, he proposed to do the same thing under his own flag and asked if he had American sanction to proceed.[12] Medina believed that Central America would eventually be united under one strong political leader. The question then became whether the United States preferred to deal with Maximilian's French monarchy, a displaced group of Confederates hungry to reestablish slavery, or Medina, the only one that asserted support for democracy in Central America? Baxter would inherit the consequences of Medina's ambition.

⸺   ⸺

One of the issues that preoccupied all American diplomats in Central America was the southern transcontinental railroad and the proposed isthmian canal. One railroad was a reality. First opened in 1855, the Panama Railroad crossed the isthmus at Panama—then part of Colombia—and became the fashionable method of transportation, despite its shortcomings. Offering a rough ride and frequently interrupted service, it was still faster and more reliable than mule trains over mountain trails. The completion in 1869 of the Transcontinental Railroad across the United States reduced some of the demand for passenger and freight traffic. Still, there was demand for future commerce because the existing railroad across Panama was small and its size limited Central American potential.

Creating a competing Honduran Interoceanic Railroad under British leadership had implications for the economy of both the region and the hemisphere. First supported by President Cabañas and long advocated by American George Squier, the proposed railroad across Honduras was to extend from Puerto Cortés on the Caribbean to the Gulf of Fonseca on the Pacific side, originally laid out to pass through the important city of Tegucigalpa.[13] Squier negotiated an agreement to build and manage the enterprise as early as 1853, but it fell to British interests to finance and move the plan forward. President Medina indebted Honduras to British investors for nearly $25,000,000, creating a debt service that outstripped Honduras' annual gross revenue of $400,000.[14] Payments would need to come from revenues generated from the operation of a railroad that was not yet built. The situation was made more serious by graft, much of the borrowed money being siphoned off before it ever reached the railroad builders, thereby making it nearly impossible for the railroad to be completed.[15]

The United States and Great Britain were both interested in harvesting the resources of Honduras and securing access to expeditious routes across the isthmus. In 1850 the two Anglo powers signed a convention that supported construction of a canal or railway across the isthmus and agreed to protect it so long as it remained neutral.[16] Further, the commercial rivals found it expedient to cooperate in principle, signing the "Treaty of Friendship, Commerce, and Navigation," on July 4, 1864, to further guarantee the neutrality of the railroad. This move was intended to place the world's leading Anglo maritime powers in a position to shield the important trans-American commercial lifeline from disruption by foreign and domestic disputes. Whether this agreement would actually serve the purpose intended or simply remain a paper deterrent was as yet untried.[17] José María Medina was pleased. He adopted former President Cabañas' dream of a railroad that would bring commercial success and he was willing to risk the destabilization of his government with its tenuous financing.[18]

The other issue was the long dreamt of trans-isthmian canal. The opening of the Suez Canal after ten years of well-publicized construction on November 17, 1869, had a remarkable impact on Americans. This success demonstrated that a canal could break through narrow continents, joining oceans together to avoid long circum-continental voyages. Suddenly it seemed plausible that the East and West coasts of America might too be joined. The natural route would cross the Central American isthmus, a route jubilantly projected by promoters to cut the trip around Cape Horn from months to days. The cost of construction was projected at between $60 and $100 million.[19] Here there was another opportunity for international cooperation among the Anglo maritime powers. The United States had in 1850 via the Clayton-Bulwer Treaty acknowledged their direct competitive interests with Great Britain in the creation of a trans-isthmian canal. Though the treaty outlined a cooperative future for the two nations in either a railway or canal venture, there was limited trust attached to the document.[20] Both saw a neutral railroad or canal across the isthmus to be in everyone's best interest, while either endeavor controlled by any single power might prove disastrous.

By the 1860s a British company was actively working to construct the Honduran Interoceanic Railroad, but no private firm from either nation had begun a canal. The United States made surveys of the potential canal route. During Baxter's tenure in Honduras, in January 1870 the gunboat USS *Nipsic* and the tender USS *Guard* with geologists, engineers, and officers of the Coast Survey comprising the Darien Expedition went to the isthmus to reconnoiter possible routes. Their reports sobered those lobbying for a quick assumption of risk. The challenges were better identified, the costs clarified, and the political need for treaties legitimized to show a much more difficult enterprise awaited those daring enough to undertake it. By the time the expedition returned in June, the interest of the public was quickly subsiding in light of ongoing local political instability, earthquakes, and the concern that the environment was not conducive to Anglo-style business.[21] Until the railway was complete, the primary means of travel across Honduras was via pack animal traversing mountainous country on poorly improved trails.

———

Henry Baxter placed his business affairs in the care of his brother Witter and was ready to assume his duties in a remarkable two weeks. On June 1, 1869, Baxter wrote to Secretary of State Hamilton Fish that he was departing for Honduras.[22]

Just getting to the place of his new appointment proved arduous. Baxter went ahead of his wife and daughters, taking his 13-year-old son Harry with him. Father and son traveled across the continent on the newly opened Transcontinental Railroad, taking just days to pass through territory that in 1849–50 took Baxter over ten months to transit. The mild discomforts of rail travel presented a remarkable contrast to the stress and pain of being responsible for a group trekking through unsettled country. The worst logistical problems the former 49er faced involved selecting a ship aboard which to reach Honduras.

The Baxters sailed from San Francisco, both of them experiencing sea sickness on the voyage. They arrived in the harbor of La Unión, on Salvador's Pacific Coast, by steamer *Guatemala* on July 1. In his correspondence he threaded a line between optimism and realism, frequently addressing Vi's concern that she might not like Honduras: "I find as yet the Country presents as favorable appearance as I had expected (you know my ideas were not very exalted) and I trust when you come you will not be disappointed. But you must understand that I am not yet introduced to Honduras."[23]

On July 3 Henry and Harry left La Unión by small boat, crossing the Bahía de la Unión (Union Bay) and following the La Brea estuary inland, arriving in Honduras for the first time. Happily, this transit of a waterway by open boat was—unlike the "Commodore's" experience at Fredericksburg—completed without anyone shooting at him. He secured mules, the services of a guide and translator, and cooking utensils and provisions to feed the party on the trip. They twisted through mountains and valleys, fording rivers via narrow mule trail through Nacaome, Mansanita, and La Venta.[24] They arrived in the valley of Tegucigalpa on the evening

10. Mission to Honduras, 1869–1873

of July 8. Baxter took responsibility for the legation office and public property in Tegucigalpa—52 miles away from the capital of Comayagua—and assumed is duties on July 10.[25]

He left no first impressions of Tegucigalpa, a city built in an undulating valley, surrounded by the steep, low mountains. Founded by the Spanish on the site of an existing native village in 1578, the city was 3,281 feet above sea level and, at 14°06' north latitude, only 965 miles (1555 km) north of the equator. The tropical highlands, the latitude, elevation, and the sheltered valley allowed Tegucigalpa to maintain remarkably pleasant average temperatures between 77°F and 86°F. The valley was less humid than the coastal areas and experienced an annual rainy season that extended from May through October. Baxter wrote to Elvira that she and the children would enjoy "a delightful climate. I think it cannot be surpassed."[26] The mountain slopes were forested, with farming in the valleys and mining among the elevations.

We might infer what Henry Baxter saw upon his arrival in Tegucigalpa based upon William Wells' experience:

> We entered a paved street bordered with handsome stone and plastered adobe houses the walls painted blue red cream color or white after the fancy of the proprietor. The grated balconies, narrow grass grown sidewalk, regularly tiled roofs, paved patios, the peculiar and simple style of architecture, the cries of street venders, the equestrian display, and the dark eyed, *mantilla'd* faces gazing listlessly upon us from the cool prisonlike residences reminded me more of Havana than any city I had yet seen in Central America....
>
> The streets are all named and the town struck me at first glance as an exception to the usual ruined deserted appearance of Central American cities. This is the head-quarters of fashion and gayety in Honduras.[27]

Baxter took over the legation from Richard H. Rousseau, a Kentucky lawyer from Louisville. He was also the older brother of the late Union General Lovell Harrison Rousseau, who was best known for his role in the Battle of Shiloh and for a volatile temper that clouded his post-war service in the United States Congress. He had received 21 votes at the 1864 Republican National Convention for Lincoln's Vice-Presidential running mate. General Rousseau returned to the army and died just weeks after overseeing the turbulent 1868 election as commander in charge of the Department of Louisiana.[28] This military connection gave Rousseau and Baxter something in common, easing the indoctrination of the later to the politics and duties of his diplomatic post.

Baxter wrote to Elvira about the experience in staying with Rousseau:

> Well dearest you are anxious to hear how I like Honduras and especially Tegucigalpa—Well Honduras is very primitive and no better than I expected to find it....
>
> I have not had time to look around sufficiently to see whether I shall be able to secure a convenient (convenient for the country) house or not. This house that is now occupied by Mr. Rousseau belongs to people who wish to occupy it this fall so that it cannot be had and if none can be secured in Tegucigalpa I must look in Comayagua when I go there although from all the information I get I think this the pleasanter place for a residence.... My impression is from what I have seen that it will be fully up to our expectations and a place quite bearable except lonesome and very healthy—I don't want you to get the idea that you would rather remain in the states for I cannot spare you I assure you my dear wife.[29]

Two days after his arrival, Baxter wrote to Francisco Alvarado, Honduran Minister of Foreign Relations, informing him of his presence and requesting an appointment to present his credentials to President Medina. Alvarado invited the general to visit with the President at Comayagua on August 18.

Outgoing minister Rousseau introduced Baxter to Secretary Alvarado, who in turn presented him to President Medina. He was received "cordially." Baxter congratulated Medina on the development of Honduras, its mineral resources, and the prospect of the early completion of the Interoceanic Railroad. With excellent harbors on either coast, Baxter assured Medina that the railroad was the essential element necessary to insure Honduras' future prosperity.[30]

Medina and Baxter got along from the start. The two were nearly the same age, shared the same birthday (September 8), and both had led armies in combat. Beyond this, the men could not have been more different. Though strongly partisan, Baxter was a firm believer in democracy. As a Republican he saw the need for a strong federal government, abhorred slavery, highly valued social and economic order, and believed that the promotion of energetic business and the extraction of natural resources were essential. Medina was liberal by comparison to some of his predecessors, but craved power and wished to maintain his as long as he could. He yearned

President/General José María Medina had grand ambitions for the economic prosperity of Honduras through creation of the Honduran Interoceanic Railway. But graft among his supporters and his own political ambitions to unite the isthmus under his leadership inspired a series of wars and revolutions that made Henry Baxter's time in Honduras memorable.

for a return to a united Central America with himself at its head. Since both men valued order and had fought to hold a country together, Medina had a strong bond with Baxter. Throughout his assignment in Honduras, Baxter rarely criticized Medina's actions though they subverted democracy in favor of autocracy, because he saw the need for a strong central authority to unite the fractured loyalties of the political landscape. This is not to say that Baxter favored all that Medina did, but he restricted his dispatches and letters to the facts with interpretation of the mood of the population as filtered through his contacts rather than as a matter of personal opinion.[31]

The unstable situation in Central America was illustrated by one of Baxter's first actions. He requested that all official correspondence henceforth be sent in care of George A.K. Morris & Company at Amapala, on Honduras' Pacific coast, rather than through La Unión, San Salvador. With Salvador and Honduras periodically in conflict, the change would be more reliable and safer from espionage. It would also save additional postage fees required by Salvador.[32]

10. Mission to Honduras, 1869–1873

On August 27 Baxter requested the appointment of a Consular Agent at the port of Amapala. He felt that this additional appointment was necessary because: (1) the inadequate regulation of trade was causing losses in duties to the United Sates and losses to shipping companies, and (2) revolution in Nicaragua could spread to adjacent nations and the high level of unemployment in the port of Amapala could lead to uprisings. In other words, the agent would provide security for both American citizens and American trade should the situation destabilize. Baxter requested and was granted approval to appoint Morris to the new position.[33]

Even the presence of young Harry did not alleviate Henry's loneliness for a stable family life. Through the summer and fall Baxter agonized over Elvira's anticipated trip to Honduras with the girls. He wrote to her repeatedly about travel arrangements, and then waited anxiously as few letters came in reply. When he did hear from Elvira, it was in a cluster of letters from Minooka, Chicago, Jonesville, and Detroit. She appeared to be having the time of her life and traveling everywhere except to join her husband. Henry sent $500 to Witter to help her with travel expenses. Baxter departed Tegucigalpa to collect his wife and three daughters on November 15. He went overland to Omoa, then by ship to New Orleans where he met them and shared Christmas before returning to Omoa on January 5, 1870.

The expected quick return to Tegucigalpa proved optimistic. As William Wells suggested, so Baxter learned that tropical fevers took their toll on those unused to the climate:

> The fevers of the country are the tertiana or every other day fever resembling in its effects and mode of attack the worst form of fever and ague of the Western United States and the calentura a type of the same.... The symptoms of Central American fever are cold shudderings varied by quick flushes of heat and sickness at the stomach. If the patient has taken cold they are reckoned dangerous. An intolerable headache, weakness, of the limbs, aching of the joints, dizziness, and general debility attend the attack.[34]

Baxter's daughter Jennie fell sick with malaria and remained so for weeks. He stayed with her in San Pedro, about 42 miles inland. On February 9 he wrote that she "is now recovering and we hope will soon be able to ride again."[35] But it was March 10 before Baxter was finally back in Tegucigalpa. Central America was quickly illustrating its challenges for the Michiganders.

Henry Baxter's impressions of the people of Honduras were not positive. His first week in Tegucigalpa he wrote to Elvira:

> I hardly know about living yet, but of this set down as a fact that the servants are a worthless, lazy, dirty set and you will long for home many times. A good house keeper would be a great acquisition.[36]

Although his opinion improved as he and his family came to know the people and the country, this initial prejudice based on contemporary American standards and Victorian perceptions of propriety mark him as a man of his time and culture.

Life in Honduras posed significant challenges for the Baxters. The state religion of Honduras was Catholicism, although other faiths were guaranteed tolerance via the Honduran Constitution.[37] Yet the dominance of the Catholic faith was problematic for Presbyterians because there were no Protestant churches where public worship was held.

So too did the general ambivalence of some members of the community bother Baxter:

> No church but Catholic Mass and that every day in the week. The Sabbath by the people here is appropriated for recreation and pleasure. Tell [Rev E. W.] Childs I would give well I don't know what, good attention at least, to sit one Sabbath in his church and I would so like to be with the Sabbath school again and the evening prayer meetings. I think of them often and trust I ever may. They have been a source of great comfort and pleasure and I trust of good to me. Oh, it is so different here.[38]

Henry wrote that the "surroundings of the Sabbath we hardly have here although we endeavor to heed it ourselves and ... make a community of ourselves."[39] Baxter held services for his family in his home, which also doubled as the consulate. This was a necessity as, to quote Squier, "The priests [of Honduras] are generally the most liberal part of the population. Their influence, however, is small."[40] As Baxter found, liberal priests were not particularly welcome among the small republics.

Article 33 of the Honduran national constitution forbid a President from succeeding himself, so Medina's partisans repealed the clause in August 1869, allowing him to be elected to another four year term. He was inaugurated on February 1 and the period of relative peacefulness in Honduras began a steady deterioration. As early as December 1869 political disturbances began to occur in Olancho and Paraiso. Largely fomented by Nicaraguan exiles, these early acts against Medina were easily brushed aside, but they were indicative of many troubles on the horizon.[41]

A primary focus of Baxter's diplomatic agenda was the creation of an extradition agreement between the United States and Honduras. On January 27 Fish wrote to Baxter, giving him the authority to negotiate. In April Baxter presented the plan and reported that it was favorably received. As the summer wore on, Baxter moved the Extradition Convention toward completion.

He reported that the Interoceanic Railroad was progressing. The first of three sections (at the eastern end) were expected to be completed early in 1871. The railroad would aid American movement across the continent since it was shorter than the Panama route, and therefore would facilitate communication with China and the Far East. However, he was concerned that the British interest in the railroad would help them gain influence in Honduras. He recommended that American interests and authority be solidified by establishing a Pacific naval station in the Bay of Fonseca on Tiger Island at Amapala. The importance of the island lay in its strategic location on the route of American steamers running between San Francisco and Panama. He was in favor of actually taking ownership of Tiger Island, if necessary to create a permanent American presence.[42]

Unfortunately, 1870 ended with a tragedy. Baxter reported to Fish that he had received word from Minister Resident at Salvador General A.T.A. Torbert that two American citizens were assassinated in western Honduras near the border with Salvador. Dr. T.C. Ledyard and Robert N. Bell—both dentists from Ceres, New York—were killed near the town of Sensenti while bound for Honduras.[43] The cause of the murder was robbery, and it sparked sharp reaction in the states. The *New York Herald* editorialized,

10. Mission to Honduras, 1869–1873

The lives of foreigners are held at too cheep a rate by the majority of the citizens of the Spanish American Republics, and it is time they were taught a severe lesson, and now there is a fitting opportunity.[44]

In April 1871 Baxter was informed that the bodies of the two men would be recovered by family. Though at the time Honduras and Salvador were at war, Baxter aided the families in their efforts to the best of his ability.[45] One of the two murderers was arrested. Despite the *Herald*'s agitation, no military intervention occurred.

⇒ ⇐

The year 1871 was a good one for the Baxters. Henry had Elvira and the kids with him in Honduras, temporarily bringing his diplomatic life and home life together. He was fortunate in the choice of rented residence. He lived in part of a home occupied by former Honduran President General José Trinidad Cabañas, whose two liberal terms—March 1 to July 6, 1852, and December 31, 1853, to June 6, 1855—were marked by efforts at civil reform and the first attempt to build a railroad across Honduras. Earlier in his career, Cabañas had helped Francisco Morazán unite Central America and served in the governments of both Salvador and Honduras. Up until his death he remained a staunch advocate of unification, raising the ire of some for his outspokenness.

Tegucigalpa was among the most developed and comfortable cities in Honduras. Baxter choose to reside in Tegucigalpa instead of the capital because of the culture, connections, and climate that it offered. Illustration from William V. Wells, *Explorations and Adventures in Honduras and El Salvador* (New York: Harper and Brothers, 1857).

They lived up the hill to the north of Tegucigalpa's city center. There the elite of the community congregated, living in thick adobe-walled homes built in the Spanish style with stables in the back and an interior courtyard suitable for the children to play in and for Henry to plant fruits, vegetables, and flowers. The masonry walls kept the houses cool during the day, while a refreshing evening breeze made it a pleasure to watch the setting sun cast mountain shadows across the city.

From this vantage point they had a spectacular view of the city to the south, with the painted exteriors of the churches of Iglesia los Delores (1732) and St. Michael Archangel (1782) visible on days when low hanging clouds or torrential rain did not obscure them. When Henry was not required by business to take one of the steep winding stone-paved streets downtown, they were close enough to the European colony and their Honduran friends to visit, or for the children to take music lessons and overnight with friends. Business was conducted in the home as American and British citizens with problems sought Henry out.

They did their best to adapt to Honduran culture. Yet they sent home descriptions of the culture that focused on the contrasts to the world they left in America. Henry noted washer women who did the laundry in the river by beating each item with rocks that invariably crushed buttons, cooks who bought food only for a single day's consumption, and the many articles common in the United States that were not available in Honduran markets.

This is the only period during which we know much about the Baxter home, because Henry's daughter Carrie (age 11) kept a journal as part of her lessons. Though it only covers three months, it is very enlightening about the family routine.

The most stable day in the Baxter week was Sunday, when Henry officiated at church services. Every Sunday evening Henry quizzed Jennie, Carrie, and Harry on their Bible lessons and assigned new ones to be mastered by the following week. If Henry was away from home on legation business, no services were held.

The children adopted some Honduran ways. Jennie, Carrie, and eventually little Lottie went with local girls to bathe in the river once a week, a routine that they came to look forward to. Harry took up hunting with his friends, specializing in birds. They all were introduced to Honduran festivals, which were both a curiosity and source of entertainment. As elite visitors to Honduras, the Baxters were invited to many social functions. The children particularly liked the custom by which Hondurans gave gifts to those that visited their homes.[46] Carrie wrote that the entire family assumed the traditional schedule of city dwellers in Tegucigalpa:

> The way we take our meals here is, when we first get up in the morning we have tea or coffee then about ten o'clock we have breakfast, at four dinner and then at eight tea.[47]

During the day Carrie and Jennie studied music with an English woman. The girls also studied Spanish, which at first was slow going, but picked up as the girls made Honduran friends. Carrie played with paper dolls, often entertaining younger sister Lottie whom she also dressed, taught letters, spelling, and writing. Letter writing was something taken seriously, though not as seriously as receiving letters from the diplomatic courier every two weeks. Failing to receive mail from home brought gloom to the household. After dinner the family rode their horses, played whist or cribbage, or received visitors. Sometimes Henry read to the children.[48]

But there were disturbing developments at home that mirrored the situation in Honduras. Henry had to watch the political state of affairs, particularly events that might impact

10. Mission to Honduras, 1869–1873

the Interoceanic Railway. He was way from home in Comayagua more than he wished dealing with international politics and he and Elvira developed debilitating headaches and chills, signs that they had contracted malaria.

⸻

The situation in Central America was deteriorating. A growing number of exiled dissidents from neighboring countries created problems. Leaders of both Salvador and Honduras refused to live up to international agreements. President Medina and President Francisco Dueñas of Salvador simply hated each other. The tension that this antipathy caused along the Honduran/Salvadoran border built until the Interoceanic Railroad requested military protection for railroad employees and engineers who were threatened by the inhabitants of the area.[49]

In late 1870 the continued courage of former President Cabañas who called for reform and refederation of the Central American republics created additional problems. His passionate appeals at a time when war among the republics was again approaching led to a remarkable incident in both his life and Henry Baxter's. According to Baxter family tradition, an angry mob came for Cabañas at the residence he shared with Baxter. They demanded that the elderly Cabañas be turned over to them. Baxter had no personal security, so he strapped on his Civil War sword and sidearm and stood in the gateway to the house's courtyard. He handed his hat to his 14-year-old son Harry, who stood behind him as he drew pistol and sword and dared the crowd to advance and take Cabañas, literally over his dead body. This kind of machismo had exactly the right impact on people who respected a brave, passionate man. The mob backed down.[50] General Cabañas died in early January 1871, leading Carrie to comment in her diary,

A protégé of Francisco Morazán, President José Trinidad Cabañas was one of Honduras' most conscientious leaders. Today Cabañas is honored with his portrait on the Honduran 10 Lempira note because of his vision for creating economic independence and his courage in standing up for democracy. Henry Baxter shared Cabañas' home and courageously defended the outspoken former president from public unrest when others were afraid to do so. Baxter maintained friendships with both President Medina who subverted democracy in Honduras to support his ambitions to reign over a consolidated Central America and ex–President Cabañas who opposed Medina for his incursions upon democracy.

> General Cabañas is dead. He was a former president and was a very good man, respected by all. He lives in this very house. Papa has just received an invitation to go to his mass for the repose of his soul at eight o'clock tomorrow evening.[51]

Though he was among the foreigners who were potentially at risk in these unsettled times, Baxter had risen above vulnerability, achieving security for both himself and his family by a show of his own personal courage, persistence, and respect for a prominent Honduran.

To cool the growing tensions and protect foreign nationals, Baxter recommended that the Honduran government: (1) not allow local government officials to speak against foreigners or the railroad; (2) allow foreigners to carry arms and be placed on the same legal footing as officials of the government; (3) settle jurisdictional differences between local natives and officials of the railroad; and (4) keep soldiers on station to guard the railroad and construction material.[52] He received minimal support largely because Medina had little real control over local matters.

On February 7, Baxter received a letter from Francisco Alvarado, Honduran Minister of Foreign Relations, informing him that the treaty between Honduras and Salvador had been suspended. A proclamation issued by President Medina listed multiple grievances. Baxter warned Fish that war was imminent.

The causes of the conflict related primarily to the interrelationship of individuals in the governments of the two countries. Honduras had expelled persons for political misdemeanors who found refuge in Salvador and were employed there by agents of the government. They were stationed on the border and collected disaffected persons from Honduras, threatening the security of the latter country.

The concern over unrest in Honduras created a growing insecurity among Anglos. Vastly outnumbered by the natives and protective of the gains they had made in commerce, most Americans were quick to call for help if they sensed that a change of political power was in the wind. Most called for a naval ship, a movable platform for guns and men that provided protection while the ex-patriot continued to do business despite the civil unrest.

A call for protection came on December 24, 1870. George Morris in Amapala wrote that one of the "periodical revolutions" was on the horizon and that it was prudent to provide for the "safety of each place where considerable property" is held.[53] The property of foreigners was always targeted during these revolutions, and therefore a man-of-war should be summoned to provide security. Morris requested that Baxter contact either the admiral commanding the Pacific Squadron or authorities in Washington and request that a ship be sent to the Bay of Fonseca.

Baxter warned Fish that American citizens and property were in danger. Unprotected merchandise belonging to Americans in Honduras and Salvador was stored at La Unión and Amapala. He recommended that the United States send a ship of war to the Bay of Fonseca to offer protection as needed and renewed his support for creating a naval base and a free port on Tiger Island. The American press expressed concern that foreign property could not be secured if a formal declaration of war were issued.[54]

On February 8, 1871, *Alcance a la Gaceta No. 19* (published in Comayagua) printed a Honduran indictment of Salvadoran behavior, accusing Salvador of negotiating and acting in bad faith.[55] Honduras had had enough of Salvador's interference and was ready for war.

On February 10, Alvarado wrote to Baxter, trying to convince him that America should support Honduras and force Salvador to back down. He argued that refugees from the Honduran provinces of San Miguel and La Unión crossing the frontier were the root cause of these problems. There was a serious threat of invasion from Salvadorian troops at San Miguel under General Forencio Xatruch, leader of the opposition party in Honduras. Alvarado argued that Honduras could defend itself, but it could not guard the railroad enterprise from harm. In early March Baxter went to Comayagua to make his case for protection of the railway in company with British officials. There was little more he could do without involving the United States.

Baxter also wrote to the authorities in Salvador and reminded them of the 1864 treaty, reiterating that the United States would be unhappy if Salvador and Honduras were to go to war. Since the Salvadorans believed that America would not intervene, the thinly veiled threat had little impact. They responded on March 6 that the railroad neutrality issue was overshadowed by more egregious Honduran breaches of neutrality. This response threatened the railroad and left little room for diplomatic intervention. If meaningful dialogue were to occur, it would have to be precipitated by a show of naval or military force.

Baxter wrote Fish on April 1 indicating that all attempts at a peaceful settlement between Salvador and Honduras had failed. War was declared by Honduras on March 5 after a Salvadoran force crossed the border and attacked a small group of Honduran police protecting workmen on the Interoceanic Railway at Goascoran. Honduran forces attacked and were repulsed at Pasaquina, Salvador. President Medina commanded Honduran forces in person with some success. Yet, the Hondurans were steadily pushed back.[56]

On May 22 Alvarado reported that Salvadoran General Mirondas' troops invaded Honduras and occupied Goascoran. Alvarado argued that President Medina had not fortified the Honduran capital because the presence of the Interoceanic Railway made it a neutral city. Alvarado asked Baxter to place the capital under protection of the United States.[57] Under pressure to save his country from being overrun by stronger Salvadoran forces, President Medina instructed Alvarado to try his last option. With the enemy quickly approaching, Alvarado wrote a note later that day asking Baxter for permission to raise the American flag over the public square in Comayagua as a sign of the protection of the United States.[58] They gambled that the American who had barred an unruly mob from taking the feeble Cabañas from his sick bed might just have the audacity to extend his country's protection to the railroad and the capital without any resources to enforce either. This would make Salvadoran forces wonder if they had assessed America's intentions correctly and potentially risk full American intervention.

On March 26 Baxter replied that he would consult with General Torbert in Salvador about the idea of providing protection to Comayagua. But with regard to raising the flag of the United States over the capitol immediately, he could not give such permission as it exceeded his authority. He would, however, inquire if the Department of State would authorize this action.[59] Since it would take weeks to get permission to do this from Washington, Baxter had adroitly sidestepped a thorny involvement while maintaining American sympathy for the Medina regime and doing what he could with General Torbert to represent American interests and assert protection of the railroad enterprise. In truth, the American diplomats did not believe that American protection would attach itself to the railroad until the work was completed and functional.[60]

Tegucigalpa was occupied by General Xatruch on March 30. Over 300 Hondurans joined the invading forces. Many citizens had fled the city, but on April 2 some of those remaining declared against President Medina and in favor of General Xatruch, proclaiming him provisional President. Xatruch formed a cabinet and appointed a new governor and municipal officials.[61] Baxter wrote,

> This morning Gen. Xatruch with an army now numbering about one thousand men, together with the provisional government will march toward the valley of Comayagua expecting to meet the Honduran forces (of what number I am not informed) either at San Antonio or La Raz in the Valley. I have no reliable news of the condition of affairs in Salvador.[62]

Guatemala threatened to join the war to support Salvador. United States Consul Silas Hudson asked for a naval vessel to help protect Americans there.[63]

But the war brought unintended consequences. Salvadorian President Dueñas was toppled from power on April 15, as the result of the poor performance of his armies. Dueñas and General Martínez took refuge in the house of General Torbert. General Santiago González formed a provisional government. By then, General Xatruch asserted control of six departments of Honduras and claimed to be strong enough to resist the return of President Medina. In this, Baxter stated "I think he is over estimating his ability."[64]

Medina was expected to return to the capital when news of the change in Salvadoran government reached him. The "legitimate government" of Honduras was then meeting in Santa Barbara, where it had removed on April 4 as the Salvadoran army approached.[65]

The flow of news within the country was unreliable

> it being very difficult to get couriers to make the trip, and then procured often failing to make connection with steamers for Panama owing to the many detentions, and often difficulties in procuring passage from La Brea across the bay to Amapala which was the case with my last courier, which will account for the detention of dispatches.[66]

Baxter's sense of how the political situation would resolve itself turned out to be correct. General Xatruch and his supporters retreated on the night of May 19. President Medina reoccupied the capital a few days later. On the evening of May 20 a force of about 400 Hondurans quietly reoccupied Tegucigalpa, leading Baxter to report "Medina may be considered as entirely re-established."[67]

On June 5 Secretary Alvarado proclaimed the war over and peace restored throughout the country. Baxter wrote him a congratulatory letter, expressing his pleasure at the termination of the conflict "secured by the able leadership and command and the true courage and valor of her noble soldiers."[68] Baxter hoped that unity and sense of purpose established during the conflict would continue during the ensuing peace.

With peace restored, he informed Washington that he intended to take a trip to see his family off on their return to the United States and personally review the progress of the Interoceanic Railway.

⇒ ⇐

The return of normalcy soon brought Baxter back to the protracted negotiations over the extradition convention. The document was signed on March 15, delayed because the Spanish copy included incorrect wording and correcting the document was secondary to the Honduran government's effort to win the war. The convention included basic mechanisms for retrieving convicted criminals from the territory of the other, as long as there was proof the person was convicted of any one of a long list of crimes including murder, rape, arson, piracy, mutiny, fraud, burglary, forgery, counterfeiting, or embezzlement. The convention excluded any "offence of a political character." Article IV stated that persons having committed crimes in the country they were resident in could be tried and serve their sentences in that country before being extradited.[69]

Since his wife was bound for the states and the convention was an international agreement of some importance, Henry had Elvira carry it to Washington personally. This arrangement—and the fact that Henry claimed her traveling expenses as a business expense of the legation—later led to a sharp exchange with the Department of State, to whom this seemed a self-serving extravagance. Not cowed by the rebuke he received, Baxter replied that departmental guidelines stated that treaties were important and should be delivered in person or by special messenger. Given the disorganized state of the mails after the recent conflict, to Baxter his actions not only fit within policy, but also made excellent sense. The department was to eventually honor his request for reimbursement for Mrs. Baxter's traveling expenses, illustrating that his military experience had taught him how to outfox government bureaucrats.

That fall he passed another landmark. He wrote his 12-year-old daughter Carrie, "It does not seem to me that I have passed my fiftieth birth day, but this is not very old after all though it seems so to youth."[70] He had achieved a lot in half a century and had every reason to believe that his future would be just as bright as his past had been.

However, Henry Baxter could not hide his loneliness. Carrie, Jennie, and Harry were all in school at Lake Forest, on the shore of Lake Michigan 30 miles north of Chicago. Elvira and Lottie were in Michigan. He was alone in Honduras with only "the pleasure of writing and receiving letters" to keep him company.[71] His consternation was nearly palpable in the fall of 1871 when he learned that much of Chicago had burned on October 8–10. His children could see the glow of the flames from Lake Forest, but until their letters arrived six weeks later Henry had no way of knowing that they were safe.[72]

Still, he tried to be the best father he could, writing in response to Carrie's request to be exempted from keeping a diary for school:

> Now my dear Carrie, you don't want me to do that, and you would regret it very much if I did for it will be such a satisfaction after your school days are passed and will be a source of improvement all the time. So I shall take it for granted that you have not asked me for the excuse. That is right, isn't it?[73]

A long way away he might be, but that did not soften the general's discipline for his troops.

= =

The situation became "very quiet and satisfactory" after the brief war concluded and the attempted revolution was quelled.[74] This despite an uprising of about "three hundred desperadoes" led by a man named Sambrano, a Xatruch leader who had the group "burning and plundering to considerable extent toward the Pacific coast."[75] The Honduran military was able to take Sambrano into custody and kill, disperse, or capture his group.

The war-related labor shortages had disrupted construction of the Interoceanic Railway. Baxter reported that the builders found it "almost impossible" to find workmen to continue and so it was "not progressing very rapidly just now, very little being done on the second, and nothing on the third section."[76]

The unsatisfactory result of the war with Salvador and the equally abysmal conduct of

President Medina in maintaining power against the constitutional authority led him to offer his position up for reelection in October. The referendum would only allow the people to decide if he would complete the remaining two years of his second term, not allow other candidates to declare as opposition. Medina was reelected, probably through chicanery, and many Hondurans were displeased.

Flush with his victory, Medina sought from the government of Salvador "an indemnity for his services in overthrowing Dueñas."[77] This claim was considered "preposterous" and began again another downward spiral of relations between the two countries. Many Central Americans believed that Medina wanted to become dictator of a consolidated Central America, a theory that had basis in fact.[78]

The election and Medina's continued bad behavior inflamed the insurgents, who reorganized and became stronger. Four to seven hundred were reportedly active in early October. They defeated the army, alarming the people of Honduran cities where citizens formed militia groups to defend their homes. Of more concern, the movement was beginning to take on political overtones that could threaten the Honduran government. Baxter wrote to Carrie,

> I have not been out of Tegucigalpa since I came back from Amapala ... and since that the country has been in such an unsettled state that I have not thought it best to leave. The Indians have been very troublesome and the people of Tegucigalpa have been quite as scared as they were during the revolution while you were all here. It is not all over yet but I am in hopes it will be very soon.[79]

By December the group of "Indians and desperadoes" had been attacked and dispersed by the military several times, only to use the challenges of the mountainous terrain to retreat, reassemble, and return to the offensive with little apparent loss of strength. Southern Honduras was destabilized and there were rumors that Salvador and Guatemala would unite to overthrow Medina.[80] Mail was increasingly difficult to send or receive because desperadoes interfered with travel.

⇒ ⇐

On February 9 President Medina addressed the Honduran Congress. In his message, he extolled the rule of law in Honduras and the growing reputation of the country among the international community, most notably "European and American governments."[81] He argued that small nations were based in law and that law must be the basis of decisions. Yet there were situations where the chief executive must use his own discretion in the national interest, such as the defense of the nation against an invading enemy. His actions in retaining power were in the best interest of the people.[82]

That winter the Honduran government signed a treaty with the "insurgent leaders of the Indian faction that had for some time been disturbing the peace of the country and committing serious depredations."[83] The treaty signed in La Paz in December offered amnesty to the insurgents under condition that within 15 days they laid down their arms, returned to their homes, and took responsibility for any further actions against the government.[84] This quelled most of the internal strife, but the persistent rumors of possible war between Salvador and Honduras continued. Baxter reported, "The prevailing opinion [is] that there will be a peaceful solution of all questions of differences, and that amicable relations may be maintained."[85] But the distaste Medina had for President Don Santiago González of Salvador made a reconciliation impossible. By March it was clear that "the press of Salvador being especially bitter against President Medina, and it has been thought very probable that Salvador and Guatemala were likely to unite to make war upon Honduras, (which now is believed to be almost certain) and for the sole purpose to displace President Medina."[86]

González had come to power in April 1871, displacing Dueñas via coup. The González regime organized a convention in October 1871 that drafted a liberal republican constitution guaranteeing citizens basic rights. Under the new constitution, González was elected President for a two year term and inaugurated on February 1, 1872. However, only a small group of the potential electorate qualified to vote, a point that would remain an issue. Salvadoran troops had worked with Honduran troops to help control the rebellious Indian population along the border, both countries agreeing on the need to maintain order. However, González and Medina fell out over unification of the Central American republics. Medina saw himself as the ultimate leader of any such union. González and the leaders of the other Central American republics disputed this, each feeling more qualified, appropriate, or ambitious. They came to despise Medina for his ambition to seize control of their nations. President Miguel García Granados of Guatemala became a close ally of González. When delegates from the republics—all except Nicaragua—met to consider union in the spring of 1872, the resulting discussions were "too full of petty detail, and [their outcome] will never be accepted by all the States."[87]

The spark that finally ignited war was based in religion. The government of Guatemala found the Jesuit Order's allegiance to Catholicism over secular government a source of continuous intrigue. In February Guatemala decided to expel all Jesuits from the country. This example was followed—despite dubious constitutional authority to do so—by Salvador on March 12. Both Nicaragua and Honduras opposed this move. Honduran troops began to collect along the border with Salvador and rumors of impending war grew. Thomas Biddle, United States Consul in Salvador, wrote on March 20, "The unhappy controversies as to the Jesuits threaten serious discord" among the republics.[88]

On March 25 President Medina declared war. The causes included slights at the La Unión meetings, the recent treaty of mutual support between Salvador and Guatemala, and the harboring of Honduran political dissidents in Salvador. Medina ended all official relations with Salvador, closed Honduran borders, declared martial law, and placed the army on a "warfooting." War was "universally considered inevitable" by Hondurans in opposition to Medina who anticipated that his actions would eventually result in his overthrow.[89] Biddle saw the conservative Honduras as the aggressor, refusing to listen to reason regarding the Jesuit expulsion, an issue he felt illustrated Salvadoran liberalism. He felt Medina was attempting to use war as a way to unite factions at odds in his own country and to divert their antipathy toward a foreign government. With a higher population, he predicted that the Salvadorans would be able to raise and equip a larger army and would defeat the Hondurans. On April 2 President González called out the Salvadoran militia and on April 5 mobilized it for action. He was immediately criticized by opposition in his own country for his usurpation of legislative power as established in the constitution enacted one year before. On April 25 González declared war.[90]

The ongoing political issues within Honduras and the international dispute continued to impact the work on the Interoceanic Railway. Baxter reported that the work was "not being pushed with special energy, and certainly its speedy completion from present appearances cannot be anticipated."[91]

The situation quickly deteriorated. President Granados of Guatemala followed with his own declaration of war. A confident President José María Medina led the Honduran army in the field personally. He gave executive authority in the government to Cresencio Gómez. The Salvadoran army was massed near the southwestern Honduran border at Chaletenango and Sensuntepeque. On May 1 Salvadoran General Espinosa moved into Honduran territory, routing what little resistance was met. Meanwhile, General Estrever marched from La Unión toward Amapala. On May 3 or 4 Salvadoran General Don Juan Antonio Medina invaded Honduras at Sabana Grande (about 28 miles south of Tegucigalpa). He surprised and defeated a division of the Honduran Army on May 6. The strategic Pacific port of Amapala surrendered on May 7.[92] Honduras was cut off from the Pacific.

On May 11 Evaristo Carazo arrived in San Salvador, attempting on behalf of Nicaragua to mediate a cessation of hostilities. The effort was unsuccessful despite the support of American counsels Thomas Biddle and Silas Hudson.[93]

Honduran President Medina was in the department of Gracias with the main army attempting to defend against Guatemalan forces as Salvadoran General Medina swept north. On May 9 Baxter witnessed the unopposed occupation of Tegucigalpa. On the 12th General Espinosa occupied Comayagua, forcing President pro tem Gómez, the cabinet, and officials of government to flee. As each Honduran department was occupied, it declared against the government of Medina and committed to support a provisional government formed under Céleo Arias. The invasion evolved into a Salvadoran-sponsored revolution.[94]

Now an experienced observer of Central American politics, Baxter reported that the revolution in Honduras backed jointly by Salvador and Guatemala might just succeed, *if* those governments "can keep their own republics quiet for a sufficient time."[95]

Finally on May 27 President Medina attacked Comayagua. After a battle that lasted "many hours," his army was repulsed with severe losses. He was forced to retire, abandoning the field to the invaders.[96]

Both the revolutionaries and their combined Salvadoran-Guatemalan sponsors thought President Medina finished. Revolutionary Hondurans set about forming a new permanent government. Both the Salvadoran and Guatemalan armies returned home, leaving only 800 men to guard the provisional government in Comayagua. Curiously, they seemed little worried by the fact that the former government headed by President pro tem Gómez was still at large, nor by rumors that President Medina had retired to a stronghold at Omoa. Baxter refused to commit to the belief that President Medina was gone permanently.[97]

In a culture where the personal animosities between national leaders could easily lead to war, the internal jealousies and desires for power left the new government a weak confederation. Baxter could not contain some contempt for the situation when he reported that "the revolution in Honduras is the result of personal dislikes and the desire for personal power, rather than of any desire for the public welfare."[98] Obtaining reliable information was impossible. Medina and his government were reported variously in Omoa or Truxillo. On June 21 a rumor spread that Salvador was in the midst of a revolution.[99] By early July the invading forces and their provisional government held the south while Medina held the north, creating an uneasy balance of power that shifted each day. The governments of Salvador and Guatemala were tottering. A more fluid political situation is almost impossible to imagine.

July 1872 was Henry Baxter's most interesting month as American Consul in Honduras. On July 13 Baxter asked Fish for "instructions as under what circumstances it would be proper for me to recognize a new Government in case the revolution should succeed."[100] Work on the railroad was suspended and a British man-of-war was reportedly on the north coast protecting that section of the work. Baxter's communication with Washington via the port of Amapala resumed when the Salvadoran-Guatemalan-backed revolutionary government had control of southern Honduras. But sometime after July 13 the territory between Tegucigalpa and the Pacific Coast was occupied and controlled by "an armed force of Indians, estimated from four to six hundred, commanded by one Barona, professedly acting in the interest of President Medina, but appearing to act entirely upon their own responsibility."[101] Baxter anticipated having weeks of diplomatic communications waiting for him in Amapala and on August 10 sent a special courier to the coast hoping to renew communication with the outside world. This courier had a very difficult time of it, being captured by Indians and imprisoned for five days. His arms, money, and valuables were stolen, but the official correspondence was untouched. He made it to Amapala, where he sent Baxter's dispatches and picked up those from Washington. To avoid recapture, he took a circuitous route, traveling at night in the most dangerous areas. He reached Tegucigalpa on September 2.

What Baxter had to report was both shocking and confusing. Barona's Indians attacked Tegucigalpa on July 30. Baxter guarded his retinue at home while a battle between three hundred Indians and 50 soldiers backed by the armed citizens of the city was fought for an hour and a half. Barona's Indians were defeated and retreated, but not far, leaving the citizenry in continual fear that the attack might be renewed. Baxter concluded that "Honduras now has a revolution within a revolution."[102]

Medina was not the only one with problems. González found his citizenry harder to control when he returned and in July he suspended the constitution and resumed dictatorial powers in order to remain in the Presidency. Before long González's enemies were deported.

Meanwhile the primary revolution continued. On July 10 Salvadoran General Juan Antonio Medina, who acted under the authority of provisional Honduran President Céleo Arias, attacked Omoa. The castle at Omoa fired its cannons in defense, killing a few Salvadorans and striking the residence of the British Consul General. The Salvadorans assembled all the women and children of the town in the main street and threatened to kill them if the fort did not capitulate. On July 15 the castle surrendered. However, in an unexpected twist, as soon as he had possession of the fort, Salvadoran Juan Antonio Medina (aka Medinetta) declared himself Provisional President of Honduras, began appointing ministers, and threatened foreign merchants. He forced President Crescencio Gómez to inaugurate him on July 17. Some supposed that this arrangement was part of a secret agreement with former President Medina, as a means of returning to power, or at least subverting the power of the provisional government. This interpretation was supported by the report that one of the Presidents Medina—in charge of the second provisional government—with six hundred troops was defeated at Santa Barbara in northeastern Honduras by an army of the first provisional government led by Salvadoran General Espinoza. On August 2, former President José María Medina was captured at Puerto Cabello and was brought to Comayagua on August 9. Baxter reported that this news was "celebrated by a general ringing of bells and firing of cannon."[103] The other Medina (aka Medinetta) was "driven from the country," escaping to Salvador where he was imprisoned.[104]

The provisional government of Honduras instituted a series of measures intended to regain order. All men ages 18 to 50 were called to take up arms to support the government, with heavy penalties for those that refused. Communication and commerce with the towns that served as strongholds for displaced President Medina—Omoa, San Pedro, and Port Cortés—was suspended. The government complained that the directors of the Honduras Interoceanic Railroad had not been neutral during the conflict, giving aid to former President Medina. In all, it appeared that a strong central government was again in place.

By early September provisional President Céleo Arias intended to reconvene Congress and use that body to try former President Medina. The new government wanted to make an example of the old leader, and in this way satisfy his detractors at home and his opponents in Salvador and Guatemala. The idea that this would promote long term stability in the country was dubious.

Problems for President González in Salvador continued. In early September he called for a new constitution that would provide an air of legitimacy in light of his unwillingness to be hemmed in by the current constitution, which had been adopted the previous October. The changes he wished included the extension of the Presidential term from two to four years, Presidential control of the press, the ability to activate the army and militia as he wished, and a myriad of smaller, but important, extensions of his authority. Within days, Vice President Méndez, "a virtuous man, honorable, energetic, and talented, with the esteem of the whole community," was shot in the back in a public street, assassinated because of his role in either maintaining or subverting González's power. At the time of his death, he was in charge of all government departments save only foreign relations.

There was widespread despair that this instability would not end. Hondurans were concerned that the war had disrupted daily life. As the story of L.E. Burkman, the American superintendent of railroad carpenters, illustrated, provisional troops had little self-control:

> After the suspension of the works I was ordered by Mr. James Douglas, the engineer in Chief of this District…, to take an account of stock in the District Store. On the 18th of July … a small party of soldiers entered the town under the command of one Leandro Rodrigues … acting under the provisional Government as Governor of this Department. They come to the Station saying that there [sic] mission was to establish peace and order. Some goods belonging to a native merchant of this place were in the company's premises. The said Governor Leandro Rodrigues expressed a desire to see them, they were shown to him, he then left, but soon returned with the merchant in irons, accompanied by some of his officials in a state of drunkenness, and entered the store, and commenced to plunder the effects of this merchant. Upon seeing me seated at my desk, he drew his sword and ordered me to leave the premises. Seeing the condition they were in I thought it best to comply; I rose to put on my coat, when he commenced beating me over the head and back with his sword, screaming in fury, Leave! Leave! Leave! I got to the door, and out on the walk leading to the gate, he following me beating me all the way, thereby raising contusions on my head, and raising welts upon my back so that I was unable to attend to my duties for some days. Whilst being driven out of the station in this manner, there were outside … some twenty soldiers under the orders of Francisco Rodrigues, brother of the above mentioned Governor. He was mounted having a rifle cocked and pointed towards the gate. On seeing his brother following me down the walk toward the gate inflicting these outrages upon my person, he eased his rifle and said "Que Burkman" and put his rifle to his shoulder evidently recognizing me. After passing through the gate, this Governor ceased beating me. I then escaped to a frenchmans house who kindly dressed my bruises, and while there concealed I saw from the window this Governor in company with his officials going round the public square shouting "Viva La Patria" and so intoxicated that in endeavoring to draw his revolver to shoot a harmless Belize negro, who at the time was passing, shot his own brother through the cheek.[105]

Baxter sought justice for Burkman, arguing that the Honduran government was responsible for protecting foreigners and that they should demonstrate resolve to do so by arresting and prosecuting those responsible. The rapidly changing political landscape led to a polite acknowledgement and platitudes, but there was apparently no real effort expended. The government needed all the supporters it could get.

The management of the Interoceanic Railway struggled to maintain progress despite the repeated changes in governmental authority, as well as challenges with terrain, climate, and vast fluctuations in the availability of labor. These challenges drove the bonds funding the project from a high over $80 to a reported low under $40. With no prospect of a stable socio-political climate to work in, the decision was made to give it up. William J. Bain, the agent for sections two and three of the railroad construction project, wrote Baxter on August 29 to tell him the directors in England had instructed him to turn over all plans to the government of Honduras. He was to return at once to England with his staff. "This would seem for the present," wrote Baxter, "to put an end to the prospects of the Interoceanic Railway in Honduras."[106] With the departure of the engineers and workmen, the general contractors Maury Brothers and McCaudlish gave up and the project lay dormant well into the following year.

This came at a time when Americans were realizing that they could unseat the British as the primary beneficiary of Central American trade. New Orleans was the heir apparent to this trade and the *New York Times* examined the gains that could be made by focusing on American development of individual Central American states. Of Honduras' aggregate imports and exports of $2,750,000—the lowest among Costa Rica, Nicaragua, and Guatemala—the United States could claim only a small percentage. The British exodus created an opportunity for American entrepreneurs to capture a greater part of the trade in Honduran exports. Conversely, Honduras held potential for consumption of American exports of provisions and manufactured goods. The merchants of New Orleans were encouraged to use the pending establishment of a new steamship line to Central American ports as the basis "for a complete commercial conquest of all these States."[107] Baxter saw the potential and supported it, but American business moved slowly. However, the end of the war gave the British company heart to go forward again. In October the order to withdraw British subjects working on the railway was rescinded, and the construction began again, albeit at a slow pace.

Normal routine reasserted itself in Honduras. Elections in December allowed the legislature to hold a new session in January or February. But by November Baxter's only communication with the provisional government had been a brief note from the new Foreign Minister Ponciano Leiva indicating that Baxter could communicate with him as necessary. The fact that the new government made no request to be officially recognized by the United States puzzled both Baxter and the Department of State. Both expected a rapid request to insure that the government be seen as legitimate and stable on the international stage, and Baxter prepared accordingly. Finally late in November Baxter received a letter from President Grant to be presented to Provisional President Arias to assure him of continued good relations between the two governments.[108]

Baxter presented Grant's letter personally to Arias on December 9, assuring him that the United States desired the peace and prosperity of the republic and that cordial relations be maintained between the two. On December 11, Arias returned the favor, bringing his cabinet to visit Baxter.[109]

With affairs apparently in good order, on November 30, 1872, Henry Baxter asked the State Department for 60 days leave of absence to deal with personal business. He felt that his three year absence from his home more than justified a brief leave. The request was granted, but Baxter was not able to get away. The return of civil unrest created an "unsettled state of the country [that] has not permitted me to take advantage of this leave within the prescribed time, owing to the insecurity of travelling from this to the coast with my family."[110]

In December he learned that the legations of the Central American countries were to be combined. On December 18 he wrote to Senator Chandler (R–Michigan) asking for help to obtain this combined position that—with a salary of $10,000—would have been a significant step up. Chandler wrote in February, "You are the man I wish to hold the position and my influence will look to that end."[111]

By late January 1873 no elections had been scheduled and there were uprisings in several departments. The legation's mail was disrupted. The general contractor for the railway had "thrown up the whole affair" and the work halted again. Employees were being retained pending a government attempt to obtain a new loan in Paris.[112]

On February 12 Baxter wrote to a new Secretary of Foreign Affairs—Juan N. Venero—trying to resolve claims by three Americans against the Honduran government. The losses included personal injury, failure to fulfill a contract, and outright theft of money and materials. Baxter encouraged Venero to settle the claims. Again mired in growing political turmoil, these claims received scant attention.

The result of the 1872 overthrow of Medina was the return of liberal government in Guatemala and Salvador. Céleo Arias was elected Honduran President on July 26, 1872, and began to consolidate power. Medina remained imprisoned for "conspiring against the Government."[113] Other prominent Hondurans were arrested for "heading and instigating a conspiracy to overthrow the present government and to release ex-President Medina from prison" which caused "quite an excitement" lasting several weeks.[114] On March 18, 1873, the Honduran government issued a call for a constitutional assembly with an address by President Arias, stating the need for the people to choose wise representatives.

Baxter learned on March 29 that the previous extradition agreement he had negotiated with the government of Honduras had failed to pass the United States Senate. He received full written authority to negotiate a new extradition agreement. He immediately contacted Foreign Minister Vinero and commenced.

On June 4, 1873, Baxter signed the convention for extradition of criminals he had negotiated. The convention was not approved by the Senate until February 9, 1874.[115]

On May 22, 1872, Congress consolidated the Central American diplomatic missions. The decision was based in part upon the recent crisis during which American diplomats in multiple countries tried unsuccessfully to bring the nations to peaceful terms. But the policy was also a return to the belief that the Central American countries should be consolidated and that this could best be encouraged by a single diplomat that worked patiently toward

10. Mission to Honduras, 1869–1873

that end. The fact that this consolidation would allow the administration to save money on diplomatic salaries was an added bonus.[116] With the consolidation pending, Baxter gave up as impractical his planned visit home, stating, "As the mission in Honduras is to be so soon discontinued that I shall find my time so entirely and necessarily occupied with my duties here that I shall not be able to avail myself" of the leave.[117]

Henry Baxter received his official recall on June 26, 1873. The archives and property of the legation were left in charge of José Sotero Lazo, an artist who accompanied Wells on his 1855 trip across Honduras.[118] He left George A.K. Morris in Amapala as commercial agent and was told by Foreign Minister Vinero that this arrangement would be honored, but it was not. Another filibustering expedition was off the east coast aboard the American steamer *General Sherman*. Honduras was again moving toward a state of war with its neighbors, as evidenced by a June 17, 1873, decree by President Arias.[119] Baxter's departure left a lot for the combined consul to deal with.

Henry Baxter closed his mission, as did former Ministers Jacob Blair of Costa Rica and Thomas Biddle of San Salvador. The three journeyed home together with their families aboard the steamship *Rising Star* with Consul Harrington of Aspinwall, Colombia (now Colón, Panama) in August. They had a final audience at the State Department.[120]

By the time of his departure, the Interoceanic Railway had been restructured and was running between Puerto Cortés and Potrevillo, a distance of 54 miles. The new contract signed in London on July 12, 1873, provided a revised structure for administrating the project, but was not particularly helpful in attracting additional funds to complete the work. Potential backers were concerned: (1) the political instability of the region would not allow the work to be completed; (2) there was a suspicion that most of the money never reached the railway, much of it being siphoned off by graft; and (3) there was little hope that Honduras could repay the debt. In order to keep the work going, 1,000 tons of railway iron held at Amapala was sold to fund continued work on Section 3, the Pacific end of the railroad.[121] The construction was to continue for years before completed from sea to sea.

Losing his position because Congress consolidated Central American legations was one thing, but learning that his replacement was a former Confederate army officer turned Republican was too much. Baxter was replaced by Colonel George Williamson (1829–1890), a native of South Carolina who moved to Louisiana before the Civil War, lobbied the Texas legislature to secede, and commanded a regiment under Confederate General Kirby Smith in the Western Theater of the war.[122] Grant appointed Williamson to help build his southern support for reelection in 1872. Baxter had made a substantial financial contribution to Grant's reelection campaign. He expressed his discontent to Senator Zach Chandler in Washington. Chandler indicated that he would see to Baxter's future appointment.[123]

Williamson used the 52nd anniversary of Central American independence and the upcoming centennial of the founding of the United States as an entrée to talk with the foreign ministers of the several nations about the benefits to be accrued through the peaceful combination of smaller republics under one government.[124]

Williamson reported to Hamilton Fish, "The universally professed sentiment is in favor of the union, except among the office-holders" who would be the ones whose power, influence, and potential for graft would be most immediately curtailed by such an arrangement.[125] There were many political and practical impediments to unification, including problems with communication, significant debts, corruption, and the lack of a common identity.[126] The seemingly unending revolutions continued through Williamson's appointment, as they would for decades to come.

Williamson concluded that the right person was needed to unite the republics, and that the only person with the public spirit and political acumen to have achieved it was former President Cabañas. Central America would remain divided and the conflicts would continue, becoming an object of derision in the United States and the American companies that wished to do business there. By the early twentieth century, writers and filmmakers would make the frequent revolutions in Central America a recurrent punch line to a seemingly unending joke among nations.

The continuing unrest led the *New Orleans Picayune* on September 4, 1873, to quip,

> These countries are thus kept in a continued state of alarm, and the people naturally feel indignant that the United States Government does not take some means to prevent these hostile intents upon its republican neighbors, with which otherwise their relations are entirely of a friendly nature; more especially as none of the Central American States have any naval force like Spain to defend their coasts.
>
> The people say it is unworthy of a great nation like the United States and the leading power on the American Continent.[127]

The Arias regime did not last long due to the machinations of President Justo Rufino Barrios of Guatemala. El Salvador and Guatemala invaded Honduras in early 1874, forcing President Arais to surrender Comayagua on January 13.[128] In another strange twist of fate, former President José María Medina was freed from prison and joined the Salvadorans in the invasion of Honduras.[129] In 1878 he was executed for his continued political agitation.

America remained heavily involved in Central America after Baxter's mission, but skirted intervention in local intrigues in part because of Baxter's example of 1872. Baxter's decisions to defend ex–President Cabañas personally, but to refuse President Medina's request to raise the American flag over the capitol were correct in every regard and had proven the test of time in a country where there were 64 separate presidencies and a number of juntas between 1839 and 1900.[130]

11

Ended All Too Soon

The return to the United States coincided with the Panic of 1873. The general upheaval in business grew to a banking crisis in the fall, causing the failure of many railroads, high unemployment, and a depression that was to last for five years. This was not a particularly good time to be an out of work diplomat.

The *Jonesville Independent* welcomed him home in August 1873:

> He is looking hale and hearty—no older than when he went away, four years ago.... The General is now engaged in hand shaking, which he does in that hearty way which is well remembered by his friends who welcomed his return from California and from the army. Everybody is glad to see him, and he appears equally so on meeting his old time friends and neighbors of Jonesville.[1]

Henry brought home with him "numerous specimens of tropical birds and animals" which he showed around the community.[2]

He had arrived home in time to reenter local Michigan politics. He made multiple public appearances, most notably speaking at a reunion of the 18th Michigan Volunteer Infantry when they convened at Jonesville on August 28. Baxter lauded what Jonesvilleites contributed to the war effort, particularly championing the "substantial aid rendered during the country's hour of peril" by his wife and other women of the community. "The General was cheered lustily, and a number [of veterans] went forward and shook his hand, not having met with him since his return from Honduras."[3]

In the fall of 1873 he used his connections and continued popularity to reclaim his former position as Hillsdale County Register of Deeds (1873–1876). His increased status from the appointment to Honduras and the machinations of his friends and family in Jonesville helped. The backlash over his contrived loss in 1868 also played a part in reclaiming the office. The Baxters assumed a comfortable life, devoid of the excitement of a place where the political landscape seemed stuck in continual earthquake.

The action was the part of the game that Henry loved and in Jonesville he missed it. He was soon making his best efforts to obtain another diplomatic post. Now with undeniable experience, his sights returned to Europe, the most important realm of world diplomacy. His local knowledge now extended into the Grant Administration, with a power base in an increasingly geographically dispersed set of family, friends, Michiganders, veterans, and federal office holders.

The return to Michigan was both joyful and sad. He was able to renew relationships with old acquaintances and see family again. He was nearer his children and had the comforts of home. The Baxters continued to be influential in their state. Both Witter and Benjamin were active with the state educational system, as well as managing lucrative law practices. All were active in the Republican Party and Henry resumed his work with veterans groups.

Jonesville was on the forefront of economic development, having opened the "first cotton cloth manufactory in the Northwest."[4] Jonesville was still on the forefront of important social issues, having invited Susan B. Anthony to help organize a local suffrage society as part of the crusade for universal female suffrage.[5]

Now with a population of 1,800 and a thriving commercial and industrial economy, Jonesville was no longer the rude village that Baxter had come to as a boy and his family was no longer just local gentry, they had achieved statewide and national prominence.

⇉ ⇇

On October 16 Baxter bought the James Gay and Lawson Withington lumber yard, located on the north side of Chicago Street not far west of the St. Joseph River and adjacent to the north-south line of the Fort Wayne, Jackson, and Saginaw Railroad.[6] Within a stones' throw to the southeast was the site of the mill where he started his mercantile career nearly 40 years before. An advertisement in the *Independent* that November read,

> Henry Baxter, dealer in all kinds of lumber, dressed flooring, siding, etc.
> Yard & office opposite the Ft. WJ & S RR Depot, Jonesville, Mich.[7]

In the years after the great Chicago fire of 1871 and the dramatic growth of towns on the western prairies that Baxter had traversed in his youth, lumber was in high demand. Being located adjacent to railroad connections put him in an ideal situation to ship his product anywhere. Best of all, he was in a lucrative business that allowed him time to continue in local elected office and to exert his influence.

Whether his diplomatic post heightened his sense of status or his growing family dictated it, Henry's boundless energy boiled over into an expansion of the family home on East Street. He remodeled the existing one story structure and added a second floor so that it "now looms up among the lofty buildings."[8] Not only was his home in one of the most fashionable Jonesville neighborhoods, its expansion made him competitive with his neighbors, including E.O. Grosvenor, now President of Michigan's Board of State Building Commissioners who were building the new state capitol, the cornerstone of which was laid on October 2, 1873.

Between his lumber business, his position as Hillsdale County Register of Deeds, and the rebuilding of his family home, Henry was very busy that fall and early winter. Yet, what he desired most was another diplomatic post and he awaited word that the newly reelected Grant would find a place for him.

⇉ ⇇

The world continues on without all of us eventually. The year 1874 would see the world continue without Henry Baxter. Robust man that he was, a lifetime of activity and stress left him open to an opportunistic disease.

Henry Baxter had suffered a debilitating fever during the 1849 Gold Rush, had been shot three times during the Civil War, and had struggled with malaria in Honduras. In Decem-

11. Ended All Too Soon

ber he contracted a cold that turned into pneumonia. There was no expressed fear for his recovery. He received treatment at home, but grew weaker, dying on Thursday, December 30, 1873.

The shock of the sudden death of a man who had so often stood firm in the face of physical challenges took everyone by surprise. Word spread quickly, drawing mourners to Jonesville.

Perhaps the best summary of his life was provided by the *Jonesville Independent*:

> In his younger days he was the sole light of the younger people, and many pleasant incidents are yet related by those gray-haired men who were among the early settlers of this county, and companions of the General....
>
> He was 52 yrs. Old on the 8th day of Sept. last, but looked much older. He was one of the best of men—honest, unassuming, social, and generous to a fault. His funeral will take place from the Presbyterian Church, at 10 o'clock AM on Friday (tomorrow).[9]

Baxter's second in command in the 7th Michigan presented a tribute. Sidney Vrooman described Baxter as well liked, a man that stood up for men's welfare. He related with feeling how Elvira had given her husband a Bible before he went off to war, and how appropriate that was for this man to have carried it with him through so many battles, and to have drawn strength from it in Central America. E. W. Childs—former pastor of the Jonesville Presbyterian Church—delivered an hour long funeral sermon. Henry was laid to rest on a hillside at Sunset View Cemetery on Friday, January 2, next to his infant son Eddie and close to his father Levi. An 18-foot granite obelisk was erected on Baxter's grave beneath the oaks and maples.

The prominence of the Baxter family—specifically Henry, Witter, and Benjamin—was extolled in the obituary published by the *Jackson Daily Citizen* which stated "the family is one of the most conspicuous in the history of the state."[10] The *New York Times* carried an obituary, one of the few Jonesville citizens to have been memorialized in this way. Henry had indeed made it on to the national stage.

No one knew it at the time, but Baxter's long sought appointment as minister to a European nation was on its way to him, illustrating that his service in Honduras had been considered good, for Secretary of State Hamilton Fish would not have reappointed him to a more responsible position among those coveted European posts had he not felt him capable. His appointment to Holland arrived days after his death.

Henry Baxter left no will. On January 6, 1874, Elvira petitioned the probate court successfully to have Jonathan B. Graham of Jonesville named estate executor. Graham was an old friend of the family, a prominent farmer and businessman engaged with the Jonesville Woolen Mills, a former state legislator, a member of the Michigan Constitutional Convention of 1850, and a man active in local politics. The tentative value of the personal and real estate was estimated at $8,000.[11]

He left his family with a reasonable, though not extravagant, legacy. Graham had the property inventoried and appraised by Jonesville's most prominent citizens, Ebenezer O. Grosvenor (Republican leader, banker, and former Lieutenant Governor) and George C. Munro (Democratic leader, General of the militia, and businessman) on February 4. In addition to his Jonesville his home, he had land associated with his business that were together valued at $4,100. The assets of his business totaled $16,448.47, including $1,500 in the hands of his brother Witter, and a $5,000 life insurance policy. After the debts were settled, his widow Elvira was awarded $1,745.38 and each of the four children $872.69 in cash on May 16, 1878.[12]

Baxter's life was one of ever expanding growth in personal knowledge and experience that led him to significant achievements. Much as the temptation exists to focus on his Civil War experiences as the climax, like many generals of that war his more lasting achievements occurred in his post-war career.[13] His foray into the local political world was overshadowed by his diplomatic service in Central America, where a man of his temperament and brand of leadership was greatly respected. Had he not died early, he would have reached the European stage, the epicenter of world politics. Surely he would have proved himself worthy there.

⇒ ⇐

The passage of time in Hillsdale County did not immediately erase Henry Baxter from memory. "He was a general favorite with the citizens," was recorded in the *History of Hillsdale County* (1879), "and had the faculty of making himself dear to all his acquaintances either in civil, military or private life."[14] Those characteristics carried his memory onward for generations.

Jonesville remembered Baxter in a variety of ways. Memorial books in his honor were placed in the Jonesville District Library. Contributions in his honor were made to erect the soldiers and sailors monument in the central park only a few blocks north of his family home and across Chicago Street from the Presbyterian Church that was so much a part of his life. For years, the caretakers of Sunset View Cemetery took special care of his grave. During the American bicentennial a chain painted red, white, and blue was erected around his monument.

Short is memory, and especially brief is the recollection of what heroes accomplish. Yet those that served with him did not forget, and that created something of a stir among Michigan units the Grand Army of the Republic when two posts claimed him as their namesake. On March 28, 1883, Post 119 was chartered in Charlevoix as the "Baxter" post. As later recounted by Post Commander G.H. Green, the post was named for the general

> from the fact that a number of our boys was with him in the crossing of the river at Fredericksburg and other engagements. And in naming our Post we considered the name of "<u>Baxter</u>" a sufficient designation as no other soldier of that name distinguished himself as your late husband did.
>
> In the Roster we noticed the names of Custer, Burnside, Wadsworth, Sedgwick, McCook, Garfield, McPherson, and many other Generals—hence we deemed it proper that the name of "<u>Baxter</u>" alone was all that was necessary to distinguish so great a man as he was—His name standing as conspicuous in history as other Generals whose names adorn many of our Posts.[15]

The letter was dated September 8, 1884, Henry Baxter's 63rd birthday.

The post that had trespassed on sacred territory was Jonesville GAR Post 219, which was chartered on January 7, 1884, as the "Henry Baxter" post. Most troublesome to Post 119 was that Post 219 had not only received Elvira's blessing, but that she and her children had donated a "portrait of General Henry Baxter, a gallant soldier, in honor of whom this Post has been named."[16] Elvira also presented a "beautiful flag."[17] The controversy created tensions between the two posts that were not ended until Post 219 was disbanded in 1913 as the number of Civil War veterans in Fayette Township dropped too low to support it. With his sensitivity to the honors bestowed upon him by the officers and men of his commands during his lifetime, Henry would have been touched by this rivalry after his death. With his excellent sense of humor, he would have noted sheepishly that the biggest battle of his career was not at Antietam, Fredericksburg, Gettysburg, or Fair Oaks, it was for use of his name after his death.

Henry's brothers were always his closest cohorts. Witter died in his sleep on February 6, 1888, and was buried in Jonesville. He was mourned as "one of the most prominent citizens in Southern Michigan" politics and education. Like Henry, the *New York Times* printed his obituary.[18] Oldest brother Benjamin lived the longest. He died in Dearborn, Michigan, on June 10, 1902, age 87, and was buried in Tecumseh.[19] Although the brothers were elected to state offices in Michigan, there was no further move toward the national stage after Henry's death.

Among his friends and business associates, the best remembered was former Honduran President Trinidad Cabañas. Though he preceded Henry Baxter in death by two years, he outlived his American friend in the hearts of his countrymen because of his liberal reforms, his honest administration, and his support of the economic development of his country. Today his bust is prominently displayed in Tegucigalpa and his face graces the front of the Honduran 10 Lempira note.

Henry Baxter, his family, and his early allies emigrated to Michigan before statehood, developed the state's resources as they built their own financial capacity, and elbowed their way onto the economic and political elevator of statehood and rode it as far up as they could. That none became governor is a testament to their fierce partisanship and stubbornness that kept them from

Having witnessed his father's bravery in defending former President Cabañas against incredible odds, Henry Baxter's son Harry fell in love with the machismo of military life and Central America. In 1876 he received an appointment as a lieutenant in the Salvadoran Army. He lived as an American expatriate, making infrequent trips to the United States. He was in Guatemala in 1892, but lost touch with his family. His fate is unknown. *Courtesy of Charles Henderson.*

compromising as the world changed. But they played important roles in forming Michigan and the Republican Party, each new opportunity adding to their extended local knowledge of politics.

Henry was the most adventurous and dynamic, a practical leader who learned from his experiences and applied that knowledge as he moved forward, first to the far west, then into combat, and lastly into Honduras. That he got on well with people and earned their respect is clear. But the fact that he among others saw his future guided by providence and that by using what he learned he could push himself, his family, his state, and his country to new levels of power and influence, marks him as a man of this time. Yet, the fact that he—with the least formal education among his family—attained the greatest heights, says something about the man and how he applied the extended local knowledge that he gained through an eventful life. The fact that his death marked the gradual erosion of the influence of Jonesville on the national and international stages illustrates the difference that one person can make.

The nearly constant upward trajectory of his life survived the transitions from businessman to explorer, politician to general, and from civic leader to diplomat. His achievements before and after the Civil War illustrates that the venturist was just as successful as West Pointers, but had a dynamic character that transcended his stunted rise through the ranks of the general officers. His life was truly one that illustrated a venturesome spirit and the grit to match.

Chapter Notes

Introduction

1. This distinction belongs to the crossing at Fredericksburg rather than the crossing of the Niagara River at the Battle of Queenston Heights (October 13, 1813) because the initial landing at Queenston was made before dawn and it is arguable that the defenders were not entrenched. Michael Hurley, "Battle of Queenston Heights: The Americans Lead the First Charge into Battle," *Esprit de Corps* (September 2012): 26.

2. Willis F. Dunbar, *Michigan: A History of the Wolverine State* (Grand Rapids: William B. Eerdman's, 1970), 385.

3. The pastoral motif and its impact on the American experience addressed by Leo Marx, *Machine in the Garden: Technology and the Pastoral Ideal in America* (New York: Oxford University Press, 1964), 24–35.

4. Calvinist Puritanism and the development of a spectrum of Protestant faiths that nicely fit the precepts of a capitalist economy are illustrated in Melvin Stokes and Stephen Conway, *The Market Revolution in America: Social, Political, and Religious Expressions, 1800–1880* (Charlottesville: University Press of Virginia, 1996), 3.

5. Lewis O. Saum, *The Popular Mood of Pre-Civil War America* (Westport, CT: Greenwood Press, 1980), 3–26.

6. Frederick Jackson Turner, *The Frontier in American History* (New York: Henry Holt and Company, 1921), 2–3.

7. Drew R. McCoy, *The Elusive Republic: Political Economy in Jeffersonian America* (Chapel Hill: Published for the Institute of Early American History and Culture, Williamsburg, Virginia, by the University of North Carolina Press, 1980), 168.

8. E. Richard Brown, *Rockefeller Medical Men: Medicine and Capitalism in America* (Berkeley: University of California Press, 1979).

9. Mark Van Rhyn, *Beyond the Battlefield: Post-War Careers of Middle Rank Civil War Generals*, Ph.D. dissertation, University of Nebraska, 2003, 4.

10. Larry Tagg, *The Generals of Gettysburg: The Leaders of America's Greatest Battle* (Campbell, CA: Savas, 1998), 25; Steven E. Sodergren, "Great Is the Shovel and Spade": The Adaptation of Union Soldiers to Combat Conditions, 1864–5, Ph.D. dissertation, University of Kansas, 2006, 6–7. Sodergren discusses Earl Hess' assertion that Union soldiers drew upon models from their civilian lives for inspiration in how to meet Civil War adversity. See Earl Hess, *The Union Soldier in Battle: Enduring the Ordeal of Combat* (Lawrence: University Press of Kansas, 1997), 195.

Chapter 1

1. *History of Delaware County, New York* (New York: W.W. Munsell & Company, 1880), 49, 284.

2. Ibid., 286.

3. Ibid.

4. *History of Hillsdale County, Michigan* (Philadelphia: Everts & Abbott, 1879), 147.

5. *History of Hillsdale County*, 148; *Portrait and Biographical Album of Hillsdale County, Michigan* (Chicago: Chapman Brothers, 1888), 967–968; W.A. Whitney and R.I. Bonner, *History and Biographical Record of Lenawee County, Michigan* (Adrian, MI: W. Stearns and Company, 1879), 84–85; Deed dated October 8, 1831, Lenawee County, Michigan, Register of Deeds.

6. *Laws of the Territory of Michigan* (Detroit: Sheldon M'Knight, 1833), 527.

7. *State of Michigan Gazetteer & Business Directory for 1856-7* (Detroit: H. Huntington Lee & Company and James Sutherland, 1856), 128.

8. *History of Hillsdale County*, 140.

9. Ibid., 127, 140, 148; *Jonesville Independent*, March 6, 1862.

10. *Report of the Pioneer Society of the State of Michigan*, Vol. IV (Lansing: W.S. George & Company, 1883), 254; George N. Fuller, *Economic and Social Beginnings of Michigan: A Study in the Settlement of the Lower Peninsula During the Territorial Period, 1805–1837* (Lansing: Wynkoop Hallenbeck Crawford Company, 1916), 77.

11. Harriet Martineau, *Society in America*, Vol. I (New York: Saunders and Otley, 1837), 236.

12. *Report of the Pioneer Society of the State of Michigan*, Vol. V (Lansing: W.S. George & Company, 1884), 254.

13. *History of Hillsdale County*, 148; *Hillsdale Standard*, March 11, 1862; *Delaware (NY) Gazette*, July 1, 1835.

14. *Early History of Michigan, with Biographies of State*

Officers, Members of Congress, Judges and Legislators (Lansing: Thorp and Godfrey, State Printers and Binders, 1888), 80.

15. Clarence Edwin Carter, *The Territorial Papers of the United States*, Vol. XII: The Territory of Michigan, 1829–1837 (Washington: GPO, 1945), 687–689; Fuller, *Economic and Social Beginnings*, 254.

16. Dury, *White Pigeon*, 52–54; *History of St. Joseph County, Michigan* (Philadelphia: L.H. Everts and Company, 1877), 65; Deeds dated October 1 and October 24, 1839, St. Joseph County, Michigan, Register of Deeds.

17. *History of Hillsdale County*, 127.

18. Fuller, *Economic and Social Beginnings*, 285–286.

19. John T. Blois, *Gazetteer of the State of Michigan* (Detroit: Sydney L. Rood & Company, 1838), 26.

20. 1840 Census of White Pigeon, Michigan; Deed dated June 9, 1841, St. Joseph County, Michigan, Register of Deeds.

21. *Acts of the Legislature of the State of Michigan, Passed at the Annual Session of 1847* (Detroit: Bagg & Harmon, Printers to the State, 1847), 47–49.

22. *Hillsdale Standard*, March 11, 1862; First Presbyterian Church Records, 1836–1936, Bentley Historical Library.

23. *Jonesville Independent*, January 1, 1874.

24. *History of Hillsdale County*, 148.

25. *Ibid.*

26. Martin J. Hershock, *The Paradox of Progress: Economic Change, Individual Enterprise, and Political Culture in Michigan, 1837–1878* (Athens: Ohio University Press, 2003), 61–69.

27. Letter from Robert McClelland to Alphaeus Felch, April 13, 1854, Alpheus Felch Papers, 1806–1896, Bentley Historical Library.

Chapter 2

1. Christopher Herbert, "'Life's Prizes Are by Labor Got': Risk, Reward, and White Manliness in the California Gold Rush," *Pacific Historical Review* 68, no. 1 (2011): 339–340.

2. *Michigan Telegraph*, February 3, 1849.

3. *Hillsdale Whig Standard*, February 20, 1849.

4. *Ibid.*

5. *Ibid.*

6. John Cumming, *The Long Road to California: The Journal of Cephas Arms Supplemented with Letters by Traveling Companions on the Overland Trail in 1849* (Mount Pleasant, MI: John Cumming, 1985), xiv-xv.

7. *Hillsdale Whig Standard*, February 20, 1849.

8. *Hillsdale Whig Standard*, March 13, 1849.

9. *Ibid.*

10. John G. Gardner vs. Henry Baxter, Isaac B. Adams, and Ebenezer O. Grosvenor, Case #133 (1847), Hillsdale County Circuit Court, State of Michigan Archives; Levi Baxter vs. Adam Howder, Case #220 (1847–1849), Hillsdale County Circuit Court, State of Michigan Archives.

11. *Hillsdale Whig Standard*, June 26, 1849.

12. *Frontier Guardian*, May 2 & 30, 1849.

13. Louis J. Rusmussen, *California Wagon Train Lists*, Vol. I (Colma, CA: San Francisco Historic Records, 1994), 64–65; John Cumming, personal communication, February 20, 1983; Cumming, *Long Road*, viii, 137–139.

14. Cumming, *Long Road*, 3.

15. *Ibid.*

16. *Ibid.*

17. *Ibid.,* 11.

18. *Hillsdale Whig Standard*, December 11, 1849.

19. *Ibid.*

20. *Ibid.*

21. *Ibid.*

22. *Ibid.*

23. *Ibid.*

24. *Ibid.*

25. *Ibid.*

26. *Ibid.*

27. *Ibid.*

28. *Ibid.*

29. *Ibid.*

30. *Ibid.*

31. Cumming, *Long Road*, 35–37.

32. *Ibid.,* 42.

33. *Hillsdale Whig Standard*, August 14, 1849.

34. *Ibid.*

35. Cumming, *Long Road*, 43.

36. *Ibid.,* 43–44.

37. *Ibid.,* 50.

38. *Ibid.,* 49.

39. *Kalamazoo Gazette*, September 28, 1849.

40. Cumming, *Long Road*, 50.

41. *Ibid.,* 52.

42. *Ibid.,* 53.

43. *Ibid.,* 54.

44. *Ibid.*

45. *Ibid.,* 58.

46. *Ibid.,* 60.

47. *Ibid.,* 62–63.

48. *Ibid.,* 73–74.

49. *Ibid.,* 75.

50. *Ibid.,* 77.

51. *Ibid.,* 78–79, 86.

52. *Ibid.,* 80–81, 87.

53. *Ibid.,* 70.

54. *Ibid.,* 70–71, 85.

55. *Ibid.,* x.

56. *Ibid.,* 82.

57. *Hillsdale Whig Standard*, January 29, 1850.

58. Cumming, *The Long Road*, 88.

59. *Ibid.*

60. *Ibid.,* 89. "Quondam" is Latin for once. "Caput et calces" refers to his kind of shoes.

61. *Ibid.,* 90–91.

62. *Ibid.,* 91–93.

63. *Ibid.,* 92.

64. *Ibid.*

65. *Ibid.,* 95.

66. *Ibid.,* 97–98.

67. Cumming, *Long Road*, 97–98, 101, 120; Edward Leo Lyman, *The Overland Journey from Utah to California: Wagon Travel from the City of the Saints to the City of Angels* (Reno: University of Nevada Press, 2004), 59.

68. Cumming, *Long Road*, 99.

69. *Ibid.*

70. *Ibid.,* 100.

71. *Ibid.*, 101–103.
72. *Ibid.*, 102.
73. *Ibid.*, 102–103, 105.
74. *Ibid.*, 106.
75. *Ibid.*, 106, 121.
76. Cumming, *Long Road*, 121; Ormsby later died while returning to Michigan from California when the SS *Central American* foundered enroute from Panama to New York in September 1857. See http://wellerharvey.wordpress.com/stories/%E2%80%A2-dr-caleb-ormsby-and-the-ss-central-america/.
77. Cumming, *Long Road*, 121.
78. *Ibid.*, 106–108.
79. *Ibid.*, 108.
80. *Ibid.*, 108–109.
81. *Ibid.*, 109.
82. *Ibid.*
83. *Ibid.*, 113–114.
84. *Ibid.*, 115–116.
85. *Ibid.*, 117.
86. *Ibid.*
87. *Ibid.*, 96.
88. *Ibid.*, 118.
89. *Ibid.*, 124.
90. *Ibid.*
91. Cumming, *Long Road*, 118.
92. *Hillsdale Whig Standard*, October 29, 1850; Cumming, *Long Road*, 125.
93. Cumming, *Long Road*, 96–97.
94. *Ibid.*, 97.
95. *Ibid.*, 120.
96. *Ibid.*, 126.
97. *Hillsdale Whig Standard*, October 29, 1850; *Jonesville Telegraph*, October 16, 1850; Cumming, *Long Road*, 132–136.
98. *Jonesville Telegraph*, February 11, 1851, & March 25, 1851, & July 8, 1851.

Chapter 3

1. *Portrait and Biographical Album of Hillsdale County, Michigan* (1888), 990.
2. Hershock, *Paradox of Progress*, 53–57; Jay C. Martin, *Sailing the Freshwater Seas: A Social History of Life Aboard the Commercial Sailing Vessels of the United States and Canada on the Great Lakes, 1815–1930*, Ph.D. dissertation, Bowling Green State University, 1995, 16–32.
3. Hershock, *Paradox of Progress*, 15, 22–23, 38.
4. *Ibid.*, 14–54.
5. *Jonesville Telegraph*, May 9, 1850.
6. *Ibid.* Hershock rightly characterizes the friction between the Democratic and Whig Parties as part of a search for order in which these political entities sought to identify and eradicate the sources of societal anxiety incidental to the rapidly changing times. Hershock, *Paradox of Progress*, 52.
7. *Jonesville Telegraph*, October 21, 1851.
8. Margaret Sterne, "From Jonesville to Frankfort on the Main: The Political Career of William Walton Murphy, 1861–1869," *The Quarterly Review of the Michigan Alumnus* (Spring 1959): 260.
9. "A Slave-Catcher Defeated," *Liberator*, November 22, 1839; *History of Hillsdale County, Michigan* (1879), 127.
10. *Jonesville Telegraph*, April 4, 1851.
11. The quote is from "Pickings by the Way," *Michigan Farmer*, January 1, 1853; The statistics are from *Census and Statistics of the State of Michigan, May 1854* (Lansing: George W. Peck, 1854), 112–123.
12. *Michigan Farmer*, January 1854.
13. Leonard L. Richards, *The Slave Power: The Free North and Southern Domination, 1780–1860* (Baton Rouge: Louisiana University Press, 2000), 192–194.
14. Floyd B. Streeter, *Political Parties in Michigan, 1837–1860* (Lansing: Michigan Historical Commission, 1918), 190. That Christiancy of Monroe knew of Levi Baxter of White Pigeon through legal matters as early as 1846 is shown by letter from Christiancy dated January 12, 1846, contained in *Journal of the Senate of the State of Ohio*, 1st Session, 44th General Assembly (Columbus: C. Scott and Company, 1846), Appendix, 45–47. They later served in the Michigan Senate together.
15. "To the People of the State of Michigan!" *Hillsdale Whig Standard*, July 4, 1854.
16. *Proceedings at the Celebration of the Fiftieth Anniversary of the Birth of the Republican Party, at Jackson, Michigan, July 6, 1904; Together with a History of the Republican Party in Michigan* (Detroit: Detroit Tribune, 1904), 44.
17. Hershock, *Paradox of Progress*, 76, 126–127; Streeter, *Political Parties*, 191; *American (Jackson) Citizen*, July 5, 1854.
18. *Hillsdale Standard*, July 18, 1854.
19. Streeter, *Political Parties*, 192–193.
20. Robert B. Ross, *The Early Bench and Bar of Detroit, from 1805 to the End of 1850* (Detroit: Richard P. Joy and Clarence M. Burton, 1907), 28.
21. *Ibid.*
22. *Jonesville Independent*, November 13, 1873; Birdseye View of Jonesville, Michigan, 1872, from the collection of the Clarke Historical Library, Central Michigan University; Deed and abstract for Lots 14 & 15 Registered October 13, 1856 and October 11, 1856, Lytles Platt, Fayette Township, Hillsdale County, Michigan.
23. *State of Michigan Gazetteer & Business Directory for 1856-7* (Detroit: H. Huntington Lee & Company and James Sutherland, 1856), 136.
24. *Ibid.*, 128, 136–137.
25. John I. Knapp and R.I. Bonner, *Illustrated History and Biographical Record of Lenawee County, Michigan* (Adrian, MI: Times Printing Company, 1903), 221; *Portrait and Biographical Record of Lafayette and Saline Counties, Missouri* (Chicago: Chapman Brothers, 1893), 374–375.
26. *Ibid.*, 137.
27. 1860 Federal Census, Jonesville, Michigan, June 22, 1860.
28. Ralph M. Powers, Jr., *Jonesville Union School at Jonesville, Hillsdale, County, Michigan* (Jonesville, MI: Ralph M. Powers, 2008).
29. *Hillsdale Whig Standard*, September 30, 1856; "The Republican Convention," *Jackson Citizen*, April 3, 1856.
30. *Hillsdale Whig Standard*, October 21, 1856 and October 28, 1856.
31. *Proceedings at the Celebration of the Fiftieth*

Anniversary of the Birth of the Republican Party, at Jackson, Michigan, July 6, 190, 73–74.

32. *Hillsdale Whig Standard*, October 28, 1856.

33. *Proceedings of the Republican National Convention Held at Chicago, May 16, 17, & 18, 1860* (Albany: Weed, Parsons and Company, 1860), 2, 9, 11, 37, 109, 123, 140.

34. *Portrait and Biographical Album of Hillsdale County, Michigan* (1888), 995.

Chapter 4

1. As indicated by the 1860 federal census, the six Old Northwest states of Ohio, Indiana, Illinois, Michigan, Wisconsin, and Minnesota had 17.1 percent of the pre-war population of the United States, and 24 percent of the total population of the Union after secession. *Population of the United States in 1860; Compiled from the Original Returns of the Eighth Census* (Washington: GPO, 1864), iv.

2. Fred A. Shannon, *The Organization and Administration of the Union Army, 1861–1865* (Gloucester, MA: Peter Smith, 1965), 27.

3. Records of the Michigan Military Establishment Seventh Michigan Infantry: Letters—59–14 Box 100, Folder 3, State of Michigan Archives, Letter to General John Robertson from John H. Waterman, April 26, 1861.

4. Shannon, *Organization and Administration*, 35–36.

5. David G. Townshend, *The Seventh Michigan Volunteer Infantry: The Gallant Men and Flag in the Civil War, 1861 to 1865* (Fort Lauderdale: Southeast Publications, 1993), 7.

6. *Jonesville Telegraph*, June 20, 1861.

7. Shannon, *Organization and Administration*, 45–46, 156–171.

8. Letter to General John Robertson from Nathaniel B. Eldridge of the "Rough and Ready Guards" of Lapeer, April 29, 1861, Seventh Michigan Infantry: Letters—59–14, Box 100, Folder 3, Doc 9, State of Michigan Archives; John Robertson, *Michigan in the War* (Lansing: W.S. George and Company, 1880), 99, 270.

9. "Remarks of Gen. Shafter before the Thomas Post G.A.R., March 18, 1902," William R. Shafter Papers, Bentley Historical Library.

10. Letters dated July 2–3, 1861 and July 10, 1861, Samuel Chase Hodgman Papers, A-180, Archives and Regional History Collection, Western Michigan University.

11. *Ibid.*

12. Henry Baxter to Elvira Baxter, June 30, 1861, Henry Baxter Collection MSS 894, L. Tom Perry Special Collections, Brigham Young University, Provo, Utah.

13. Charles Curtis Letter, July 16, 1861, Curtis Papers, Mss. Cc-78, Box 1, Diary 1861, Clarke Historical Library, Central Michigan University.

14. *Ibid.*

15. *Monroe Commercial*, August 8, 1861.

16. *Hillsdale Standard*, August 13, 1861.

17. Curtis Papers, Mss. Cc-78, Box 1, Diary 1861.

18. *Monroe Commercial*, August 15, 1861.

19. "The Old Seventh," *Monroe Commercial*, May 20, 1915.

20. Curtis Papers, Mss. Cc-78, Box 1, Diary 1861.

21. Curtis Papers, Mss. Cc-78, Box 1, Diary August 23, 1861.

22. Curtis Papers, Mss. Cc-78, Box 1, Diary September 2, 1861.

23. *Monroe Commercial*, September 19, 1861; Curtis Papers, Mss. Cc-78, Box 1, Diary August 23, 1861.

24. *Monroe Commercial*, September 19, 1861.

25. *Ibid.*

26. *Ibid.*

27. *Ibid.*

28. *Ibid.*; Letter dated September 10, 1861, Hodgman Papers, A-180.

29. *Monroe Commercial*, September 19, 1861.

30. The Journal of M.S. Rice, Company I, 7th Michigan, February 18, 1902, 7th Michigan Volunteer Infantry subject file, Monroe County Museum, 7.

31. *Monroe Commercial*, September 19, 1861.

32. *Ibid.*

33. *Ibid.*

34. *Ibid.*

35. Letter September 10, 1861, Hodgman Papers, A-180.

36. Shannon, *Organization and Administration*, 125. William Shafter remembered that one of his men broke into tears when told he would have to go into combat armed with one of the dysfunctional Belgian rifles. "Remarks of Gen. Shafter before the Thomas Post G.A.R., March 18, 1902."

37. "Unpublished Autobiography of Robert C. Knaggs, 7th Michigan Infantry," University Archives and Regional History Collection, Western Michigan University, Mrs. Katherine Havel Collection, 26.

38. "Unpublished Autobiography of Robert C. Knaggs, 7th Michigan Infantry," 27, 29; Townshend, *Seventh Michigan*, 17.

39. "Unpublished Autobiography of Robert C. Knaggs, 7th Michigan Infantry," 27; Gary L. Ecelbarger, *Frederick W. Lander: The Great Natural American Soldier* (Baton Rouge: Louisiana State University Press, 2000), 128.

40. Journal of M.S. Rice, Company I, 7th Michigan, 10.

41. *Ibid.*; Townshend, *Seventh Michigan*, 22.

42. *Hillsdale Standard*, October 15, 1861.

43. Ecelbarger, *Frederick W. Lander*, 128–129; "Remarks of Gen. Shafter before the Thomas Post G.A.R., March 18, 1902."

44. Letter from Chester H. Bangs to Miss Augusta Allen, September 29, 1861, "Headquarters, 7th Mich V, Camp Benton," MS# Bb-83.B2, Clarke Historical Collection, Central Michigan University.

45. "Unpublished Autobiography of Robert C. Knaggs, 7th Michigan Infantry," 27.

46. *Jonesville Telegraph*, September 9, 1861; Lewis was editor and publisher of the *Western Rural* (1863–69) an endeavor in which he failed financially, then moved on to the *Chicagoan/Universe*, then in 1870 the *Young Folk's Rural/Weekly*. Franklin W. Scott, *Newspapers and Periodicals of Illinois, 1814–1879* (Urbana: Franklin W. Scott, 1910), 80, 91–92, 105; "Robert F. Johnstone," *Pioneer Collections: Report of the Pioneer Society of the State of Michigan*, Vol. IV (Lansing: Thorp & Godfrey, 1883), 437; J.C. Holmes, "A Sketch of the *Michigan Farmer*," *Pio-*

neer Collections: Report of the Pioneer Society of the State of Michigan, Vol. VII (Lansing: Thorp & Godfrey, 1886), 101; John D. Hicks, The Populist Revolt: A History of the Farmer's Alliance and the People's Party (Minneapolis: University of Minnesota, 1931), 98. Both Witter Baxter and Lewis were honorary members of the Hillsdale College Amphictyon literary society. Other members included Zachariah Chandler, Lewis Cass, Ebenezer Grosvenor, and other prominent Michiganders of the day. History of the Amphictyon Society of Hillsdale College, Hillsdale, Michigan (Chicago: Smith & Colbert, 1890), 60.

47. Floyd B. Streeter, Political Parties in Michigan, 1837–1860, 139; Early History of Michigan with Biographies of State Officers, Members of Congress, Judges and Legislators (Lansing: Thorp & Godfrey, 1888), 484–485; Tom S. Applegate, A History of the Press of Michigan Prepared for the Centennial (Adrian, MI: Times Steam Presses, 1876), 29.

48. Les Hutchinson and Connie James, Jonesville Sesquicentennial Historical Record (Jonesville, MI: Hutchinson and James, 1978), 25.

49. Jonesville Telegraph, October 31, 1861.

50. Franklin W. Scott, Newspapers and Periodicals of Illinois, 1814–1879 (Urbana: Franklin W. Scott, 1910), 80, 91–92, 105.

51. History of Hillsdale County, 131; Sterne, "From Jonesville to Frankfort on the Main," 253–258; Jay Sexton, Debtor Diplomacy: Finance and American Foreign Relations in the Civil War, 1837–1873 (New York: Oxford University Press, 2005), 122.

52. Rudolph J. Schroeder, Seven Days Before Richmond: McClellan's Peninsula Campaign of 1862 and its Aftermath (Bloomington: iUniverse, Inc., 2009), 4–6; Richard B. Irwin, "Ball's Bluff and the Arrest of General Stone," in Battles and Leaders of the Civil War, Vol. II (New York: Thomas Yoseloff, 1956), 123–134; Townshend, Seventh Michigan, 24.

53. Letter dated October 27, 1861, by unidentified member of 7th Michigan Infantry, Jean Meyer Richards Collection, A-1704, Archives and Regional History Collection, Western Michigan University.

54. Ibid.

55. Curtis Papers, Mss. Cc-78, Box 1, Diary 1861, undated entry.

56. Ecelbarger, Frederick W. Lander, 129–137; "Unpublished Autobiography of Robert C. Knaggs, 7th Michigan Infantry," 27.

57. "Unpublished Autobiography of Robert C. Knaggs, 7th Michigan Infantry," 26.

58. Townshend, Seventh Michigan, 26.

59. Monroe Commercial, December 12, 1861, in Townshend, Seventh Michigan, 29–31.

60. Schroeder, Seven Days Before Richmond, 6.

61. Monroe Commercial, December 12, 1861.

62. Henry Baxter to Elvira Baxter, December 31, 1861, Henry Baxter Collection MSS 894.

63. "What Michigan Has Done for the Union," New York Herald-Tribune, November 27, 1861.

Chapter 5

1. Letter dated January 12, 1862, Hodgman Papers, A-180.

2. Letter dated February 13, 1862, Hodgman Papers, A-180. General Stone's arrest and over six month imprisonment without trial was largely political. Stone was later reinstated and returned to service, though his military career never recovered.

3. Hillsdale Standard, March 11, 1862; Jonesville Telegraph, March 6, 1862.

4. Henry Baxter to Elvira Baxter, March 20, 1862, Burton Historical Collection, Detroit Public Library.

5. Jonesville Telegraph, April 17, 1862.

6. Mary A. Livermore, My Story of the War: A Woman's Narrative of Four Years Personal Experience as a Nurse in the Union Army (Hartford, CT: A.D. Worthington and Company, 1889), 109.

7. Jonesville Telegraph, May 29, 1862.

8. Livermore, My Story of the War, 122, 133, 136, 143–144, 155.

9. Letter from Charles Curtis dated March 2, 1862, Charles Henry Curtis Papers, Cc-78.

10. Letter dated March 9, 1862, Hodgman Papers, A-180; Schroeder, Seven Days Before Richmond, 19; Monroe Commercial, March 27, 1862, in Townshend, Seventh Michigan, 35–36.

11. The Journal of M.S. Rice, Company I, 7th Michigan, 11.

12. "Unpublished Autobiography of Robert C. Knaggs," 29; Letters dated March 10, 1862, March 16, 1862, and March 20, 1862, Hodgman Papers, A-180; Monroe Commercial, March 27, 1862, in Townshend, Seventh Michigan, 34–35; Paul H. Carlson, "Pecos Bill": A Military Biography of William R. Shafter (College Station: Texas A&M University Press, 1989), 17. The captured officer was Major E.B. Pendleton, Commissary Department, Provisional Army of the Confederate States of America. War of the Rebellion Series II, Volume VIII (Washington: GPO, 1899), 60. Hereafter cited as OR.

13. Henry Baxter to Elvira Baxter, March 20, 1862, Burton Historical Collection.

14. Ibid.

15. Ibid.

16. Monroe Commercial, March 27, 1862, in Townshend, Seventh Michigan, 36.

17. "Unpublished Autobiography of Robert C. Knaggs," 29; Letters dated March 10, 1862, March 16, 1862, and March 20, 1862, Hodgman Papers, A-180; Monroe Commercial, March 27, 1862, in Townshend, Seventh Michigan, 34–35. In a letter home Henry Baxter indicated that new muskets had been received as early as November 13, 1861, just after the disastrous Balls Bluff affair. The author has uncovered no explanation and interprets this to mean that some newer weapons were received in November, but that the bulk were not obtained until spring. Henry Baxter to Elvira Baxter, November 14, 1861, Henry Baxter Collection MSS 894.

18. "Unpublished Autobiography of Robert C. Knaggs," 27–29; Letter from Charles Curtis dated March 2, 1862, Curtis Papers, Cc-78. The letter contains some items written after March 2.

19. Charles Curtis Diary, March 25, 1862, Curtis Papers, Mss. Cc-78.

20. Ibid., April 6, 1862.

21. Ibid.

22. Records of the Michigan Military Establishment

Seventh Michigan Infantry: Letters—59–14 Box 100, Folder 2, Doc 43 State of Michigan Archives, Letter to General John Robertson from Colonel I.R. Grosvenor, April 15, 1862.
  23. Charles Curtis Diary, April 8, 1862, Curtis Papers, Mss. Cc-78.
  24. Henry Baxter to Elvira Baxter, May 2, 1862, Henry Baxter Collection MSS 894.
  25. Charles Curtis Diary, May 6, 1862, Curtis Papers, Mss. Cc-78.
  26. *Ibid.*
  27. *Ibid.*, May 6 and 7, 1862.
  28. *Ibid.*, May 8, 1862.
  29. John B. Jones, *A Rebel War Clerk's Diary at the Confederate States Capital*, Vol. II (Philadelphia: J.B. Lippincott, 1866), 125.
  30. Townshend, *Seventh Michigan*, 42.
  31. Charles Curtis Diary, June 1, 1862, Charles Henry Curtis Papers, Mss. Cc-78; Townshend, *Seventh Michigan*, 39.
  32. *Ibid.*, 44.
  33. Charles Curtis Diary, June 1, 1862, Curtis Papers, Mss. Cc-78, Box 1, Diary 1861.
  34. *Ibid.*
  35. *Ibid.*
  36. Townshend, *Seventh Michigan*, 41.
  37. *Ibid.*, 44.
  38. Charles Curtis Diary, June 1, 1862, Curtis Papers, Mss. Cc-78, Box 1, Diary 1861.
  39. *Ibid.*, Diary, June 19, 1862.
  40. Schroeder, *Seven Days Before Richmond*, 220–225.
  41. *Ibid.*, 224–254.
  42. Charles Curtis Diary, July 1, 1862, Curtis Paper.
  43. Schroeder, *Seven Days Before Richmond*, 263–270.
  44. Charles Curtis Diary, July 1, 1862, Curtis Papers.
  45. *Ibid.*
  46. "Unpublished Autobiography of Robert C. Knaggs," 31; The Journal of M.S. Rice, 17.
  47. "Unpublished Autobiography of Robert C. Knaggs," 31.
  48. Herman J. Viola, ed., *The Memoirs of Charles Henry Veil: A Soldier's Recollections of the Civil War and the Arizona Territory* (New York: Orion Books, 1993), 17–18.
  49. Schroeder, *Seven Days Before Richmond*, 352–357.
  50. Charles Curtis Diary, July 1, 1862, Curtis Papers.
  51. Schroeder, *Seven Days Before Richmond*, 358–369.
  52. *Ibid.*, 369–371, 383; Townshend, *Seventh Michigan*, 48.
  53. Schroeder, *Seven Days Before Richmond*, 386.
  54. Charles Curtis Diary, July 4, 1862, Curtis Papers; Letters dated July 3, 1862, Hodgman Papers, A-180.
  55. Charles Curtis Diary, July 4, 1862, Curtis Papers.
  56. OR Series I, Volume XI, Part I, 811.
  57. Charles Curtis Diary, July 1 & 4, 1862, Curtis Papers.
  58. Townshend, *Seventh Michigan*, 49–50, 59. An article published after Grosvenor's death indicated that General Halleck had refused to grant any furloughs, and this was the reason McClellan denied the request. The article entitled "Last Reunion of Gallant Seventh" *Monroe Record-Commerical*, June 17, 1915, actually quotes Talcott E. Wing, editor, *History of Monroe County, Michigan* (New York: Munsell & Company, 1890), 452–453. This history was written when Grosvenor was still alive.
  59. Charles Curtis Diary, July 14, 1862, Curtis Papers.
  60. Records of the Michigan Military Establishment Seventh Michigan Infantry: Letters—59–14 Box 100, Folder 2, Doc 39 State of Michigan Archives, Letter to Governor Austin Blair from Brigadier General John Sedgwick, July 12, 1862.
  61. Shannon, *Organization and Administration*, 164.
  62. Records of the Michigan Military Establishment Seventh Michigan Infantry: Letters—59–14 Box 100, Folder 2, Doc 39 State of Michigan Archives, Letter to I.M. Howard from Captain Henry W. Nall, October 28, 1862.
  63. Mark De Wolfe Howe, *Touched With Fire* (Cambridge: Harvard University Press, 1946), 59.
  64. Wing, *History of Monroe County*, 452–453.
  65. Reed, *Bench and Bar of Michigan*, 583.
  66. *OR* Series I, Vol. XI, Pt. II, 80–82.

Chapter 6

  1. Schroeder, *Seven Days Before Richmond*, 427–433.
  2. Charles Curtis Diary, August 4 and 7, 1862, Curtis Papers; Schroeder, *Seven Days Before Richmond*, 432–434, 443–445.
  3. Schroeder, *Seven Days Before Richmond*, 444–445.
  4. *Ibid.*, 446, 453.
  5. *Ibid.*, 452–454.
  6. *Ibid.*, 453–454, 456; "Unpublished Autobiography of Robert C. Knaggs, 7th Michigan Infantry," 32–33; *Jonesville Independent*, September 11, 1862.
  7. Charles Curtis Diary, September 8, 1862, Curtis Papers.
  8. *Jonesville Independent*, September 11, 1862.
  9. *OR*, Vol. 19, 321–322.
  10. *Ibid.*
  11. Charles Curtis Diary, September 20, 1862, Curtis Papers.
  12. "Unpublished Autobiography of Robert C. Knaggs," 33–35.
  13. *OR*, Vol. 19, 322.
  14. James M. McPherson, *Crossroads of Freedom: Antietam* (New York: Oxford University Press, 2002), 3.
  15. The Journal of M.S. Rice, 21.
  16. McPherson, *Crossroads of Freedom*, 8–9; Jones, *A Rebel War Clerk's Diary*, 154.
  17. Jack D. Welsh, *Medical Histories of Union Generals* (Kent, OH: Kent State University Press, 1996), 22.
  18. *Portrait and Biographical Album of Hillsdale County, Michigan* (1888), 990.
  19. *Jonesville Independent*, September 25, 1862.
  20. *Ibid.*, October 9, 1862.
  21. Townshend, *Seventh Michigan*, 75–76.
  22. Records of the Michigan Military Establishment Seventh Michigan Infantry: Letters—59–14 Box 100, Folder 2, State of Michigan Archives, Letter to Governor Austin Blair from Quartermaster Charles Walker, September 30, 1862.
  23. *Jonesville Independent*, October 9, 1862.
  24. Welsh, *Medical Histories of Union Generals*, 23.
  25. *Jonesville Independent*, November 6, 1862.

26. *Jonesville Telegraph*, September 14, 1865.
27. "Unpublished Autobiography of Robert C. Knaggs," 31; National Archives, Baxter Personnel File, War Department Order Number 379 from the Adjutant General's Office on December 5, 1862 and War Department Order Number 5 from the Adjutant General's Office on January 5, 1863.
28. "Unpublished Autobiography of Robert C. Knaggs," 32; Shafter was commissioned as First Lieutenant of Company I when the 7th Michigan Volunteer Infantry was mustered in. Robertson, *Michigan in the War*, 270.
29. Livermore, *My Story of the War*, 234.
30. Francis A. O'Reilly, *The Fredericksburg Campaign: Winter War on the Rappahannock* (Baton Rouge: Louisiana State University Press, 2003), 2. Charles Curtis Diary, November 10, 1862, Curtis Papers.
31. Charles Curtis Diary, November 11, 1862, Curtis Papers.
32. *Jonesville Independent*, December 18, 1862.
33. Ibid.
34. Ibid.
35. O'Reilly, *Fredericksburg Campaign*, 5–11.
36. Edwin B. Coddington, *The Gettysburg Campaign: A Study in Command* (New York: Scribner's, 1968), 48.
37. O'Reilly, *Fredericksburg Campaign*, 24–25.
38. Ibid.
39. Ibid., 25–26.
40. Ibid., 30–37.
41. Ibid.
42. Ibid., 34–42.
43. *Jonesville Independent*, December 25, 1862; *New York Times*, December 12, 1862.
44. O'Reilly, *Fredericksburg Campaign*, 44–49.
45. Ibid., 50–53.
46. Ibid., 52–54.
47. *Jonesville Independent*, December 25, 1862; *New York Times*, December 12, 1862; O'Reilly, *Fredericksburg Campaign*, 54.
48. Ibid.
49. *Jonesville Independent*, December 25, 1862; *New York Times*, December 13, 1862; O'Reilly, *Fredericksburg Campaign*, 54–58, 61.
50. O'Reilly, *Fredericksburg Campaign*, 54–59.
51. *Jonesville Independent*, December 25, 1862; *New York Times*, December 13, 1862; O'Reilly, *Fredericksburg Campaign*, 54–58, 61–63.
52. O'Reilly, *Fredericksburg Campaign*, 63–65.
53. Ibid., 65.
54. *Jonesville Independent*, December 25, 1862; *New York Times*, December 13, 1862; O'Reilly, *Fredericksburg Campaign*, 54–58, 61–67. O'Reilly says the guns went off at 5:00 a.m. The *New York Times* says 5:30 a.m.
55. O'Reilly, *Fredericksburg Campaign*, 66–67.
56. Ibid., 66–68.
57. OR, Vol. 21, 221, 282; *New York Times*, December 13, 1862.
58. Letter from C.G. Birbeck of Co. C., 7th Michigan, printed in the *Jonesville Independent*, December 25, 1862.
59. OR, Vol. 21, 262, 282; O'Reilly, *Fredericksburg Campaign*, 68–69.
60. *Jonesville Independent*, December 25, 1862; *New York Times*, December 12, 1862.
61. Harold A. Small, *The Road to Richmond: The Civil War Memoirs of Maj. Abner R. Small of the 16th Maine Volunteers, With his Diary as a Prisoner of War* (Berkeley: University of California Press, 1959), 61.
62. *New York Times*, December 13, 1862; O'Reilly, *Fredericksburg Campaign*, 70–73, 76.
63. O'Reilly, *Fredericksburg Campaign*, 69.
64. Ibid., 73.
65. Ibid., 73–76.
66. Ibid., 78.
67. OR, Vol. 21, 282; O'Reilly, *Fredericksburg Campaign*, 68–69, 79.
68. OR, Vol. 21, 282.
69. OR, Vol. 21, 282; *Jonesville Independent*, December 25, 1862.
70. O'Reilly, *Fredericksburg Campaign*, 79–80–81.
71. Gary W. Gallagher, ed., *Fighting for the Confederacy: The Personal Recollections of General Edward Porter Alexander* (Chapel Hill: University of North Carolina Press, 1989), 170–171. Alexander was arranging artillery on Marye's Heights at the time the river crossing took place. Clearly, his appreciation of the sight came in part from his background as an artillerist.
72. OR, Vol. 21, 282; *Jonesville Independent*, December 25, 1862; O'Reilly, *Fredericksburg Campaign*, 80–82.
73. OR, Vol. 21, 282; *Jonesville Independent*, December 25, 1862; O'Reilly, *Fredericksburg Campaign*, 80–81.
74. OR, Vol. 21, 282.
75. Ibid., 282–285.
76. Oliver O. Howard, *Autobiography of Oliver Otis Howard, Major-General, United States Army*, Vol. 1 (New York: Baker & Taylor Company, 1908), 323.
77. Ibid., 282.
78. O'Reilly, *Fredericksburg Campaign*, 81.
79. Stephen B. Oates, *A Woman of Valor: Clara Barton and the Civil War* (New York: Macmillan, 1994), 107; "Burnside's Army," *New York Herald-Tribune*, December 15, 1862.
80. *New York Times*, December 13, 1862; Townshend, *Seventh Michigan*, 99. Confederate government clerk John B. Jones in Richmond wrote that Robert E. Lee reported by telegraph that Union troops had not crossed at 3:00 p.m. but half an hour later he expected them to do so that evening or the next day. Jones, *A Rebel War Clerk's Diary*, 210–211.
81. Townshend, *Seventh Michigan*, 99.
82. According to the *New York Times*, December 13, 1862, the river was "not three hundred yards wide." OR, Vol. 21, 282; *Jonesville Independent*, December 25, 1862; O'Reilly, *Fredericksburg Campaign*, 82.
83. Oates, *A Woman of Valor*, 107.
84. OR, Vol. 21, 282; *Jonesville Independent*, December 25, 1862; O'Reilly, *Fredericksburg Campaign*, 82–83; "From Washington," *New York Herald-Tribune*, December 15, 1862; Townshend, *Seventh Michigan*, 99.
85. OR, Vol. 21, 282–284.
86. James Longstreet, *From Manassas to Appomattox* (Bloomington: Indiana University Press, 1960), 302–303.
87. Townshend, *Seventh Michigan*, 98.
88. *New York Times*, December 14, 1862.
89. "Monthy Record of Current Events," *Harpers WWVII* (Harper & Brothers, 1863), 269–270; "Forlorn

Hope," *Frank Leslie's Illustrated Newspaper* 378 (December 27, 1862): 216–217.
    90. *Jonesville Independent*, December 25, 1862.
    91. O'Reilly, *Fredericksburg Campaign*, 102–126.
    92. Jones, *A Rebel War Clerk's Diary*, 210.
    93. *Ibid.*, 211.
    94. O'Reilly, *Fredericksburg Campaign*, 127–245.
    95. *OR*, Vol. 21, 284–285; O'Reilly, *Fredericksburg Campaign*, 102–126, 246–332.
    96. O'Reilly, *Fredericksburg Campaign*, 434–450.
    97. *Ibid.*, 450–456.
    98. Jones, *A Rebel War Clerk's Diary*, 214.
    99. Letter from Robert G. Shaw dated December 12, 1862, in Russell Duncan, *Blue-Eyed Child of Fortune: The Civil War Letters of Colonel Robert Gould Shaw* (Athens: University of Georgia Press, 1994), 269.
    100. The Journal of M.S. Rice, 24.
    101. *New York Times*, December 13, 1862.
    102. *OR*, Vol. 21, 221.
    103. *New York Times*, December 14, 1862.
    104. *Ibid.*
    105. *OR*, Vol. 21, 264.
    106. Robert G. Carter, *Four Brothers in Blue* (Austin: University of Texas Press, 1978), 193.
    107. D.G. Crotty, *Four Years Campaigning in the Army of the Potomac* (Grand Rapids: Dygert Brothers & Company, 1874), 72.
    108. *Jonesville Independent*, December 25, 1862.
    109. *Jonesville Telegraph*, September 14, 1865.
    110. *Jonesville Independent*, December 25, 1862.
    111. *Jonesville Telegraph*, September 14, 1865.
    112. Letter from General John W. Geary, Camp near Fairfax, Virginia, December 26, 1862, in William A. Blair, ed., *A Politician Goes to War: The Civil War Letters of John White Geary* (University Park: Pennsylvania State University, 1995), 76.

Chapter 7

    1. Small, *The Road to Richmond*, 77.
    2. Small, *Road to Richmond*, 79.
    3. *Ibid.*, 80.
    4. *Ibid.*
    5. Notarized statement of A.K. Kinne, MD, January 25, 1863, contained in Henry Baxter's personnel file, National Archives and Records Administration; *Hillsdale Standard*, February 3, 1863.
    6. *Ibid.*; Henry Baxter to Elvira Baxter, February 15, 1863, Henry Baxter Collection MSS 894.
    7. *Ibid.*, March 19, 1863.
    8. *Ibid.*
    9. *Journal of the executive proceedings of the Senate of the United States of America, 1862–1864*, March 12, 1863, 284. From http://memory.loc.gov/cgi-bin/query/D?hlaw:2:./temp/~ammem_JpI2.
    10. Letter Henry Baxter to Elvira Baxter, March 29, 1863, Burton Historical Collection, Detroit Public Library, Detroit, Michigan.
    11. *Ibid.*
    12. "The New Generals," *New York Times*, April 5, 1863.
    13. Letter from Thomas Jones dated March 18, 1863, in Richard M. Trimble, *Brothers Until Death: The Civil War Letters of William, Thomas, and Maggie Jones, 1861–1865* (Macon: Mercer University Press, 2000), 46.
    14. *Ibid.*, Diary February 22, 1863.
    15. *Ibid.*, Letter February 27, 1863.
    16. *Ibid.*
    17. Small, *Road to Richmond*, 84.
    18. Coddington, *Gettysburg Campaign*, 33.
    19. The Journal of M.S. Rice, 26.
    20. Henry Baxter to Elvira Baxter, April 12, 1863, Henry Baxter Collection MSS 894.
    21. *Ibid.*
    22. *Ibid.*, Letter April 14, 1863.
    23. *OR*, Vol. 25, Pt. 2 (Washington: GPO, 1889), 229.
    24. Paul Taylor, *Glory Was Not Their Companion: The Twenty-Sixth New York Volunteer Infantry in the Civil War* (Jefferson, N.C.: McFarland, 2005), 113–115.
    25. Coddington, *Gettysburg Campaign*, 38–30.
    26. Taylor, *Glory*, 115–116.
    27. *OR*, Vol. 25, Pt. 1, 276.
    28. *Ibid.*
    29. Small, *Road to Richmond*, 92.
    30. Taylor, *Glory*, 122.
    31. Small, *Road to Richmond*, 93.
    32. Henry Baxter to Elvira Baxter, September 3, 1863, Henry Baxter Collection MSS 894.
    33. Henry Baxter to Elvira Baxter, May 28, 1863; Henry Baxter Collection MSS 894; *Annual Report of the Adjutant General of Michigan, for the Year 1863* (Lansing: John A. Kerr & Company, 1863), 3.
    34. Coddington, *Gettysburg Campaign*, 5–10.
    35. Small, *Road to Richmond*, 93–94.
    36. Coddington, *Gettysburg Campaign*, 130–131, 209–210; Small, *Road to Richmond*, 97.
    37. Small, *Road to Richmond*, 69–76.
    38. Ken Bandy and Florence Freeland, *The Gettysburg Papers* (Dayton: Morningside Bookshop, 1978), 259–260.
    39. *Ibid.*, 259–260; Coddington, *Gettysburg Campaign*, 228; *OR*, Vol. 39, Part 1, 243–257.
    40. Coddington, *Gettysburg Campaign*, 260–265.
    41. Tagg, *The Generals of Gettysburg*, 24. Tagg states that Baxter's Brigade marched in after Paul's Brigade, but it does not match up with accounts by Small and Baxter.
    42. Small, *Road to Richmond*, 98–99; Abner Doubleday, *Chancellorsville and Gettysburg* (New York: Charles Scribner's Sons, 1882), 142–143; Coddington, *Gettysburg Campaign*, 261–267.
    43. Small, *Road to Richmond*, 98–99; Doubleday, *Chancellorsville and Gettysburg*, 142–143; Coddington, *Gettysburg Campaign*, 261–268.
    44. Donald Pfanz, *Richard S. Ewell: A Soldier's Life* (Chapel Hill: University of North Carolina Press, 1998), 304–306.
    45. Robert Wynstra, *The Rashness of That Hour: Politics, Gettysburg, and the Downfall of Confederate Brigadier General Alfred Iverson* (El Dorado Hills, CA: Savas Beatie, 2010), 210–212.
    46. *OR*, Vol. 39, Part 1, 243–257.
    47. *OR*, Vol. 39, Part 1, 307–309.
    48. Tagg, *Generals of Gettysburg*, 24.
    49. Wynstra, *Rashness*, 218.
    50. Coddington, *Gettysburg Campaign*, 288–289;

Darrell L. Collins, *Major General Robert E. Rodes of the Army of Northern Virginia: A Biography* (El Dorado Hills, CA: Savas Beatie, 2008), 265–266.

51. *OR*, Vol. 39, Part 1, 2,92–293, 307–309; Collins, *Major General Robert E. Rodes*, 265–270.

52. Doubleday, *Chancellorsville and Gettysburg*,142–143; Pfanz, *Richard S. Ewell*, 305; Collins, *Major General Robert E. Rodes*, 270.

53. Doubleday, *Chancellorsville and Gettysburg*, 142–143.

54. Collins, *Major General Robert E. Rodes*, 233; George G. Meade, *The Life and Letters of George Gordon Meade*, Vol. II (Big Byte Books, 2014).

55. Wynstra, *Rashness*, 239.

56. *OR*, Vol. 39, Part 1, 307–309; Tagg, *Generals of Gettysburg*, 24–25. The flags of the 23rd North Carolina were among those captured. Collins, *Major General Robert E. Rodes*, 272; Wynstra, *Rashness*, 242, 245.

57. *OR*, Vol. 39, Part 1, 309–310.

58. *OR*, Series I, Vol. 27.

59. Doubleday, *Chancellorsville and Gettysburg*, 289–291.

60. *OR*, Vol. 39, Part 1, 307–309.

61. Small, *Road to Richmond*, 98–99.

62. Meade, *The Life and Letters of George Gordon Meade*, Vol. II.

63. Ibid., 100.

64. Bandy and Freeland, *Gettysburg Papers*, 246; Welsch, *Medical*, 253.

65. *OR*, Vol. 39, Part 1, 307–309; Wynstra, *Rashness*, 244–245.

66. Small, *Road to Richmond*, 100–101.

67. Meade, *The Life and Letters of George Gordon Meade* Vol. II.

68. Doubleday, *Chancellorsville and Gettysburg*, 148–149.

69. *OR*, Vol. 39, Part 1, 307–309.

70. "Unpublished Autobiography of Robert C. Knaggs," 35–38.

71. *OR*, Vol. 39, Part 1, 307–309.

72. *OR*, Series 1, Vol. 27, Part 1, 309–310; Taggs, *Generals of Gettysburg*, 25.

73. Small, *Road to Richmond*, 103.

74. *OR*, Vol. 39, Part 1, 307–309; Coddington, *Gettysburg Campaign*, 333.

75. Coddington, *Gettysburg Campaign*, 333, 427.

76. *OR*, Vol. 39, Part 1, 307–309.

77. Ibid.

78. Coddington, *Gettysburg Campaign*, 423, 448.

79. *OR*, Vol. 39, Part 1, 307–309.

80. Coddington, *Gettysburg Campaign*, 486–490, 493.

81. *OR*, Vol. 39, Part 1, 307–309.

82. Ibid.

83. Small, *Road to Richmond*, 107.

84. Augustus C. Paul (formerly of the 23rd Kentucky Volunteers) was on June 1, 1863, appointed assistant adjutant-general of volunteers, serving on the staff of General Henry Baxter. He participated in the battles of the Wilderness, Spotsylvania Court House, and Mine Run, during which he was captured and spent eleven months in southern prison camps. *Reports of Committees of the House of Representatives for the First Session of the Forty-Eight Congress, 1883–84*, Vol. II, 48th Congress, 1st Session, House of Representatives Report No. 524 (Washington: GPO, 1884). Paul was the son of Brigadier General Gabriel R. Paul of Newport, Kentucky, and the general—now blind from wounds received at Gettysburg—wrote to Green C. Smith on January 5, 1865, asking for assistance to obtain the exchange of his son. Lincoln endorsed the request "if it can be without detriment" *Collected Works of Abraham Lincoln*, Vol. 8 (New York: Abraham Lincoln Association, 1953), 311. A. Paul was not released until the end of the war.

85. *OR*, Series 1, Volume 27, Part 1, 309–310; Tagg, *Generals of Gettysburg*, 25.

86. *OR*, Series I, Vol. 27.

87. *OR*, Vol. 39, Part 1, 291.

88. "The New Military Aspect," *New York Times*, September 28, 1863.

89. Frederick S. Daniel, *The Richmond Examiner During the War; or the ORitings of John M. Daniel* (New York: Frederick S. Daniel, 1868), 90–91.

90. Daniel, *Richmond Examiner*, 96–97.

91. Stephen E. Ambrose, ed., *A Wisconsin Boy in Dixie: The Civil War Letters of James K. Newton* (Madison: University of Wisconsin Press, 1961), 90.

92. Sterne, "From Jonesville to Frankfort on the Main," 256–257.

93. Jay Sexton, *Debtor Diplomacy: Finance and American Foreign Relations in the Civil War, 1837–1873* (New York: Oxford University Press, 2005), 122–123.

94. Henry Baxter to Elvira Baxter, September 5, 1863, Henry Baxter Collection MSS 894.

95. Ibid., August 4, 1863.

96. Small, *Road to Richmond*, 116.

Chapter 8

1. Small, *Road to Richmond*, 125.
2. Ibid., 126.
3. Ibid.; *OR*, Vol. 33, Part 2, 737–738, 785.
4. Small, *Road to Richmond*, 130.
5. Ibid.
6. Ibid.
7. *OR*, Vol. 42, 188.
8. Robert McBride, *In the Ranks: From the Wilderness to Appomattox Court-House* (Cincinnati: Walden & Stowe, 1881), 30.
9. McBride, *In the Ranks*, 31.
10. Small, *Road to Richmond*, 132–133.
11. *Jonesville Telegraph*, May 19, 1864; *Portrait and Biographical Album of Hillsdale County, Michigan* (1888), 991; Welsh, *Medical*, 23; Richard E. Matthews, *The 149th Pennsylvania Volunteer Infantry Unit in the Civil War* (Jefferson, N.C: McFarland, 1994), 145.
12. Small, *Road to Richmond*, 132–133.
13. *Jonesville Telegraph*, May 19, 1864.
14. McBride, *In the Ranks*, 37.
15. *OR*, Vol. 36, Part 1, 119–188.
16. Noah A. Trudeau, *The Last Citadel: Petersburg, Virginia, June 1864-April 1865* (Boston: Little, Brown, 1991), 192.
17. Sodergren, "Great Is the Shovel and Spade," 85–86.
18. Ibid., 48–65.

19. "Gala Day With the Fifth Corps," *Philadelphia Inquirer*, September 17, 1864, as reproduced in Eric A. Campbell, ed., *"A Grand and Terrible Dramma": From Gettysburg to Petersburg: Civil War Letters of Charles Wellington Reed* (New York: Fordham University Press, 2000), 269, 375–379.
20. Campbell, *"A Grand, Terrible Dramma,"* 264–265.
21. James C. Mohr, ed., *The Cormany Diaries: A Northern Family in the Civil War* (Pittsburgh: University of Pittsburgh Press, 1982), 477.
22. Sommers, *Richmond Redeemed*, 180.
23. Henry Baxter to Elvira Baxter, September 17, 1864, Henry Baxter Collection MSS 894.
24. Campbell, *"A Grand and Terrible Dramma,"* 267.
25. Ibid., 268.
26. Sommers, *Richmond Redeemed*, 190, 223–224.; Campbell, *"A Grand and Terrible Dramma,"* 265–275.
27. Trudeau, *Last Citadel*, 220.
28. Ibid., 253.
29. Walt Alexander, Letter from Watertown, New York, November 16, 1864, Ms#2n-95, Clarke Historical Collection, Central Michigan University.
30. Trudeau, *Last Citadel*, 253.
31. James I. Robertson, Jr., ed., *The Civil War Letters of General Robert McAllister* (New Brunswick, N.J.: Rutgers University Press, 1965), 533.
32. Henry Baxter to Elvira Baxter, December 6, 1864 Henry Baxter Collection MSS 894.

Chapter 9

1. Ervan L. Jordan, *Black Confederates and Afro-Yankees in Civil War Virginia* (Charlottesville: University of Virginia Press, 1995), 242–251; Trudeau, *Last Citadel*, 324.
2. *Inaugural Addresses of the Presidents of the United States* (Washington: GPO, 1989), [June 17, 2012].
3. Henry Baxter to Elvira Baxter, January 1, 1865, Henry Baxter Collection MSS 894.
4. Ibid.
5. *OR*, Vol. 51, Part 1, 286, 288 and Vol. 46, Part 1, 96–97.
6. *OR*, Vol. 51, Part 1, 286, 288.
7. *OR*, Vol. 46, Part 1, 96–97 and Vol. 51, Part 1, 286, 288.
8. Trudeau, *Last Citadel*, 319–320.
9. Ibid., 320–321.
10. *OR*, Vol. 46, Part 1, 96–97 and Vol. 51, Part 1, 286–289, 291–292; Trudeau, *Last Citadel*, 321–322.
11. *OR*, Vol. 46, Part 2, 519.
12. *OR*, Vol. 46, Part I, 96–97.
13. Ibid.; Trudeau, *Last Citadel*, 330–354.
14. George A. Townsend, *Rustics in Rebellion: A Yankee Reporter on the Road to Richmond, 1861–65* (Chapel Hill: University of North Carolina Press, 1950), 246.
15. *OR*, Vol. 46, Part 1, 892.
16. Ibid., 97, 892.
17. Ibid., 893.
18. Ibid., 97–98, 889–890, 893.
19. Townsend, *Rustics in Rebellion*, 256.
20. *OR*, Vol. 46, Part 1, 893.
21. Paul Andrew Hutton, *Phil Sheridan and His Army* (Lincoln: University of Nebraska Press, 1985), 18–19,

150–152. Examples of Sheridan's dismissal of otherwise competent officers include Warren, Alfred T.A. Torbert, and William Averell. The reasons for Warren's removal from command were the subject of a court of inquiry seventeen years later. The court exonerated Warren.
22. Trudeau, *Last Citadel*, 385.
23. *OR*, Vol. 46, Part 1, 894.
24. Ibid., 894–895.
25. Letter Daniel Bentz to David Broey, April 26, 1865, Ms#2a-33, Clarke Historical Collection, Central Michigan University.
26. *OR*, Vol. 46, Part 1, 895.
27. J. David Hacker, "A Census-Based Count of the Civil War Dead," *Civil War History* 57 (December 2011): 307–348.
28. Beth G. Crabtree and James W. Patton, eds., *Journal of a Secesh Lady: The Diary of Catherine Ann Devereux Edmondston, 1860–1866* (Raleigh: North Carolina Department of Cultural Resources, 1979), 694–695.
29. Thomas Reed Turner, *Beware the People Weeping: Public Opinion and the Assassination of Abraham Lincoln* (Baton Rouge: Louisiana State University Press, 1982), 45–47.
30. The secret feelings that southerners expressed in diaries, journals, and letters upon Lincoln's assassination are best illustrated by Carolyn Lawton Harrell, *When the Bells Tolled for Lincoln: Southern Reaction to the Assassination* (Macon, Georgia: Mercer University Press, 1997).
31. Small, *Road to Richmond*, 180.
32. *WR*, Vol. 46, Part 1, 98.
33. Henry Baxter to Elvira Baxter, May 4, 1865, Henry Baxter Collection MSS 894.
34. The Richmond newspapers are held in the Henry Baxter Collection MSS 894.
35. Sally A. Brock Putnam, *Richmond During the War: Four Years of Personal Observation* (New York: G.W. Carleton & Company, 1867), 386.
36. Small, *Road to Richmond*, 180; *OR*, Vol. 46, Part 1, 98.
37. Small, *Road to Richmond*, 180–181.
38. Ibid., 181–182.
39. Civil War Letters of Mack and Nan Ewing, MS 2008-46, Box 4, Folder 13, Archives of Michigan.
40. Larry M. Logue and Michael Barton, eds., *The Civil War Veteran: A Historical Reader* (New York: New York University Press, 2007), 10–11.
41. *OR*, Vol. 46, Part 3, 1292.
42. "The New Provisional Corps," *New York Times*, July 9, 1865; *OR*, Vol. 46, Part 3, 1302–1303.
43. Ibid.
44. *Jonesville Telegraph*, January 1, 1874; *Journal of the Executive Proceedings of the Senate of the United States of America from February 13, 1866, to July 28, 1866, Inclusive*, Vol. XIV, Part II (Washington: GPO, 1887), 857; "The Army," *New York Times*, July 29, 1866.
45. *Jonesville Telegraph*, August 10, 1865.
46. "Reconstruction," *Jackson Citizen Patriot*, August 8, 1865.
47. Photocopied statement dated August 25, 1865, noted filed in Hillsdale County by W.W. Brewster, Clerk, on July 3, 1866, in the collection of Charles Henderson.
48. Alfred Chandler's thesis presented in the *Visible*

Hand (Cambridge: Belknap Press of Harvard University Press, 1977) of middle managers that grew to administer the development of late-nineteenth century America has been applied to Union Generals of the Civil War by Van Rhyn, "Beyond the Battlefield," 2–3.

49. *Jonesville Telegraph*, September 14, 1865.
50. Deed Registered November 3, 1865, Fayette Township, Hillsdale County, Michigan.
51. Statistics were compiled from Robertson, *Michigan in the War.*
52. Ibid.
53. Records of the Michigan Military Establishment Seventh Michigan Infantry: Reports—59–14 Box 100, Folder 6, Doc 4–6, State of Michigan Archives, Letter to Men of the 7th Michigan from Colonel Norman Hall, July 9, 1864.
54. Grouverneur Warren to Henry Baxter, April 30, 1866, Correspondence with the War Department, May 1866, Henry Baxter Collection MSS 894.
55. Henry Baxter to Olivia Gardner, May 3, 1866, Henry Baxter Collection, MSS894.
56. *Jonesville Telegraph*, May 3, 1866.
57. "Union Mass Meeting," *New York Times*, September 4, 1866; "The Boys in Blue," *New York Times*, September 20, 1866.
58. "The Hillsdale Soldiers and Sailors' Convention," *Jonesville Independent*, September 27, 1866.
59. Logue and Barton, *Civil War Veteran*, 281–291; "Patriots for Revenue," *New York Times*, January 1, 1893.
60. "Patriots for Revenue," *New York Times*, January 1, 1893; Logue and Barton, *Civil War Veteran*, 294.
61. Logue and Barton, *Civil War Veteran*, 304–306.
62. "The State Convention," *Jonesville Independent*, June 11, 1868; "Legislative Nominations," *Jonesville Independent*, August 13, 1868.
63. "Legislative Nominations," *Jonesville Independent*, August 13, 1868; "County Convention," *Jonesville Independent*, August 20, 1868.
64. "Letter from Wm. R. Montgomery" and "Wm. R. Montgomery," *Jonesville Independent*, August 20, 1868.
65. "A.S. Welch," *Jonesville Independent*, July 2, 1868; "Hon. A.S. Welch," *Jonesville Independent*, September 3, 1868.
66. "Senator Chandler at Hillsdale," *Jonesville Independent*, September 3, 1868.
67. "The Riot at Hillsdale," *Jonesville Independent*, September 10, 1868.
68. Ibid.
69. "Rail Road!" *Jonesville Independent*, October 8, 1868.
70. "Jackson, Fort Wayne, and Cincinnati Railroad," *Jonesville Independent*, October 22, 1868.
71. "Location of the Jackson, Fort Wayne, and Cincinnati Railroad," *Jonesville Independent*, December 10, 1868; "Wail On!" *Jonesville Independent*, December 24, 1868.
72. *Jonesville Independent*, October 29, 1868.
73. "Election Returns," *Jonesville Independent*, November 5, 1868; "The Village of Fayette," *Jonesville Independent*, November 12, 1868; "Register of Deeds," *Jonesville Independent*, November 26, 1868.
74. "Register of Deeds," *Jonesville Independent*, November 26, 1868.
75. Allan Nevins, *Hamilton Fish: The Inner History of the Grant Administration* (New York: F. Ungar, 1957), 107.
76. Ibid., 111.
77. John Y. Simon, ed., *The Papers of Ulysses S. Grant: Volume 19: July 1, 1868-October 31, 1869* (Carbondale: Southern Illinois University Press, 1995), 440–441.
78. Sterne, "From Jonesville to Frankfort on the Main," 258–260.
79. Applications and Recommendations for Public Office, RG-59, National Archives and Records Administration, letter dated April 12, 1869.
80. Deed Recorded March 16, 1869, Fayette Township, Hillsdale County, Michigan.
81. *The Tribune Almanac for 1868* (New York: Tribune Association, 1868), 87.

Chapter 10

1. "Washington," *Jackson Citizen Patriot*, April 16, 1869.
2. Henry Baxter to W.B. Davis, May 14, 1869, Microcopy 219, Roll 22, Dispatches from United States Ministers to Central America, 1824–1906, National Archives and Record Administration, 1956.
3. "Honduras," in *The American Annual Cyclopedia and Register of Important Events of the Year 1872*, Vol. XII (New York: D. Appleton, 1873), 380.
4. Nevins, *Hamilton Fish*, 1.
5. Ibid., 127–128.
6. Richard Rousseau to W.B. Davis, Letter May 6, 1869, Microcopy 219, NARA.
7. Dana G. Munro, *The Five Republics of Central America: Their Political and Economic Development and Their Relations with the United States* (New York: Oxford University Press, 1918), 121–122.
8. Dario Aquiles Euraque, *Merchants and Industrialists in Northern Honduras: The Making of a National Bourgeoisie in Peripheral Capitalism, 1870s-1972*, dissertation, University of Wisconsin–Madison, 1990, 35–36.
9. https://history.state.gov/departmenthistory/people/chiefsofmission/honduras.
10. Munro, *Five Republics,* 122–122; Thomas Biddle to Hamilton Fish, December 11, 1871, *Papers Relating to the Foreign Relations of the United States Transmitted to Congress with the Annual Message of the President, December 2, 1872* (Washington: GPO, 1873), 504; Hubert Howe Bancroft, *The Works of Hubert Howe Bancroft: Vol VIII, History of Central America, 1801–1887* (San Francisco: History Company, 1887), 324–325.
11. Hector Francisco Trejo and María Emildre Torres de Paz, *Historia de Honduras* (San Pedro Sula, Honduras: Editorial Coello, 2009), 102. Behind this uprising were Florence Xatruch, Francisco Dueñas, and Rafael Carrera, opponents of Medina's regime. Mario Arnoldo Bueso Yescas, *Santa Rosa de los Llanos: Cuña de la República* (Tegucigalpa: Graficentro Editores, 2005), 29.
12. Correspondence from U.S. Minister Resident Honduras to Sec. Seward, September–November 1866, Despatches from United States Ministers to Central America, 1824–1906, Microcopy 219, Roll 22, Honduras, NARA, 1956.
13. Euraque, *Merchants and Industrialists*, 4, 54.

14. "Honduras," in *The American Annual 1872*, 380.
15. Trejo and Torres, *Historia de Honduras*, 2009, 103, 112.
16. E.G. Squier, *Honduras Interoceanic Railway* (London: Trubner & Company, 1857), 99.
17. Charles I. Bevans, *Treaties and Other International Agreements of the United States of American, 1776–1949*, Vol. 8 (Washington: Department of State Publication 8590, 1971), 880–887.
18. Mario Arnoldo Bueso Yescas, *Santa Rosa de los Llanos: Cuña de la República* (Tegucigalpa: Graficentro Editores, 2005), 29–30.
19. Nevins, *Hamilton Fish*, 327; The various routes of the proposed canal were widely debated in the press. Perhaps the most conservative view may be found in "Ship Canal Routes" *Internal Revenue Record and Customs Journal* 11, no. 23, June 4, 1870, 181.
20. Euraque, *Merchants and Industrialists*, 43–44.
21. Nevins, *Hamilton Fish*, 327; "Central America" *New York Times*, March 22, 1871.
22. Baxter to Fish, June 1, 1869, Henry Baxter Collection MSS 894.
23. Henry Baxter to Elvira Baxter, July 2, 1869, Henry Baxter Collection MSS 894.
24. William V. Wells, *Explorations and Adventures in Honduras Comprising Sketches of Travel in the Gold Regions of Olancho and a Review of the History and General Resources of Central America* (New York: Harper and Brothers, 1857), 146–152.
25. All we know about the property of the United States in Tegucigalpa comes from a brief mention in the correspondence of Baxter's predecessor. Rousseau to Fish, April 13, 1870, Microcopy 219, Roll 22, NARA.
26. Henry Baxter to Elvira Baxter, August 22, 1869, Henry Baxter Collection MSS 894.
27. Wells, *Explorations and Adventures in Honduras*, 179–181.
28. Baxter to Fish, May 10, 1869, Microcopy 219, Roll 22, NARA; Rousseau to Fish, April 13, 1870, Microcopy 219, Roll 22, NARA; Henry Baxter to Elvira Baxter, July 12, 1869, Henry Baxter Collection MSS 894; "Death of Hon. R.H. Rousseau, of Kentucky." *New York Times*, September 20, 1872, 2; Dan Lee, *Kentuckian in Blue: A Biography of Major General Lovell Harrison Rousseau* (Jefferson, N.C.: McFarland, 2010), 12–13, 213–214.
29. Henry Baxter to Elvira Baxter, July 12, 1869, Henry Baxter Collection MSS 894.
30. Baxter to Fish, August 18, 1869, Microcopy 219, Roll 22, NARA; Rousseau to Fish, April 13, 1870, Microcopy 219, Roll 22, NARA; Medina to Baxter, August 10, 1869, Microcopy 219, Roll 22, NARA; Henry Baxter to Elvira Baxter, July 12, 1869, Henry Baxter Collection MSS 894.
31. Yescas, *Santa Rosa de los Llanos*, 19–20.
32. Baxter to Fish, July 24, 1869, Microcopy 219, Roll 22, NARA.
33. *Ibid.*, August 27, 1869.
34. Wells, *Explorations and Adventures in Honduras*, 548–549.
35. Baxter to Fish, February 9, 1870, Microcopy 219, Roll 22, NARA; Letter from L.E. Burkman dated December 5, 1872, as an enclosure to Baxter to Venero, February 12, 1873, Microcopy 219, Roll 22, NARA.
36. Henry Baxter to Elvira Baxter, July 12, 1869, Henry Baxter Collection MSS 894.
37. Ephraim George Squier, *Honduras; Descriptive, Historical, and Statistical* (London: Trubner & Company, 1870), 276.
38. Henry Baxter to Elvira Baxter, October 22, 1869, Henry Baxter Collection MSS 894.
39. *Ibid.*, August 22, 1869.
40. Squier, *Honduras*, 276.
41. Bancroft, *History of Central America*, 454–455.
42. Baxter to Fish, August 13, 1870, Microcopy 219, Roll 22, NARA.
43. Baxter to Fish, March 10, 1870 & April 27, 1870, Microcopy 219, Roll 22, NARA, December 1, 1870. Alfred Thomas Archimedes Torbert (1833–1880) from Delaware was an 1855 graduate of West Point who achieved brigade command in the eastern theater early in the Civil War. He and Baxter participated in multiple campaigns together. After the war he was posted United States Minister Resident at El Salvador, then later to Havana, and Paris. Both Baxter and Torbert diligently called the attention of their respective countries to the guarantees of neutrality for the Interoceanic Railroad.
44. "Assassination of Two American Citizens in Honduras," *New York Herald*, December 21, 1870.
45. Baxter to Fish, Letter April 15, 1871, Microcopy 219, Roll 22, NARA.
46. Carrie Baxter Journal, January 30, 1871, Henry Baxter Collection MSS 894.
47. *Ibid.*, January 9, 1871.
48. Carrie Baxter Diary, January-February 1871, Henry Baxter Collection MSS 894.
49. Bancroft, *History of Central America*, 455.
50. Charles S. Henderson interview, November 3, 1983.
51. Carrie Baxter Diary, January 15, 1871, Henry Baxter Collection MSS 894.
52. Baxter to Alvarado, January 17, 1871, Microcopy 219, Roll 22, NARA.
53. George A.K. Morris to Henry Baxter, Letter December 24, 1870, Microcopy 219, Roll 22, NARA.
54. Baxter to Fish, February 7, 1871, and Morris to Baxter, December 24, 1870, Microcopy 219, Roll 22, NARA; "Central America" *New York Times*, March 22, 1871.
55. Circular of the Governments of Nicaragua and Costa Rica," *Alcance a la Gaceta No. 19*, February 8, 1871.
56. Baxter to Fish, April 1, 1871, Microcopy 219, Roll 22, NARA; "Letter from Belize," *New York Times*, April 30, 1871.
57. Alvarado to Baxter, May 24, 1871, Microcopy 219, Roll 22, NARA.
58. *Ibid.*; Bancroft, *History of Central America*, 455; The tendency to run to the United States for protection under the Monroe Doctrine was not new. Similar requests for protection or annexation by the United States had been made by El Salvador when under threat from Mexico in 1822 and by El Salvador Nicaragua, and Honduras in 1849. Walter LaFeber, *Inevitable Revolutions: The United States in Central America* (New York: W.W. Norton, 1993), 24–25.
59. Baxter to Alvarado, May 26, 1871, Microcopy 219, Roll 22, NARA.

60. Bancroft, *History of Central America*, 454–455.
61. Baxter to Fish, April 3, 1871, Microcopy 219, Roll 22, NARA.
62. Alvarado to Baxter, May 24, 1871, Microcopy 219, Roll 22, NARA.
63. Baxter to Fish, April 22, 1871, Microcopy 219, Roll 22, NARA.
64. *Ibid.*, May 2, 1871.
65. *Ibid.*
66. *Ibid.*
67. *Ibid.*, May 22, 1871.
68. Baxter to Alvarado, June 7, 1871, Microcopy 219, Roll 22, NARA.
69. Extradition Convention July 24, 1871, Microcopy 219, Roll 22, NARA.
70. Henry Baxter to Carrie Baxter, Letter November 28, 1871, Henry Baxter Collection MSS 894.
71. *Ibid.*
72. *Ibid.*
73. *Ibid.*
74. Baxter to Fish, September 1, 1871, *Papers Relating to the Foreign Relations of the United States Transmitted to Congress with the Annual Message of the President, December 2, 1872* (Washington: GPO, 1873), 301.
75. *Ibid.*, September 1 and December 4, 1871, *Papers 1872*, 300–301.
76. *Ibid.*, September 1, 1871, *Papers 1872*, 301.
77. Bancroft, *History of Central America*, 457.
78. *Ibid.*
79. Henry Baxter to Carrie Baxter, November 28, 1871, Henry Baxter Collection MSS 894.
80. Baxter to Fish, December 4, 1871, *Papers 1872*, 301–302.
81. "Message Directed by the Hon. Sr. President of the Sovereign Congress at its Fourth Gathering" *Legislative Bulletin of the Republic of Honduras*, February 19, 1872; Baxter to Fish, March 11, 1872, *Papers 1872*, 302.
82. "Message Directed ...," *Legislative Bulletin of the Republic of Honduras*, February 19, 1872; Baxter to Fish, March 11, 1872, Microcopy 219, Roll 22, NARA.
83. Baxter to Fish, March 11, 1872, *Papers 1872*, 302.
84. "Amnesty" *Honduras Gacete*, January 7, 1872, 3; enclosed with Baxter to Fish, March 11, 1872, Microcopy 219, Roll 22, NARA.
85. Baxter to Fish, March 11, 1872, *Papers 1872*, 302.
86. *Ibid.*
87. Biddle to Fish, Letters December 11, 1871; March 12 and April 20, 1872, *Papers 1872*, 502–503, 518–519, 530; "Central America," *New York Times*, August 15, 1872.
88. Biddle to Fish, March 20, 1872, *Papers 1872*, 519.
89. Baxter to Fish, March 30, 1872, *Papers 1872*, 302; Biddle to Fish, April 10, 1872, *Papers 1872*, 524.
90. Biddle to Fish, April 10, April 19, and May 11, 1872, *Papers 1872*, 524–534.
91. Baxter to Fish, March 30, 1872, *Papers 1872*, 303.
92. *Ibid.*; Biddle to Fish, December 11, 1871, 502; Biddle to Fish, April 19, 1872, May 11, 1872, & May 20, 1872, *Papers 1872*, 527, 531, 535.
93. *Ibid.*, May 11, 1872, 534–535.
94. Baxter to Fish, May 15, 1872, *Papers* 303; Biddle to Fish, May 11, 1872 & May 20, 1872, *Papers 1872*, 531, 535.
95. Baxter to Fish, May 15, 1872, *Papers 1872*, 303.
96. *Ibid.*, 303–304.
97. *Ibid.*, June 12, 1872, 304.
98. *Ibid.*, 304–305.
99. *Ibid.*, June 21, 1872, 305; "Central America," *New York Times*, June 25, 1872.
100. Baxter to Fish, July 13, 1872, Microcopy 219, Roll 22, NARA.
101. Baxter to Fish, August 10, 1872, *Papers 1872*, 305.
102. *Ibid.*, June 21, 1872, 305; "Central and South America," *New York Times*, June 25, 1872.
103. Baxter to Fish, June 21, 1872 & September 6, 1872, *Papers 1872*, 305, 306; Biddle to Fish, August 8, 1872, *Papers 1872*, 543; "Central and South America" *New York Times*, August 2, 1872; "The San Salvador and Honduras Difficulties," *New York Times*, August 17, 1872.
104. Baxter to Fish, September 6, 1872, *Papers 1872*, 306.
105. Letter from L.E. Burkman dated December 5, 1872, as an enclosure to Baxter to Venero, February 12, 1873, Microcopy 219, Roll 22, NARA.
106. Baxter to Fish, September 6, 1872, *Papers 1872*, 306.
107. "Central American Trade—Its Value $15,000,000," *New York Times*, September 22, 1872.
108. Baxter to Fish, November 6, 1872, Microcopy 219, Roll 22, NARA.
109. *Ibid.*, November 22, 1872.
110. Baxter to Fish, March 10, 1873, Microcopy 219, Roll 22, NARA.
111. Zachariah Chandler to Henry Baxter, February 12, 1873, Henry Baxter Collection MSS 894.
112. *Ibid.*, January 30, 1873.
113. "Central America" *New York Times*, April 22, 1873.
114. Baxter to Fish, March 31, 1873, Microcopy 219, Roll 22, NARA.
115. *Journal of the executive proceedings of the Senate of the United States of America*, 43rd Congress, February 9, 1874, 243–244.
116. *New Orleans Daily Picayune*, August 2, 1873; *Congressional Globe*, Volume 66, Part 2 February 21, 1872, 1168.
117. Baxter to Fish, May 27, 1873, Microcopy 219, Roll 22, NARA.
118. *Ibid.*, June 26, 1873; Wells, *Explorations and Adventures in Honduras*, 46.
119. Baxter to Fish, June 30, 1873, Microcopy 219, Roll 22, NARA; Baxter to Venero, June 19, 1873, Microcopy 219, Roll 22, NARA.
120. *New Orleans Daily Picayune*, July 31 and August 2, 1873; "National Hotel," *Washington Critic Record*, August 11, 1873.
121. *Appleton's Annual Cyclopaedia and Register of Important Events of the Year 1875*, Vol. XV (New York: D. Appleton, 1877), 387.
122. "Washington: Colonel Williams," *New York Herald*, May 20, 1873; E.W. Winkler, editor, *Journal of the Secession Convention of Texas* (Austin: Austin Printing Company, 1912), 120–123; http://history.state.gov/departmenthistory/people/williamson-george-mcwillie.

123. Zachariah Chandler to Henry Baxter, February 12, 1873, Henry Baxter Collection, MSS 894.

124. "Washington: Colonel Williams," *New York Herald*, May 20, 1873.

125. Williamson to Fish, September 14, 1873, *Executive Documents Printed by Order of the House of Representatives, 1874–75*, Second Session, Forty-Third Congress (Washington: GPO, 1875), 96–97.

126. Williamson to Fish, June 24, 1874, *Foreign Relations of the United States, 1874* (Washington: GPO, 1874), 172–174.

127. "Panama," *New Orleans Picayune*, September 4, 1873.

128. R.G. Huston, *Journey in Honduras and Jottings Along the Way* (Cincinnati: Robert Clark & Company, 1875), 26–27; Trejo and Torres, *Historia de Honduras*, 103.

129. *Executive Documents Printed by Order of the House of Representatives, 1874–75*, 179.

130. Thomas P. Anderson, *Politics in Central America* (Westport, CT: Greenwood Press, 1988), 110.

Chapter 11

1. "Returned," *Jonesville Independent*, August 7, 1873.

2. Ibid.

3. "Reunion of the 18th," *Jonesville Independent*, August 28, 1873.

4. *The American Exchange and Review*, Vol. XXIII, March 1873-August 1873 (Philadelphia: Review Publishing Company, 1873), 262.

5. Ann D. Gordon, ed., *The Selected Papers of Elizabeth Cady Stanton and Suson B. Anthony. Volume II: Against an Aristocracy of Sex, 1866 to 1873* (New Brunswick, N.J.: Rutgers University Press, 2000), 316–317.

6. *Jonesville Independent*, January 1, 1874; *Portrait and Biographical Album of Hillsdale County, Michigan* (1888), 991; Lot 20 Fayette Township, Warranty Deed, Registered October 21, 1873, Hillsdale County Register of Deeds.

7. *Jonesville Independent*, November 6, 1873.

8. Ibid., November 13, 1873, and January 1, 1874.

9. *Jonesville Independent*, January 1, 1874.

10. "Death of Gen. Henry Baxter," *Jackson Daily Citizen*, January 2, 1874.

11. Petition for Appointment of Administrator, Probate Court of Hillsdale County, Michigan, January 6, 1874.

12. Baxter Estate, Probate Court of Hillsdale County, Michigan, 1873–1889; Register of Deeds, Hillsdale County, Michigan, Liber 108, 503.

13. Van Rhyn, Beyond the Battlefield, 9.

14. *History of Hillsdale County*, 128.

15. G.H. Green to Elvira Baxter, Letter September 8, 1884, Henry Baxter Collection, MSS 894.

16. W.W. Wade and C.G. Birbeck to Elvira Baxter, February 22, 1884, Henry Baxter Collection, MSS 894.

17. G.H. Green to Elvira Baxter, September 8, 1884, Henry Baxter Collection, MSS 894.

18. "Found Dead in his Bed," *New York Times*, February 8, 1888.

19. *Michigan Biographies*, Vol. I (Lansing: Michigan Historical Commission, 1924), 62–63; Death Certificate of Benjamin Levi Baxter, June 10, 1902, State of Michigan Archives; *Petersburg Sun*, June 13, 1902, in the obituary index of the Monroe County Museum.

Bibliography

Manuscripts

1820 and 1830 Federal Census of Delaware County, New York, 87A-88.

1840 Federal Census of White Pigeon, St. Joseph County, Michigan.

1850 and 1860 Federal Census of Jonesville, Hillsdale County, Michigan.

Alexander, Walt. Letter from Watertown, New York, November 16, 1864, Ms#2n-95, Clarke Historical Collection, Central Michigan University.

Bangs, Chester H. Letter to Miss Augusta Allen, September 29, 1861, "Headquarters, 7th Michigan, Camp Benton," MS# Bb-83.B2, Clarke Historical Collection, Central Michigan University.

Baxter, Elvira. Death Certificate, December 12, 1915. State of Michigan Archives.

Baxter, Harry. Emergency Passport Application, 1877–1907, Collection Number ARC Identifier 1187503, NARA Series M1834, Roll #11, Vol. 18, www.Ancestory.com.

Baxter, Henry. Applications and Recommendations for Public Office, RG-59, National Archives and Records Administration.

Baxter, Henry. Collection MSS 894, L. Tom Perry Special Collections, Brigham Young University.

Baxter, Henry. Estate. Probate Records, Hillsdale County, Michigan, 1873–1889.

Baxter, Henry. Letter to Elvira Baxter, March 20, 1862, Burton Historical Collection, Detroit Public Library.

Baxter, Henry. Letters. Microcopy 219, Roll 22, Dispatches from United States Ministers to Central America, 1824–1906, National Archives and Record Administration, 1956.

Baxter, Henry. Personnel File. National Archives and Records Administration.

Baxter, Levi. Estate. Probate Records, Hillsdale County, Michigan, 1862–1870.

Bueso Yescas, Mario Arnoldo. *Santa Rosa de los Llanos: Cuña de la Republica*. Tegucigalpa: Graficentro Editores, 2005.

Curtis, Charles. Papers. Mss. Cc-78, Box 1, Diary 1861, Clarke Historical Library, Central Michigan University.

Deeds 1843–1873. Fayette Township, Hillsdale County, Michigan, Register of Deeds.

Deeds 1831. Lenawee County, Michigan, Register of Deeds.

Deeds 1839–1841. St. Joseph County, Michigan, Register of Deeds.

Detroit, Hillsdale, and Indiana Railroad. Minutes. Clarke Historical Library, Central Michigan University.

Ewing, Mack and Nan. Civil War Letters. MS 2008-46, Box 4, Folder 13, Archives of Michigan.

Felch, Alpheus. Papers, 1806–1896. Bentley Historical Library, University of Michigan.

First Presbyterian Church Records, 1836–1936. Bentley Historical Library, University of Michigan.

Grand Army of the Republic, 1876–1945. Record Group 63-19, State Archives of Michigan.

Henderson, Charles S. Oral history interview with Jay Martin, November 3, 1983.

Hillsdale County Circuit Court Records, 1844–1849, State of Michigan Archives.

Hodgman, Samuel Chase. Papers. A-180, Archives and Regional History Collection, Western Michigan University.

Knaggs, Robert C. Unpublished Autobiography of the 7th Michigan Infantry. Mrs. Katherine Havel Collection, A-261, Archives and Regional History Collection, Western Michigan University.

Records of the Michigan Military Establishment Seventh Michigan Infantry. State of Michigan Archives.

Rice, M.S. Journal. Company I, 7th Michigan, February 18, 1902, "7th Michigan Volunteer Infantry subject file, Monroe County Museum.

Seventh Michigan Infantry. Letter to General John Robertson from Nathaniel B. Eldridge of the "Rough and Ready Guards" of Lapeer, April 29, 1861. Letters—59-14, Box 100, Folder 3, Doc 9, State of Michigan Archives.

Seventh Michigan Volunteer Infantry Association. Book of Reunion, 1886–1927. Transcript in the collection of the Monroe County Museum.

Shafter, William R. Papers. "Remarks of Gen. Shafter before the Thomas Post G.A.R., March 18, 1902." Bentley Historical Library, University of Michigan.

Sunset Cemetery Records. Fayette Township, Jonesville, Michigan.
Tuller, Artimedorus. Papers, 1793–1855, Bentley Historical Library, University of Michigan.
Unknown author. Letter dated August 7, 1861, Ms #Bb83.S43, Clarke Historical Library, Central Michigan University.
Unknown author. Letter dated October 27, 1861, Jean Meyer Richards Collection, A-1704, Archives and Regional History Collection, Western Michigan University.

Periodicals

Albany Argus, 1813.
Albany Register, 1810.
Alcance a la Gaceta (Comayagua, Honduras), 1871.
American (Jackson) Citizen, July 5, 1854.
Congressional Globe (Washington, D.C.), 1835.
Flake's Bulletin (Galveston, Texas) 1868.
Frontier Guardian (Council Bluffs, Iowa), 1849.
The Golden Rule (Albany, New York), 1846.
Hillsdale Standard, 1849–1874.
Hillsdale Whig Standard, 1849–1856.
Honduras Gacete (Tegucigalpa, Honduras), 1871–1873.
Ithaca Journal, 1824.
Jackson Citizen, 1856, 1874.
Jackson Citizen Patriot, 1865–1869, 1879, 1889, 1899.
Jonesville Independent, 1862–1983.
Jonesville Telegraph, 1850–1874.
Kalamazoo Gazette, 1849.
Legislative Bulletin of the Republic of Honduras, 1872.
Liberator (Boston, Massachusetts), 1839.
Michigan Farmer (Detroit), 1853–1854.
Michigan Telegraph (Kalamazoo), 1849.
Milwaukee Sentinel, 1843.
Monroe Commercial, 1861–1863, 1915.
New Orleans Daily Picayune, 1873.
New York American, 1834.
New York Herald, 1870–1873.
New York Herald-Tribune, 1861.
New York Times, 1862–1873, 1888, 1893.
The Northern Monthly (Newark, New Jersey), 1864.
United States Service Magazine (New York, New York), 1865.
Washington Critic Record, 1873.

Secondary Sources

Acts of the Legislature of the State of Michigan, 1839. Detroit: John S. Bagg, 1839.
Ambrose, Stephen E., ed. *A Wisconsin Boy in Dixie: The Civil War Letters of James K. Newton.* Madison: University of Wisconsin Press, 1961.
American Annual Cyclopedia and Register of Important Events of the Year 1872, Vol. XII. New York: D. Appleton, 1873.
American Biographical History of Eminent and Self-Made Men of the State of Michigan. Cincinnati: Western Biographical Publishing Company, 1878.
American Exchange and Review, Vol. XXIII, March 1873-August 1873. Philadelphia: Review Publishing Company, 1873.
Anderson, Thomas P. *Politics in Central America.* Westport, CT: Greenwood Press, 1988.
Annual Report of the Adjutant General of Michigan, for the Year 1863. Lansing: John A. Kerr & Company, 1863.
Applegate, Tom S. *A History of the Press of Michigan Prepared for the Centennial.* Adrian, MI: Times Steam Presses, 1876.
Appleton's Annual Cyclopaedia and Register of Important Events of the Year 1875. Vol. XV. New York: D. Appleton, 1877.
Bancroft, Hubert H. *The Works of Hubert Howe Bancroft: Vol VIII, History of Central America, 1801–1887.* San Francisco: History Company, 1887.
Bandy, Ken, and Florence Freeland. *The Gettysburg Papers.* Dayton: Morningside Bookshop, 1978.
Beath, Robert B. *History of the Grand Army of the Republic.* New York: Bryan, Taylor & Company, 1889.
Bevans, Charles I. *Treaties and Other International Agreements of the United States of American, 1776–1949*, Vol. 8. Washington: Department of State Publication 8590, 1971.
Blair, William A., ed. *A Politician Goes to War: The Civil War Letters of John White Geary.* University Park: Pennsylvania State University, 1995.
Blois, John T. *Gazetteer of the State of Michigan.* Detroit: Sydney L. Rood & Company, 1838.
Bonner, Richard I., ed. *Memoirs of Lenawee County*, Vol. I. Madison: Western Historical Association, 1909.
Brown, E. Richard. *Rockefeller Medical Men: Medicine and Capitalism in America.* Berkeley: University of California Press, 1979.
Campbell, Eric A., ed. *"A Grand and Terrible Dramma": From Gettysburg to Petersburg: Civil War Letters of Charles Wellington Reed.* New York: Fordham University Press, 2000.
Carlson, Paul H. *"Pecos Bill": A Military Biography of William R. Shafter.* College Station: Texas A&M University Press, 1989.
Carter, Clarence Edwin. *The Territorial Papers of the United States*, Vol. XII: The Territory of Michigan, 1829–1837. Washington: GPO, 1945.
Carter, Robert G. *Four Brothers in Blue.* Austin: University of Texas Press, 1978.
Chandler, Alfred. *The Visible Hand.* Cambridge: Belknap Press of Harvard University Press, 1977.
Coddington, Edwin B. *The Gettysburg Campaign: A Study in Command.* New York: Scribner's, 1968.
Collected Works of Abraham Lincoln, Vol. 8. New York: Abraham Lincoln Association, 1953.
Collins, Darrell L. *Major General Robert E. Rodes of the Army of Northern Virginia: A Biography.* El Dorado Hills, CA: Savas Beatie, 2008.
Cooper, Phillip L. *The Antecedents of Council Bluffs, Iowa: From Exploration to Town Charter*, Masters. Omaha: University of Nebraska, February 1973.
Crabtree, Beth G., and James W. Patton, eds. *Journal of a Secesh Lady: The Diary of Catherine Ann Devereux Edmondston, 1860–1866.* Raleigh: North Carolina Department of Cultural Resources, 1979.
Crotty, D.G. *Four Years Campaigning in the Army of the Potomac.* Grand Rapids: Dygert Brothers & Company, 1874.
Cumming, John. *The Gold Rush: Letters from the Wolver-

ine Rangers to the Marshall, Michigan, Statesman, 1849–1851. Mount Pleasant, MI: Cumming Press, 1974.
Cumming, John. *The Long Road to California: The Journal of Cephas Arms Supplemented with Letters by Traveling Companions on the Overland Trail in 1849*. Mount Pleasant, MI: John Cumming, 1985.
Daniel, Frederick S. *The Richmond Examiner During the War; or the Writings of John M. Daniel*. New York: Frederick S. Daniel, 1868.
Dempsey, Jack. *Michigan and the Civil War: A Great and Bloody Sacrifice*. Charleston: The History Press, 2011.
Documents Accompanying the Journal of the Senate of the State of Michigan at the Annual Session of 1841, Vol. I. Detroit: George Dawson, 1841.
Doubleday, Abner. *Chancellorsville and Gettysburg*. New York: Charles Scribner's Sons, 1882.
Dunbar, Willis F. *Michigan: A History of the Wolverine State*. Grand Rapids: William B. Eerdman's Publishing Company, 1970.
Duncan, Russell. *Blue-Eyed Child of Fortune: The Civil War Letters of Colonel Robert Gould Shaw*. Athens: University of Georgia Press, 1994.
Dury, Wayne L. *White Pigeon*. St. Joseph, MI: St. Joseph Historical Society, 1994.
Dusseault, John H. *The Thirty-Ninth Infantry in the Civil War*. Somerville, MA: Somerville Journal Print, 1908.
Early History of Michigan, with Biographies of State Officers, Members of Congress, Judges and Legislators. Lansing: Thorp and Godfrey, State Printers and Binders, 1888.
Ecelbarger, Gary L. *Frederick W. Lander: The Great Natural American Soldier*. Baton Rouge: Louisiana State University Press, 2000.
Euraque, Dario A. *Merchants and Industrialists in Northern Honduras: The Making of a National Bourgeoisie in Peripheral Capitalism, 1870s-1972*, dissertation. Madison: University of Wisconsin, 1990).
Executive Documents Printed by Order of the House of Representatives, 1874–75. Second Session, Forty-Third Congress. Washington: GPO, 1875.
Flint, Henry M. *The Railroads of the United States; Their History and Statistics*. Philadelphia: John E. Potter and Company, 1868.
Foreign Relations of the United States, 1874. Washington: GPO, 1874.
Fuller, George N. *Economic and Social Beginnings of Michigan: A Study of the Settlement of the Lower Peninsula During the Territorial Period, 1805–1837*. Lansing: Wynkoop Hallenbeck Crawford Company, 1916.
Gallagher, Gary W., ed. *Fighting for the Confederacy: The Personal Recollections of General Edward Porter Alexander*. Chapel Hill: University of North Carolina Press, 1989.
Gilpin, Alec Richard. *The Territory of Michigan*. East Lansing: Michigan State University Press, 1970.
Gordon, Ann D., ed. *The Selected Papers of Elizabeth Cady Stanton and Suson B. Anthony. Volume II: Against an Aristocracy of Sex, 1866 to 1873*. Vol. II. New Brunswick, N.J.: Rutgers University Press, 2000.
Gordon, Thomas F. *A Digest of the Laws of the United States*. Philadelphia: Thomas F. Gordon, 1827.
Goss, Warren Lee. "Yorktown and Williamsburg" in *Battles and Leaders of the Civil War*, Vol. II. New York: Thomas Yoseloff, 1956.
Grant, Ulysses S. *Personal Memoirs of U.S. Grant*. New York: Charles L. Webster & Company, 1994.
Greeley, Horace. *Proceedings of the first Three Republican National Conventions of 1856, 1860, 1864*. Minneapolis: Charles W. Johnson, 1893.
Harrell, Carolyn L. *When the Bells Tolled for Lincoln: Southern Reaction to the Assassination* Macon: Mercer University Press, 1997.
Hawes, George W. *Michigan State Gazetteer and Business Directory for 1860*. Detroit: F. Raymond & Company, 1859.
Herbert, Christopher. "'Life's Prizes Are by Labor Got': Risk, Reward, and White Manliness in the California Gold Rush." *Pacific Historical Review* 68, no. 1 (2011): 339–340.
Hershock, Martin J. *The Paradox of Progress: Economic Change, Individual Enterprise, and Political Culture in Michigan, 1837–1878*. Athens: Ohio University Press, 2003.
Hess, Earl. *The Union Soldier in Battle: Enduring the Ordeal of Combat*. Lawrence: University Press of Kansas, 1997.
Hicks, John D. *The Populist Revolt: A History of the Farmer's Alliance and the People's Party*. Minneapolis: University of Minnesota, 1931.
Hinchman, T.H. *Banks and Banking in Michigan*. Detroit: William Graham, 1887.
History of Calhoun County, Michigan. Philadelphia: L.H. Everts & Company, 1877.
History of Delaware County, New York. New York: W.W. Munsell & Company, 1880.
History of Hillsdale County, Michigan. Philadelphia: Everts & Abbott, 1879.
History of St. Joseph County, Michigan. Philadelphia: L.H. Everts and Company, 1877.
Howe, Mark De Wolfe. *Touched With Fire*. Cambridge: Harvard University Press, 1946.
Huston, R.G. *Journey in Honduras and Jottings Along the Way*. Cincinnati: Robert Clark & Company, 1875.
Hutchinson, Les, and Connie James, *Jonesville Sesquicentennial Historical Record*. Jonesville, MI: Hutchinson and James, 1978.
Hutton, Paul A. *Phil Sheridan and His Army*. Lincoln: University of Nebraska Press, 1985.
Inaugural Addresses of the Presidents of the United States. Washington: GPO, 1989.
Irwin, Richard B. "Ball's Bluff and the Arrest of General Stone." In *Battles and Leaders of the Civil War*, Vol. II. New York: Thomas Yoseloff, 1956.
Jones, John B. *A Rebel War Clerk's Diary at the Confederate States Capital*, Vol. II. Philadelphia: J.B. Lippincott, 1866.
Jordan, Ervan L. *Black Confederates and Afro-Yankees in Civil War Virginia*. Charlottesville: University of Virginia Press, 1995.
Journal of the Executive Proceedings of the Senate of the United States of America. 43rd Congress, February 9, 1874
Journal of the Executive Proceedings of the Senate of the United States of America from February 13, 1866, to July

28, 1866, Inclusive. Vol. XIV, Part II. Washington: GPO, 1887.
Journal of the Executive Proceedings of the Senate of the United States of America, 1869–1871. Washington: GPO, 1871.
Journal of the House of Representatives of the United States. 1st Session, 22nd Congress. Washington: Duff Green, 1831.
Journal of the Senate of the State of Ohio. 1st Session, 44th General Assembly. Columbus: C. Scott and Company, 1846.
LaFeber, Walter. Inevitable Revolutions: The United States in Central America. New York: W.W. Norton, 1993.
Laws of the Territory of Michigan 1833. Detroit: Sheldon M'Knight, 1833.
Laws of the Territory of Michigan, Vol. III. Lansing: W.S. George & Company, 1874.
Lee, Dan. Kentuckian in Blue: A Biography of Major General Lovell Harrison Rousseau. Jefferson, N.C.: McFarland, 2010.
Livermore, Mary A. My Story of the War: A Woman's Narrative of Four Years Personal Experience as a Nurse in the Union Army. Hartford, CT: A.D. Worthington and Company, 1889.
Logue, Larry M., and Michael Barton, eds. The Civil War Veteran: A Historical Reader. New York: New York University Press, 2007.
Longstreet, James. From Manassas to Appomattox. Bloomington: Indiana University Press, 1960.
Lyman, Edward Leo. The Overland Journey from Utah to California: Wagon Travel from the City of the Saints to the City of Angels. Reno: University of Nevada Press, 2004.
Martin, Jay C. Sailing the Freshwater Seas: A Social History of Life Aboard the Commercial Sailing Vessels of the United States and Canada on the Great Lakes, 1815–1930, Ph.D. dissertation. Bowling Green: Bowling Green State University, 1995.
Martineau, Harriet. Society in America, Vol. I. New York: Saunders and Otley, 1837.
Matthews, Richard E. The 149th Pennsylvania Volunteer Infantry Unit in the Civil War. Jefferson, N.C.: McFarland, 1994.
Marx, Leo. Machine in the Garden: Technology and the Pastoral Ideal in America. New York: Oxford University Press, 1964.
McBride, Robert. In the Ranks: From the Wilderness to Appomatox Court-House. Cincinnati: Walden & Stowe, 1881.
McClellan, George B. "The Peninsular Campaign." In Battles and Leaders of the Civil War, Vol. II. New York: Thomas Yoseloff, 1956.
McCoy, Drew R. The Elusive Republic: Political Economy in Jeffersonian America. Chapel Hill: Published for the Institute of Early American History and Culture, Williamsburg, Virginia, by the University of North Carolina Press, 1980.
McPherson, James M. Crossroads of Freedom: Antietam. New York: Oxford University Press, 2002.
Michigan Adjutant General's Department Report, 1859–1861. Lansing: State of Michigan, 1861.
Michigan Biographies, Vol. I. Lansing: The Michigan Historical Commission, 1924.
Michigan Pioneer and Historical Collections, Vol. XXVI. Lansing: Robert Smith and Company, 1896.
Michigan State Gazetteer and Business Directory for 1863–64. Detroit: Charles F. Clark, 1863.
Mohr, James C., ed. The Cormany Diaries: A Northern Family in the Civil War. Pittsburgh: University of Pittsburgh Press, 1982.
Moore, O.W. Journal of the Senate of the State of Michigan, 1850. Lansing: R.W. Ingals, State Printer, 1850.
Moore, O.W. Journal of the Senate of the State of Michigan, 1853. Lansing: George W. Peck, 1853.
Munro, Dana G. The Five Republics of Central America: Their Political and Economic Development and Their Relations with the United States. New York: Oxford University Press, 1918.
Nevins, Allan. Hamilton Fish: The Inner History of the Grant Administration. New York: F. Ungar, 1957.
Oates, Stephen B. A Woman of Valor: Clara Barton and the Civil War. New York: Macmillan, 1994.
O'Reilly, Francis A. The Fredericksburg Campaign: Winter War on the Rappahannock. Baton Rouge: Louisiana State University Press, 2003.
Orton, Edward. An Account of the Descendants of Thomas Orton, Windsor, Connecticut, 1641. Columbus, OH: Nitschke Brothers, 1896.
Papers Relating to the Foreign Relations of the United States Transmitted to Congress with the Annual Message of the President, December 2, 1872. Washington: GPO, 1873.
Pfanz, Donald. Richard S. Ewell: A Soldier's Life. Chapel Hill: University of North Carolina Press, 1998.
Pioneer Collections: Report of the Pioneer Society of the State of Michigan, Vol. IV. Lansing: Wynkoop Hallenbeck Crawford Company, 1906.
Pioneer Collections: Report of the Pioneer Society of the State of Michigan, Vol. VII. Lansing: Thorp & Godfrey, 1886.
Platt, James E. Journal of the Senate of the State of Michigan, 1847. Detroit: Bagg & Harmon, 1847.
Population of the United States in 1860; Compiled from the Original Returns of the Eighth Census. Washington: GPO, 1864.
Poremba, David Lee. On-the-Road Histories: Michigan. Northampton, MA: Interlink Publishing Group, 2006.
Portrait and Biographical Album of Hillsdale County, Michigan. Chicago: Chapman Brothers, 1888.
Powers, Ralph M. Benaiah Jones III: American Frontiersman, 1795–1861. Jonesville, MI: Ralph M. Powers, 1981.
Proceedings at the Celebration of the Fiftieth Anniversary of the Birth of the Republican Party, at Jackson, Michigan, July 6, 1904; Together with a History of the Republican Party in Michigan. Detroit: Detroit Tribune, 1904.
Proceedings of the Republican National Convention Held at Chicago, May 16, 17, & 18, 1860. Albany: Weed, Parsons and Company, 1860.
Putnam, Daniel. A History of the Michigan State Normal School at Ypsilanti, Michigan, 1849–1899. Ypsilanti: Daniel Putnam, 1899.
Putnam, Sally A. Richmond During the War: Four Years of Personal Observation. New York: G.W. Carleton & Company, 1867.
Reed, George Irving. Bench and Bar of Michigan: A Vol-

ume of History and Biography. Chicago: Century Publishing and Engraving Company, 1897.
Report of the Pioneer Society of the State of Michigan, Vol. IV. Lansing: W.S. George & Company Printers and Binders, 1883.
Report of the Pioneer Society of the State of Michigan, Vol. V. Lansing: W.S. George & Company, 1884.
Report of the Proceedings and Debates in the Convention to Revise the Constitution of the State of Michigan, 1850. Lansing: R.W. Ingals, State Printer, 1850.
Reports of Committees of the House of Representatives for the First Session of the Forty-Eight Congress, 1883–84. Vol. II. 48th Congress, 1st Session. House of Representatives Report No. 524. Washington: GPO, 1884.
Richards, Leonard L. The Slave Power: The Free North and Southern Domination, 1780–1860. Baton Rouge: Louisiana University Press, 2000.
Robertson, James I., Jr., editor. The Civil War Letters of General Robert McAllister. New Brunswick, New Jersey: Rutgers University Press, 1965.
Robertson, John. Michigan in the War. Lansing: W.S. George and Company, 1880.
Ross, Robert B. The Early Bench and Bar of Detroit, from 1805 to the end of 1850. Detroit: Richard P. Joy and Clarence M. Burton, 1907.
Rusmussen, Louis J. California Wagon Train Lists, Vol. I. San Francisco Historic Records, 1994.
Saum, Lewis O. The Popular Mood of Pre-Civil War America. Westport, CT: Greenwood Press, 1980.
Schroeder, Rudolph J. Seven Days Before Richmond: McClellan's Peninsula Campaign of 1862 \ and its Aftermath. Bloomington: iUniverse, 2009.
Scott, Franklin. Newspapers and Periodicals of Illinois, 1814–1879. Urbana: Franklin W. Scott, 1910.
Scott, James W.T. "Baxter Family Notes." New York Genealogical and Biographical Record (April 1907).
Senate Report No. 16. 55th Congress, 3rd Session, February 16, 1899.
Sexton, Jay. Debtor Diplomacy: Finance and American Foreign Relations in the Civil War, 1837–1873. New York: Oxford University Press, 2005.
Shannon, Fred A. The Organization and Administration of the Union Army, 1861–1865. Gloucester, MA: Peter Smith, 1965.
Simon, John Y., ed. The Papers of Ulysses S. Grant: Volume 19: July 1, 1868-October 31, 1869. Carbondale: Southern Illinois University Press, 1995.
Small, Harold A. The Road to Richmond: The Civil War Memoirs of Maj. Abner R. Small of the 16th Maine Volunteers, with His Diary as a Prisoner of War. Berkeley: University of California Press, 1959.
Sodergren, Steven E. 'Great Is the Shovel and Spade': The Adaptation of Union Soldiers to Combat Conditions, 1864–5, Ph.D. dissertation. University of Kansas, 2006.
Sommers, Richard J. Richmond Redeemed: The Siege at Petersburg. Garden City, N.Y.: Doubleday & Company, 1981.
Squier, E.G. Honduras; Descriptive, Historical, and Statistical. London: Trubner & Company, 1870.
Squier, E.G. Honduras Interoceanic Railway. London: Trubner & Company, 1857.
State of Michigan Gazetteer & Business Directory for 1856–7. Detroit: H. Huntington Lee & Company and James Sutherland, 1856.
Steere, Edward. The Wilderness Campaign. Harrisburg, PA: Stackpole Company, 1960.
Stephenson, Anders. Manifest Destiny: American Expansionism and the Empire of Right. New York: Hill and Wang, 1995.
Sterne, Margaret. "From Jonesville to Frankfort on the Main: The Political Career of William Walton Murphy, 1861–1869." The Quarterly Review of the Michigan Alumnus (Spring 1959): 253–258.
Stokes, Melvin, and Stephen Conway. The Market Revolution in America: Social, Political, and Religious Expressions, 1800–1880. Charlottesville: University Press of Virginia, 1996.
Streeter, Floyd B. Political Parties in Michigan, 1837–1860. Lansing: Michigan Historical Commission, 1918.
Tagg, Larry. The Generals of Gettysburg: The Leaders of America's Greatest Battle. Campbell, CA: Savas, 1998.
Taylor, Paul. Glory Was Not Their Companion: The Twenty-Sixth New York Volunteer Infantry in the Civil War. Jefferson, N.C.: McFarland, 2005.
Townsend, George A. Rustics in Rebellion: A Yankee Reporter on the Road to Richmond, 1861–65. Chapel Hill: University of North Carolina Press, 1950.
Townshend, David G. The Seventh Michigan Volunteer Infantry: The Gallant Men and Flag in the Civil War, 1861 to 1865. Fort Lauderdale: Southeast Publications, 1993.
Transactions of the State Agricultural Society of Michigan; with reports of county agricultural societies, for the year 1856, Vol. 3. Lansing: Hosmer & Kerr, 1857.
Trejo, Por Hector Francisco, and Maria Emildre Torres de Paz. Historia de Honduras. San Pedro Sula, Honduras: Editorial Coello, 2009.
Trimble, Richard M. Brothers Until Death: The Civil War Letters of William, Thomas, and Maggie Jones, 1861–1865. Macon: Mercer University Press, 2000.
Trudeau, Noah A. The Last Citadel: Petersburg, Virginia, June 1864-April 1865. Boston: Little, Brown, 1991.
Tucker, Spencer C. Brigadier General John D. Imboden: Confederate Commander in the Shenandoah. Lexington: University of Kentucky Press, 2003.
Turner, Frederick Jackson. The Frontier in American History. New York: Henry Holt and Company, 1921.
Turner, Thomas R. Beware the People Weeping: Public Opinion and the Assassination of Abraham Lincoln. Baton Rouge: Louisiana State University Press, 1982.
Van Rhyn, Mark. Beyond the Battlefield: Post-War Careers of Middle Rank Civil War Generals, Ph.D. dissertation. University of Nebraska, 2003.
Viola, Herman J., ed. The Memoirs of Charles Henry Veil: A Soldier's Recollections of the Civil War and the Arizona Territory. New York: Orion Books, 1993.
Walton, Cindy Lou. The Hillsdale County Fair in the Eyes of the Woman's Congress and Friends, 1851–2007. Bloomington: Author House, 2009.
War of the Rebellion: A Compilation of the Official Records of the Union and Confederate Armies. Washington: GPO, 1881–1901.
Wells, William V. Explorations and Adventures in Honduras Comprising Sketches of Travel in the Gold Regions of Olancho and a Review of the History and General

Resources of Central America. New York: Harpers and Brothers, 1857.

Welsh, Jack D. *Medical Histories of Union Generals.* Kent, OH: Kent State University Press, 1996.

Whitney, W.A., and Bonner, R.A. *History and Biographical Record of Lenawee County, Michigan,* Vol. I. Adrian: W. Stearns & Company, 1879.

Wilder, I.W. *Journal of the State of Michigan, 1855.* Lansing: Hosmer & Fitch, 1855.

Wing, Talcott E., ed. *History of Monroe County, Michigan.* New York: Munsell & Company, 1890.

Wright, Elizur. *Myron Holley; and What He did for Liberty and True Religion.* Boston: Elizur Wright, 1882.

Wynstra, Robert. *The Rashness of That Hour: Politics, Gettysburg, and the Downfall of Confederate Brigadier General Alfred Iverson.* El Dorado Hills, CA: Savas Beatie, 2010.

Index

Numbers in ***bold italics*** indicate pages with photographs.

Abbot, Captain 43
abolition 34–36, 38, 41, 42, 124
Adams and Company Express 59
Adrian, Michigan 12, 17, 26
African Americans 36; soldiers 124
Aker, Peter P. 18, 22
Albany, New York 10
Aldrich, Amos 39
Alexander, Edward 87
Alexander, Walt 121
Alexandria, Virginia 62, 76–77
Algoma 22
Alleghany Mountains 49
Allen, Michigan 11
Allen's Farm 69
Altoona 49
Alvarado, Francisco 151–152, 158–160
Amapala, Honduras 152–154, 158, 160, 162, 164–165, 169
Amelia Court House 129
Amelia Springs 129–130
American Fur Company 23
Ames, Iowa 138
Anderson, Robert 73
Andersonville, Georgia 109
Ann Arbor, Michigan 10, 29
Anthony, Susan B. 172
Antietam 74, 77–81, 85, 92, 98, 175
Antietam Creek 130
Appomattox, Virginia 130–*131*
Appomattox Court House 130, 132
Appomattox River 126
Arias, Céleo 164–170
Arlington Heights, Virginia 134
Arms, Cephas 19, 22–31
Armstrong's Mill 121, 126
Army of Northern Virginia 68–69, 76–77, 93, 114–115, 126, 130, 132
Army of the James 121
Army of the Potomac 48–53, 57–59, 62, *63*, 69, 72, 76–77, 80–83, 88, 91, 93–94, 96–100, 102–103, 114–115, 117–118, *131*, 132, 136
Arrowsmith, T.V. 62
Aspinwall, Columbia 169
Augusta 65
Austria 140
Ayers, Romeyn 128, 136

Bacon, Dr. Syrus 48
Bahía de la Unión (Union Bay) 150
Bain, William J. 167
Baker, A.J. 18, 22, 39
Baker, Col. Edward 53–54
Ball, Col. William B. 82–83
Ball's Bluff 54, 61; battle 58, 66
Ball's Crossroads 134
Baltimore, Maryland 49, 102
Baltimore and Ohio Canal 60
Baltimore and Ohio Railroad 52, 136
Baltimore and Washington Railroad 49
Bangs, Chester H. 51–52
Bankhead, Henry C. 106
Barksdale, William 85, 91
Barns, Mrs. 102
Barnum, Dr. Bolivar 48
Barona 165
Barrios, Justo Rufino 170
Barton, Clara 89, 94
Bates, James L. 100, 103, 116, 118
Battle Creek, Michigan 12
Baxter, Alice Beaumont 35, 40
Baxter, Antoinette 10, 12, 35, 59
Baxter, Benjamin Levi 6, 8, 9, 10, 12, 40, 59, 137, 172–173, 175
Baxter, Carrie L. 39, 48, 156–157, 161–162
Baxter, Charles E.K. 10, 35, 59
Baxter, Clara 10, 35, 59
Baxter, Edwin Warren 39, 141, 173

Baxter, Elizabeth 10, 12, 35, 59
Baxter, Elvira Ellen "Vi" 39, 46, 48, 55, 58–59, *63*, 64, 80, 97, 99, 102, 113, 120, 122, 124, 133, 141, 143–144, 150–151, 153, 155, 157, 161, 173–174
Baxter, Florence 10, 35, 59
Baxter, Francis (1742) 5
Baxter, Francis (1823) 6
Baxter, Helen N. 6, 12, 35, 59
Baxter, Henry Grange 39, 48, 150, 153, 156–157, 161, *175*
Baxter, Jennie H. 39, 48, 153, 156, 161
Baxter, John 5, 6
Baxter, Levi, Jr. 5, 6, 7, 8, *9–15*, 22, 33–40, 52, 58–59, 125, 137, *139*, 141, 173
Baxter, Levi, Sr. 5
Baxter, Lois 6, 10
Baxter, Lois Francis 6, 10, 12, 35–36, 59, 144
Baxter, Lois "Lottie" Francis 39, 156, 161
Baxter, Mary Jane 6, 12, 59
Baxter, Nancy Ann 6
Baxter, Narcissa 6
Baxter, Susan E. 10, 12, 35
Baxter, William 5
Baxter, Witter Johnston 6, *9*, 12–14, 35–42, 59, 137, *139*–142, 150, 153, 172–175
Baxter, Aldrich, & Company 39
Bay of Fonseca 145, 154, 158
Bayne, Thomas M. 100
Beach, Alexander 40
Beaman, Fernando C. 41, 143–144
Beaumont, Abram Lovett 35
Beaver Creek, Utah 28
Beisel, George W. 14
Belgian rifles 49, 61
Bell, Robert N. 154
Belle Plain, Virginia 83
Bennet, J.E. 143–144

Benton, Col. William P. 50, 54
Bentz, Daniel 132
Berea Church 103
Berkeley Plantation 70
Berryville, Virginia 60
Bethesda Church 118
Biddle, Thomas 163–164, 169
Big Muddy River 29
Bills, Perley 13
Bingham, Kingsley 38, 41
Bitter Spring 30
Blacks and Whites Station 133
Blair, Austin 34, 41, 56, 73–75, 79, 94, 102, 136
Blair, Jacob 169
Blair Guard 45
Boatswain's Swamp 68
Bolivar, Virginia 79
Bolivar Heights 60
Booth, John Wilkes 132
Bostwick, Lucius A. 47
Boughton, Selleck C. 6, 11
"Boys in Blue" 140
Brainard, Wesley 85
Branch County 14, 142
Brand, Nathan 39
Brandy Station 102, 114
Branegan, George 36
Brant, Joseph 5
Brent, Winifred Lee 94
Bridger, James 25
Briggs, Henry S. 113
Bristoe Campaign 114
Brotherhood of Soldiers 140
Brown, John 61
Brown, Joseph W. 6, 9
Brownsville, Michigan 6, 7
Brownsville, Texas 133
Buchanan, James 42
Buford, John 104
Bull Run 44, 53, 77
Burkeville, Virginia 124
Burkeville Junction 133
Burkman, L.E. 166
Burns, William W. 69
Burnside, Ambrose 58, 81–84, 86–87, 90–92, 96, 174
Burr Oak, Michigan 43, 45
Burr Oak Rangers 45
Butler, Benjamin 120–121
Butler, Walter 5

Cabañas, José Trinidad 148–149, 155, 157–159, 170, 175
Calhoun Pass (Cajon Pass) 30
California 22, 25, 26, 28, 29, 30–32, 33, 39, 50, 147, 171
California Gold Rush 2, 16–33, 172
Cambridge Junction 7
Camp Benton 50, 51, 58
Camp Monroe 47–48
Canada 122

Cape Horn 149
Carazo, Evaristo 164
Caribbean 149
Carrera, Pres. Rafael 148
Carr's Creek, New York 5
Casey, Silas 66
Cash Spring 30
Cass, Lewis 7
Castellanos, Victoriano 148
Catholicism 153, 163
Cedar River 19
Cemetery Hill 108–110
Cemetery Ridge 108–110
Centerville, Virginia 77
Central America 33, 144–145, 146–149, 151–153, 155, 157, 162–164, 167–170, 173–175; Canal 145, 147
Ceres, New York 154
Chadlock, Dr. Gilbert 79
Chain Bridge 77
Chaletenango 164
Chamberlain, Joshua 128, 136
Chancellorsville, Virginia 98–101, 103
Chancellorsville Campaign 101
Chandler, Zachariah 41, 53, 102, 142, 144, 168–169
Charles City Courthouse 76
Charlestown, West Virginia 60, 99
Charlevoix, Michigan 174
Chase, Salmon 57
Cheeseman's Creek 64
Cherry Creek Massacre 5
Cherry Hill 5
Chesapeake Bay 57, 62, 82
Chicago, Illinois 8–10, 15, 38, 41, 59, 153, 161; fire of 1871 161, 172; Fort Dearborn 8
Chicago Road (US-12) 5, 7–12, 15, 34, 39
Chickahominy River 66–68, 70, 76
Childs, the Rev. E.W. 154, 173
China 154
Chino Hills 31
Christiancy, Isaac P. 37–38, 41
Clark's Mountain 114
Clayton-Bulwer Treaty 150
Cleveland, Ohio 48
Cleveland and Pittsburgh Rail Road 48
Coe, George A. 41
Cold Harbor 118
Coldwater, Michigan 15, 58, 142
Cole, T.G. 47
Colfax, Schuyler 144
Collins, C.J. 26
Colombia 149, 169
Colón, Panama 169
Colquitt's Salient 127
Comayagua, Honduras 147–148, 151, 157–160, 164–165

Comstock, C.B. 88
Concord, Michigan 9, 12
Confederate Congress 124
Congress 11, 15, 37, 38, 42, 44, 54, 55, 99, 136, 145–147, 151, 168–169
Congress, USS 62
Connecticut 43
Cooley, G.C. 18, 21
copperheads 142
Cormany, Samuel 119
Costa Rica 148, 167, 169
Couch, Darius N. 72, 85, 93, 99
Coulter, Richard 103, 116–118, 120, 128
Council Bluffs, Iowa 18–19
Crapo, Henry H. 135
Crawford, Samuel W. 119, 12–123, 125–126, 128
Crotty, D.G. 93
Cuba 80
Culpeper, Virginia 114
Culpeper Centreville Express 114
Culpeper Courthouse 80–81, 102
Culp's Hill 109–110
Cumberland 52
Cumberland, USS 62
Curtenius Guard 44
Curtis, Charles 46–48, 54, 63–65, 67–69, 73, 77–78, 81, 98
Custer, George Armstrong 52, 174
Cutler, Lysander 104, 106–107

Dabney's Mill 125, 136
Dallas, Capt. Charles 30
Dana, Brig. Gen. Napoleon 59, 65–67, 69–71, 77, 80
Danville, Virginia 129
Danville Railroad 119
Darien Expedition 150
Dartmouth College 10, 12
Davis, Jefferson 58, 68, 81, 102, 122, 124, 126, 128–130, 133
Dearborn, Michigan 175
Deep Run 86
Delaware 121
Delaware County 5
Delhi, New York 5, 10
Democracy 152
Democratic Party 33–34, 37–38, 121, 139, 142–143, 173; Antislavery Democrats 41
Denison, Andrew 116
Dennis, James 141
Detroit, Michigan 6, 8, 9–11, 13, 15, 17, 34, 38, 44, 46, 48, 94, 102, 138–139, 153
Detroit Advertiser 17
Detroit, Hillsdale, and Indiana Railroad 140
Detroit River 35
Detroit Tribune 67

Index

Devil's Gate 24
Dibble, A.M. 18
Dickison, C.J. 135
Dinwiddie Court House 125, 127; battle 127
Doney, Mr. and Mrs. Thomas 39
Donner Party 26
Doty, Captain 28
Doubleday, Abner 104, 106–107, 109–112
Douglas, James 166
Douglas, Stephen 37
Draft 60
Dueñas, Francisco 157, 160, 162–163
Dumfries, Virginia 83

Early, Jubal 100–101, 105
East Windsor, Connecticut 5
Eastern Michigan University 17, 138
Ebersol, David 47
Edmondston, Catherine 132
Edward's Ferry 50–51, 53, 61
Edwardsburg 48
18th Massachusetts 119
18th Mississippi 86–87
8th Florida 87
8th Massachusetts 113
88th Pennsylvania 103, 107, 113, 116, 120, 125
89th New York 84, 87
87th Pennsylvania 91
83rd New York 103, 107, 113, 116
El Salvador 147–148, 150, 152, 154–155, 157–160, 162–166, 168, 170, *175*
11th Pennsylvania 103, 106, 113, 116–120, 125–126
Elmira, Virginia 101
Ely's Ford 101, 116
Emancipation Proclamation 81
Emmitsburg 104
Emory, Lieutenant 90
Erie Canal 33
Espinosa, General 164–165
Estrever, General 164
Etham's Landing 65
Evans, Brig. Gen. Nathan 54
Ewell, Richard 105, 109–110, 116
Ewing, Andy 135
Exchange Bank 36
"extended local knowledge" 2, 3, 17, 19, 22, 23, 32, 33, 48, 135, 145, 176
Extradition Convention 154, 160, 168

Fair Oaks 68, 70, 74, 80, 175
Fair Oaks Station 66–67, 69, 74
Fairchild, Harrison 87
Fairfax Court House 134
Falmouth, Virginia 81–82, 96, 101

Far East 154
Farmington, Michigan 45
Farmville 130
Fayette, Michigan 143
Fayette House 36; *see also* Jonesville Exchange
"Fayette Mill" 8, 11, *13*, *139*
Fayette Republican 142
"Fayette Rovers" 17–33, 42
Fayette Township 34, 36, 38, 40–41, 137, 175
Fayette Union School *see* Jonesville Union School
Federal Republic of Central America 148
Fenton, William F. 46
Ferrer, Francisco 148
Ferrero, Edward 122
15th New York Engineers 84, 86–87
15th Vermont 113
5th Massachusetts Battery 120
5th North Carolina 106
5th U.S. Artillery 73, 120
5th New York Engineers 83–84
50th New York Volunteer Engineers 85
51st Massachusetts 113
59th New York Volunteers 90–92
57th New York 84, 86, 111
57th Pennsylvania 126
1st Minnesota 50
1st New York Light Artillery 120
1st Rhode Island Light Artillery 51
1st U.S. Artillery 73
Fish, Hamilton 144–147, 150, 154, 158–159, 164, 169, 173
Five Forks 127–128, *131*, 136
Fletcher Chapel 100
Flint, Michigan 45
Florida 138, 142
"Forlorn Hope" 1, *88*, 93, 144
Fort Archer 120
Fort Bridger 25
Fort Davison 120
Fort Dushane 120–121
Fort Hall 25
Fort Henry 58
Fort Laramie 19, 23–24
Fort Stedman 126–127
Fort Sumter 42–43, 73, 93
Fort Wadsworth 120
Fort Wayne 44–47
Fort Wayne, Jackson, and Saginaw Railroad 137, 140, 172
Fortress Monroe 62, 74, 76
14th Vermont 113
45th New York 106
42nd New York 59, 71, 77, 79, 90, 92
46th Massachusetts 113

46th New York 84, 87
4th United States Artillery 70, 108, 120
Foust, Benezet R. 103
France 148
Frankfort, Germany 53, 113, 140, 144
Franklin, William 57, 65, 68, 71, 77, 82, 86, 92
Frederick, Maryland 104, 111
Fredericksburg, Virginia 1, 2, 81–85, 98, 100, 114, 116, 150; Battle of 1, 80, 87–88, *90*–92, 94–95, 97–98, 101, 134, 174–175
Fredericksburg Campaign 82, 93
Free Democrats 37–38
Free-Soil Party 14, 37, 38, 41, 52
French, Gen. William 92
frontier 3
Fugitive Slave Rendition Law 38

Gabriel Mission 31
Gaines Mill 68–69
Gale, Henry 18
García Granados, Miguel 163
Gardner, John G. 13–14, 36
Gardner, Ransom 15
Garfield, GAR Post 174
Garnett, Richard 69
Garnett's Hill 69
Gay, James 172
Geary, Gen. John 94
General Sherman 169
General Survey Act 8
"Genesee Mills" 13
George, Austin 39
George, Elvira Ellen "Vi" *see* Baxter, Elvira Ellen "Vi"
George, Roxanna Smith 39
George A.K. Morris & Company 152
Georgetown 77
Georgia 123
Germania Ford 116
Germany 53, 113, 140, 144
Getty, G.W. 117
Gettysburg, Pennsylvania 103, 104, *105*, 106, 108, 112–113, 115, 136, 138, 175
Gibbon, John 78
Gibbs, Lydia 10
Glendale 70–71, 74; battle 71
Glenn, Captain 108
Globe Tavern 118
Goascoran, Honduras 159
Gómez, Cresencio 164–165
González, Don Santiago 160, 162–163, 165–166
Gordon, John 126–127
Gorman, Willis 53, 102
Gracias a Dios Department 148, 164
Graham, Jonathan B. 34, 173

Grand Army of the Republic 140, 174
Grand Island, Nebraska 20
Grand River 8, 12
Grant, George W. 103,
Grant, Ulysses S. 58, 99, 102, 115–120, 122, 124–125, 127, 129–130, 132, 143–146, 167, 169; administration 171
Gravelly Run 127
Gravelly Run Church 128
Gravelly Run Farm 125
Great Britain 149–150, 167
Great Lakes 33–34, 44
Great Salt Lake 18, 24–25
Great Western Stage Company 9
Green, G.H. 174
Gregg, David 120, 125
Gregory, Henry 18, 24
Griffin, Charles 116, 128, 133, 136
Grosvenor, Ebenezer Oliver 36, 38, 40, 42, 135, 137, *139*–141, 172–173
Grosvenor, Ira R. 42, 44, 47, 49, 51–52, 54–56, 59–63, 66–67, 70, 72–75, 94
Grosvenor and Company 36
"Grosvenor's Union Guard" 42
Guard, USS 150
Guardiola, José Santos 148
Guatemala 145, 147–148, 162–168, 170, *175*
Guatemala 150
Gulf of Fonseca 149
Gulf of Honduras 145

Hale, E.M. 40, 80
Halifax Road 119
Hall, James 104
Hall, Norman 73, 77–79, 81, 85–89, 91–93, 99, 101, 138
Halleck, Henry 74, 76, 82, 135
Halstead, G.W. 17–18, 22
Hampton, Virginia 62
Hampton Road 62
Hancock, Winfield S. 99, 109–110, 121
Hanover Court House 134
Harington 169
Harpers 91
Harpers Ferry, West Virginia 52, 60, 77, 103
Harrisburg, Pennsylvania 49
Harrison's Island 53, 54
Harrison's Landing 68, 70, 72, 74–77
Hartman, Andrew 18
Harvey, H.C. 58
Hatchers Run 121, 125–127, 129
Hawksville 123
Haxall's Landing 72
Hayes, Joseph 136
Hays, Alexander 110

Hazard, John G. 70
Heintzelman, Gen. Samuel 62, 65, 69, 72
Helena 113
Hernandez Spring 30
Herr Ridge 104
Heth, Henry 117, 119
Hewitt, H.L. 12
Hill, A.P. 104–105, 110, 125
Hill, D.H. 66–68
Hillsdale, Michigan 8, 9, 11–12, 14–15, 17, 34–36, 38, 41, 135, 137, 139–140, 142–143
Hillsdale County 7, 8, 11, 13–14, 16, 18, 34, 36, 38–42, 47, 52–53, 97, 137, 139–144, 171, 174
Hillsdale County Agricultural Society 40–41
Hillsdale County Fair 40
Hillsdale County Gazette 12, 34
Hillsdale County Register of Deeds 139–144, 171–172
Hillsdale County Republican Convention 40, 139–144
Hillsdale Standard 58
Hillsdale Township 41
Hillsdale Whig Standard 15, 17–18, 22, 37, 40–41, 47, 51,
Hobby, Dr. Allen 39
Hodgman, Samuel 45–46, 63
Holland 173
Holley, Clarissa Gregg 35
Holly, Myron 35
Holmes, Oliver Wendell, Jr. 74
Holseudingen, John G. 38
Homer, Michigan 9, 35
Homer and Jonesville Plank Road Company 35
Honduran Interoceanic Railroad 149–150, *152*
Honduras 2, 144–145, *146*–151, 152–173, 175–176
Hood, Gen. John Bell 65
Hooker, Gen. Joseph "Fighting Joe" 67–68, 71, 73, 76, 82, 96, 98–103
Howard, Jacob 38
Howard, Gen. Oliver 78, 85, 88, 93, 104, *105*–109
Howard, William A. 144
Howland, William T. 36
Hudson, Silas 160, 164
Hudson, Michigan 9, 136
Huger, Benjamin 69, 71
Humphrey, Andrew 120, 125
Hunt, Henry 84–87, 89, 90–91
Hunt, Jefferson 27–28
Hunt, Thomas 45, 74, 79

Iglesia los Delores 156
Illinois 9, 19, 53
Imboden, John D. 109
Independence, Missouri 16

Indiana 8–9, 11, 14, 43, 50
Inestroza, Francisco 148
Interoceanic Railroad 152, 154, 157, 159–161, 163, 165–167, 169
Iowa 19
"Iowa Rangers" 20
Iowa State University 138
Iron Brigade 104
Isthmian Canal 149
Iverson, Alfred 106–107

Jackson, Stonewall 58, 60, 68, 70–71, 76–77, 83–84, 98–99
Jackson, Michigan 6, 9, 36–37, 102
Jackson Daily Citizen 173
Jackson, Fort Wayne, and Cincinnati Railroad 142
James River 64, 68–71, 74, 118, 133–134
Jarratt's Station 123
Jefferson's Rock 61
Jennings, Gilbert S. 100
Jericho Mill 118
Jetersville, Virginia 129
Johnson, Andrew 121, 133, 135, 144, 148
Johnston, Jane Campbell 6
Johnston, Joseph E. 62, 66, 68, 113, 126, 129
Johnston, Lois 5
Johnston, Mary 6
Johnston, William 5
Johnston, Witter 5, 6
Jones, Benaiah 8
Jones, L.M. 18
Jones, Lois 8
Jones, Thomas 97
Jonesville, Michigan 7–12, 15–*18*, 19, 22, 26, 29, 31, 33–36, 39–42, 44–45, 51–52, 58–59, 79–80, 97, 135–138–142, 153, 171–176; business 13–15; politics 7, 12, 142
Jonesville Academy 17
Jonesville District Library 174
Jonesville Exchange 36; *see also* Fayette House
Jonesville GAR Post 174
Jonesville Independent 39, 51, 58, 94, 97, 171
"Jonesville Light Guard" 42, 44–45
Jonesville School Board 40
Jonesville Telegraph 34–36, 44, 52
Jonesville Union School 17, 31, 34, 35, 39, 142
Jonesville Volunteer Fire Department 40
Jonesville Woolen Mills 173

Kalamazoo, Michigan 17, 23, 38
Kalamazoo River 8
Kalamazoo Road 11

Index

Kanesville, Iowa 19
Kansas 41
Kansas-Nebraska Act 37–38, 41
Kanyon Creek 25
Kellogg, Charles 12, 14
Kellogg, Edwin 12, 14
Kellogg, George 12
Kellogg, John A. 128, 139
Kellogg, Mary Jane *see* Baxter, Mary Jane
Kentucky 121, 151
Kinnie, A.K. 97
Knaggs, Robert 50, 52, 54, 61–62, 67, 78, 100, 108–109, 133
Knight, Z.B. 38
Knox County 28
"Knox County, Illinois Company" 19
Knoxville 21

La Brea 160
La Brea estuary 150
La Paz 162
La Plaisance Bay Pike 7
La Raz 160
La Unión 150, 152, 158, 164
La Venta 150
Lafayette, Marquis de 63
Lafr, Jacob 35
Lake Baw Beese 11
Lake Erie 8, 10, 15, 48
Lake Forest 161
Lake Huron 10
Lake Michigan 7, 8, 10, 15, 35
Lake Shore and Michigan Railway 14–15, 139
Lake Superior 34
Lander, Frederick 50–52, 54
Landon, Henry 47, 67
Lansing, Michigan 34, 139
Lapeer, Michigan 43, 45
Las Vegas, Nevada 27, 29
Latham, Ira 18
Latin Americans 147
Laws of the Territory of Michigan 6
Lazo, José Sotero 169
Leavens, S. 40
Ledyard, T.C. 154
Lee, Col. Raymond 51, 78, 80
Lee, Robert E. 68–69, 71–72, 76, 79–83, 91–92, 98, 100–103, 109, 111–112, 114–119, 124, 127–130, 131–132, 143
Leesburg, Virginia 50, 53–54, 60
Leiva, Ponciano 167
Lenawee County 7, 8, 11, 14, 40
Leonard, Samuel 101, 103, 116–117
Leslie's 91
Lewis, H.N.F. 52
Lewis, J.S. 17–18
Libby Prison 133
Liberty Party 35

Lincoln, Abraham 42–44, 53, 55–57, 76–77, 79, 81–83, 94, 96–98, 103, 111, 114–116, 121–122, 124, 127, 132–134, 148, 151
Lincoln Calvary 56
Litchfield, Connecticut 10
Litchfield, Michigan 9
Litchfield Township 39
Little Bethel 62
Little Round Top 110, 136
Little Salt Lake, Utah 28
Livingston County 38
Lockwood, Jonathan 11
Logan Loop Mountain 50
London, England 169
London, Michigan 73
Longstreet, James 70, 83–84, 91, 110, 114
Los Angeles, California 27
Lossing, Benson J. 74
Louisiana 121, 151, 169
Louisiana Territory 37
Louisville, Kentucky 151
Loup River 19
Lowe, Thaddeus 58
Lutheran Theological Seminary 104
Lyle, Peter 100, 103, 107–108, 115
Lynchburg, Virginia 130
Lyon, Lucius 10
Lyster, Winifred 1

Macomb County 33
Macy, Major 90–91
Magruder, John 69
Maine 43
Malvern Hill 67, 70–72, 74, 76; battle 72
Manassas 60
Manassas Junction 44, 57, 62
Manchester 133
Manheim, Pennsylvania 132
"manifest destiny" 2
Mansanita 150
Mariposa 31
Marsh Creek 104
Marshall, Michigan 17
Martineau, Harriet 8
Martínez, General 160
Marx, Karl 113
Marye's Heights, Virginia 87, 92
Maryland 49–50, 60, 77, 81, 94, 102
Mason, Michigan 44, 99
Massachusetts 93, 96
Maumee River 7, 8
Maury Brothers 167
Maximilian, Ferdinand 148
Maximilian, Joseph I 148
May Queen 48
Maysville, Kentucky 36
McAllister, Robert 122
McBride, R.E. 117

McCandlish 167
McClellan, George 53, 55, 57, 60, 62–66, 68–74, 76–77, 79–82, 98, 121
McClelland, Robert 15
McCook, GAR Post 174
McCormick, Dr. William 27
McCoy, Thomas 120, 128, 130, 132
McDowell, Irvin 57, 84
McGaffey, Neal 11
McInnis, Anna Bella 6
McKieney, John 38
McLean House 130
McNaughton, M.A. 37
McPherson, GAR Post 174
McPherson Ridge 104, 106
Meade, Maj. Gen. George 92, 99, 103–104, 107, 109–110, 112, 114–116, 118–120, 125, 127
Meagher, Thomas 91
Medal of Honor 67, 80
Medina, Gen. Don Juan Antonio (Medinetta) 164–165
Medina, Pres. José María 148–149, 151–152, 154, 157–160, 162–166, 168, 170
Méndez, Vice President 166
Merced River 31
Meridian Hill 49, 61
Merrimac, USS 65
Mexican War 3, 4, 14, 16, 26, 45, 74, 78, 96
Mexico 148
Michigan 2, 9, 19, 55, 59, 93, 99, 102, 122, 135, 141, 172, 174, 176; education 175; politics 171, 175; statehood 12; territory 2, 9
Michigan Agricultural Society 41
Michigan Board of Education 35, 41
Michigan Central Railroad 15
Michigan City, Indiana 9
Michigan Constitutional Convention of 1835 11
Michigan Constitutional Convention of 1850 34, 173
Michigan Farmer 36
Michigan Legislature 7, 10, 12, 14, 34, 35, 38
Michigan Manual Labor School 10
"Michigan, My Michigan" (poem and song) 1
Michigan Soldier's Relief Association 59
Michigan Southern Railroad 14–15, 35, 39
Michigan State Militia 43–44; 1st M.V.I 43, 44, 135; 2nd M.V.I 135; 3rd M.V.I 135; 4th M.V.I 42, 72; 5th M.V.I 44; 6th M.V.I 43–44, 49; 7th M.V.I (4th Regi-

ment) 1, 43–55, 47–51, 53, 58–59, 61–67, 69–82, 85–*88*, 89–*90*, 91–97, 99, 102, 138, 143, 173; 8th M.V.I 135; 9th M.V.I 135; 10th M.V.I 135; 11th M.V.I 135; 12th M.V.I 135; 13th M.V.I 135; 14th M.V.I; 15th M.V.I; 16th M.V.I 135; 17th M.V.I 135; 18th M.V.I 135, 171; 19th M.V.I 135; 20th M.V.I; 24th M.V.I 102; 27th M.V.I 135
Michigan State Normal School *see* Eastern Michigan University
Michigan Territorial Convention of 1834 10
Middletown 104
Miles, Mr. 20
Miles, Nelson A. 122
military reconnaissance balloon 65
milling 6
Milwaukee Sentinel 17
Mine Run 114, 116
Mine Run Campaign 114
Minooka 153
Mirondas, General 159
Mississippi 44, 46
Mississippi River 44, 99, 102
Missouri 23, 103
Missouri Compromise of 1820 37, 41
Missouri River 19
Moesch, Joseph A. 103, 116
Mohave Desert 30
Monitor, USS 62
Monocacy 136
Monroe, Michigan 7, 15, 35, 37, 39, 42, 44, 46–48, 52, 73, 100, 114, 138; county 7, 14, 33
Monroe Commercial 17, 46–47, 73
Monroe Doctrine 140, 147–148
Monroe Light Guard 44
Monroe Trail 7
Montes, José Francisco 148
Montgomery, William 141–143
Morazán, Francisco 148, 155, *157*
Morell, George 72
Morgan, John 114
Morgan's Forty 37
Morley, Frederick 102
Mormons (Church of Jesus Christ of Latter-Day Saints) 18, 25–27, 147
Morris, George A.K. 153, 158, 169
Morrow, Henry 102, 138
Mosherville, Michigan 9
"Mountain Fever" 29
Munro, George C. 34, 39–40, 42, *139*, 142–143, 173
Murphy, Ellen 35
Murphy, William W. 13, 18, 35–36, 38–42, 52–53, 113, *139*–141, 144

Nacaome, Honduras 150
Nagle, Henry 69
Napoleon III 148
Napoleon, Michigan 51
Native Americans 19, 23, 25, 26, 27, 29, 31, 33, 147
New Amsterdam 145
New Hampshire 43
New Jersey 43, 121
New Orleans, Louisiana 133, 153, 167
New Orleans Picayune 170
New York 5, 50, 61, 102, 121–122, 139, 145
New York City, New York 15
New York Herald-Tribune 55
New York Times 91, 93, 97, 167, 173, 175
Newberryport, Massachusetts 39
Newton, John 109, 115
Nicaragua 145, 147–148, 153–154, 163–164, 167
Niles, Michigan 9
19th Massachusetts 50, 59, 66, 71, 85, 87, 90–93
19th Pennsylvania 107–108, 111
90th Pennsylvania 100, 103, 107, 113, 116, 120
94th New York 120
97th New York 103, 106–107, 109, 113, 116, 120, 125
9th Massachusetts 120
Nipsic, USS 150
Norfolk, Virginia 62, 65
Normandy, France 89
North Adams, Michigan 9
North Anna, Virigina 83
North Carolina 81, 126, 129
Northrup, Charles 111
Nottoway Court House 132–133
Nottoway River 123

Oak Grove 68
Oak Hill 106
Oak Ridge 106–107
Oakland County 33, 38
observation balloon 50, 58
Ocean 48
Odd Fellows 14
Oesterle, Frederick 54
Ohio 8, 14, 43, 48–49
Olancho, Honduras 154
Old Northwest Territory 42, 59
Olds, James 11
Omoa, Honduras 153, 164–166
Onderdonk, J.T. 18
O'Neil, Edward A. 106
149th Pennsylvania 108
104th New York 120
190th Pennsylvania 132

117th Pennsylvania 128, 130, 132
107th Pennsylvania 120, 125
106th Pennsylvania Volunteer Infantry 78
136th Pennsylvania 100
127th Pennsylvania Volunteers 90
Orange and Alexandria Railroad 57, 80
Ormsby, Dr. Caleb 29
Orton, Elizabeth M. 10, 12, 35, 59
Orton, Miles 10
Orton, Samuel G. 10
Oscaloosa 20
Osseo, Michigan 9, 12
Overland Campaign 116, 118

Pacific 149
Pacific Springs 25
Packer, Henry 36
Palmer, Alonzo 51
Palmetto Ranch 133
Pamunkey River 68, 118
Panama 33, 149, 154, 169
Panama Railroad 149
Panic of 1873 171
Panic of 1837 12
Paraiso 154
Paris, France 168
Parke, John 120–121
Partridge, James Rudolph 147
Pasaquina, Salvador 159
Patrick, Marsena 88
Paul, Augustus 111
Paul, Gabriel 103, 107–108, 111–112
Pawnee 19
Peach Orchard 69, 74
Peeble's Farm 119, 121
Pendleton, E.B. 60
Pendleton, George 121
Peninsula Campaign 57, 73
Penniman, E.J 41
Pennsylvania 48–49, 77, 102–104
Pennsylvania Central Railroad 49
Petersburg, Virginia 118–124, 126–129, 133–134, 140
Pettigrew, J. Johnston 104
Philadelphia, Pennsylvania 36, 38, 138
Pickett, George 127–128
Pickett's Charge 110
Pierce, Franklin 147
Pinkerton, Allan 63
Pittsburgh, Pennsylvania 48–49
Pittsford, Michigan 9
Platt, H.W. 17–18
Platt, Zephaniah 13
Platte River 19, 21, 23
Plattsville, Iowa 19
Pleasonton, Alfred 82, 102–103
Plummer, William 87
Point of Rocks 60
Pollack's Creek 100

Pollack's Mill 101
Pontiac, Michigan 45
pontoons 83–84, 89–*90*
Pope, John 76–77
Popular Springs Church 119, 121
Poolesville, Maryland 50
Port Cortés 166
Port Hudson 113
Port Huron, Michigan 43, 44
Porter, Andrew 68–69, 72
Potomac River 50, 52–54, 55, 60, 62, 77, 83, 99, 103, 111
Potrevillo 169
Prairie Creek 20
Prairieville, Michigan 45
Prairieville Rangers 45
Presbyterian Church 5, 10, 14, 35, 37, 39, 48, 58, 138, 142, 153, 173–174
Presidential Election of 1860 41, 42
Presidential Election of 1864 121–122
Presidential Election of 1868 142, 151
Presidential Election of 1872 169
Prince Edward Court House 130
"progress" 3
"providence" 2, 23, 31, 114, 132, 176
Provisional Corps 136
Provo, Utah 26–27
Prussia 140, 144
Puerto Cabello 165
Puerto Cortés 149, 169

Quebec 5

railroads 10, 14, 33
Raisin River 6–8
Ralph, Calvin R. 17–18, 29, 31
Rapidan River 114–115
Rappahannock River 1, 82–84, 86, *88*, 89–*90*, 92–94, 97–101, 114
Reams Station 121
Reconstruction 138, 140
"Red Mills" 6, 7
Redfern, John 14
Reed, Charles 120
Reeves & Selfridge 136
Republican National Convention: (1856) 41; (1860) 38, 41, 51; (1864) 151
Republican Party 6, 35–38, 41–42, 52, 58–59, 81, 102, 121, 135, 137, *139*, 141–144, 152, 169, 172, 173, 176
Republican State Committee of Michigan 38
Revolutionary War 5
Reynolds, John F. 99–100, 103–105, 138

Rhoades, George B. 116
Rice, Melvin S. 48, 50, 79, 93, 98
Richardson, Israel 50
Richardson, John 66–67, 70–71
Richmond, Virginia 57, 62, 65, 68, 69, 70, 73–74, 76, 79, 81, 82–83, 92–93, 98, 100, 103, 115–117, 119–120, 123–124, 126–129, 133–134
Richmond and Danville Railroad 129, 133
Richmond and York River Railroad 66–67, 69
Richmond Examiner 113
Richmond, Fredericksburg and Potomac Railroad 81–82
Ricker, Samuel 53
Ricketts, R. Bruce 122
Ripon, Wisconsin 36–37
Rising Sun 169
River, James 121
Roanoke Island, North Carolina 58
Robertson, John 43, 63, 73–74, 142
Robinson, John 100–103, 106–112, 115–116, 118
Rodes, Robert *105*–106
Rodrigues, Francisco 166
Rodrigues, Leandro 166
Root, Adrian 103
Rothschild, Baron 53
"Rough and Ready" Lapeer Guard 45
Rousseau, Lovell Harrison 151
Rousseau, Richard 148, 151–152
Rowanty Creek 125, 127
Rowe, Harrison 19
Rowlson, H.B. 40
"rugged individualist" 3
Ruggles, George D. 136

Sabana Grande 164
Sacramento, California 16, 18, 23, 26
St. Francis, Missouri 18
St. Joseph County 11, 14
St. Joseph River 7, 8, 12–13, 36, 137, *139*, 172
St. Lawrence River 33
St. Louis, Missouri 22
St. Michael Archangel 156
Saline, Michigan 9
Salt Lake City, Utah 18, 24–26
Sambrano 161
San Antonio 160
San Francisco, California 26, 33, 150, 154
San Miguel 159
San Pedro 153, 166
San Salvador 145, 164, 169
San Union 159
Sand Lakes 11

Santa Barbara 160, 165
Santa Fe, New Mexico 27
Sauk Trail 8
Sault Ste. Marie, Michigan 34
Savage Station 69–70, 74
Saylors Creek 130
Scales, Alfred M. 108
Schoolcraft, Michigan 48
Scipio Township 41
Secessionists 42, 60, 63, 73
2nd Maine Battery 104
2nd United States Sharpshooters 84
Sedgwick, John 59, 65, 66, 70–73, 75–76, 99, 118, 174
Selfridge, John 144
Selfridge, Lois F. *see* Baxter, Lois Francis
Selfridge, Robert 144
Selfridge, Robert Oliver 36–37
Selfridge, Baxter, & Company 144
Seminary Ridge 104, 106–108
Seminole War 96
Senate 145
Sensenti, Honduras 154
Sensuntepeque, El Salvador 164
Seven Days, Battle of 72, 74
Seven Pines 66–68
Seventh Michigan Volunteer Infantry Association 75
17th Mississippi 87
7th Mississippi 67
71st Pennsylvania 71
Seward, William H. 53, 57, 120
Seymour, Turman 72
Shafter, William 45, 51, 60, 67, 80
Sharp, Salmon 14
Sharps rifles 49, 61
Sharpsburg, Maryland 77
Shenandoah Valley 60, 68, 76
Sheridan, Philip 127–130, 132
Sherman, William T. 123
Shiloh, Tennessee 150
Ship Point 62, 64
Sickles, Dan 110
Sidney Plains, New York 5, 6, 10
Sigel, General Franz 82
Sill, I.B. 35
Sinclair, William 40
Sioux Indians 19
Sisson, Cook 8, 11
Sisson, Thomas 11
16th Maine 120, 125, 134
16th Pennsylvania Calvary 119
16th Vermont 113
66th New York 84
Skinker's Neck, Virginia 83
"slave power" 16, 37
slavery 14, 16, 33, 34–36, 37, 50, 60, 102, 133, 141, 147, 149, 152; Abolition 34–36, 38, 41, 42, 124; Slocum, Henry 71–72

Small, Abner 101, 107–108, 115–116, 134–135
Smith, G.W. 68–69
Smith, Helen *see* Baxter, Helen N.
Smith, Kirby 133, 169
Smith, Orson K. 29–30
Smith, S.N. 78
Soldier's Aid Society 59
South Carolina 42, 73, 169
South Mountain 104
South Pass, Rocky Mountains 24–25
South Side Railroad 119, 121, 125, 127, 129
Southern transcontinental railroad 149
Spain 147
Spaniards 30–31, 33, 147, 151, 156
Spanish-American War 78–80
Spanish Rancho 31
Spanish Trail 28–29
Spotsylvania Court House 118
Springfield rifles 61
Squier, George 149, 154
Stafford Heights 86
stampede 20–25
Stanley, H.S. 39
Stanleyville 104
Stannard, George J. 113
Stanton, Edwin 127, 135–136
State Department 145–147, 161, 168–169
states rights 102, 141
Steele, Capt. Amos 99
Stewart, James 108
Stockton, California 31
Stone, Gen. Charles P. 50, 53–54, 58
Stone, Roy 107
Stony Creek Depot 119
Stoughton, William L. 144
Strickland, Randolph 41
Strong, A.K. 48, 55, 61
Stuart, Jeb 68, 100, 102–103
Stuart's cavalry 100
Stuyvesant, Peter 145
"success" 3
Suez Canal 149
suffrage 172
Sully, Alfred 71
Sumner, Gen. Edwin 59, 66–67, 69–72, 76–77, 82–83, 86, 88, 92
Susquehanna River 5
Sussex Court House 123
Sutter's Mill, California 16
Swan, Elias S. 14
Sykes, George 72, 92, 110

Taneytown, Maryland 77
Taylor, Captain 29
Tecumseh, Michigan 6–8, 9–12, 13, 36, 137, 175
Tecumseh Literary Institute 12
Tegucigalpa, Honduras 147–151, 153, 155–156, 159–160, 162, 164–165, 175
Tennessee 58, 121
10th Massachusetts 50
10th Pennsylvania Reserves 84
Texas 169
Third Delaware 119
Thirds, William 48
13th Massachusetts 101, 103
13th Vermont 113
39th Massachusetts 113, 120–121, 125–126
Tiger Island 154, 158
Tilton, William S. 117
Tinoco de Contreras, José Gregorio 147
Toledo, Ohio 15, 46, 48
Torbert, Alfred T.A 154, 159–160
Townsend, George 128
Transcontinental Railroad 149–150
Trans-Isthmian canal 150
Treaty of Friendship, Commerce, and Navigation 149, 159
Treaty of Guadalupe Hidalgo 26
Truxillo 164
Tulare Valley 31
Tullahoma 113
Tunnicliff, Dr. Joseph 102
Turner, Dick 133
Tuscola, Michigan 45
Tuscola Company 45
Tuscola Volunteers 45
12th Massachusetts 100–101, 103, 106–108, 111, 113, 116, 118
12th Vermont 113
20th Massachusetts 51, 59, 66–67, 70–71, 74, 78, 90–92
20th North Carolina 106–107
21st Mississippi 87
26st New York 100–101
23rd North Carolina 106–107

"under the oaks" 6, 38, 58
Underground railroad 38
Union City, Michigan 12
Union Guard 44
United States Engineer Battalion 84
United States Ford 101
United States Sanitary Commission 59
United States Senate 138, 142, 168
United States Soldiers and Sailors Protective Society 140
University of Michigan 10, 12, 14, 31, 137
Utah Valley 26

Van Buren, Martin 10
"venturist" 3, 5, 13, 16, 17, 19, 22, 24, 28, 33, 122, 125, 135, 141, 147, 176
Vicksburg, Mississippi 112–113, 143
Vincent, Thomas 135
Venero, Juan N. 168–169
Virgin River 29
Virginia 52, 56, 60–61, 80–81, 102, 109, 123, 127
Virginia, CSS 62
Vrooman, Sidney R. 45, 47, 58, 77, 81, 173

Wade, William W. 45
Wadsworth, James S. 110, 116, 174
Wainwright, Charles S. 138
Walbridge, David 38
Waldron, Henry 141–142
Walker, Quartermaster Charles 79
Walker, William 148
War Department 57
War of 1812 78
Warren, Gouverneur K. 72, 115–116, 118–123, 125–128, 132, 138, 141
Warrenton, Virginia 81–82
Washburn, Mary 5
Washburne, Elihu B. 120
Washington, Gen. George 63
Washington D.C. 38, 43, 48–50, 52–55, 59, 61–63, 76–77, 80, 82, 102–103, 111, 117, 130, 134, 144, 158–161, 165
Washtenaw County 33
Waterman, John 43
Wayne County 33, 38
Webb, Alexander S. 109
Welch, Adonijah S. 17–23, 26–27, 29, 31, 35, 39, 138, 142
Weldon and Petersburg Railroad 118
Weldon Railroad 118, 123, 125
Wells, William 151, 153, *155*, 169
West Canada Creek 5
West Point 3, 51, 65, 73, 96, 99, 100, 103, 109, 136, 176
Western Rural 53
Weymouth, Captain 87, 91
Wheelock, Charles 103, 107, 109, 116
Whig Party 14, 16, 34, 37–38, 41
White House Landing 68
White Oak Swamp 69–70, 74
White Pigeon, Michigan 9–12, 13, 15
"White Pigeon Academy" 14
White Pigeon Paper Company 11
Wilcox, Cadmus 117
Wilderness 100, 136; battle 116, 118; Tavern 116
Willcox, Orlando B. 139

Willet, Marinus 5
William, Issac 31
Williams, Alpheus S. 102
Williamsburg, Virginia 65, 65
Williamson, George 169–170
Willow Spring 30
Wilmington, North Carolina 118–119

Winans, Frazey 46–47, 74
Wisconsin 139
Withington, Lawson 172
women, role of in the Civil War 48, 59, 89, 94, 122, 171
Woodbury, Daniel 84–87, 90
Wright, Mr. 39

Xatruch, Forencio 159–161

York River 64–65
Yorktown, Virginia 62–65, 69
Ypsilanti, Michigan 9, 17, 80, 94, 97, 117

www.ingramcontent.com/pod-product-compliance
Ingram Content Group UK Ltd.
Pitfield, Milton Keynes, MK11 3LW, UK
UKHW050526150426
5217IPUK00026B/1824